About the author

Never far from the public eye since kicking the All Blacks to victory at Cardiff in 1972 as a 21-year-old, Joe Karam has been a public advocate for David Bain since 1996. Karam was named by the *New Zealand Herald* in 2007 and TV3 in 2009 as one of their New Zealanders of the Year, and his assertion that the first Bain trial was a travesty was vindicated by the Judicial Committee of the Privy Council and David's subsequent acquittal.

TRIAL BY AMBUSH

THE PROSECUTIONS OF DAVID BAIN

JOE KARAM

HarperCollins*Publishers*

Disclaimer

The opinions expressed in this book are those of the author or of other persons and are not those of the publisher. The publisher has no reasonable cause to believe that the opinions set out in the book are not the genuine opinions of the author or of those other persons.

HarperCollinsPublishers

First published in 2012
by HarperCollins*Publishers (New Zealand) Limited*
PO Box 1, Shortland Street, Auckland 1140

Copyright © Joe Karam 2012
Joe Karam asserts the moral right to be identified as the author of this work.
All rights reserved. No part of this publication may be reproduced, stored in a retrieval system or transmitted in any form or by any means, electronic, mechanical, photocopying, recording or otherwise, without the prior written permission of the publishers.

HarperCollinsPublishers
31 View Road, Glenfield, Auckland 0627, New Zealand
Level 13, 201 Elizabeth Street, Sydney NSW 2000, Australia
A 53, Sector 57, Noida, UP, India
77–85 Fulham Palace Road, London W6 8JB, United Kingdom
2 Bloor Street East, 20th floor, Toronto, Ontario M4W 1A8, Canada
10 East 53rd Street, New York, NY 10022, USA

National Library of New Zealand Cataloguing-in-Publication Data

Karam, Joe, 1951-
Trial by ambush : the prosecutions of David Bain / Joe Karam.
Includes bibliographical references.
ISBN 978-1-86950-834-0
1. Bain, David Cullen, 1972- —Trials, litigation, etc. 2. Trials
(Murder)—New Zealand. 3. Mass murder—New Zealand—Dunedin.
4. Evidence (Law)—New Zealand. 4. Judicial error—New Zealand.
I. Title.
364.1523099392—dc 22

ISBN: 978 1 86950 834 0

Cover design by Christa Moffitt, Christabella Designs
Front cover image by Getty Images; back cover images by Fairfax Photos
Typesetting by Springfield West

Printed by Griffin Press, Australia

70gsm Classic used by HarperCollins*Publishers* is a natural, recyclable product made from wood grown in sustainable forests. The manufacturing processes conform to the environmental regulations in the country of origin, Finland.

Trial by Ambush is a remarkable book. Essentially there are three themes running through it. The first is the exhaustive analysis of the evidence relied on by the Crown at both trials. Secondly, it is an exploration of how the police and the judicial system failed David Bain. Thirdly, it is a testament to Joe Karam's tenacity, intelligence and determination to see justice prevail.

I have some personal knowledge of Joe's approach to the investigation. In April 1997 Joe published his first book on the case, *David and Goliath*, in which he was highly critical of the evidence given by two police officers. As a consequence he and his publishers were sued by the officers for defamation.

When Joe came to see me to defend the claim I was initially sceptical. However, I was impressed by the extent to which Joe had thought through all the issues that I raised and the detached and analytical way he presented his arguments.

There was a two-week hearing before a jury in the High Court in 2000. Joe gave evidence setting out the basis for his beliefs and why he considered that the views expressed in his book were correct. The jury believed him and threw out the claims.

I thought then, and still do, that this was an important decision for all of us. I suggested to the jury that the right to criticize the police was a fundamental right and an important safeguard in the democratic process.

Over the next few years Joe and the defence team prepared a compelling dossier highlighting the systemic flaws in the police investigation and compelling new evidence indicating David's innocence.

One of the principal themes running through this book is the failure of the New Zealand appellate system to provide David Bain with the protection that we are entitled to expect. The judgment delivered by the Court of Appeal in 2003 was deeply flawed and profoundly disappointing. Its failure to address the new evidence and arguments raised by the defence team inevitably raised issues about our judicial system being overly protective of the police and being reluctant to acknowledge the deeply flawed process that had led to a conviction that should have been overturned.

The Privy Council subsequently overturned the Court of Appeal decision. As the Privy Council rarely interfered with decisions involving criminal convictions, this was in itself highly unusual. However, the judgment analysed and rejected each of the grounds relied on by the Court of Appeal, concluding that a substantial miscarriage of justice had actually occurred.

Trial by Ambush takes us through the serious and systemic shortcomings in the police investigation and presentation of evidence at the first trial. As a consequence, an innocent man was convicted and spent 13 years in jail. This significant failure by the police was, in turn, endorsed by a compliant Police Complaints Authority.

Whether or not these failures were deliberate, they nevertheless demonstrate how such institutions can fail to meet their obligations to ensure a fair and dispassionate trial.

If Joe's curiosity had not been triggered by that story in the *New Zealand Herald* in 1996, David's conviction would never have been overturned. So this is also the remarkable story of a man who became convinced of a major miscarriage of justice and was determined to ensure that justice would ultimately be done.

CONTENTS

PART ONE

GUILTY AS SIN

CHAPTER 1

OPERATION EVERY

Visitors to downtown Dunedin today will be impressed by the imposing structure that houses the Criminal Investigation Branch (CIB) of the Dunedin police. It was not so grand in 1994, when the CIB operated out of the fifth floor of the old Electricity Department building in a labyrinth of offices and narrow corridors.

It was to this fifth floor, at about 10.30 on the morning of Friday, 24 June 1994, that Bob Clark was delivering his 22-year-old nephew, David. It was day four of 'Operation Every', the police code-name for its investigation into the execution-style killings of five people in an old ramshackle house at 65 Every Street, Andersons Bay, Dunedin, which was instigated when David had reported the deaths on a 111 emergency call the previous Monday morning.

The four days of Operation Every had been four days of living hell for David, the sole survivor of the tragedy. He had been doing everything he could to help the police in their inquiries, and had already had three extensive interviews with one of the officers assigned to Operation Every. He had been treated as a witness to the tragedy — a young man who had lost everyone he loved, in horrifying circumstances.

He had no reason, on that Friday morning, to fear this latest meeting, and neither did his uncle Bob Clark who drove David to the police station. It was, as far as David knew, simply another interview in the inevitable series of interviews that were necessary as the police attempted to unravel the mystery of how and why the family had been killed. Certainly, neither of them had any reason to feel anything but confidence in the police.

Now, that morning in the Dunedin CIB, David was separated from his uncle and ushered into an interview room with two detectives he had not previously encountered. The horror that began four days earlier was about to get much, much worse.

This was no friendly chat.

'You have the right to remain silent but anything you do say may be used in evidence against you,' David was told. 'You are entitled to consult and instruct a lawyer without delay. Do you understand?'

'Yes,' David replied.

But did he really, at that moment, understand at all?

Operation Every, headed up by Detective Chief Inspector Peter Robinson and Detective Senior Sergeant Jim Doyle, had begun on the previous Monday, 20 June, at about 7.45 a.m. when Sergeant Murray Stapp of the Dunedin police, responding to David's 111 emergency call, reported the discovery of five bodies in the Every Street house.

In the front living room was the body of Robin Bain, 58, father of the family. Fully dressed, one shot in the left temple, he was lying on the floor on his right side, a pool of blood on the carpet adjacent to his head and a .22 rifle at approximately right angles next to his body.

In the main bedroom down the hall was the mother, Margaret Bain, 50, tucked up in bed, wearing a nightgown. She had apparently been shot while asleep. One shot had gone through her left eye, and blood streamed over her face and out of her nostrils.

In the downstairs bedroom was the eldest daughter, Arawa Bain, 19, fully clothed, one shot through her forehead just above her right eyebrow. She had been shot while kneeling on the floor about midway between her bed and the entrance to her room.

The second daughter, Laniet Bain, 17, fully clothed, was found tucked up in bed with three shots to her head: one into the left cheek, one just above her left ear and a third into the top of her head in the middle of her skull.

The youngest child, Stephen Bain, 14, was found lying on the floor of his bedroom clad in black underpants with a white T-shirt wrapped about his neck. Shot twice, the first bullet had gone into and through the palm of his left hand before gouging a laceration from front to back across his scalp. The second and fatal bullet was directed down into the top of his head.

In a sixth room was the survivor, David Bain, 22 years old, still talking to the 111 operator when Sergeant Stapp and his team made entry to the house. He was apparently suffering from shock and trauma but appeared to be otherwise uninjured. The family dog and cat were running free in the house.

Up until that moment, life had been busy and normal for David Bain. The budding classical singer, university student, keen runner and member of a loving if disorganized family had had an active weekend. He'd been out on Friday evening shooting a video and having coffee with friends, and on Sunday, the day before the tragedy, he'd been up early for a run to St Clair Beach, about 5 km from his Andersons Bay home, where he was joined by his dad and Stephen for the Midwinter Polar Plunge. Those southern waters are cold enough in summertime, but the hardy locals always turn out in good numbers for this annual event. In 1994 it was a fine, sunny day and there was a large crowd. David's father Robin didn't swim, but Stephen and David both plunged in. Afterwards, David changed into clothes brought over by his dad in the van and then joined two friends who drove him off to the University of Otago where he spent the afternoon rehearsing for a production in which he was leader of the male chorus.

His two sisters were working at a café in town that Sunday afternoon, and so after the rehearsal at about five o'clock he joined them and the three went home together, stopping at the supermarket on the way. Laniet, unusually, was coming home to spend the night. Aged 17, she had left home a year earlier and had lived at various flats around Dunedin, although then, in June 1994, she was living at least part of the time in the schoolhouse at Taieri Beach with her father and another young man.

The evening was relatively uneventful for David. The family was having fish and chips for dinner and Arawa was supposed to go and get them, but she was called out babysitting and so David and Laniet drove together to collect the evening meal. They chatted outside the fish and chip shop while they waited.

Monday morning began as usual, as David struggled out of his warm bed shortly after 5.30 a.m. into the freezing Dunedin morning. After four or five years being an *Otago Daily Times* delivery boy, that was just part of his routine and he dressed, put on his Walkman and headed out the front door with the family dog Casey.

As usual, that morning it took him about an hour to deliver the 150 or so papers, which were delivered in the normal fashion without incident. Arriving back home, he swung automatically into his normal daily routine. His hands were black with printer's ink from handling the raw, hot-off-the-press newspapers so, as usual, he kicked off his shoes, hung up the yellow *ODT* delivery bag in his room and went downstairs to the room that combined the bathroom, laundry and lavatory and washed them in cold water and soap over the hand-basin.

He then put on a load of washing as he did most mornings. In front of the washing machine was a pile of clothes, the weekend collection of a family of six. It comprised all sorts of items ranging from underwear to old towels, jerseys, trousers and swimming togs.

He sorted out a bunch of 'coloureds' from the pile and put them in the machine along with the red sweatshirt he had worn on the paper round. The 'whites' he left in the cane laundry basket on the floor. One item among these was a white long-sleeved sweatshirt he had been given as a member of a production of *The Gondoliers* at the Opera Live Society earlier that year. It was not included in the wash, although later the police would say it had diluted blood on its right shoulder and sleeve.

A couple of scoops of laundry powder, a flick of the switch, push the dial in to get the old tub started, and it was back upstairs to his bedroom. He noticed a light coming from his mother's room and thought he might make her a cup of tea before getting ready to go to university. He reached his own room. His light switch was the old-fashioned pull-cord variety, tucked away behind the door. He reached around, pulled it on — and there was the scene signalling his life was about to change forever.

The wardrobe doors were wide open and on the floor in front of the wardrobe were a pile of bullets, the packet they had been in, and the trigger lock that secured his .22 rifle, all of which should have been in the wardrobe. Startled. Incredulous. Alarmed. The house was consumed in silence, still pitch-black except for the slither of light coming out of his mum's bedroom entrance. He ran to that light down the hallway, calling out to her. But as he approached he saw blood streaming down her face and out of her nostrils. Her eye was distended like a big red bubble. She did not respond to him.

That, at least, was David's version of events given to the police during the week.

About 15 or 20 minutes later, at 7.09 a.m., the Telecom emergency call centre in Christchurch received a call from a young man who was so off the wall they thought it might be a hoax or a drugged-out freak. 'I came home and they're all dead,' he wailed. 'Who do you want?' they asked. 'I don't know, anyone, please help me,' came the garbled response. The Telecom operator put him through to St John Ambulance in Dunedin.

Just over three hours later, at 10.30 a.m., David was carried out of the house and put into an ambulance. With him in the ambulance was Detective Sergeant Greg Dunne who had been appointed officer in charge of witnesses.

Dunne, who would stay with David for the rest of that long day and conduct interviews with him throughout the coming days, was asking questions and taking notes. Another detective was there, too, for a start, in the ambulance and at the CIB offices, and he had his notebook out as well. David had difficulty talking; Dunne recorded that he seemed to have lost his voice. He complained of a sore head. At one point, David broke in on Dunne's questions, asking, 'Can you tell me what has happened?' Dunne told him: 'You're right, Mum and Dad are dead.'

Dunne was present at 11 a.m. when Dr Pryde, the police doctor, examined David in a full body strip-search, taking intimate body swabs and genital samples in the process. David was still wearing the same clothes he had been found in: white socks, bike shorts underneath black rugby shorts and a white T-shirt with 'Queen's Baton Relay Run' on it. These were seized by Detective Ross. David was photographed by the police photographer and his fingerprints were taken.

At noon, Dunne sat David down in an interview room and asked him questions nearly all afternoon, till about 4.30 p.m. David signed the notes made by Dunne as being true and correct. Finally, about 10 hours after he had discovered the bullets in his room and run in fear to his mother, his Uncle Bob collected him. Bob was married to Jan, David's mother's younger sister. Uncle Bob and Aunty Jan took David to their home in the seaside suburb of St Clair, where their two teenage daughters also lived.

The next day, Tuesday, 21 June, Greg Dunne went out to the Clarks' house and after first speaking to the Clarks he took down another statement from David from 2.35 p.m. till about 5.30. Dunne had by this time been briefed by Operation Every HQ, so the questioning is sharper, more acute, more finely directed, although David would not have noticed. He was simply trying to help the nice policeman. It was late in this interview that David would make statements that would have a very significant bearing on the turn of events.

> *Dunne:* How do you explain the 25 minutes in the house before you called the ambulance?
>
> *David:* I don't know. Slow.
>
> *Dunne:* Run through actions/timing.
>
> *David:* I can't tell you anything about the time. Recently, I have been spacing out. It has happened in the last couple of months. Last time it happened was at the Symphonia. I don't remember two movements. The people I was with said I was watching the show. Before that, all I can think of is when time flew, went by very quickly. I can't tell when it starts or ends.
>
> *Dunne:* Have you sought medical attention for this?
>
> *David:* No, it only happened two weeks ago. I have talked to [name suppressed — a female friend of David's] about it.

The interview did not have long to run. They had discussed family finances, Robin and Margaret's relationship, the various habits of different members of the family, the family dynamics, who got on best with whom, who used the computer in the house and what each individual used it for. Every little detail of the family's life was discussed, and, being the only one left, David did all he could to help.

> *Dunne:* Do you know of any extra-marital relationships?
>
> *David:* No, Mum didn't have any. I don't know about Dad; I knew very little about what Dad thought or did.
>
> *Dunne:* Was your mum a homeopath?
>
> *David:* Yes, touch for health massage, and natural remedies for any ailment.
>
> *Dunne:* Without harping on about it, Dave, can you think of any reason why you said that your whole family had been killed to the 111 lady, when you had only seen or knew about Mum and Dad?
>
> *David:* I don't know.

After Dunne left the Clark home that afternoon, David had a conversation with his Uncle Bob about what might have happened. This came about because the *Otago Daily Times* had, as would be expected, prominently featured this dramatic and bizarre event. More details of the massacre had been released by the police and were included in graphic fashion. The locality of the bodies, the number of shots fired and even some diagrammatic depictions of where they were found were included. David was shocked to learn that Laniet had been shot three times and Stephen had apparently tried to fight off his assailant after the first shot failed in its objective, and that Arawa, too, was out of bed.

Stephen must have woken up just before the first shot was fired at him and, while he still lay in bed with his head on the pillow, he successfully pushed away the tip of the rifle with his left hand, causing the bullet to go directly through the palm of his hand and then into his head at about the hairline. It gouged a 20 mm deep, 50–60 mm-long gash from front to back across the top of his scalp, before lodging itself in the pillow where it was located.

Bleeding profusely, with two serious injuries, the head one of which would have made it virtually impossible for him to see, Stephen had flailed about, possibly trying to fight off his assailant, causing huge volumes of blood to be left on the bedding and about his room.

David became deeply distressed seeing and reading the grisly details of his family's demise. He was also concerned about why it might have taken 20 minutes for him to call 111 after he got home. So his uncle called Detective Sergeant Dunne, telling him David wanted to see him. Dunne went back to St Clair about 9.30 p.m. that evening and found David very upset, crying and distressed, according to his notes of the meeting.

It was at this meeting Dunne told David that the police had already ruled out a stranger to the house being responsible and that it was either David or his father who must have done it. According to Dunne's notes, David said: 'If only I had run home I might have been able to save them.'

Dunne recorded that 'he wants to blame someone but doesn't know who to blame', seemingly a reference to David blaming himself for not getting home in time to save his family.

Later that night, David told members of his family that if it was his father he could never forgive him.

CHAPTER 2

THE ARREST AND ITS AFTERMATH

It had been a long week, filled with police interrogations, sleeplessness, headaches, nightmares. The funerals were scheduled for the Saturday, and David was involved with the extended family, a victim support officer and the undertaker, helping with those arrangements.

And then came Friday and the visit to the Dunedin CIB. His Uncle Bob was taken away for a coffee with Detective Senior Sergeant Jim Doyle, the officer directing inquiries for Operation Every, while in a separate room on the fifth floor of the old building David was confronted by two detectives he had not previously met. No longer the friendly, helpful Greg Dunne, this time David faced Detective Neil Lowden and Detective Sergeant Kallum Croudis, who read him his rights and David said he understood. The interview began.

For the most part Croudis asked the questions and Lowden made notes of the interview, although occasionally they swapped roles. The exact typewritten transcript of the questions and answers is given in Appendix A.

The allegations covered in this statement are obvious. Aside from matters stated as factual evidence, the most dramatic and revealing segment is the reference by Croudis to the missing 15 to 20 minutes, followed by the question: 'Is that an explanation for what happened to your family that morning?' The police belief was revealed in an instant: David killed his family after returning from the paper round, in the period of time that he was not able to account for. According to this theory, either he was lying when he said he couldn't remember, or he had suffered a blackout and his mind had blocked from his memory the terrible deeds he had committed.

The allegations put to David as being 'factual' evidence for which an explanation was sought were as follows:

- Your fingerprints have been found in blood on your firearm.
- There is a bloodstained fingerprint on the washing machine.
- There are indications of blood from clothing that appears to have been pushed into the washing machine.
- Agreement that David did wash clothes on Monday morning and that the wash included socks and a sweatshirt belonging to David and a jersey belonging to Arawa.
- Blood was found on the back of the T-shirt David was wearing when the police arrived.
- Blood was also on the sole of one of the socks David was wearing.
- A spot of blood was on the black rugby shorts he was wearing.
- Blood was in the porcelain hand-basin in the bathroom.
- A considerable amount of blood was on a large green towel hanging in the bathroom.
- Blood was smeared on the door surround in Stephen's room.
- A pair of formal gloves was found in Stephen's room heavily blood-stained.

It was at this point it would seem that David finally understood the legal warning he had been given and requested a solicitor. He was asked who he wanted, but he didn't know any solicitors. A list was provided. Bob Clark, David's uncle, knew Michael Guest, a criminal lawyer in Dunedin. Guest was located, with the assistance of Jim Doyle, on business at the courthouse. He came quickly to the CIB offices and consulted with David. He immediately put a stop to any further questioning.

Croudis then gave Guest a written list of further questions that he wanted to ask David, but Guest advised that David would not answer those questions.

The five written questions were:

- A lens from a set of glasses you have been wearing was found in Stephen's room. [Presumably he was going to be asked for an explanation for their presence.]
- Did you tell Val Boyd [David's aunt]: 'It could have been me. I don't know if it was me or Dad.'?
- A piece of skin similar to the piece missing from your knee was found in Stephen's room; can you explain this?

- A computer message was typed at 6.44 a.m. after you got home; did you type it?
- Did you shoot and kill the members of your immediate family?

Then Croudis asked if a medical examination could be conducted on David, saying that he wanted the general practitioner to view injuries observed on Monday to establish further bruising and to examine the soles of his feet.

Guest again, on David's behalf, declined.

At precisely 1.46 p.m., about three hours after Bob and David had arrived at the CIB, Croudis formally charged David Bain with the murder of his father, mother, sisters and brother. David was told that in answer to the charges he did not have to say anything but if he did it would be taken down in writing and could be used in evidence.

Not for the first time and certainly not the last, David, before being handcuffed and led off to the cells, wearing the woolly jersey knitted for him by his mum that would come to stigmatize him over the ensuing years and make him the butt of much national ridicule, answered Croudis: 'No, I'm not guilty.'

THE POWER TO PROSECUTE

Once the decision to charge and arrest David was taken, after only four days of inquiries and in the face of his continued cooperation and absolute claims of innocence, there could be no turning back for Operation Every. The battle lines were drawn. 'Paper boy delivers death to family' screamed the headlines. The police, having settled on a culprit, focused on a successful prosecution.

The dangers of the police developing a guilty mindset are perhaps best illustrated in the Arthur Allan Thomas case where police were found to have actually planted evidence to snare the man they believed was guilty but who was actually innocent.

In the Gisborne District Court in 1997 the Crown brought a case against five of its own officers, accusing them of corruption involving drugs and money. The case, known as Operation Vine, was found to be based on completely bogus evidence. In the foreword to a book about that case — *Presumed Guilty* by Miriyana Alexander — the counsel for the innocent accused, John Haigh QC, wrote, very appositely as far as the then still-unfolding Bain saga was concerned:

This book also raises the whole question of a need for the monitoring of investigative procedures … The power to prosecute is an awesome responsibility in terms of its impact … on each and every citizen of this country …

In regard to investigations that lead to charges and prosecution, what is required … is a degree of objectivity in every investigation. Where a mindset has developed as to the guilt of a suspect there can be no such objectivity.

An inquiry into what had gone wrong with the case was also commissioned. It was undertaken by District Court Judge Russell Callander, who noted in his report:

The decision to charge is the single most important decision made in the course of criminal proceedings. It lies at the very core of a system of Justice …

Once the decision to charge has been made the storm begins: irreversible tides will engulf the main players, changing their lives forever …

A deluge of media scrutiny, personal distress, family tension, financial burden and community pressure will take an inevitable toll …

The fear and consequences of criminal court proceedings and their outcome are profound. An eventual dismissal of the case is no consolation to an accused person.

The Bain case was no ordinary case: five people, slain in the dark of night in their own home, in one of Dunedin's better suburbs. No sign of drugs. No alcohol involved. Only one survivor, who presented as helpful, articulate, intelligent, diligent and who had nothing in his past to suggest that he would be capable of or have reason to commit this slaughter of his entire family. While it would have been totally remiss if David had not been treated as a suspect, even if only on the basis that he was the 'last man standing', one would not expect any conclusion to be reached in haste in such complex circumstances.

The decision to lay charges in any circumstances is never, or at least *should* never, be taken lightly. For homicide investigations, the police have the Homicide section of the *Criminal Investigation Manual*, the 'A to Z' of the serious crime detection work. It states that, as a general principle, the officer in charge of the investigation is responsible for interviewing the offender. Croudis and Lowden were acting under the instructions of DCI Peter Robinson and DSS Jim Doyle. However, no mention is made of any consultation with Robinson, which in such a serious high-profile case is bewildering.

The *Manual* also says that before making an arrest the officer in charge should read and evaluate relevant witnesses' statements; consider evidence-identification, fingerprints, corroboration, exhibits, photographs, plans, and murder weapon. He or she should evaluate results from specialists such as fingerprint experts and the pathologist, and scientific analysis from forensic scientists. Significantly, it says that where scientific or other expert opinion is the main evidence against a suspect, reports should be obtained in writing. He or she should also evaluate results of the interviews with the alleged offender and any search of a person's vehicle, home or workplace which has been undertaken. It states that he or she should ensure that the ingredients of homicide are satisfied and also that a prima facie case is established. In a case with only two possible suspects a prima facie case against one suspect must necessarily include the positive elimination of the other. The officer in charge should also consider what defences may be available and any outstanding inquiries that would require attention *before an arrest is made.*

Once the arrest happens, a tipping point has been reached from which there is no turning back and as a result of which the implications are serious and wide-ranging.

It is very unusual for the police to change their mind once charges have been laid.

In the history of homicide investigation in New Zealand the Bain case represented one of the most complex ever confronted by the New Zealand Police. There have been other family slayings and also some isolated mass killings in New Zealand but, the Arthur Allan Thomas case aside, they did not need solving for the reason that the perpetrator either committed suicide or gave himself up, as is the norm in such cases.

In terms of mass family killings, perhaps the most notable also occurred in the 1990s, one being the case of the Schlaepfer family near Pukekohe and the other that of the Ratima family in Masterton. On 20 May 1992 64-year-old Brian Schlaepfer shot or stabbed his family, killing his wife, his three sons, aged 39, 33 and 31, as well as one of his sons' wife and his grandson, aged 11. Another grandchild would probably have been killed, but she was hiding in a wardrobe talking on the telephone to the police. When the police arrived, the 64 year old had shot himself and was dead. The motive for the mass killing was never totally clear, but it was ascertained that Schlaepfer suffered from depression in the lead-up to the slayings.

On 26 June 1992 Raymond Ratima killed seven people in their home including his own three sons who were aged six, four and two at the time. He left his three sons on his wife's bed with a Bible on top of them. The mass killer was eventually subdued and at his court hearing he expressed remorse for his actions. Apparently, his behaviour was quite out of character for him. In the period before the tragedy there had been a serious argument between Ratima and his wife and he was forced out of their home. He felt as though his world was crashing down and after looking to social services and lawyers for help he was in despair. After days of little sleep and food, his mind apparently turned to revenge and murder.

The slayings of 13 people at Aramoana near Dunedin were a different kind of homicide, not family related but indiscriminate killings perpetrated by a man whose past behaviour indicated serious antisocial personality disorders. He was shot by the police. At Raurimu in 1997 a young man running naked in the neighbourhood killed members of his family and other people indiscriminately. This person had a long history of psychiatric instability. He was apprehended and judged to be insane at his trial.

But, in this case, as already indicated from the records of Detective Dunne, there were two suspects: David the survivor or Robin the father, found with the gun lying on the floor beside him. In order to be sure it was one, the other would need to be positively eliminated.

In that interview room, way back in 1994, Detectives Lowden and Croudis had just exercised that 'awesome responsibility' in one of the most perplexing and serious cases in New Zealand's criminal case history. On the basis of the statements of an extremely traumatized 22 year old, armed with theories that had not been tested as stipulated by the *Criminal Investigation Manual*, without the benefit of scientific forensic reports from the relevant experts, and before all witnesses had been found or interviewed, they charged David Bain with the murder of his family.

The decision made that day would lock David into a system that would affect him for the rest of his life and cause him to engage in a combat with the criminal justice system from behind bars that would last for just a few days short of 15 years.

His extended family, including his parents' siblings, would also be victims of that decision. So, too, were David's friends at the time and those he has made since. The taxpayers of New Zealand have seen untold millions of their dollars go up in smoke as a result.

The power to prosecute is indeed awesome and with it should come an equally awesome degree of propriety, expertise, objectivity and accountability.

With all that in mind, we can ask: what did the officers involved with Operation Every know that gave them grounds to be so certain of David's guilt? Eleven matters of evidence were put to David in the interview before he asked for a lawyer, and there were four more that he declined to answer on the advice of his just-appointed lawyer, Michael Guest.

On their face, or 'prima facie' as the law puts it, these items of evidence appear incriminating. However, it would seem as though the detectives, in making the decision to lay charges, did not give consideration 'beyond face value', because there were a multitude of matters that remained unanswered. Some examples are:

- The very first point postulated that his fingerprints were found on the gun '*in blood*'. What tests had been done to warrant this statement?
- Then there is the statement that '*a considerable amount of blood was found on a green towel hanging in the bathroom*'. Had any tests been done on this towel? How old was the blood? More importantly, perhaps, whose blood was it? Was it even connected with the killings?
- Then to the questions that David did not answer, the first of which says that '*a lens from a pair of glasses you [David] have been wearing was found in Stephen's room*'. What was the evidential foundation for this?
- There is the statement David allegedly made to his other aunt, Val Boyd, '*It could have been me. I don't know if it was me or Dad.*' What was the evidence for this allegation?

- The next matter in the unanswered questions relates to a piece of skin found in Stephen's room said to be '*similar to the skin missing from David's knee*'. The detective wanted David to explain this. David had not been investigating the crime scene. Is a similarity in appearance sufficient to make an arrest? Whose skin was it? Had any tests been done?
- Finally in the unanswered list there was the matter of the message on the computer, '*typed onto the computer at 6.44 a.m. after you got home*'. Was there a firm evidential foundation for this allegation about the timing?

So, at the time of David's arrest, the information and evidence before the police can be broadly characterized as falling into three categories:

1. Information of an unequivocal nature. For example, that blood was present in certain places and on certain items and that there was a message on the computer.

2. Information which was insufficiently complete to judge its relevance, significance and also how it correlated with other evidence. For example, whose blood was it and what would that reveal in the context of other evidence?

3. Information indicating avenues of inquiry that had not even commenced or which were in such an early stage that nothing could yet be gleaned of a useful or definitive nature. By way of examples, there is the piece of skin found in Stephen's bedroom, on which at the time no tests had been conducted but which the police apparently assumed was David's; and on another front, suggestions of unusual and possibly very relevant information regarding the family dynamics.

Were the Operation Every heads justified in proceeding with the arrest when they did or, on the other hand, had they become besieged with a *guilty* mindset that caused them to act prematurely and imprudently?

It is clear from the interview conducted by Croudis and Lowden on the day of the arrest and from those between David and Greg Dunne earlier, that three factors dominated the detectives' belief that David was guilty of the five murders.

The first was that David had said to the 111 operator 'they are all dead — I came home and they're all dead', and yet he told Dunne that he had only seen his mother and father dead. This was construed as a lie, a belated attempt to cover up the deed, one of those elementary giveaway mistakes that even the most sophisticated of felons always makes.

The second point relates to the 'missing 20 minutes', the period of time between when David got home and when he called 111. It was believed that this was when David committed the killings, and that again he was lying or had a blackout and couldn't remember doing it. This belief can be gleaned directly from the question to David: 'You could not account for 15 to 20 minutes. Is that an explanation for what happened to your family that morning?' David answered: 'No, it's a question of what happened to me.'

The third crucial aspect that caused the detectives to be so sure was to do with blood:

- Bloody fingerprints on the rifle.
- Bloodstained fingerprint on the washing machine.
- Bloody clothing pushed into the washing machine.
- Blood on the 'Queen's Baton Relay Run' T-shirt David was wearing.
- Blood on the black rugby shorts he was wearing.
- Blood on the sole of the sock he was wearing.
- Blood on a towel in the bathroom.
- Blood on the door surround in Stephen's room.
- Bloodstained gloves found in Stephen's room.
- Blood in the hand-basin.

Ten different bloodstains were put to David that Friday, showing the reliance placed by Operation Every on these matters for their belief that David was the killer.

INVESTIGATING THE CRIME

A large inquiry team was established on the first morning by Detective Chief Inspector Peter Robinson, head of the Dunedin CIB, and officer in charge of Operation Every.

DSS Jim Doyle was made second in charge, responsible for coordinating the inquiry, assimilating and redirecting inquiries as information came to hand and ensuring the overall efficiency of the operation. The 2IC is said to be the busiest man in the team.

Detective Sergeant Milton Weir was appointed as officer in charge of the scene investigation, essentially involving the house and section at 65 Every Street.

Peter Hentschel, a forensic scientist from ESR (Institute of Environmental Science and Research) in Christchurch, was called in to assist Weir with the crime scene investigation and spent almost the entire first week at the scene.

Dr Alec Dempster was the pathologist who first examined the bodies at the scene and then conducted postmortems on the five victims and compiled his official reports.

Kim Jones, from the fingerprint section of the New Zealand Police in Wellington, was consulted as the fingerprint expert.

Robert Ngamoki, of the Police Armoury in Wellington, was the ballistics expert.

Then there were the other aspects that needed attention, such as general inquiries in the neighbourhood. Scene guards were posted to monitor and record the comings and goings into and out of the address. A number of police photographers were detailed to the inquiry at the scene and their efforts resulted in thousands of still photos as well as about an hour of video tape recording. Police photographers were at the mortuary to take photos during the autopsies conducted by Dr Dempster. There was an officer detailed to be in charge of each body. They were each under the control of the officer in charge of bodies Detective McGregor, who in turn, according to the *Manual*, was responsible to the officer in charge of the scene, Detective Sergeant Milton Weir.

The duties of the officer in charge (OC) of bodies are very explicitly set out in the *Manual*. These include not only a thorough list of duties at the scene, but also procedures for removal of the body, attendance at the postmortem and the collection and recording of bodily samples.

An exhibits officer was established to record and label every item gathered by detectives at the crime scene and elsewhere. Hundreds of exhibits were generated.

A computer expert from Otago University was called in to examine the family computer.

Then there were what in police lingo are called area canvass inquiries —

essentially door knocking and setting up road blocks in the vicinity of a crime to locate and interview potential witnesses.

All of these functional operations were under way within the initial days of the inquiry.

THE FIRST MORNING

On that freezing mid-winter Monday morning of 20 June 1994, as a result of the 111 call made by David at 7.09 a.m., four armed police officers led by Sergeant Stapp smashed the window beside the front door of 65 Every Street and made entry at about 7.35 a.m. By 7.45 a.m. it had been reported to the police control that there were five dead family members and one survivor.

The call went out from the police control room to top brass who, in some cases no doubt, forewent their breakfast and rushed to the office. DCI Robinson as head of the CIB took control and called for a briefing at police headquarters at 8.15 a.m. By this time the names of the dead were known. Robinson appointed himself officer in charge, with Doyle as his deputy. As many as 30 detectives may have been present at this very first gathering of the team who would make up Operation Every. Also at the briefing was the pathologist, Dr Alec Dempster.

At the scene, Constable Van Turnhout had been sent to observe David and make notes.

The first four officers to the scene — Stapp, Wylie, Andrew and Stephenson — having cleared the house by about 7.40 a.m., let in ambulance staff to assist the survivor, and to check the other five to make sure they were actually dead and therefore would not require medical attention. They were required to give statements to detectives detailed to the case and then were sent for trauma counselling as a result of having had to suffer the ordeal of being first to discover and report the gruesome situation.

Detective Kevin Anderson was sent to the scene as the temporary scene control officer. Detective Sergeant Milton Weir had been appointed as officer in charge of the scene at the 8.15 a.m. briefing, but did not arrive at 65 Every Street until about 9.45.

In the meantime, immediately following the 8.15 briefing, Robinson, Doyle and Bernie Hill, the local Superintendent of Police, went directly to Every Street. They went into and through the entire house, inspecting each of the rooms in the house and looking in on Van Turnhout in David's bedroom. This tour took place between 8.50 a.m. and 9 a.m., whereupon the three top brass returned to HQ and held another briefing at 9.15 a.m.

DS Weir was at this briefing as well and following it he went to the scene which at that point became properly controlled, more than two hours after it had been discovered and not before something like 14 or 15 individuals had access to one degree or another. The pathologist, Dr Dempster, arrived about the same time as Weir but was not allowed to enter the house until 12.05 p.m.

The bodies were removed later that day and autopsies carried out late into the night, the final one not completed until the following morning. Dr Dempster and the police at that stage believed they were dealing with a murder/suicide and that David was, as he had told them, an innocent and lonely survivor.

A FAMILY IN SHOCK

But then, on the Friday afternoon, David was charged with the murders. The final vestiges of his previous identity fell away. No longer was he a son or a brother; no longer was he a university student or a musician or an athlete. Now he was nothing but a remand prisoner facing five counts of murder. His family was dead; at times, David wished he was dead, too.

The following day, Saturday, there was to be a combined funeral service for Robin, Margaret, Arawa, Laniet and Stephen. David had been involved in planning the service, but now he was unable to attend. Who made that decision has never been made clear, but it must be debatable whether he could be legally denied the right to attend his family's service, for he was, after all, still an innocent person in the eyes of the law.

By this time, the extended family from each of his parents' sides had descended upon Dunedin. They, too, were severely traumatized by the week's events. Perhaps understandably, David's uncles and aunts appear to have bought into the condemnation of their nephew; after all it was their brother or sister, Robin and Margaret, who had been murdered. None of them knew David very well, if at all, and any affinity or favour would quite naturally belong with their brother or sister, rather than the nephew who the police obviously 'knew' had 'done it'. It is understandable that Robin's brothers and sister would have trouble accepting the alternative, that their own sibling had murdered his family before taking his own life.

Two of David's uncles were the executors of Robin and Margaret's will, between them representing both sides of the extended family: Michael Bain, one of Robin's two brothers, and John Boyd who was married to Valerie, one of Margaret's three sisters. They had quite a job ahead of them, for Robin and Margaret had accumulated assets that were spread far and wide around the globe. They were assiduous hoarders of artefacts and memorabilia, and there was also a considerable array of photo albums and videos recording the lives of the Bain family.

The situation facing Michael Bain and John Boyd deserves some attention for like nearly everything else relating to the events that were set in motion that June Monday in 1994, it was by no means simple, and in fact may be virtually unprecedented.

Robin Bain had two brothers and a sister. The family grew up in Island Bay in Wellington and then in Otaki, a village just north of Wellington, and were of staunch Presbyterian stock. Back in those days, growing up through the 1950s and 60s, both Robin and Michael owned rifles, and they regularly went tramping with their .303s in tow.

Robin went to training college and became a teacher. He was very active in the Presbyterian Church and in 1964–65 went as a lay missionary to Papua New Guinea for the first time. He met Margaret in Dunedin and they married in 1969. They had their first child, David, on 27 March 1972, and a year later shifted to PNG where their three other children were born. They remained in PNG for 15 years, returning to New Zealand for holidays three times. It was just before they moved to PNG in 1973 that Michael was appointed by Robin as an executor of his will.

Michael Bain had worked his way up to a senior position in the Air Force. He lived at the Woodbourne air base in Blenheim with his family for some years before moving to Wellington where he lived at the time of the deaths in 1994. Like the rest of his family, he had seen very little of Robin over the years, and barely knew the children at all. Michael had not seen Margaret since 1988. He never visited them in Dunedin and despite the fact that Robin spent a couple of weeks with him in January of 1994 when they painted their mother's house in Otaki, he did not know that Robin and Margaret's marriage had been on the rocks for some years.

John Boyd, of course, was not a blood relative of any of David's family.

He enjoyed a successful career as a bank officer for over 40 years. He barely knew David's family at all.

But here they both were in June of 1994 with the responsibility of resolving the estate of Robin and Margaret in the most highly charged circumstances one could imagine.

John Boyd and his wife Val arrived in Dunedin the day after the deaths and stayed at the Clarks' where David was also resident. Michael Bain did not arrive until the Thursday. That same afternoon Michael and John visited the lawyers who would act for the estate. Whether at the time of that meeting they had an inkling from the police that David was to be charged is unknown. They certainly knew that the police had decided it was either Robin or David.

The wills left everything belonging to Robin and Margaret, in the event that they both died, to the remaining family, meaning that if David had not been charged, the entire estate would have been his as the sole surviving beneficiary. But under the circumstances it was something of a nightmare because he was still the sole beneficiary pending the outcome of the charges against him.

One can imagine the state of the Clark household on the Friday when David was arrested. The funeral plans were thrown into chaos as David had been quite involved with those preparations and now he could not even attend. Of course there were meetings with the police and also the obvious trauma for all concerned at the incredible rush of events that surrounded the week. A murder in one's neighbourhood of somebody known is traumatic enough. For Margaret and Robin's siblings and their families it must have been a dreadful week, made even more brutal by the fact that they had been harbouring the apparent killer under their own roof. The emotions must have been nearly at breaking point by that Friday night.

On the other hand, maybe there was also some relief. Rather than a long drawn-out investigation with the associated intense media scrutiny, perhaps resulting in unpleasant revelations about the lives of their brother and sister, at least under these circumstances they could begin to move forward. With an arrest having been made, the matter would now be sub judice and perhaps there was some hope that David might enter guilty pleas, thereby saving everyone the tribulations associated with a high-profile murder trial.

But David did not plead guilty. He maintained his innocence. So his uncles and aunts, and in particular Michael Bain and John Boyd as trustees of the estate, were confronted with a most difficult conundrum. Should they support their surviving blood relation or should they support the police against him and stand by their own brother and sister, David's parents?

The dilemma is both moral and legal. It is impossible in this forum to ascertain the legal position; even judges may find it difficult. The moral one is just as difficult. The trustees of an estate have as their primary responsibility a duty to the beneficiaries of that estate. But in this case there was only one and he had been charged with killing the very people from whom he would stand to benefit. The estate was endowed with ample funds that could have been used to assist David's defence. But then the executors had to decide whether to use those funds to defend the person alleged to be the killer, or accept that he was guilty as charged and leave him to fight on his own.

It was a weighty question which may be without precedent, and the answer probably lay in that murky world of gut feeling. If his family believed he was guilty it would be counter-intuitive to spend money defending him. On the other hand, as he steadfastly maintained his innocence, should he not be entitled to the best possible defence?

So as David acclimatized himself to life on remand as a high-profile, at-risk killer in the dungeons of the old Dunedin remand prison, a variety of forces were at play on the outside determining his fate.

Time was rushing by at a frantic pace as the week drew to an end. After David's arrest on Friday, DCI Robinson met with the family.

On Saturday, as the funerals were in progress, the case against David continued to be built. Jim Doyle and Milton Weir carried out reconstructions at the crime scene, concluding that Robin was shot as he knelt in front of a red chair, by a person hiding behind adjacent curtains that separated the little computer alcove from the lounge proper. Weir, being of similar stature to Robin, played his part and he had no trouble reaching the trigger of the rifle when re-enacting a suicide scenario. Although the *Manual* states that experts should attend reconstructions, Dr Dempster, the most relevant expert, was not present.

On Saturday afternoon following the funerals, the family were taken through the Every Street house by the police. Already a shambles before the tragedy, the house was now virtually uninhabitable. In the process of the scene inquiry collecting evidence it had been virtually wrecked. Doors had been removed and sent to the ESR for examination. Whole door frames had been sawn off with a chainsaw for the same reason. Carpets had been lifted and so the old wooden structure was reduced to its bare bones. A large container and tent were set up on the front lawn containing the considerable array of family artefacts and possessions. What to do with them? It must have seemed at once heartbreaking and overwhelming.

On the question of David's guilt, the family quickly took their position, accepting the police's version of events. On Tuesday, 28 June Michael and Peter Bain along with John Boyd visited David in prison. They asked him point blank if he had done it. David denied responsibility. They also discussed what to do with the house. David told his uncles he had no desire to keep the house.

The police finished their scene examination and collecting evidence from the house by 30 June, and their surveillance of the property ended on that date. The estate paid for security guards to protect it from squatters or other ghoulish intruders for the following week.

Meanwhile, the executors, Michael Bain and John Boyd, took advice to the effect that the property would be more valuable if the house was removed than if it was standing derelict and dismantled. They had the option of bulldozing it to the ground or burning it. Quite obviously, the former would have cost a lot more and so they arranged with the fire service to have it burnt. From the executors' point of view it may have been the prudent decision, but it certainly did not help David.

The house at 65 Every Street was burnt to the ground in a blaze of publicity just a week later, an eerie and spectacular sight. Coming so soon after David's arrest it gave the chilling impression of being the final step in a sort of exorcism of evil — the evil one is behind bars and the scene of his evil deeds is eliminated from sight. Conservative Dunedin could carry on with life as though this aberration had never happened.

THE DEFENCE

And so, as week two turned into week three, the collateral forces were combining to render David's position very lonely indeed. All he now had, apart from the friends who visited and supported him emotionally, was his lawyer Michael Guest, whom he had never heard of until the day of his arrest.

Guest came from a distinguished legal family in Dunedin. His father, and maybe even his grandfather, had been lawyers in Dunedin. His brother Stephen was an academic lawyer working in London.

He was admitted to the Bar in 1972 and in 1987 became a District Court judge in Invercargill, at 36 the youngest to have been appointed to such a position. He resigned after only two years in controversial circumstances apparently related mainly to financial matters. He is quoted in a newspaper article on 9 December 2001 as saying 'I was technically insolvent. I could not carry on as a judge.'

Having resigned, being in impecunious circumstances and needing to rebuild his career, he moved to Tauranga where he worked doing mostly legal aid casework. In 1992, with the dust having settled in his home town, he moved back to Dunedin and set up practice there again where his family were well established and where old blood runs deep.

David of course knew none of this and nor did he know of another case that Guest was involved in at the very same time he became David's lawyer. That case resulted in the Otago District Law Society bringing six charges against Guest for professional misconduct on a case during the years 1993 and 1996. The charges related to his honesty and integrity. The hearing was before the Law Practitioners Disciplinary Tribunal and took place over a number of days in July, August and September 2001.

The case was a particularly sad affair. Two new mothers had been sent home from hospital with the wrong babies. It was even more distressing for the mothers because it was many months before the mistake was identified by which time they had become attached to the infant in their care. The woman Guest represented was a poorly educated solo mother for whom he received legal aid. However, he told his client that he had been refused and took a fee from her as well.

Guest was represented by the very highly regarded barrister, George Barton QC. Nevertheless, the tribunal found against him in December 2001 and, despite his appeal, he was struck off.

The tribunal made many damning comments that impinged on his integrity. It said he left a clear impression of obfuscation by quantity of words, rather than of truth by simple narration of facts …

This was actual misconduct by Mr Guest in the course of his legal practice … a manipulation of his client, to his best advantage … in the belief that he [Guest] would be able to get away with it because of [his client's] limited intelligence and ability to understand and complain and that it involved deliberate lying and deceit, motivated by self-interest.

The years went by and after two stints as a Dunedin City Councillor, in 2009 he applied to the Law Society to be reinstated. Although his application was viewed with some caution by the body, he gained a partial right to practise, which did not satisfy him. He gathered about 90 letters in support of what he claimed to be his new-found redemption as a man of good moral fibre and ethical stature. He swore an affidavit to this effect.

However, in this affidavit, he also made an untrue claim regarding his conduct while practising in Tauranga. The Law Society decided that he was not reformed at all, that this was a clear example of more of the same, and his application was denied.

So, at the very time of David's arrest and trial, Guest was indulging in the conduct that resulted in his ultimate disgrace. He was also struggling to reconstruct his life financially and in the eyes of his peers. It may be that such a high-profile case was seen by him as a golden opportunity to achieve both. A further example of his cavalier behaviour is that he accepted money for and agreed to allow the making of the inside story of his defence of David Bain to a television documentary maker, meaning that during preparation for the trial and even during the trial itself he was distracted by performing for the cameras. In this documentary he talks about having 'a quick flick' through documents disclosed to him by the police.

David, locked in the cells of Dunedin's remand prison, was oblivious to Guest's background or his nefarious conduct at the time, and had little option but to put his faith in his lawyer. In the meantime, Operation Every marched into full stride, preparing for the depositions hearing set down for October of 1994, and this brought into play the next range of forces that would come to bear on the case: the Crown Prosecutor's office and expert analysis by the ESR scientists of the exhibits collected by the police. At the completion of the depositions hearing David was committed for trial.

PART TWO

THE FIRST TRIAL

CHAPTER 3
THE FIRST TWO DAYS

THE STAGE IS SET

And so, after almost a year of investigation, the trial began on 8 May 1995 in the Dunedin High Court. It involved forensic analysis that took the police as far as Melbourne to obtain the most up to date DNA testing, and about 80 witnesses. Of these, only three were called by Michael Guest in defence of his client: David himself; Dr Paul Mullen, a forensic psychiatrist from Melbourne; and Kyle Cunningham, a young bloke who had been living at the Taieri Beach schoolhouse with Robin and Laniet at the time of the tragedy.

The Crown Prosecutor at the first trial was Bill Wright who had graduated from the University of Otago in 1969 and who had been involved in Crown work since 1970. He cleverly packaged the case against David in a simple format. There were three planks, he said, upon which the case was built. He said it was like three points of a triangle:

1. There was a mass of evidence implicating David as the killer.
2. There was no evidence suggesting that Robin was involved in any way.
3. It was highly unlikely that Robin could have committed suicide.

This triangle was predicated on the way the whole inquiry had been run, as explained to David by Greg Dunne a year earlier that it was either David or Robin. The Crown proposition, of course, could be put another way: We know it was either Robin or David, but it is clear that it was not Robin so therefore it *must* have been David.

To set the scene we must retreat to 27 April 1995, just over a week before the trial began, when Wright wrote a letter to the registrar of the High Court that was copied to Michael Guest. The letter was to inform the court of the final list of witnesses the prosecution intended to call and at the same time note changes to the evidence from that presented at the depositions hearing the previous year.

It also listed additional evidence to be provided by some witnesses. Dr Dempster, the pathologist, for example, would now say (in addition to what was contained in his actual report) that in regards to the death of Robin, the site and location of the entry wound were both unusual in suicide, something he had not indicated in the pre-trial hearing, and on the same matter an ambulance officer would give evidence that he had attended 20–30 suicides by shooting and that he had never before seen a wound in this position. Imagine the defence counsel's consternation at having this quite profound and technical evidence thrown at him just a week before trial, leaving him no time to have it peer-reviewed by experts of his own.

The Crown Prosecutor, though, was onto it. He knew that the death of Robin Bain was the key to the trial. If the Crown could convince the jury that Robin did not kill himself, only one possibility remained — David shot him. On the other hand, a reasonable possibility that Robin did shoot himself could spell disaster for the prosecution.

In all, 24 witnesses were specifically referred to in the letter as either adding to or otherwise amending the evidence they had tendered in sworn testimony at the depositions hearing. Of relevance as we get into the evidence at the trial, neither Dr Pryde nor DS Milton Weir is mentioned in this letter.

In respect to photographs, the letter heralded only one new photo from those which had been exhibited at the depositions hearing. This was photo number 62 and it, too, will take on significance as the evidence unfolds. There was another notable feature about Photo 62 in the letter which was that it was the only photo produced for trial that did not have a caption explaining its significance and relevance. All other photos were described; for example, Photo 72 had a caption which read 'Staining on electric blanket switch and container'.

The trial began with an order from the presiding judge that all witnesses were to be excluded from the court except for the police officers in charge of the case: DSS Jim Doyle and DS Milton Weir.

THE CROWN OPENING

Bill Wright's opening address to the jury occupied about three hours, and in the course of it he took the defence completely by surprise and turned the psychology of the case upside down.

In 1995 the courts did not make a record of counsel's opening and closing addresses and so the following rendition of Bill Wright's opening address to the jury is taken from his own handwritten notes which he attached as an exhibit to an affidavit tendered to the Court of Appeal for the hearing that took place in 2002. In the affidavit he stated: '*I do not believe I departed from them in a material way.*'

These notes record that he began by setting out what the Crown intended to prove, commencing with a brief background description of each member of the family. As to Laniet he said — '*finished school and had part time employment*'. He told the court that '*an estrangement had taken place between Margaret and Robin. There had been marital discord for many years.*'

He then went on to describe what he called '*the somewhat unusual behaviour*' of the accused in and around the time of the murders. This included the fact that David had discussed with some friends having occasional déjà vu experiences, that he had gone into a trance for about 20 minutes at a concert and that he had seen the movie *Schindler's List* on 29 May 1994. He repeated what David had told the police that he could not account for the 20 minutes after he arrived home before he called 111. And then in the few days after the murders Wright suggested that David's behaviour was also unusual in that he wanted to get Arawa's friends together to celebrate what would have been her twentieth birthday had she lived, and also the manner of his involvement in the funeral arrangements.

He went through the evidence the police found within a few days which '*nominated the accused as the killer*' and '*excluded Robin*' and also made it '*most unlikely*' that Robin had committed suicide.

He ran through all the blood evidence telling the jury how David could not offer an explanation for any of it.

He told them that '*two droplets of blood were found on the upper surfaces of one sock*' (the white socks David was wearing when found), that this blood had been tested and was the blood of either Laniet or Stephen.

He told them how the fingerprints of each of the four fingers of David's left hand were on the forward area of the wooden part of the rifle pointing downwards and that these prints were made in blood; that is, the blood was on the fingers and deposited onto the rifle, not the other way round. He called these '*positive prints*'.

He described the house — '*dilapidated and in grave state of disrepair*'. He said the front room of the house '*assumed special significance for the family — apparently it had been the practice of Robin Bain to go to this room in the mornings for the purpose of praying*'.

He told them that there was no blood on Robin Bain's shoes or socks, that the only blood on him was a very small amount — '*drop of blood on fingernails*'. No fingerprints were found on the computer. The computer was turned on at 6.44 a.m. The copy of the *ODT* delivered to 65 Every Street that day was found folded up on a shelf in the hallway just outside the door to '*the accused's*' room.

Stephen's room occupied a considerable amount of time. He recounted that there were two shots. That this room was very heavily bloodstained throughout: '*Considerable blood — over Stephen, floor, bed, bunks — there is a lot of blood.*' White dress gloves were found on the floor soaked in blood. There was a lens found that matched the frames and the other lens found on a chair in David's room. His notes state the lens was '*found on the floor in room on top of material — clear — hard to see in photos.*'

He tells of the stockinged footprints found with luminol tests.

- '*two — in Margaret's room going out*
- *one — in hallway*
- *two — in Laniet's room — one in one out. All right foot.*'

He tells of the bloodstains on David's clothes and injuries he was found to have. Blood on the back of the T-shirt, in the crotch area of the black rugby shorts, and the socks — '*don't know which sock was on which of his feet*', one of the socks had '*droplets of blood — these fallen vertically — either Stephen's or Laniet's*'. This is the second mention of these 'droplets'.

Dr Pryde commenced examining David at the CIB at 11.00 a.m. on the day of the tragedy and according to Wright noted the following:

- '*Bruising to right temple — 3 cm*
- *Bruising above right eye*

42

- *Bruising to right cheek below eye*
- *Skin abrasion inner aspect of right knee'*

He says Dr Pryde *'took various samples from the accused'*.

He then comes to a heading — *'Reconstruction'*

'We know the accused completed his paper round the morning of 20 June. He was back at 65 Every Street at 6.42 a.m.'

He speculates as to the order in which the deaths occurred, and says it was either Margaret, Stephen, Laniet then Arawa or Laniet, Margaret, Stephen (then back to Laniet's room) then Arawa. He says he certainly went back into Laniet's room after being in Stephen's.

In respect to Robin, his notes say: *'It will never be known with certainty when Robin Bain was shot in relation to the others. He could have been first or last.'* He qualified this according to his notes by telling the jury, *'there would have been sufficient time in the missing 15–20 minutes for the accused to have killed his father first and then the others. However, there are two important pieces of evidence which would indicate Robin Bain was killed some time after the four.*

'Robin Bain's body was still relatively warm compared to the others according to the ambulance.

'Washing machine — earliest accused could have put it on was 6.42 a.m. — when police arrived — 7.34 a.m. at latest, it was not going.

'Therefore the clothes put in prior to the accused going to deliver his papers.'

The above passage is the final passage in the extensive notes Mr Wright made for his opening address to the jury.

THE FIRST RULING

During the course of trials judges are often required to make rulings usually as a result of protests made by the defence, or in some circumstances by the Crown. Justice Williamson was required to make eight rulings during this trial, and the first of them arose immediately upon the completion of the Crown's opening address.

Guest had two complaints and both related to timing matters. The first was the issue arising out of the closing remarks that David may have put the washing on *before* he went on his paper round. The significance of this is that David cannot have done the washing until after Stephen had been killed, which Guest of course thought, up to the point in time he heard this, was after the paper round.

This was news to Guest and of course to David. The only evidence the police had about the washing was what David himself had told them — that after he came home he went directly downstairs, to the bathroom/laundry, washed his hands and put on a wash of coloured items including the red sweatshirt he had worn on the paper run.

Guest asked the judge that he make a ruling that the Crown should confirm whether or not it was alleged that all five were shot after the paper round or whether they were saying four were shot before he left and one upon his return. Clearly, in addition to what is recorded in his notes, Wright must have signalled this new theory in more detail for Guest to have lodged the protest.

The other complaint made by Guest was that Wright had said that David was back at 65 Every Street at 6.42 a.m., a time matter that will become very significant.

The judge ruled against Guest, saying in his ruling the jury could decide what they believed once they had heard all the evidence.

The judge in his written ruling recorded that '*the defence was concerned it would be some time before it would have the opportunity to challenge these facts*'. It can be presumed he meant to say 'challenge these allegations'.

Guest's concern about the issue of when the killings were supposed to have happened was very live and real. He had always been led to believe that the killings occurred, or were alleged to have occurred, in the 'missing 20 minutes'. The first he ever heard of the 'four before and one after' theory was in the last seconds of Wright's opening address just minutes before the first witness was to be called.

The main issue arising from this was that it threw the whole theory of the case as it had been into chaos. Guest's plans for cross-examination would have been thrown into utter turmoil.

Think about the ramifications. The psychology of the case was turned upside down. It is one thing to suggest a person who suffers from trances and premonitions and the like suffers a kind of temporary mental aberration during the missing 20 minutes and does some terrible thing that his mind has blacked out. It is totally another to suggest that the executions were planned and premeditated so as to escape detection by laying the blame with his father and into the bargain being so cold and callous that he could take his dog and deliver 150 newspapers after having just executed his mother and siblings and with the intention of returning home to then deal to his father.

The first scenario raises the spectre of a mentally frail person suffering a period of derangement or temporary insanity. The second requires the person to be an out and out psychopath: that is the psychology of it. Guest was defending an entirely unheralded proposition.

Right from the beginning of the inquiry it was obvious that various incidents that are known to have occurred would need to be correlated with each other in order to establish a sequence of events, which in turn would assist in determining one of the most important issues in any case — opportunity. It has been famously said, long ago, that in solving murder cases there are three predominant factors — motive, means and opportunity. Opportunity is the opposite of alibi and simply means the possibility that a particular deed could have been carried out by a particular person at a given time. Obviously, if a person has an alibi for an event or action then, at the very least, an alternative explanation for that event must be sought. It was an accepted fact that David Bain did do his paper round on the morning of the murders, therefore if any event crucial to the murders occurred while he was absent he would have an alibi.

Another factor was the time of the deaths. Obviously, if it could be shown that the killings all happened during the period when David was known to be on his paper round, then he cannot have been the killer. But regarding this new scenario where the Crown were having a bob each way as to when the family were murdered, the defence was faced with enormous problems. A big gap between the deaths fitted one of the scenarios and no gap at all fitted the other.

Imagine if some of the bodies were still warm and had therefore been dead just a short time, say a maximum of two hours, whereas others were stiff with rigor mortis which normally takes about six or seven hours to set in, then this would open up various alternative theories in respect to the sequence of deaths. For example, if it could be established that Robin was killed first, a possibility flagged by Wright in his opening address, then clearly he could not have killed the others.

45

Another matter is that as the rifle and ammunition were kept in a wardrobe in David's bedroom, Robin, if he was the killer, had to wait till David went on his paper round to have access to it.

David, if he were the culprit, had to commit the murders either before his paper round or after it. That means before about 5.30 a.m. or between 6.45 a.m. and 7 a.m. after he got home. Robin's opportunity was the hour between (about) 5.45 and 6.45 a.m. when he knew that David would be absent from the house on his paper round.

So it is only fair to acknowledge that the sudden change in the Crown theory about when the murders were alleged to have taken place was a bombshell to Guest and made his defence of David much more difficult. He had always believed, and been led to believe, that the case he was defending was, as stated by Croudis when David was arrested, that the missing 15–20 minutes between about 6.45 and 7 a.m. accounted for the deaths of the five family members.

Perhaps just as notable is that the Crown itself was hedging its bets. Serious misgivings about the theory on which David was charged must have existed for the Crown to advance the alternative scenario articulated in its opening address.

On this note the trial began. The first round had clearly gone in favour of the Crown before even the first witness was called. But then it got down to the slow, arduous and sometimes very boring process that goes to make up a case in a modern criminal trial.

THE FIRST WITNESSES

The following account of the trial covers every witness called to give evidence and endeavours to impart all of the salient testimony from the trial.

But first, an explanatory note on terminology. The evidence of a witness being led through their deposition statement or brief of evidence by the side calling them is referred to as 'evidence in chief'. Once that stage is finished the other side is free to ask questions of the witness and this is known as 'cross-examination'. At the completion of cross-examination further questioning of the witness is permitted by the leading counsel but questioning at this time is restricted to matters that have been raised in cross-examination. This is called 're-examination'.

The police were down to call their three photographers, Gardener,

Chilton and Bachelor, first but, very unusually, their evidence was not required. Guest must have agreed to this. Milton Weir eventually produced the photographs and video for trial even though he never held a camera or developed a photo at any stage.

So, as it turned out, registered surveyor Reece Gardner was first up. He acted under instructions from Weir to draw up a plan of the house, with various overlays showing the location where bodies, bullets, blood and footprints were found. His evidence was read by consent, meaning that his statement was read to the jury by the court registrar and that he was not required for cross-examination.

George Barbara, a police constable in the CIB, then gave evidence as the officer in charge of exhibits. He produced a list of exhibits along with a record of the movements of the exhibits as they passed in and out of his possession. About 160 exhibits were produced at this trial by the Crown.

Then came Frances Edwards, the emergency call centre operator who spoke to David for 26 minutes after first putting him through to the St John Ambulance in Dunedin. Guest did cross-examine her, but really only for effect. An interesting factor to bear in mind is that David was evidently so scared he wanted to keep talking to her until help arrived. The witness said she would normally hang up after passing the call through to the emergency services, but in this case because of the apparent extreme distress of the caller she stayed with him and did not hang up until she heard the police enter his room.

Next was Gary Barker, from the Telecom call centre in Christchurch, who produced evidence of the length of that call, which was 26 minutes.

The fifth witness was Thomas (Tom) Dempsey, the ambulance officer in the St John Ambulance call centre who took the call from David when Edwards passed it through at 7.10 a.m. All Dempsey confirmed was that he was the person who took the call, a recording of which was played to the jury. The transcript of the call became Exhibit 571. It read as follows:

St John: St John Ambulance. Can I help you?
Caller: Help, they are all dead.
St John: What's the matter?
Caller: They are all dead. I came home and they are all dead.
St John: Whereabouts are you?

Caller: Every Street. 65 Every Street. They are all dead.

St John: Who's all dead?

Caller: My family, they are all dead. Hurry up.

St John: Okay. Every Street. That runs off Somerville Street?

Caller: Yes.

St John: What phone number are you calling from?

Caller: 454 2527.

St John: 454 2527. And your last name?

Caller: Bain.

St John: Bain. Okay. We are on our way.

Caller: Please hurry up.

St John: Okay, Mr Bain, we will be there very shortly.

This transcript of the conversation between David and Tom Dempsey was made by the police on the day of the killings and Dempsey signed it the following day as being a true and accurate account of the recording on the cassette tape that was made of the call. The recording lasts almost exactly one minute. The conversation between David and Frances Edwards from Telecom that took place before the call was transferred to St John and after St John had hung up was not recorded. Guest asked one question of Tom Dempsey which was of no consequence.

THE FIRST FOUR POLICE

Then came the first four officers who arrived at the scene: Stapp, Stephenson, Wylie and Andrew. A number of matters are of interest.

Before going in they armed themselves with pistols. They were able to see the body of Robin Bain through the front window with the rifle beside it when they shone a torch in the window. They could hear a distressed voice calling for help from the front window on the opposite side of the front door. They couldn't open the front door so Stapp smashed a window beside it and was able to reach in and open it from the inside. It was still pitch-black. The first thing Stapp did when he got in the door was to check out the room where the live person was. Here is what he said in evidence.

'There was a male person in the area of the window that faces the front of the house, [at] the bottom of the bed … He was lying on the floor … in a foetal position. I ran to him. I stopped about a metre from him, I had my revolver pointed out and pointing in his direction.' He described him as convulsing and shaking, and wailing hysterically, 'They're all dead, they're all dead.' He then said that Constable Andrew stayed with him until the ambulance officers were let in to look after him and that he then went with Wylie through the rest of the house.

Stapp said that in Margaret's room the dog was sitting beside the bed. On seeing him it stood up, snarling and barking at him. Stapp says the only noises in the house were the person in room B (David) crying and the dog barking.

There was no sound of the washing machine going when he got to the laundry. The lights were on, according to him, in the room where Robin lay, David's room, the hallway, Margaret's room and the kitchen. The bathroom he couldn't remember. At about 7.45 a.m. he got another officer to tie the dog up on the front porch. The total time he was in the house was about 20 minutes. He confirmed that his shoes were never checked for bloodstains.

Stephenson was pretty fuzzy, quite understandably, in his recollections. He recalled seeing the dog roaming around from room to room. He went past Robin's body and poked his head and torch through the curtains and saw the computer making a glow. He also confirmed the very distressed state David was in. Stephenson's shoes were never checked for bloodstains either.

Then it was Wylie's turn. He and Stephenson had been the first officers to get to Every Street, although there was already an ambulance there, but the ambulance people had been instructed to wait until the police arrived.

Wylie has no recollection of going into the bathroom, although Stapp said they went in there together. 'He covered me while I took a torch,' Stapp had said. Wylie says he saw David having a convulsion after coming back upstairs. He then took the ambulance officer through the house to carefully check each body without disturbing anything by placing his fingers either on the wrist or the neck pulse.

Les Andrew, the last of the four police officers to give evidence, spent all his time in the room where David was. David was sitting on the floor holding the phone when Andrew first got there. The head of the bed is on the far left-hand corner as you look into the bedroom from the doorway and the bed is on a slight angle, meaning that the foot of the bed is about 300 mm out from the wall. At that point on the wall is a window through which the officers had been able to speak to David from outside before they made entry. Under the window was a dresser with staggered sharp corners. There was also a blue suitcase standing against the wall between the bed and the wall, making the gap between the bed and the wall even narrower.

Soon after Andrew's arrival he observed David shaking violently for about 10 to 15 seconds in what he thought was some kind of fit.

David then crashed backwards down between the bed and the wall. Andrew rushed over, rolled David over onto his side and then dragged him out and put him in the recovery position at the foot of the bed. He checked his pulse. All Andrew could say was '*there was one*', referring to David's pulse, meaning he was alive, although he had gone very limp.

Andrew says, and the Crown went on to make something of it, that David's eyes did not change like other people's did when he had seen them having a fit. 'They stayed the same, they were normal. They didn't sort of roll back or quiver or change as I have seen before,' he said. Andrew went on to say that David may have banged his head when he crashed between the bed and the wall, but if he did it would have been the back of the head. He also did not notice 'contact of any substance' between David's body and any objects as he dragged him out.

Another point made, confirmed by other witnesses, was that the light bulb in the bedroom was very dim. When the two ambulance officers came in, Andrew tried to turn the light on, thinking that it was off. However, instead of turning the light on he actually turned it off because it was already on. That gives an indication of how dark it was in the room even with the light on. A similar situation existed in the bathroom/laundry.

So the vital points to emerge from these four police were: David was wailing and hysterical. He had a fit, according to Andrew, which was described as odd because his eyes didn't change. He crashed down between the bed and the wall. If he bumped his head, Andrew said it would have been on the back. He then went into a semiconscious state after being dragged out of the narrow opening by Andrew.

In a direct question from Guest, Andrew agreed there was no suggestion on his part that David was 'doing a Hollywood'. None of the officers had their shoes checked to see whether they had trodden in blood. A dog and cat were roaming about the house. Finally, and perhaps crucially, Stapp maintained he went down to the laundry by 7.30. This, however, was in conflict with the Telecom woman's evidence that she hung up as soon as police entered, and Telecom's records show that to be at 7.36 a.m. It would have been at best another two minutes before Stapp got down to the laundry. This point Guest failed to elicit. Not making it allowed the impression to remain in the jury's mind that David must indeed have put the washing machine on before the paper run.

AMBULANCE OFFICERS

Next came the four ambulance officers: Chief Ambulance Officer Craig Wombwell, Ray Anderson, Jan Scott and John Dick. Wombwell was the first to give evidence. He had been a paramedic at that time for 21 years. He was the first ambulance officer into the house with Anderson. He went straight to David and said the room was very dark. 'I don't remember the light being on ... we were using our torches.' When he first got to David he appeared to be unconscious. He checked his pulse and it was normal and strong, between 70 and 80 bpm. He then said David did not present as a person who had just had a fit or had suffered from medical shock.

Wombwell then went with Wylie to check the bodies in the rest of the house. It was now about 7.45 a.m. The description Wombwell gave of the warmth or otherwise of Robin's body was slightly muddled. He said, 'Robin felt warmer than he looked like he should. His appearance was one similar to that of being dead for a long time, not a short time. I am talking about half an hour. To my initial touch he was warmer than I expected.'

Then he went to Margaret's room and said she was cool but not cold. She was tucked up underneath bedclothes in a water bed.

Stephen, though, was lying almost naked on his bedroom floor in this freezing cold, draughty house. He, too, according to Craig Wombwell, was cool but not cold, about the same temperature as Margaret. The same description applied to Laniet and Arawa. *Cool but not cold.* He summarized as follows: 'As regards temperature, the first one [Robin] I thought felt warmer than the others.'

Wombwell then went outside and arranged for two more ambulance officers to come in who relieved from about 10 a.m. till 10.20, during which time David complained of having a sore head. Wombwell said in evidence, 'I had a look but I didn't see any abrasion or mark.'

Guest's main attack on Wombwell was related to the implicit proposition that David may have been faking a fit. He put directly to Wombwell whether he was suggesting this was what happened. Wombwell replied somewhat ambiguously, 'No, there is no way I could say he was putting it on or could not. Couldn't make a definite statement either way.'

He confirmed to Guest, however, that he believed Robin had died within the last hour, and that he had told a police officer that at the time. This view he said was based on his very long experience of attending dead bodies and feeling their temperature. Unscientific certainly, but what was important was the relative warmth between the four others compared to Robin. It gave the very clear impression there had been quite some time between the deaths of Robin and the other four, based on his description of the others as 'cool but not cold'.

Wright re-examined Wombwell to reinforce the possibility that it may have been a fake fit that Andrew witnessed.

The next ambulance officer, Ray Anderson, who was only with David a very short time, said he saw him have a fit or seizure which he says was 'feigned to a degree'. In the end, under re-examination, Anderson stated point-blank 'this was in line with a purposeful fit'.

Anderson was with David for about 10 or 15 minutes between 7.45 and eight o'clock that morning. He brushed David's eyelashes to see whether he would get a reaction in an effort to judge whether he was conscious or not. He also checked David for other signs that might indicate trauma, looking all over and around David very thoroughly. However, he did not notice any bruising to David's face at this time, between 7.45 and 8 a.m.

Jan Scott, the third ambulance officer, was with David from about 7.50 a.m. until just before he was taken away at 10.20 to the CIB. She made no mention of any fitting or convulsing. David was mostly very quiet. At one stage he said he had to go to university and he also mentioned about black hands coming to get him, she said. She did not notice any bruising on his face until she got out to the ambulance at about 10.30 a.m.

The last ambulance officer, John Dick, told the court that he was with Scott and David for about two and a half hours. David complained of a headache, of being cold and feeling nauseous. He slept most of the time, Dick said. He did not move. He said he did notice a bruise on his head at some stage. He said it was very cold so they got two hot packs to put on David. Dick tried very hard to convey the impression that there was nothing wrong with David. Guest tried very hard to show that Dick was trying very hard to convey that impression.

The overall impression of Dick's evidence was that there was something dodgy about David's behaviour during those two and half hours that he was lying in the foetal position after having crashed back between the wall and the bed in front of Andrew. However, this was all based on Andrew's evidence that he had had a fit. None of them was there when the alleged fit occurred.

One thing that Guest did dispel was the Crown's attempt to suggest that David's heart rate of nearly 80 was normal and was therefore further evidence that the symptoms of stress and hysteria must have been faked. As part of his training the previous year David had undergone a physical appraisal that established his resting heart rate at about 53 beats per minute. The police obtained this report which Guest received with the discovery documents, but the Crown still tried to press home that his heart rate of 80 was normal. Guest got the ambulance officers to concede that his heart rate that morning was at least 50 per cent above its resting rate, even though it may have been about normal for many people. In other words, a person with a resting rate of 75, normal for most people, would have been about 120 by comparison, if their heart rate had raised to the same degree as David's.

DAVID TAKEN TO THE CIB

The fourteenth witness called by the Crown was the first member of Operation Every, Terry Van Turnhout, a young and inexperienced officer who was in the process of completing his detective training. He had been dispatched to the scene at 8 a.m. with very specific instructions to do nothing except watch and observe the sole survivor.

Like the others, Van Turnhout noted that he thought the lights were out when he got to 65 Every Street, when in fact they were on. He made very detailed notes in his notebook of the state of the room including drawing pictures of various items such as the bullets on the floor and other matters of interest. He actually counted the bullets and noted their precise position. He told the jury that at 8.47 a.m. the accused complained that he had a pain in his head. Van Turnhout, an hour after David had crashed onto the floor, noted a greenish bruise on David's right forehead.

At about 9 a.m. three senior police officers — Superintendent Bernie Hill, Detective Chief Inspector Peter Robinson and Detective Senior Sergeant Jim Doyle — came into the bedroom on their way out from the scene after having done a tour of the house. Van Turnhout then recorded at about 9.15 a.m. that the accused was disturbed, distressed and visibly upset. Also at about this time Van Turnhout says David asked for his glasses. He suddenly sat up and said he needed to go to university because he studied music. Van Turnhout gave evidence that he noticed a broken pair of glasses on the chair just inside the door of the bedroom.

He went on to say that at about 9.54 a.m. Weir popped into the bedroom and asked if anything in the room had been touched. Van Turnhout said that nothing had been touched apart from a pillow that he was aware of. This statement will be of note in later proceedings. At about 10.20 a.m. he assisted Detective Dunne in putting David into a carry chair and taking him from the scene out to the ambulance, which then drove the three of them to the CIB in downtown Dunedin where they arrived at about 10.29 a.m. At 10.36 a.m., according to Van Turnhout, David said, 'My father is dead, isn't he? I saw him, I saw him.' Van Turnhout does not record any reply given to David in response to this, but Dunne's notes record that he said to David: 'You are right, your mum and dad are dead.'

By this time David, Detective Sergeant Dunne and Van Turnhout were in one of the interview rooms of the CIB offices and Dunne apparently left the room for a while. While he was gone Van Turnhout said that he had a bit of a chat to David. 'We talked about David's paper run, about how long the accused was going to be at the station, whether it was going to hold him up for the next week or so; he talked about a play he was in and about ringing the producer, Mr Harry Love. I believe he was taking part in that play and wanted to ensure Mr Love was aware of what was happening.'

Dunne came back to the room with the police doctor, Dr Tom Pryde, and Van Turnhout says he was present when Dr Pryde asked David if he had got a whack on the head. David answered, 'Yes, I don't know how.' Dr Pryde then did his examination of David and left at about 11.40 a.m. when Van Turnhout had another chat with, as he called him, 'the accused', for five or six minutes when they talked about life in Papua New Guinea, his studies, and music, drama and theatre. Van Turnhout told the court that the accused appeared at ease. He didn't mention his family or what was happening. Then

Dunne and Dr Pryde came back and Van Turnhout left and he did not see the accused again.

The cross-examination was brief but Guest obtained agreement from Van Turnhout that for the whole time he was with David his eyes appeared to be glazed and his appearance and demeanour were that of a person in shock.

POLICE DOCTOR TOM PRYDE DROPS A BOMBSHELL

It was still before lunch on just the third day of the trial and the first evidence on day one was not called until nearly 3.30 p.m. but already the Crown was calling its fifteenth witness, police doctor Tom Pryde. Pryde was about to drop the first heavy bomb on David's claims of innocence, ambushing Guest in the process.

Pryde began by confirming that he had been police surgeon in Dunedin for about 25 years. He had arrived at Every Street at about 9.30 a.m. on 20 June and at about 10.30 a.m. was escorted by Weir through the house to check each body for 'life extinct'. It is interesting to note that at this time Dr Dempster, the pathologist, was also at the scene — he had been aware of the killings from 8.15, and had been waiting at Every Street since 10 a.m., but he was prevented from entering for another two hours.

After pronouncing life extinct at Every Street, Pryde went back to the CIB and as Van Turnhout described conducted an examination of David Bain. He told the jury that he explained to David he would need to examine him, obtain body and fluid samples and that these could be used as evidence by the police. He said David appeared calm and subdued and agreed to this. Pryde stated, 'He answered my questions. There was no sign of intoxication.'

He noted the three little bruises on David's face: a 3 cm bruise on the right temple; 1 cm by half centimetre bruise above the right eye; and a 1 cm by half centimetre bruise below the right eye on the cheek.

He also noted a small skin abrasion on the inner aspect of David's right knee.

Then — and this was the bombshell that came without any warning — he stated that all of these injuries were about 10 hours old at the time that he saw them at about 11.20 a.m. This meant that if he was right, the injuries occurred at about 1 a.m. when David claimed he was sound asleep in bed!

Pryde's deposition statement had given no hint that he had made this observation at the time — he had simply said they were *recent*.

It should be pointed out that our justice system provides for experts to give opinions. But, as the expression depicts, they are only one person's opinion, and so for obvious reasons they must be notified to an accused so that he or she can have the opinion tested by his or her own experts. Sometimes both sides agree; often they don't.

In this instance, Guest was ambushed by Dr Pryde's unheralded and undisclosed estimate of the age of the injuries, and so he had not had the chance to consult anyone as to its reliability or veracity. While there is no evidence of Guest protesting at the time, he did immediately fax the evidence to a pathologist he had consulted on other matters, who advised him that Dr Pryde's opinion was 'outrageously over-precise'. In notes made for the prosecution just before the trial in reference to these injuries, it is stated, 'All fresh within 12 hours' according to Dr Pryde and then it says, 'Dr Dempster will support this.'

Nevertheless, this opinion was, if believed by the jury, so significant that on its own it would be enough to convict David. It must also be put in context with the unheralded theory put up by Bill Wright at the end of his opening submissions that four were killed before the paper round and Robin killed afterwards. Here was evidence, Wright would say, that put David, rather than being sound asleep in bed as he claimed he was, involved in the fight with Stephen.

The doctor went on to explain the taking of body samples from David but did not do so in quite the detail that he had done in his deposition statement. In that earlier statement he said:

> I obtained from David Bain various body samples which included blood from his veins, hair and body samples. I also obtained swabs relating to the urethral, the glans penis and penile shaft. In a separate kit I obtained swabs from David Bain's hands to ascertain whether there was any evidence of gunshot powder residue. I inspected his nose. There was no indication of any recent nose bleed. The injuries I have referred to would not cause any bleeding.

In cross-examination Guest firstly confirmed that the skin missing from David's knee was a very superficial light graze as opposed to a gouge or laceration. He then confirmed with Pryde that the doctor had looked very carefully for debris under David's fingernails. Pryde confirmed that he had but there was none.

Pryde told Guest that he had told David the blood samples could be used in DNA testing. He agreed that he told David that he had the right to refuse any examination and to refuse giving samples. Nevertheless, Dr Pryde said, David was very cooperative.

Next up was the business of the bruising. Pryde told Guest it was at the time of his examination that he decided on 10 hours as the age of the injuries. He confirmed it was not in his deposition statement but was not pressed on its omission. He said he had based his opinion on experience.

Guest's attempts to negate this evidence probably had the effect of making it worse for his client. He asked Pryde if he could rule out the injuries being one hour old or 24 hours old. Pryde replied that he could, simply by casual inspection. So Guest moved on and asked, 'Can you rule out four hours?' Pryde came straight back with a very direct answer: 'Yes, I could. The probability for that would be practically non-existent.'

David had claimed in his police interviews that he did not have these injuries when he did his paper round. He further had said that he did not know how he got them. One possibility that Guest intended to argue was that they happened at 7.45 a.m. when he crashed down against the wall and was dragged out by Constable Andrew or alternatively when he was stumbling about the house finding his family in the dark. That was three and a half hours before Pryde examined him. Pryde had completely ruled out that time frame, leaving Guest with no explanation if Pryde's evidence stood up and was believed.

Bill Wright conducted a brief re-examination of Dr Pryde aimed at reinforcing the time of the injuries as earlier rather than later.

'Can you put a maximum or minimum time on them — can you put the figures either side?' In an answer which gives the impression of having been carefully rehearsed, Pryde said, 'The maximum probability is 10 hours and it falls off on a curve on either side of the 10 hours. Seven hours would be pretty minimal and 13 to 14 hours would be minimal on the other side.'

So there we have it. According to a man who the jury would probably consider the most believable and trustworthy witness they would hear, it was stated that David had suffered those injuries sometime between about midnight and 4 a.m. It would be a long haul back for Michael Guest from this point.

DETECTIVE ROSS COLLECTS DAVID'S CLOTHES

A short brief of evidence came next from Detective Ross, who collected David's clothes and the samples taken by Dr Pryde as exhibits. One thing he failed in was to label which sock had come from which of David's feet. This omission resulted in some difficulties at a later stage when scientists attempted to analyse blood patterns on the socks. In cross-examination, Guest had Ross agree that the blood was only on the soles of the socks, evidence in direct contrast, it will be recalled, to the claim put to the jury by Wright in his opening address. Notably, Ross's evidence in chief did not mention that the blood was only on the soles of the socks.

Ross told the court how early on the Tuesday after the killings he had to recover the socks from the exhibit officer so that ESR crime scene expert Peter Hentschel could make a visual examination of them. The same happened the following days with the clothes David had been wearing. Ross was present when the clothes were examined, and he confirmed that a smear of blood on David's black shorts was very faint and could not be seen without the assistance of special lighting.

CHAPTER 4

THE SCENE EXAMINATION

THE MINI-SCENES AND EXHIBITS

The laborious process of hearing evidence from the officers involved in the scene investigation began just before lunch on the third day of the trial. Detective Sergeant Milton Weir as officer in charge of the scene was first up to give evidence and he explained how the scene had been divided up into mini-scenes, each area having been given an initial to identify it. The room where Robin was found became Scene A; David's room Scene B; Laniet's C; the TV room/lounge at the end of the hallway D; Margaret's room Scene E; Stephen's room Scene F — which completed the upstairs area of the old two-storey house. Downstairs, Arawa's room was Scene G; the kitchen Scene H; the bathroom/laundry Scene I; the caravan where Robin lived on the weekend Scene J; and his Commer van Scene L. The letter 'S' before the scene letter stood for the word scene, he told the jury.

As exhibits were collected they were numbered according to the scene they were found in. For example, the rifle was found lying next to Robin's body in room A and so the number designated to it was SA 001, meaning that it was the first item that was seized as an exhibit in that room. For the trial, however, the exhibits were listed in order of number and the rifle became Crown exhibit number 14. This system required considerable cross-referencing. Weir explained this all to the court and to the jury.

Another factor which complicated the evidence of the scene examination was that many of the police officers worked in more than one scene. The Crown decided to call evidence by reference to each scene, meaning that most of the detectives gave evidence more than once.

In addition to this, detectives involved as scene examiners had also been in charge of various bodies and so that factor was intermingled with the evidence of scene examination.

After Weir had set the stage, a series of detectives followed, detailing the process that took place from 20 to 29 June. Weir then came back a second time, and his evidence will be covered in full later on.

THE SCENE INVESTIGATION: 20 TO 29 JUNE

PLASTIC SHEETING

Detective Kevin Anderson was sent to 65 Every Street at about eight o'clock on the morning of 20 June, temporarily appointed in charge of the scene until Weir arrived just before 10 a.m. Anderson explained that he went into the house with Weir at the time David was removed, and following that he waited outside for the arrival of plastic sheeting, used to prevent contamination of the floors during examination and removal of the bodies.

The sheeting arrived at 11.40 a.m. and Weir and Anderson laid it out through the house.

ROBIN — SCENE A

Then, at about 2.14 p.m., Anderson conducted an initial examination in Scene A where Robin's body had been found. He described the room, noting in particular the green curtains behind which were an alcove and a computer that appeared to be going. Anderson did some measurements, including noting that Robin Bain's body was 2.5 m from the door to the room and that his left buttock was 1.26 m from the green curtains. He noticed blood on the curtain and blood and bone fragments on the rifle itself. The highest of the blood spots on the curtain was 82 cm from the floor, the lowest was 51 cm from the floor and the width of the blood staining was 9 cm.

He went into the alcove and noticed a message on the computer that read: 'Sorry, you are the only one who deserved to stay.'

Just after 3 p.m., Dr Dempster the pathologist came and did a further examination of Robin Bain, and after that Robin's body was removed and taken in an undertaker's vehicle to the mortuary.

Anderson joined the ESR scientist Peter Hentschel in room A while he carried out a preliminary survey of the scene. He explained to the jury how he made the rifle safe by removing the magazine and the bullet in the breech from the rifle. Another magazine was on its edge beside Robin's right hand. He also noticed a spent cartridge shell on the floor in the alcove.

That afternoon Anderson was instructed by Weir to arrange for a computer expert to come to the house. Anderson told the jury that he contacted Martin Cox from Otago University who came to the house at about 2.10 p.m. the following day. The computer was not touched before then and remained running. Anderson then said, 'At approximately 2.16 p.m. Mr Cox carried out a number of functions and he will tell you about that.'

Anderson finished this part of his evidence by saying that a section of bloodstained carpet adjacent to Robin Bain's body was cut out and seized as an exhibit. This piece of carpet was near Robin's head and the blood had oozed from the bullet wound into a pool on the carpet.

Cross-examination raised nothing of consequence.

WASHING

Late that afternoon Anderson and another detective took down clothing from the clothesline outside the kitchen door. This was the washing that David had put through the wash and which had been hung out to dry by the police. There was a green woollen jersey among the items.

DETECTIVE MARK LODGE — OC ROBIN

Next came Detective Mark Lodge, who had been the officer in charge of Robin Bain's body. He was present when Dr Dempster examined the body and he attended the postmortem later that evening. He told the jury how he collected the body samples, including fingernail scrapings and blood samples, during the postmortem and that these were seized as exhibits. Guest had no questions for him at that stage.

MARTIN COX — THE COMPUTER EXPERT

Martin Cox was the computer expert who examined the computer with Kevin Anderson on Tuesday, 21 June. He told the jury that the computer was turned on at 6.44 a.m. on Monday. He explained that he was unable to determine the seconds so it could have been any time between 6.44.00 and 6.44.59 that the power turn-on actually occurred. He very briefly explained the method he adopted to ascertain this time and in total he would have been on the stand about seven or eight minutes. Guest had no questions for him whatsoever as he was content to have the Crown turn-on time of 6.44 a.m. locked in as firm evidence.

Detectives continued to flow onto the stand one after the other. Marie Fitchett, OC body for Margaret Bain, appeared. Together with Detective Jenny Fitzgerald, she had made a preliminary examination of room E, Margaret Bain's room.

Later that afternoon, Fitzgerald and Milton Weir examined the clothes that were in the laundry basket next to the washing machine. Each item was individually removed and recorded by her, she told the jury, and then Weir examined it. She noted that it was *dry clothing*.

STEPHEN — SCENE F

Fitzgerald was followed by Detective Michael Bracegirdle, the officer in charge of Stephen's body. Entering the house at about 3.20 p.m. on the Monday, he made considerable notes about the state of Scene F, and of Stephen's body. He stated, 'It was obvious from the amount of blood smeared and the injuries to the deceased that there had been a violent struggle.' There were no questions from Michael Guest at this stage.

Detective Jacques Legros took the stand late on the fourth day of the trial. He had conducted a preliminary examination of Stephen's room on Monday afternoon. He said it was obvious a struggle had taken place in that room. He told the jury how he had gone through Stephen's room putting marker arrows wherever he found a bloodstain. They were everywhere.

On the Wednesday he joined Weir in a detailed examination of the room. On Thursday, the day before David's arrest, he helped an electrician remove a number of light switches in the house. These were secured as exhibits.

On Friday he was assigned to removing exhibits from the Commer van, including a red anorak in which he found four keys and a shepherd's whistle on a piece of string. He also found and seized a gun target from the van which had bullet holes in it.

It appears he may have had the weekend off because his evidence then moves on to the following Monday, 27 June, when he was again continuing to search Scene F, Stephen's room. He took three sections of bloodstained carpet and also located five spent bullet shells. This is interesting because only two shots were fired in that room and so three of the shells were unaccounted for.

In cross-examination he was questioned about the target he found in the caravan and he was also questioned about the piece of skin that was found in Stephen's room. Little was added to the picture by the cross-examination.

LANIET — SCENE C

Constable Stephen Murray carried out a preliminary examination of Scene C where Laniet lay in bed with three shots to her head.

He found two live bullets in the room and he also located a small fragment of bullet lying on a leather jacket on a large black chair facing a writing desk in the room. He found another piece of lead bullet on the pillow underneath where the body had been lying.

It is significant, as we will see later, that these two sizeable lead bullet fragments were found on the Monday afternoon or early evening, the first day of the inquiry.

Hayley Stewart, officer in charge of the body of Laniet, said that Milton Weir and Constable Murray helped her remove the body from the room. Later that night she attended the postmortem, which was not completed until about midnight. There was little cross-examination.

Kevin Anderson came back to the witness box to tell the jury about his work in Scene C on Friday the twenty-fourth and Saturday the twenty-fifth with Detective Fitzgerald, who also followed up with her account of that search. Fitzgerald made the point that she never saw the room as it was before the body had been removed. Guest had no questions for Anderson or Fitzgerald.

ARAWA — SCENE G

Detective Trevor Thompson explained that he'd done a preliminary examination of Scene G, Arawa's room, which began about 3.35 p.m. on the first Monday. He said that at eight o'clock that night he found a spent shell and then, on the Thursday, he found another one. The Crown case postulated this as very significant evidence. Two shots had been fired in Arawa's room but only one met its target, the other one going through the wall. The police said this was evidence that David, no longer with glasses because by this time according to their theory his glasses had been broken and dislodged in the scuffle with Stephen, missed because of bad eyesight.

Thompson then jumped forward to 11 October 1994 when he said he attended a further examination of the computer with Martin Cox, the computer expert. Thompson says they found written documents on the computer that had been compiled by Robin, Stephen, Arawa and David. There were floppy disks of computer games that appear to belong to Stephen. He described Robin's, Arawa's and David's work as 'written essays'. Guest had no questions for Detective Thompson.

Detective Gavin Briggs was officer in charge of the body for Arawa and he noted that he protected her hands and feet with plastic bags before having her removed from the scene, and attended the postmortem the following morning. The following Monday he assisted with a reconstruction of what happened in Scene G. The Crown seemed to think the fact that a shot had missed its mark in this room was a major point and Briggs's evidence took up a considerable amount of time. This was the only reconstruction evidence that was allowed at the trial relating to the crime scene.

DAVID — SCENE B

Kevin Anderson came back for his third round of evidence, this time telling of his examination of David Bain's room on Wednesday, 22 June. He noted finding the metal glasses frame and one glasses lens on the chair in the room and he also noticed two blood spots on the duvet on David's bed. Both of these were seized as exhibits. Anderson also found a piece of cardboard which had been used as a target. This was behind the door and was also seized as an exhibit. There was very little cross-examination of Kevin Anderson.

Detective Fitzgerald also came back for the third time. She gave evidence that she assisted Anderson in his search of Scene B. Her evidence did not add to the picture at all.

THE BATHROOM/LAUNDRY — SCENE I

The first week of the trial ended with Detective Mark Lodge back on the stand, explaining that he was detailed to search the bathroom and laundry area, Scene I, on Thursday, 23 June. He pointed out blood spots in the hand-basin, a black arrow that had been placed on the washing machine near where a handprint had been found, and other details.

Lodge went into great detail describing the layout and contents of the bathroom, and the scene certainly contained some revealing evidence.

It was the hand-basin where a spot of blood was found that David had told the police he washed his hands of printer's ink when he got home from his paper round. It was also here, of course, that David, according to his statement to the police, sorted the clothing into *coloureds and whites*. The whites were in a cane basket in front of the washing machine, but these had already been inspected and seized by Milton Weir earlier in the week.

Lodge said that about 11.30 a.m. that day the police fingerprint expert Kim Jones came in to examine the print on the washing machine. A couple of hours after that, a plumber arrived and removed the taps from the bath, hand-basin and the laundry tub. Lodge went on to say that he found blood on a folded towel in the cabinet and of course there was the green towel hanging on the rail which had large bloodstains on it as well. He found four items in another cabinet which appeared to have blood on them: a pink cloth; a folded-up shower curtain; a face mask; and swimming togs. These were seized as exhibits. He also noted a Kleensak that appeared to have blood on it, which was seized also. All of the items in the cane basket that had been examined and recorded by Weir on the Monday afternoon three days previously must have been put back in the basket as Lodge records he went through them again and particularly noted the white *Gondoliers* sweatshirt which he said had blood staining on the right shoulder area. In the actual tub itself he found an old red towel and old bath mat and a white T-shirt.

On Friday he was still working in the laundry and shortly after 11 o'clock that morning — about the same time Croudis was reading David Bain his rights in the CIB a few miles away — Peter Hentschel, the ESR scientist, came in to examine the washing machine, especially to look for fibres and bloodstains. Hentschel apparently lifted two fibres and one blood spot from the washing machine and these were seized as exhibits.

On Saturday, with David locked safely behind bars and the funerals under way, Lodge was still hard at work in the laundry. He had arranged for a washing machine technician, Mark Preston, to come to the house and conduct tests. First Preston removed the side panel with a blood smear on it and water was drained from the pump. Later on Lodge found the Rawleigh's wash powder container that had what appeared to be blood on the lid. Then the washing machine technician and Lodge began the critical operation of trying to determine how long it would take for the washing machine to complete a cycle. But before doing so, Preston had to put new taps on the wall as the original ones had been removed the previous day. He obtained clothing similar to that which had been washed for the purposes of the test. He did not weigh them but believed that they were approximately the same.

The duration of the wash cycle was important because David could not, according to his version, have started it before around 6.45. The police said that it was not going when they got there at about 7.35 so if it took longer than 50 minutes this would mean that he could not have done the washing after the paper round, thereby supporting the new Crown scenario that he killed the first four and did the washing before the paper round.

The first test, done on the super wash cycle, took about 60 minutes. The following day, Sunday, they repeated the exercise and this time the cycle took about 59 minutes. However, of this, about 30 minutes was the time it took for the machine to fill with water and the other 30 minutes was the washing, rinsing and spinning.

Michael Guest asked Lodge a few questions about these tests and particularly wanted to know how noisy the washing machine was. Lodge replied: 'It was neither particularly noisy nor particularly quiet.' He also asked Lodge to confirm that the floor of the laundry was soaking wet. Lodge confirmed it was. Lodge told Guest that the palm print on the washing machine was red in colour.

In re-examination Bill Wright asked Detective Lodge if he was able to distinguish between blood that is old and blood which is diluted. 'I believe so,' Lodge earnestly replied, without explaining how. Presumably this question was directed at the blood on the shoulder of the *Gondoliers* sweatshirt that Lodge said he noticed in the cane basket in front of the washing machine.

The washing machine technician Mark Preston followed right on the heels of Detective Lodge to explain the tests he had done on the Bain washing machine. He told the jury that the washing machine was a 625 Hoover automatic, about 20 years old, and that he had done some repairs on the machine a few years beforehand. He said he was very surprised at how long the filling cycles were in the tests but said that that was not a symptom of the machine itself but rather of the water pressure coming into the house. He said he was particularly surprised because the pressure on Every Street was normally quite high.

In cross-examination Preston agreed with Guest that the water pressure on the Monday morning compared to Saturday afternoon and Sunday morning was likely to be different, which could account for the unusually long filling time that the tests took. Preston said he did not keep any records of the timing of the tests; that was done by Mark Lodge. Lodge's record showed that each time the machine was tested it took a little over 30 minutes to complete the wash cycles and the balance of the time, a little under 30 minutes, was the time it took to fill up to complete a cycle. Preston said he would normally have expected that time to have been 10 to 14 minutes, rather than the nearly 30 minutes it actually took. This would have reduced the complete cycle from about 60 minutes as it was to somewhere between 40 and 45 minutes. As Guest said to Preston, 'The timing of this washing machine cycle could be very important in this case.'

CARAVAN — SCENE J

Constable Stephen Murray told of searching the caravan, Scene J, on Tuesday, the day after the murders, later being joined by Detectives Legros and Fitzgerald in that search. Legros had received instructions from DS Milton Weir to keep an eye out for a particular type of garment, without describing what it was.

Murray found 20 spent cartridge shells in the caravan as well as one live bullet. He found two pairs of trousers which he seized as they appeared to have blood on them.

Legros then got back on the stand. Legros seemed to be Weir's right-hand man, utilized in almost every scene in the house at some stage or another. He reiterated what Murray had already told the jury.

No evidence had been offered of any reading material found in the caravan but under cross-examination Legros admitted to Guest that two books were found near Robin Bain's bunk. One was called *Death Comes as the End* and the other was called *Death at the Dolphin*. These books had been photographed but were not collected as exhibits. The first was found face down opened up, partially read. It was an Agatha Christie novel about a mysterious series of family deaths. The second was a 'whodunit' by Ngaio Marsh.

Hayley Stewart was back for another round of evidence, this time describing a search of the kitchen, which apparently found nothing of consequence.

Stephen Murray came back again to tell of searching the hallway and lounge in the main house on the Wednesday and Thursday afternoon. On Thursday night he was tasked with sending Monday's *Otago Daily Times* to Wellington to be fingerprinted. It had been found on a shelf in the hallway outside David's bedroom. No fingerprints were found on this newspaper. On Friday he assisted with a search of Margaret Bain's room and on Saturday he was instructed by Weir to seize the alarm clock from the caravan. He said that the alarm clock appeared to be set to go off between 6.30 and 6.45 a.m.

In cross-examination by Michael Guest, Murray admitted that the alarm clock was not tested to see when it did go off until just a few weeks before the trial. When the test was done, however, it was found, rather inconveniently for the police case, to have been set for 6.32 a.m.

The crime scene investigation was completed with the testimony of Senior Sergeant McDouall who gave evidence that he had searched the grounds and Commer van on the Monday of the actual killings. He gave evidence that when he searched the van on that Monday he noticed that in the front seat there was a red anorak parka and a white sweatshirt. These were examined by Milton Weir on the Friday afternoon at exactly the time David was arrested four days later and it was in the anorak pocket that the string necklace with keys on it was found. McDouall had obviously not looked in the pocket or noticed that anything was in the pocket, it would seem.

OC CRIME SCENE DS MILTON WEIR GIVES EVIDENCE

After recounting the essential evidence obtained during the crime scene examination it only remains to see how the whole thing was managed by Detective Sergeant Weir, the officer in charge. How exactly was it that this mass of evidence was said to exist against David, while none existed to incriminate Robin?

The sequence of events then, on the morning of 20 June 1994, should be kept in mind as the balance of the saga unfolds. The 111 call was received at Telecom at 7.09 a.m. and put through to St John Ambulance at 7.10 a.m. Thomas Dempsey, the ambulance officer who took the call, immediately dispatched ambulance staff and notified his superiors and the police about the call he had received. The ambulance arrived in Every Street before the police but as instructed waited on the street until the police had cleared the scene, because of course it was unclear whether this was a live armed offenders situation. So the first four police on the scene armed themselves with pistols and made entry to the house at about 7.36 a.m. — the best evidence available being the Telecom printout of the time that the call from David was terminated.

Before making entry to the house these first four officers were able to see the rifle lying on the floor next to a body in the front room through the windows in the alcove of the house. On the other side of the front door they could see a young male sitting on the floor under the window and hear his distressed, hysterical voice. At this time there were no other suspicious noises. Within a few minutes of making entry, probably by about 7.40 a.m., they had cleared the scene and the senior officer Sergeant Stapp had radioed back to headquarters the situation report, including the name of the family. Any panic by this stage should have been over. No one else was likely to get hurt, the murder weapon was on the spot — or at least that would be a very realistic assumption — and so a killer was not roaming the streets needing apprehension, and all rooms in the house were under control.

By 7.45 a.m. the chief ambulance officer had checked each of the bodies and reported that there was no pulse, no sign of life. Ambulance officers had been assigned to the sole survivor and were monitoring him. Although he appeared to be in a great state of shock and distress he was not in need of any specialized medical attention as far as they were able to ascertain. Sergeant Stapp then arranged for the one anomaly interfering with a static and untouched crime scene to be secured: he removed the dog and tied it up at the front door.

The call went out for detectives to attend a briefing at 8.15 a.m. at the CIB. The police pathologist Dr Dempster was notified and he attended this briefing held by DCI Robinson.

The dark of night had lifted. It was a very, very cold midwinter's morning in Dunedin. The house itself had no heating and was very draughty and of course did not have insulation. All reports were that it was absolutely freezing in the house — perhaps even colder than outside.

DS Weir described how he arrived at 65 Every Street at 9.45 a.m. on that fateful morning, made an initial inspection of the house and section and had a brief look in the caravan, noting that the light and radio were on. He made the decision to have David removed by carry chair because 'I realized we would probably be wanting to take possession of his clothing and if he was to be carried out a chair or a stretcher that would protect the clothing he was wearing.'

At 10.35 a.m. he accompanied Dr Pryde through the house to check the state of the deceased. Weir then told the jury that he didn't want Pryde to go all the way into Stephen's room, because 'as officer in charge of the scene I wasn't happy with people walking in and out'. Dr Pryde confirmed life extinct in Stephen from the doorway, presumably based on the information that he hadn't moved since about 7.45 a.m., some three hours earlier. If Pryde was able to do this in respect to Stephen one wonders what the purpose of taking him through the house at all was, as exactly the same circumstances prevailed for each of the other four deceased. Would a view from the door satisfy legal requirements anyway?

Weir gave a general description of the house and surrounds, emphasizing how dirty, dilapidated and smelly it was.

It was difficult to find plastic sheeting, and it didn't arrive until about 11.40 a.m. It took Weir and Anderson 20 further minutes to get it into place on the floor. Finally, at 12.05 p.m., he re-entered the house with pathologist Dr Dempster, his assistant, another police officer and the police photographer. Remember, the photographer did not give evidence, so this was the first mention of a photographer being inside the house at the scene. Dempster initially went for a quick look at each of the dead bodies, and while they were in room A they noted that the computer was going and that it had a message on it.

'Afterwards, I determined how I was going to tackle the scene examination,' Weir told the jury. He allocated duties to the available staff, and arranged for a surveyor to draw up a plan and assign a letter to each of the individual crime scenes within the greater crime scene. He said he ensured that the surveyor 'showed certain items of furniture where I thought it was relevant to show those items on the plan'.

He explained that, while he had maintained an overall supervisory role of the entire scene, he personally carried out a detailed examination of Stephen's room. He described how he had arranged for the photographer to record the investigation on videotape on that first day and for the following days as it progressed. The photographers did not give evidence and so Weir produced an edited version of the videotape which was given the exhibit number 612. He told the jury the edited version was not in chronological order.

He played the edited version to the court and gave a running commentary of matters of interest shown throughout the video. He then told the jury how at about five o'clock on the first day of the inquiry he conducted a preliminary examination of the laundry and went through the clothes that were in the washing machine and removed them. He told the jury of the various places that he had noticed bloodstains; for example, a smear of blood on the washing machine, a small drop in the hand-basin, smears on the door jambs in various areas. He said the light switch in Laniet's room and in the stairwell appeared to have blood on them, as did the post at the top and bottom of the stairs as well as on cupboards in the hall leading to Arawa's bedroom and on the door jamb of her room, and also on the light switch on that route.

He was demonstrating to the jury that at this early stage it was obvious the killer had got blood on his right arm or shoulder area and brushed against door jambs and other walls as he went about his business.

Weir then explained that Peter Hentschel, the ESR crime scene scientist from Christchurch, had arrived and that together they examined the various matters of interest. Weir decided that luminol examination should be carried out, and he helped Hentschel with the process.

He explained that luminol is sprayed onto the floor and if there is any blood present it will luminesce in a blue glow. These tests must be done in complete darkness and so they were carried out on that Monday night. Luminol was applied to the floor in Stephen's room, Margaret's room, the hallway, the stairs, kitchen and laundry. The laundry was done first and the floor showed luminescence all over, but there was no discernible pattern according to Weir. He told the jury that five footprints were found: two in Margaret's room, two at Laniet's doorway, and one in the hallway between Laniet's and Margaret's rooms. He said, 'The best way I could describe it was that of an impression similar to what you would you see of a person with a bare foot walking in the sand.' It appeared to be a right foot.

An area near the front door showed luminescence, but it didn't show up as a footprint. Room A, the room where Robin was found: no result. The TV room: no result. H (the kitchen) and G (Arawa's room) got no result either.

He then told the jury that there was a photographer present who took photos of the footprints. However, he said, 'These [the footprints] were photographed by time exposure and these were unsuccessful.'

The following day Weir hung the washing that he had removed from the washing machine onto the line in order for it to dry. The rest of that day for the most part he spent with Hentschel studying and analysing the various blood staining that was found as he had earlier described. He then went over the survey plans, indicating to the jury various matters, highlighting where blood and the five footprints had been found, as well as other items of interest.

Guest's cross-examination was not of great consequence. He queried whether the footprints could have been made by police officers' shoes, but Weir said that a shoe print would not show up toes and the ones he saw looked like the print you would see with a bare foot walking in sand. Guest tried to suggest rather lamely that rather than carrying David out in a chair he could have got clothes from the wardrobe and taken possession of his clothes that he was wearing at the scene.

Weir's second round of evidence came a few days later and as with all other police officers he was granted permission to refer to his notebook entries made at the time if he needed to refresh his memory on any matter of evidence.

He told the jury how he had decided to personally conduct the scene examination in Stephen Bain's bedroom. He began that detailed examination on the Wednesday, helped by Detective Jacques Legros. He described the room in detail and told the jury that he tasked himself 'with the identification and removal of each item in that room. There was a huge amount of material there,' he told them.

His first major discovery came with the finding of the two bloodstained white gloves under the bed. The right glove was partially inside out. Under that bed he also found a school shirt and jumper of Stephen's which were bloodstained. No matter where he looked it seems he came across blood-stained items; some with smears, some with spots of blood.

He seemed to think that the mere finding of something with blood on it was of great consequence. Of course, with Stephen bleeding profusely as he was, and flailing about as he obviously did, it was hardly surprising. Stephen was the source of all this blood and it has never been helpful in the ultimate determination of the case.

Late that Wednesday Weir said he attended a discussion at Central Police Station concerning the investigation and then he went back to the house at about eight o'clock that night with fingerprint technician Kim Jones. Jones had a machine called a Polilight which he said was an electrical apparatus that indicates the presence of blood by causing a luminescent glow. They applied the light in the laundry and confirmed the possible presence of various bloodstains and finished the day at about 10.20 p.m.

He then turned to the Thursday, the day before David was charged, and described how he arrived at Every Street about 9.30 a.m. and first of all arranged for an electrician to remove the bloodstained light switches from the house. Jones had looked at those light switches for fingerprints the previous evening but none was found. He then went to the laundry with Mark Lodge and did some more indicative tests for blood, which turned out to be positive.

Before lunch he was back in Stephen's room continuing with his detailed investigation. It wasn't long before he found the two pieces of skin on the floor and seized them as exhibits after having them photographed in position. After finding the skin he went back down to the laundry to do more tests with Mark Lodge.

The laborious description of going through item after item in Stephen Bain's bedroom continued with him telling the jury of finding blood spots on stools, pieces of paper, on a shopping bag and on a container. He said a swivel chair had both spots of blood and smears of blood on it.

Again working well into the night he got to a pile of shoes that were in front of a set of bunks on the floor next to where Stephen's body had lain. He noted that nearly all of the shoes were spotted and/or smeared with what appeared to be blood and there was even blood on the mattress of the top bunk, about one and a half metres above the floor.

While looking in that area he made a particular discovery. 'I came across a particular item, near an ice skate which is just visible in Photograph 97, it is just here [indicates where], the middle left hand of the photo, I located what appeared to be a lens from a pair of glasses. Looking at Photo 62, it is a blown up, what is meant to be a blown portion of Photo 61. You can just make out the edge of the spectacle lens just in front of the ice-skating boot.' At this point he left the witness box to show the jury, lawyers and His Honour the judge the exact location of the lens that he was pointing to in Photograph 62.

'Photo 62 was taken on the Monday as Stephen's body is still there and the lens is on the underneath side of the skate. On the Thursday the lens seen in Photo 62; that is the position I found it when I found it on the Thursday.'

Of course, the lens was secured as an exhibit and given the number SF580 and for the trial purposes became Crown Exhibit 172.

The lens was found at 8.46 p.m. on the night of Thursday, 23 June 1994 just over 12 hours before David and his uncle would begin David's final drive in a car as a free man.

Weir moved on with his evidence. On the Friday he had continued searching in Stephen Bain's bedroom but found nothing more of interest.

After lunch on Friday he went to the caravan and examined the front passenger area where he looked in the pocket of the red anorak and found a handkerchief, some fingerless gloves and a string necklace with four keys and a shepherd's whistle on it. He arranged for Legros to secure the anorak as an exhibit.

This was the anorak that McDouall had searched on the previous Monday but evidently had not bothered to look in the pocket or even felt that there might have been something in the pocket when he searched it.

On Saturday, Weir continued examining Stephen Bain's bedroom and then on Monday he and Legros did a grid search of the walls and ceilings in the room to look for any more bullet holes. This was because they had found five spent .22 bullet shells in the room yet only two shots had apparently been fired. But no bullet holes were found anywhere in the room and so no explanation was available for the presence of the three other empty shells.

THE GLASSES LENS

The main focus of Guest's cross-examination was about the finding of the glasses lens.

Guest: I now turn to the glass found in Stephen's room, the optical lens … Was the lens found under the ice-skate boot wholly or partially, when you saw it?

Weir: Partially.

Q: Look at Photos 60, 61 and 62 — from your knowledge of the scene inquiries can you confirm that those photos were taken on the Monday?

Weir: Monday the twentieth, yes.

Q: Photos 68 and 69 and 97 — it is obvious they were taken after Stephen's body had been removed.

Weir: That's correct.

Q: Do you know when Photos 68, 69 and 97 were taken?

Weir: No, I don't.

Q: You found the optical lens on the Thursday which would be the twenty-third?

Weir: That is correct. 20:46 hours.

Q: Which is Thursday evening?

Weir: Yes, 8.46.

Q: Looking at Photos 61 and 62, would you accept that because of the skate being approximately a quarter or a third under the shoe rack it is likely that it was there before any struggle took place and it is unlikely to have been disturbed?

Weir: Well, that is a possibility.

Q: It is hard to tell because of the disarray in the room?

Weir: Yes.

Q: Would you agree it is unlikely though that the skate could have been out from under the shoe rack prior to a struggle but pushed under in that position during a struggle?

Weir: Yes, I would probably agree with that.

Q: That would be because of the relative appearance of tightness under the shoe rack and the position of the stand?

Weir: Yes.

Q: Do you know what was in the black bag above the skate?

Weir: I don't think it is a black bag. I think you will find that that is a child's raincoat from memory.

Q: And the lens was found partially under that skate?

Weir: Yes, it was found as you can see it, although I accept it is difficult to see in Photo 62. That is exactly how it was.

Q: When was this Photo 62 taken in relation to finding the lens?'

Weir: Photo 62 was taken on the Monday, hang on, Photo 61 was taken on the Monday, Photo 62 is an enlargement of Photo 61.

This was the end of the cross-examination. Bill Wright had no questions in re-examination; however, the judge did. He asked Weir, 'Could you put your pen on where that lens is again?'

'Right here, Your Honour,' Weir answered as he pointed to the lens. He then added, 'I actually spoke to the police photographer this morning.

I believe one of the photo books may have a better quality photo of the remainder.'

The notes of evidence then record that the witness went to the jurors and showed them where the lens was by pointing to it with his pen on Photo 62.

It will be recalled that Bill Wright wrote to the court and Michael Guest just a week or two before the trial notifying them of various new matters and changes to the Crown evidence that had been presented at the depositions hearing. The letter contained no reference to the new evidence that would be elicited from the photo, and the attached list of photos simply referred to it as 'new photo'.

Weir's deposition statement stated he found the lens under the boot and other items. There was no suggestion it could be seen lying beside the body. Photo 62 was not included at the depositions hearing. It was for these reasons Guest was taken by surprise and questioned Weir as he did.

It will also be recalled that in Bill Wright's notes for his opening address to the jury he records that the lens was found *on top, not under items*, and in notes made of his meetings with Doyle and Weir he wrote 'left lens — on top, not under anything or hidden away', which is in contradiction with the evidence that Weir had given at the depositions hearing.

This ends the evidence of the crime scene investigation conducted under the control of Milton Weir. The reader may not be surprised to learn that the *Manual* states that one person should search each scene to avoid confusion.

The trial moved on to hearing from Maurice Clarke, a fisherman from Taieri Beach who had gone on a school camp with Robin and the children. His evidence was to the effect that although there were gun lessons and gun practice with slug guns at the school camp, Robin Bain did not take part in that activity. Nevertheless, as Legros told the jury, a blue target was found in Robert Bain's caravan that was similar to those used during this gun practice.

CHAPTER 5

FURTHER EVIDENCE: EXPERT TESTIMONY

BALLISTICS

The Crown next called Robert Ngamoki, the police armourer who had conducted ballistics and firing tests with the murder weapon and also with similar weapons in order to look at such things as the ejection pattern of the bullet shells when they were ejected from the rifle after a shot was fired. This was important to the police in respect to the bullet shell found in the computer alcove, a matter the Crown suggested proved that the rifle was fired from the alcove side of the curtains when Robin Bain was shot.

Ngamoki received the rifle and both magazines on 27 July 1994 from Kim Jones of the fingerprint section. Exhibit 16 was the five-round magazine which was in the rifle when the last shot was fired. Exhibit 25 was the 10-round magazine found on the floor beside Robin Bain's right hand. Ngamoki told the jury that the 10-round magazine was defective due to a split in the top which would cause bullets to fly out when it was being loaded.

He told the jury that the rifle weighed 3.6 kg and its total length including the silencer was 1370 mm. The barrel, he said, was 638 mm including the silencer. He explained to them the various tests he did and that in respect to the ejection pattern, the shell would fly out to the right of the rifle and slightly backwards, and when fired from shoulder height shells would travel a distance of between 1.7 and 3.6 m.

He had also tested the gunshot residue that came out the end of the barrel, or in this case the silencer, to assist with determining the firing distance of the rifle from the target. He also explained the terms 'misfeed' and 'jam' as when a bullet fails to load properly from the magazine into the breech of the rifle. He explained that in his opinion it is difficult to get the bullet out when there is a jam because the port is very narrow and sometimes you might have to use your fingernail or something similar because it is difficult to fit fingers into the breech. His evidence took quite a long time because he went into some detail on various measurements and distances, but this was the essence of it.

Cross-examination of this witness provided Michael Guest with one of his best moments during the trial. The rifle was one of the few exhibits which Guest arranged to have independently examined, and that was done by a former ESR scientist in Auckland. This resulted in him learning that the length of the rifle was 1135 mm as opposed to the 1370 mm it had been measured at by Ngamoki. The difference was 235 mm or about 8 inches. Guest had got a little green stick prepared for him, which was 235 mm long, to emphasize the error. Ngamoki of course was forced to concede that he had made a mistake in measuring the length of the rifle and Guest pounced on this most fundamental of errors to discredit the rest of his tests. Guest has very proudly related the story, to me at least, of how he debunked this witness with the use of his little green stick.

Also of interest was the fact uncovered by Michael Guest that Ngamoki had attended the scene on 29 June to assist the police with reconstructions. Under cross-examination Ngamoki said that all the shots that were fired during these reconstructions using a similar weapon were actually fired from the hip as opposed to the normal firing position from the shoulder. The reason the police did this was to emulate the position of David's left-hand fingerprints on the fore-stock of the rifle which were pointing down over the top of the rifle in the pick-up position, as opposed to having the left forward hand underneath that part of the rifle in the normal firing position.

All in all, Ngamoki's professionalism was considerably undermined as he had to produce new diagrams and concede a number of errors in his work. It is not that they had any major effect on the central question of 'Who did it — David or Robin?' But, still, at last there was a dent in the credibility of an important Crown witness.

FINGERPRINTS

Then came fingerprint technician Ross O'Hagan, who gave evidence that he took David's finger and palm prints after David's arrest.

One of the Crown's major witnesses, Kim Jones the fingerprint technician from Wellington, followed. Jones worked in the fingerprint offices of the New Zealand Police and the rifle was delivered to him almost immediately the police investigation began. Jones told the court that for seven and a half years he had worked with the examination of exhibits and identification of persons by means of their fingerprints. When he received the rifle the day after the murders, his first study of it was done using a Polilight, which is a brand name for an apparatus that emits light through a concentrated beam like a laser, and with which it is possible to set the light to a variety of wavelengths including violet light.

Jones explained to the jury: 'When I am looking for blood I would use the violet light band and at that light strength if there is a material on the gun such as blood, that contaminant absorbs that energy and admits it as fluorescence …

'When I put the Polilight onto [the gun] … I located well-defined finger-prints in what appeared to be blood on the right-hand side of the fore-end just forward of the chequered fore-grip and in an area otherwise uncontaminated.' He told them he also found a print in what appeared to be blood on the underside of the silencer.

The first lot of prints were the left-hand four fingertips of David's hand, and the one on the silencer was Stephen's middle finger.

Jones then produced to the court a photographic enlargement showing an identification comparison for fingerprints of David Bain taken at the police station on 24 June with those on the rifle. This was produced as Exhibit 577. Photo 1 on Exhibit 577 was the index finger print from the rifle and Photo 2 was David's elimination index finger print which had been lifted by O'Hagan on 24 June for evidential purposes.

Jones went on to describe that the substance in which the prints were made — which appeared to be blood — was already on the fingers and was imparted onto the rifle in an area of the rifle that had no blood on it. This is a contra-distinction that he was wishing to make between a situation where a substance, blood for example, would have been on the rifle and the fingers were placed into it. He used the phrase 'positive prints' to describe this type of print.

He told the jury that the prints were well defined and said that the fingers that imparted them onto the rifle must have had blood on them. He gave a demonstration to show that in his opinion it would be highly unlikely that those prints could have been put onto the gun by David sliding his hand under it while it was lying on the floor beside Robin Bain. The prints were on the left side of the rifle, which was the side actually on the floor when the police arrived at the scene.

At that point in Jones's evidence, the afternoon tea break took place in the court. After the adjournment he began with the following statement: 'Referring again to the four prints found on the rifle I have told you I found them in an area otherwise uncontaminated. I mean otherwise uncontaminated by blood as shown by the Polilight. The extent of the area that was uncontaminated apart from these prints, approximately the width of four fingers. The rest of the rifle … was in my opinion completely covered in its entirety with what I believe to be blood.'

He told of Stephen's print on the silencer, saying that it, too, was a positive print and that there was blood all over the silencer as well. He said the print was pointing towards the stock of the rifle at an angle of about 45 degrees.

At the house on 22 June he found the partial left-hand palm print of David Bain on the top left-hand panel of the washing machine, also in what he described as a substance which appeared to be blood. He was unable to see the colour red with the naked eye.

'I examined a computer and keyboard. I located no identifiable prints on that.' He said the keyboard was dirty and for that reason he would think it almost impossible to find prints on the keys. He said he would not expect to find prints on the keyboard because 'repeated tapping on those same keys would obliterate any initial fingerprints'.

He said he had also examined cartridge shells and he could not find any prints on any of those, partly due to the size of the objects, meaning that they were too small for a fingerprint to be left. He said he found what appeared to be blood on various light switches in the house, but he did not find any fingerprints on them.

He then produced another chart which he said was to help the jury to follow his evidence and this became Exhibit 623. The evidence of Jones the fingerprint technician occupies just over six pages of notes of evidence in the trial. The cross-examination of Jones by Michael Guest takes up four pages and began with Guest handing Jones the rifle to repeat the demonstration showing how David must have held the rifle, in Jones's opinion of course, to have made the prints. The ensuing questions would not have thrown much light on proceedings except to have had the effect of re-emphasizing that it would be an odd and unnatural way to hold a rifle to fire it.

Guest then achieved a very significant concession from Jones when he put to him that if David had picked the gun up and made the prints then dropped it into the position where it was found then that would be entirely possible. Jones agreed. Guest then said: 'There isn't just one sinister inference to draw from the fingerprints as you saw them?' Jones answered: 'There is not, sir.'

Guest moved on to the Polilight and asked the question: 'It actually fluoresces the blood?' Jones replied, 'It does, sir.'

This contention was to be of some significance many years down the track.

Guest pressed on: 'Is the Polilight fluorescing the fingerprints and the sweat and what have you, or the blood?'

'The blood is actually fluorescing,' Jones stated. 'Any fingerprints that may be in blood will fluoresce black.'

Michael Guest was on a bit of a roll with Jones at this stage and now, with the benefit of hindsight, one might say it was a shame that he was not better instructed on the subject matter. The next question and answer are also of interest: Jones was being questioned about whether he could be certain it was blood, but all he could say was that 'it appeared to be blood'.

Very poignantly, Guest then asked the following question: 'Appears through your eyes because of the colour red or reacts with a scientific test that tells you it is blood?'

Jones answered: 'I am using the machine as an initial indicator.' He was looking at the rifle for the first time on 21 June in laboratory conditions with the best lighting, and yet he was unable to say that the substance he saw was red. Despite this, according to his evidence, the gun was *entirely covered in blood.*

Guest, getting an answer which appeared to be evasive, persisted: 'Did you see red substance which appeared to be blood before you applied the Polilight?'

Again Jones could not answer in the affirmative. 'There was a material that looked like blood on the gun.'

Now, Guest asked whether he had actually seen, before applying the Polilight, a substance that appeared to be blood — that is, a red substance — on the palm print on the washing machine.

The answer this time was at least a straight one. 'In that area, no,' Jones replied.

Remember that the palm print was on the white surface of the washing machine, and even then Jones could not see any colour red. It was only when he applied the violet band of the Polilight that it appeared to be blood because in his words it fluoresced when the Polilight was shone onto it. Jones's evidence about the palm print contradicted Detective Lodge's who said it was red.

'Can you discount the possibility that the palm print was a detergent or a bleach or some substance of that nature?' Guest asked, and Jones replied in the negative.

Then after much prevarication and confusion he finally admitted that he had found a print on the computer screen that did not match any members of the Bain family, but quickly qualified the admission by telling the court that under ideal conditions 'prints can last an awful long time'. In fact, he said that the print on the computer could have originated way back to when it was in the shop. He was asked about the glasses lens found in Stephen's room and the lens and frame found in David's room but said that he had not been asked to examine those for fingerprints by the police, which seems a bit remiss. He did examine the magazines but did not find any prints on either of those.

At the end of the cross-examination the judge sought further clarification from Jones. He asked Jones to clarify what he meant when he said 'the rifle was covered in blood'. Jones answered that most of it fluoresced when he applied the Polilight.

'Could you see that without the Polilight?' the judge politely asked, repeating the question that had been earlier put by Michael Guest.

'The strap appeared to have blood on it, and visibly blood type material on the scope and barrel which certainly did not require the assistance of the Polilight,' Jones answered.

The questioning from the judge got rather interesting at this stage because Jones tried to use his befuddling technique on the judge, but Justice Williamson would not be deterred.

'Apart from the prints you have told us about, did you find any other prints on the rifle?' Williamson asked.

'I found no identifiable prints on the rifle apart from the ones I have described,' answered Jones. The judge then queried Jones about the pressure needed to leave the prints that he saw. Jones described to Justice Williamson that very light contact could make a fingerprint. By way of example he said, 'If you place your finger on the table, just the pressure that is required to change the colour of the nail is sufficient to leave a fingerprint.'

However, Jones told the judge that David's prints on the gun 'exhibited an awful lot of pressure' because 'they were well-defined'. He was unable to comment on the amount of pressure relating to Stephen's print on the silencer, notwithstanding the fact that according to him it was also well-defined and also in what appeared to be blood.

Finally, after continual pressing by the judge he admitted that he found lots of other fingerprints all over the rifle, but there was insufficient detail for him to be able to identify them. He then indicated on the rifle a series of little white arrows and said that each of those white arrows indicated where he had found ridge detail, indicating that it had been handled by somebody in that particular location. There were nine such arrows on the rifle. It was 5 p.m. and had been a long day.

FORENSIC SCIENCE

PETER HENTSCHEL

Next day the ESR scientist Peter Hentschel began his evidence in chief, which took him about two and a half hours. He was cross-examined by Guest for about three hours and then re-examined by Bill Wright and as well as that he underwent quite a grilling from the judge. He was on the stand for nearly the whole day and his evidence takes up about 10 per cent of the notes of evidence of the entire Crown case that was to convict David.

Hentschel began with the standard narration of his experience and qualifications as a forensic scientist — some 30-odd years following a master's degree in chemistry. He told the jury he made notes while at the house (although if that was true they have never been disclosed as they should have been), as he also did when he was working in his laboratory. He told them that he spent most of that first week of 20 June 1994 at Every Street.

He described the use of the substance luminol as a crime scene detection substance in the following fashion: 'It is a chemical that under certain conditions reacts with blood to produce a blue luminescence. It will react to blood that is not visible to the naked eye.' He also told the jury that in order to see the reaction, the test must be carried out in total darkness.

He went on to describe the tests done in the house. He produced drawings and charts to explain to the jury how he was able to determine that the prints they found were made by a foot with a sock on it, as opposed to a totally bare foot or a shoe. The charts and drawings were not produced as exhibits and so have never been available to be scrutinized in the future.

The shoe print which Hentschel showed the jury obviously bore little resemblance to either of the other two, and was clearly put up to the court to dispel the possibility Guest had been seeking to introduce that perhaps a policeman's boot or shoe may have made the prints. Bearing in mind Weir had said the prints resembled what you see when a person with a bare foot walks in the sand, shoe prints were pretty much ruled out already.

However, Hentschel was particularly at pains to explain how he was able to be so certain that it was a sock-clad foot rather than a bare foot that made the prints. The point of difference he relied on was that although the external perimeters looked the same, the area between the toes and the ball area of the foot is not quite so clear. The toes and instep stand out even with a sock print, but that area of identification between the toes and the ball is taken up by the sock and that is what he saw, which left him in no doubt the five prints were made by a sock-clad foot. He gave a brief description of the footprints and told the court that he recorded the length of the best print at about 280 mm.

The blood on the door jambs throughout the house was described as 'smears that appear to have been made by a bloody garment with a fairly loose knit weave'. He said the green jersey found in the clothes that had been washed, Exhibit 98, could be of the type that would cause the bloodstains that he observed on those door jambs and posts.

Of the spot of blood in the hand-basin, he said it gave the appearance 'that most likely it had been flicked onto the surface of the basin. It has not dropped onto it from a bleeding person or blood-soaked object.'

He told the jury he saw the rifle on the floor when he first arrived on the Monday afternoon. Later on he examined it in his laboratory and said: 'I observed blood on the rifle. Smears of blood were found over most parts of the rifle. As to any area where no smears of blood were found on the rifle there was an area on the forearm where there was no smearing.'

The area where there was no smearing was the area that David Bain's fingerprints were found, of course. He then went on to say: 'In fact, between the fingerprints there was a clear space', all of which suggested to him that 'the area where the fingerprints were ... had been shielded in some way'. He examined the magazine in the gun, which had no blood on it, but said blood was detected on the large 10-shot magazine found beside Robin's hands. He said he removed that blood and sent it to Dr Peter Cropp for blood-grouping tests.

Hentschel then told the jury how in his laboratory he examined the bullets and lead fragments from the heads of the deceased, those found external to the body in Laniet's room, as well as the empty cartridge shells. He went through various test-firing procedures to establish that the gun found on the floor beside Robin had fired all the bullets that caused the deaths of the family. All the bullets used were the subsonic-type ammunition with a head stamp 'W' on the base of the shell.

He looked at the skin removed from Robin Bain's hands for any evidence of gunshot residue but none was detected. He also examined the socks that David had been wearing, and applied luminol showing that minute traces of blood were identifiable all over the soles of both socks. He then measured those socks and found them to be 270 mm long from heel to toe.

No blood was found on the cycle shorts that David had been wearing underneath the black rugby shorts and there was none on the underpants either. He examined the duvet from David's bed and there were a few specks of blood on that.

He confirmed that he examined the five spent cartridge shells found in Stephen Bain's bedroom. They were all the same subsonic ammunition with the head stamp W that was used in the killings, and the shells had all been fired from David's rifle. It will be recalled that only two shots were fired there on the day of the killings.

The cardboard target found in David Bain's room also came to the attention of Peter Hentschel, and he said the holes in it were the correct size to match .22 bullet holes. Swabs had been taken from David Bain's hands by Dr Pryde, and Hentschel examined those for gunpowder residue but none was found.

He found nothing worth reporting in the lead fragments from Laniet's room.

He said that small quantities of blood were found on the light switch in David Bain's room and on the light switch from the hallway just inside the front door and also from the light switch in Arawa's room. In the kitchen there was a red substance on the light switch that appeared to be blood but it could not be confirmed. In Margaret's room on the light switch there was a red substance that was not blood. He said there was no blood on the light switch in the laundry.

He examined the white gloves that were found in Stephen Bain's room and said they were intensely bloodstained, but he could not find any evidence of gunshot residue.

Green fibres had been extracted from the fingernail scrapings taken from Stephen Bain and these were subject to special electronic tests which showed that these fibres were a match for the green jersey found in the washing machine, Exhibit 98, but they did not match any other green garments given to Peter Hentschel to examine.

The broken glasses found in David Bain's room, and also the lens found in Stephen Bain's room, were examined by Hentschel. He found no blood or anything else of interest on the spectacles frame or lenses.

Hentschel then began giving evidence about the two pieces of skin found in Stephen Bain's bedroom. Guest objected to this evidence, but the judge ruled in favour of the Crown and allowed him to proceed. The objection was based on the fact Hentschel had no medical qualifications; however, Hentschel explained that he had years of expertise and experience in matching items such as paint fragments and the like to compare them with damaged items to see if they matched. In regard to the skin, Hentschel stated 'that piece of skin could have come from that knee area' (of David Bain).

He described examining a number of items from the laundry: the face mask, shower curtain and so on, including the heavily bloodstained green towel.

He found no blood in the liquid taken from the washing machine pump or from the trap from the hand-basin or the taps that had been removed by the police.

The spent shells found in Robin's caravan were examined and five of them were of the W type and all had been fired from David's gun, the murder weapon. Two pairs of trousers from Robin Bain's caravan had small drops of blood on them as well. A white windbreaker and a sweatshirt from Robin's Commer van were negative for the presence of blood.

The blue target that had been found in Robin's van had a number of bullet holes and Hentschel gave evidence that some of those bullet holes were commensurate with having been caused by .22 bullets.

He then went on to say that all of the items on which he had found blood were handed to Dr Cropp from the ESR for blood-group testing to see if he could identify whose blood it was.

'I took blood samples from the rifle for analysis by Dr Cropp … Blood was taken from the silencer, from the front of the telescopic sight, from the barrel, from the stock near the trigger and also from the forearm where those fingerprints were found.'

In respect to the blood from 'the forearm where those fingerprints were found', it should be remembered that both Hentschel and Jones had previously told the court that the only blood in that area was the finger-prints themselves and that the area was otherwise completely free of blood including even in between the fingerprints.

At this point in his evidence he had just come back into the witness box after the lunch break. Completely out of context with his brief of evidence he was suddenly led back into discussing the footprints: 'I indicated the measuring of one of the luminol prints in the hallway of the house. I said I measured it at 280 mm. That print encompassed both the heel and the toes; that was a complete print from heel to toe.' He then gave the measurements of Robin's and David's shoes.

In cross-examination, the first thing Guest wanted to know about from Hentschel was what happened with the photos of the luminol footprints that Weir had said did not come out. Hentschel said they did come out but did not depict anything like what was actually seen with the naked eye.

Guest then wanted to know whether or not he took drawings or made notes and kept a record at the scene of what he saw when he found the footprints. Hentschel's answer was blunt and to the point: 'No.'

Guest told him he was going to call a professor who would say that he had done tests showing that luminol reacts with many other substances apart from blood. As it transpired he never did call the professor.

A much more valid attack came when Guest queried Hentschel about why, if both of David's socks were covered in blood over the soles, he would only leave a right sock print and there were no impressions at all from the left foot. His answer was unconvincing. All he could say was that maybe one sock had more blood than the other. In the end it did not really matter because Guest, as it turned out, accepted that the footprints had been made by David, arguing that they could have been put there innocently after he came home and found his family dead.

A similar distracting and rather pointless argument took place in respect to other means of testing for blood. Again Guest confidently espoused the name of the professor who he was going to call but never did. A telling, but for sad reasons only, exchange occurred in respect to Hentschel's demonstration and depictions of shoes, socks and bare-foot prints.

'Mr Hentschel, did you do those prints for us just in the last few days?'

'Yes,' answered Hentschel.

'And you are entitled as a professional expert witness to be privy to what is going on in this court; is the reason you did it in the last few days because I did my best to get 14 pairs of feet into the house before the plastic went in?'

Of course Hentschel answered as he was sure to do: 'I was asked; I don't know the reason.'

The whole court knew the reason. The complete footprint was 280 mm. It was made by a right foot wearing a sock. Robin's sock had no blood on it and was only 240 mm long, whereas David's sock did have blood on the sole and was 270 mm long, nearly a perfect match for the footprints that Hentschel had found.

It was important for the Crown to ram home to the jury that these prints were made by a bloody sock as opposed to a bare foot or a shoe. Guest, you will recall, had established that the officers at the scene did not have their shoes checked for bloodstains and he had been hopeful that he may have been able to attribute the footprints to one of these officers.

He told Guest that he could not remember receiving a call from the police at 11.45 a.m. on the day of the killings asking how long gunshot residue would last. But if he did get one, and if he did say 'after three hours, forget it', then he was only referring to a live person, he said.

Guest then told him that he was going to call scientists in relation to gunshot residue, but again he never did. The end result was that Hentschel agreed the absence of gunshot residue does not prove the person has not fired a gun.

It must have been getting close to the end of the day by the time Guest got on to the suggestion that the skin found in Stephen's room was a match for

David's knee. Discussion went on for quite some time.

Hentschel conceded that he had never seen David's actual injury, only photos. He viewed Stephen's body to look for injuries on it that might be a match and agreed that there was at least one possibility. To laypeople who have never experienced the detail of a criminal proceeding, it may strike as surprising that a scientist of 30 years' experience would try to associate the skin to the injury on an accused, but would not volunteer that he also discovered other possibilities with totally different inferences. But that is the nature of the criminal trial in New Zealand, it would seem, if the Bain case is anything to go by.

Guest then mentions another professor, the third that he said he intended to call but never did, and put to Hentschel that this professor would say that a white flake from an abrasion was totally unlike the skin found in Stephen's room. Hentschel said he would accept that from a medical person but of course the medical person never came.

The significant aspects of re-examination were both related to the footprints. 'How many times would you have used luminol in a forensic sense looking for blood?' Bill Wright asked Hentschel, who told of a large number of times over many years.

'Did you see toe definition in the luminol prints you examined in the bedroom and the hallway?'

'On most of them, yes,' was the answer. But that was not the end for Peter Hentschel, 30 years a forensic scientist, because Justice Williamson had matters he also wanted to clarify.

First, it was the bloody fingerprints.

Judge: You said the area on the firearm where ... the four fingerprints appeared, seemed or appeared to be shielded. Could you explain what you mean by that?

Hentschel: In that area of the firearm on that wood there was no smearing of any blood visible. The only blood that was observed was by way of fingerprints on that portion of that timber. The space between the fingerprints was clear; there was no blood there. And that indicated to me that that whole area had been shielded from blood being wiped across that surface.

Judge: Was the blood on the rest of the rifle smeared or sprayed in appearance?

Hentschel: It was smeared rather than sprayed.

The next matter the judge wanted to question him about was the blood on Robin's clothes.

Judge: Could all of the blood you saw on the clothing from Robin Bain had come from that injury which he had?

Hentschel: Yes. That is, as far as the upper clothing is concerned. As far as the blue trackpants is concerned Dr Cropp has examined those in greater detail than I have and he will be able to comment on that.

Finally, in the judge's quite long series of questioning it was back to those bloody footprints.

Judge: DS Weir told us about the measurements of the luminised footprints and he said the first one measured 24 cm and the second 28 cm.

Hentschel: Yes.

Judge: Do you have any comment about that?

Hentschel: The first print was not a complete print. It showed the heel area and the ball of a stockinged foot, but I did not see the toe area and that measurement would only be from the top of the ball to the heel. The other prints that I detected with luminol showed the toes as well, taken from the top of the toes to the heel.

Judge: So could all of the footprints that you saw have been made by the same foot?

Hentschel: Yes.

The judge continued to ask Hentschel a number of questions about luminol testing in general: how it works and the different reactions it gives with various items such as copper, fingerprint powder and so on. Hentschel explained that the reaction is different with each type of substance, but the reaction he saw at the Bain house was a normal reaction he would get when it reacts with blood.

DR PETER CROPP

Hentschel's long stint on the stand finally came to an end and he was immediately followed by the other scientist from the ESR, Dr Peter Cropp. He had a master's degree in chemistry and a doctorate in biochemistry and had been a forensic scientist since 1972.

He explained that he was predominantly involved with the actual testing of samples in an attempt to identify the source of the blood, although in a couple of instances he did examine exhibits and express opinions.

He received the first samples for testing on 19 July 1994, four weeks after David had been arrested, and continued receiving various samples for examination and testing right through until November of 1994.

Blood samples that had been removed from David's clothes included the white socks, which were not labelled as to which foot they had been on. Cropp noted that both socks reacted to tests, indicating blood. His evidence focused on the two spots of blood located on the sole of one sock.

But then in yet another example of evidence that went beyond a deposition statement and therefore took Guest completely unawares, he offered a view that these spots of blood on the sole of David's socks had fallen from above. There was no mention of this in his deposition statement and there was no mention either in the letter sent to the court the week before the trial. Cropp said, 'By droplets, I mean you see blood has gone on to the sock as a drop, small drop, rather than having been transferred from the floor or contact with another bloodstained surface. As to whether those two droplets I observed could be picked up by someone walking across a surface such as a bloody carpet in stocking feet, it is very, very unlikely because the edges are so well defined.'

From a scientific point of view there is a difference between blood splatter, blood drops and blood smears, and each carries different implications. Blood spatter or splatter — the terms seem to be interchangeable depending on who is talking — is a reference to airborne blood which can be blood dropping from above onto a surface, or splatter caused by pressure, as in a severed artery, or by impact, as in a bullet making contact with the flesh of an individual or by some item impacting in a pool of blood on a surface. Another situation where airborne blood can occur is what is known as 'cast-off', where blood has got onto a weapon, for example, a steel rod which is being used to strike a person. As the rod is lifted up and swung back down again, blood will cast off and cause a pattern to be sprayed across walls and ceilings. Blood smears, on the other hand, are the transfer of blood from a bloodstained surface to another surface by direct contact. For the trained scientist, much can be gleaned from the pattern of bloodstains, and the science of bloodstain analysis is highly sophisticated. Then there is blood pooling, where blood has run from a wound and pooled, for example on the floor.

Dr Cropp was the only blood splatter expert to give evidence in this trial, and his opinion that these spots were droplets that had fallen from above was telling indeed. The only reasonable explanation could be that somehow David had got himself in a tangle in the struggle with Stephen and the sole of the sock was pointing upwards and some part of Stephen was above it.

All the most significant points of evidence against David up to this point in the trial — including the age of the injuries, the skin evidence of Hentschel, the lens in Photo 62 and now the 'drops' of blood — were new matters about which Guest had no idea until the moment they were said in court. Add to that the new Crown theory that the killings began at or before 4.30 in the morning and one can see the great disadvantage under which Guest was operating.

The T-shirt that David was wearing when the police arrived at the scene had a very light smear on the lower centre rear area and this smear was only on the very upper fibres, Cropp told the jury. There is such a small amount of blood that he did not have enough to get any grouping results, but he was able to successfully complete tests showing that it was human blood. He commented also that he thought this might be a relatively old stain as opposed to one that occurred on the day in question because of the discolouration of the bloodstain.

The black rugby shorts had what he identified as 'a stain on the front outer surface running around the seam that is on the crotch of these shorts'. It also was only on the extremities of the fibres, meaning it was a light smear. Tests showed this blood could have come from Stephen, Arawa, Laniet or Margaret.

The blood on the gloves could have been from Stephen or Laniet, although of course the fact that they were found in Stephen's bedroom where there was so much blood makes it more likely that the blood on them would have been Stephen's.

A selection of blood spots from Robin's clothing was tested and it all could only have been Robin's; the same result was obtained for the group of stains from the green curtain.

The two spots from the duvet on David's bed gave no results for grouping, but one of them was shown to be human blood.

No results were obtained from the samples removed from light switches, and the spot from the hand-basin could only be proven to be human.

All the other items from the bathroom which were said to have had possible bloodstains on them — the shower curtain, face mask, towel and so on — yielded no results whatsoever.

The *Gondoliers* white sweatshirt, from the laundry basket with the whites that had not been washed, had what Cropp described as diluted blood on the right shoulder area and sleeve; but it could not even test positive for human blood. He thought this blood gave the appearance that it may have been sponged because of the dark rims around the edges of the stain.

The pair of jeans from the caravan had a small spot of blood that he identified as being Robin's blood but no results were obtained from the stain on the other trousers from the caravan.

As far as the blood on Robin Bain's hands was concerned, he did not receive any samples, he told the jury. The two samples that were collected, Exhibit 51 (the fingernail scrapings) and Exhibit 97 (from the little finger), did not get to Cropp because Hentschel decided there was not enough present for testing.

Cropp told the jury he had seen a photo of the blood on the index fingernail of Robin Bain. He couldn't reach any conclusions from this except to say that it was deposited when travelling towards the centre of the finger from the edge of the fingernail.

In cross-examination, he agreed that the blood on the back of David's T-shirt could well have been there for quite some time before the killings.

As far as the ambush evidence that the two blood spots on David's sock had fallen from above, he agreed with Guest that David's foot would need to be lifted at a considerable angle and twisted for such a thing to happen. The clear significance of Cropp's opinion that the blood had fallen on to the sock from above was, like the age of injury evidence, to put David in Stephen's room while blood was flying around. One might think a good line of questioning would have been directed at the point that if a person wearing white socks was involved in the events of that room where blood was spattered to every corner, one would expect at least one speck to have got on the top of David socks, but there was no such blood found. This questioning did not happen.

DR STEPHEN GUTOWSKI

Then a new witness took the stand for the Crown: Dr Stephen Gutowski, a DNA scientist from Melbourne, Australia. He had not provided evidence to the depositions hearing, but in March, just a few weeks before the trial commenced, Detective Chief Inspector Peter Robinson went to a Melbourne laboratory with some items and samples to have DNA tests carried out. Their procedures were more advanced than those available in New Zealand at that time. Robinson took the two pieces of skin found in Stephen Bain's room, as well as David's black rugby shorts. The results showed that the blood on the shorts could have been from any of the children but not either of the parents, and the same applied to the two pieces of skin.

PATHOLOGY: DR ALEC DEMPSTER

The jury had been subjected to a trying few days of technical expert evidence, and were now about to hear from the police pathologist Dr Alec Dempster who conducted the autopsies on each of the deceased bodies. Dr Dempster told the jury that he had been a specialist pathologist some 23 years. He was a Senior Lecturer in Pathology at Otago University. He also told the jury he had worked as a forensic pathologist in the United States, and had been involved in examining over 100 gunshot wounds. He mentioned that he was the pathologist who attended the aftermath of the Aramoana killings of 13 people that had taken place near Dunedin in November 1990.

On the day in question, he told the court that he attended the police briefing at 8.15 a.m. and arrived at the crime scene in Every Street at about 10 o'clock. He said he was not admitted to the house, however, until just after midday. He went to each of the bodies and conducted a preliminary examination.

Later on that day he conducted more detailed postmortem examinations of the bodies, except Arawa, whose postmortem was not done until the following morning. As part of the postmortem process, he took from each of the five bodies various samples and handed them to a police officer in containers. Swabs were taken from various parts of each body. The specimens were blood samples, nail scrapings, nail clippings and fibre fragments. Skin samples were taken for residue-testing purposes from Robin Bain's hands.

Dr Dempster then described his preliminary examinations and observations that he made as he was taken through the house by Detective Sergeant Weir with a police photographer. He began with Robin Bain's body lying on the floor, and noted to the jury that the gun was about 30 cm from the body, and that there was a magazine standing on its edge beside Robin Bain's right hand. He noticed a number of blood spots in the vicinity of the rifle on the floor.

He explained to the jury the blood spatter effect: 'As a bullet enters the body there is a variable amount of spatter, predominantly of blood which radiates outwards and backwards around the muzzle of the rifle for a variable distance usually regarded as up to about 900 mm or three feet.' The distance the blood travelled depended upon the nature of the weapon and the bullets used.

The green curtains, he said, contained quite large droplets of blood and tissue which had been caused as the bullet entered the deceased. He told the jury that these blood samples were examined microscopically and that fragments of bone and brain were contained in among each of the blood stains.

His view was that due to the confined area into which the pattern of blood was deposited on the curtains, he believed the blood had only travelled about two to three feet. Putting it another way, he was saying to the jury that he believed Robin's head must have been less than three feet from the curtain at the time the blood emanated from the bullet entry wound.

He observed bloodstains on Robin Bain's left hand, and went into some detail in particular about the splash of blood on the index finger of that hand. The point was that the direction of that splash was coming towards the body and could not, he said, be explained from a self-inflicted wound, but could easily be explained if the hand were not holding an object such as the gun.

He heard the noise of the computer fan when he first went into the room so he looked behind the curtains and saw the message on the computer and informed DS Weir of what he had seen.

He described the entry wound to Robin Bain as being 4 mm in diameter surrounded by a ring of soot up to 10 mm in diameter. 'This indicates to me that this is a contact wound, loose contact wound where the muzzle of the gun has been held in direct contact with the skin of the deceased.'

He then described the wound as unusual for suicide, based on the site of entry and the direction of travel, while at the same time identifying the left temple as one of the four most common places where suicide shots are found.

His description of the site of entry and the direction of travel as being highly unusual for suicide seemed to be largely based on his personal experience rather than any professional literature. 'I did not observe such an entry site in a self-inflicted gunshot wound myself in exactly this position.'

He referred to one source of literature on the subject: 'Ray and others from Washington State, Seattle.' On the basis of this data he said, 'I would suggest the chances of a self-inflicted wound in this precise site would probably be in the order of less than 5 per cent. That is quite apart from the direction of the bullet travel, which is not addressed in these articles.'

He said that he measured Robin Bain at 5 ft 9 in tall or 175 cm. At this point he used DSS Jim Doyle as a model to demonstrate how Robin Bain was shot and to explain his theory about the site of entry and direction of travel. Doyle's arm length was 780 mm. Dempster did not actually measure his height. The average arm length for people Robin Bain's height was between 715 mm and 850 mm. In this demonstration, Doyle was incapable of reaching the trigger. This demonstration had Doyle holding the rifle in his right hand with the butt on the floor with his head tilted to hold the temple against the tip of the silencer. He said sitting or squatting made it even more difficult.

Dempster told the jury that his own arm was 800 mm long and he could reach the trigger with his left hand middle finger but that this was not an easy task. He told the jury it was possible Robin Bain could have killed himself in this way but, he said, 'there are easier, much easier ways'. In summary, he said: 'I considered it unlikely that this death was self-inflicted on the basis of the anomalies in terms of the location of the weapon, location of blood spots, the location of the entry wound and its direction through the head.'

Referring to the splash of blood on the index fingernail, he said that his greatest difficulty in explaining this blood spot from the point of view of it getting there in the course of a self-inflicted wound was that it had impacted the nail with some velocity. By this he meant that if the hand was outstretched to push the trigger it would be too far away and at the wrong angle for the blood to hit it hard at the angle that it did.

He went on to describe a number of injuries on Robin Bain's hands including some bruises and abrasions. He said that they all happened at least 12 to 24 hours before his death, which he was able to ascertain because of the degree of healing that had taken place.

The stomach was effectively empty, which was what he would expect to see in the stomach 10 to 12 hours after eating an evening meal.

In regards to Robin's bladder he said that it contained about 400 ml of what appeared to be dark, relatively concentrated urine. 'I would regard that as normal overnight collection,' he said. He weighed Robin Bain at 72 kg.

Margaret Bain's bladder contained about 300 mm of urine, Dempster said. She had been shot with a contact wound through her left eye and he would have expected that she would have been immediately incapacitated as there was major destruction of important parts of the brain. Despite this, however, he told the jury she carried on breathing for a matter of minutes as she had inhaled blood into her lungs, which were quite congested.

Stephen Bain, of course, was found nearly naked on the floor with multiple bruises and injuries all over his body and so a much more detailed account followed. 'The general disorder in the room and the totality of the injuries to the deceased led me to form the opinion that the deceased had been involved in a violent struggle prior to his death,' Dempster told the jury.

Stephen was 173 cm tall and weighed 55 kg. He was slightly built, lanky, not carrying a lot of weight. Injuries were described to nearly every part of Stephen's body: the neck, shoulder, arms, legs and ankles. Interestingly, there were no injuries of any description reported on Stephen's hands, except of course for the gunshot to his left hand passing between the bones of the fingers.

Dempster said he believed Stephen had been at least partially strangled. He said there were indications in the lungs and heart and pinpoint haemorrhaging in the lining of the main airway below the vocal cords which supported an episode of serious asphyxia. He also suggested that a likely means of strangulation was by the T-shirt being pulled tightly around Stephen Bain's neck. The reason for that, as opposed to manual strangulation, was that 'there was no deep bruising on the muscles of the neck and the cartilages of the larynx were intact'. He reckoned it was unlikely but possible that the exit wound in Stephen's hand removed a piece of skin, because 'bullets don't normally act like a wad cutter'.

He said he had seen photos of the injury to David's knee — although he referred to him of course as 'the accused' — and he had seen the actual pieces of skin recovered from Stephen Bain's room. He believed the skin found in the room appeared to be thicker than the abrasion on David, and so his preference was that it originated from the back of Stephen's hand, although he could not be dogmatic on that point. 'I concede it is possible that it came from David Bain's knee,' he said to Bill Wright.

He told the jury that the bullet entered Stephen's hand while the hand was in contact with the muzzle, and he believed the bullet traversed across the top of Stephen's head, splitting the scalp without touching the underlying bone before bedding itself on the pillow where it was actually found. He believed this wound would have caused most of the blood loss which occurred in the room, although it would not have incapacitated Stephen. He said that any lacerating scalp wound causes quite significant blood loss.

There was a second shot down into the top of Stephen's head which he said would have been immediately fatal. According to the notes of evidence, Stephen's stomach contained 75 mm [sic] of food and the bladder contained 400 ml of dilute urine.

He believed that Arawa Bain was kneeling down when she was shot in the bedroom. Her stomach and bladder contents were the same quantities as for Stephen but her urine was described as dark.

In regard to Laniet, he described the three gunshot wounds as being a contact or loose contact shot to the left cheek which had penetrated beneath the base of the skull and a bullet fragment associated with the shot had just penetrated the base of the skull, causing some damage to the right temporal lobe of the brain. The second shot described was one above the left ear and this, along with the one into the left cheek, had both been fired from the left side of her body. The third shot, however, was directly down to the top of the head. The rifle would therefore need to have been held in a vertical position if her head was upright when the shot was fired. Because of the hair masking the skin he could not ascertain any distance for this shot.

The second and third wounds that he described would have been immediately fatal, he told the jury, because both wounds had destroyed major areas of the brain.

He found that her airways, like her mother's, contained a large amount of heavily bloodstained and mucoid frothy liquid. The lungs were also congested in a similar way.

These findings in regard to the congestion indicated that Laniet has survived for some time after the first of these injuries. The wound least likely to cause immediate death would be the wound on the left side of the cheek. He then expanded on these observations and stated: 'I would have anticipated that Laniet would have been making audible gurgling or similar noises as this material accumulated in the airways. This audible sound would be quite an audible sound and would in quiet circumstances be readily heard.'

Her stomach was virtually empty and her bladder contained 250 ml of urine. He recovered a number of lead fragments from her head and handed them to the police, who secured them as exhibits.

Dempster's evidence in chief ended by telling the jury that rigor mortis was fully developed in all of the bodies by the time they were removed to the mortuary. He said, 'I had arrived prepared to do cool [sic] body temperatures, but the delay in being admitted to the scene was such that I felt there was no useful advantage in doing cool [sic] body temperatures.'

Core body temperature tests are done to establish time of death.

Obviously, this is a précis of his evidence, but it covers the essential elements.

CROSS-EXAMINATION OF DEMPSTER

It was now about 10.30 a.m. on Thursday, 18 May, the ninth day of the trial. Michael Guest really and truly had his hands full. According to Dempster, it was highly unlikely Robin committed suicide, and when this factor was added to the other matters intended to show that David Bain must have been the killer, Guest was faced with major obstacles in his defence of David.

He began his cross-examination of Dr Dempster in a very positive fashion, however, by asking: 'With the certain limitations you referred to yesterday, you do accept it was possible for Robin Bain to have committed suicide?'

'I consider it possible,' Dempster answered.

Guest then said: 'You embarked yesterday on a discussion of possibilities and probabilities … you cannot completely rule out suicide?' To which Dempster also agreed.

One would think that this was a fairly successful opening gambit. However, Guest persisted and as the subject matter became more detailed, Dempster, who of course was far better versed on the matters under discussion than Guest would ever be, tied the inquisitor in knots. It turned into something akin to the local handyman arguing the toss with a world acclaimed architect on the merits of high-rise construction design.

Some good points were made during this discourse, however a close examination would suggest that they would have been so much more effective if they had been stand-alone rather than entangled among complex discussion on such things as the parabolic curve of blood splatter and the variables associated with the movement of the body and its arms in relation to the spraying of blood. One of these propositions which took Michael Guest about 85 words to pose to Dempster was tersely dismissed with the response, 'Because it would have to disobey the laws of physics.'

Most of the discussion centred on the splash of blood on the index finger. The debate raged for over an hour. Guest's tactics were aimed at getting the skilled professional to admit he was wrong, and yet he could have dealt with this issue in one or two questions had he taken a different tack. At one point in this great debate Dempster was asked a very simple and straightforward question to which there could only be one answer: 'Do you know there is no evidence in this case which has analysed the blood on the finger?' The proposition could perhaps have been better worded, but the point is clear and Dempster answered: 'I am aware.'

A follow-up question to the effect that the splash could have come from someone else could not have been discounted by the pathologist and the issue would have been all over. In addition, a link between Robin and the killings would have resulted.

However, having got Dempster to concede that he was aware this blood had never been tested, the next question was: 'We have to assume from other evidence that the blood on Robin Bain's finger is his blood and from his killing, his wound.' Of course Dempster agreed. He never suggested what this 'other' evidence may have been.

Remarkably, a little later, Guest began a new line of questioning with the words 'If the blood on Robin Bain's finger was his blood ...?' And then later on again is another question: 'Let's turn to examine the blood on the fingernail, assuming that it is Mr Bain's blood which the defence doesn't.'

Another line of questioning which never occurred but which would have been fruitful could have been directed at Dempster's own responsibilities in regard to the bloodstains that he mentioned on Robin's left hand. Guest might have said something like, 'You were fully aware when you conducted the postmortem on Robin Bain that suicide was considered a very likely scenario?' Dempster's answer would certainly have been yes, as Guest knew that at the time the postmortem was done on the first day, murder/suicide was the preferred prognosis. The next question might have been, 'Then why did you not ensure that this blood was collected for analysis like all the other blood in the house?' Dempster would probably have answered to the effect that this was the responsibility of the police, but the point would still have been strongly made.

So what useful information did Michael Guest discover during this very lengthy exchange? You will remember that Dempster demonstrated the difficulty of suicide by using Jim Doyle as a model. Guest confirmed that Dempster did not have any accurate measurements and had him agree that it would have been of some assistance had he measured Robin Bain's arms.

Dempster accepted he had not tried to replicate suicide by putting the butt of the rifle on the chair and agreed that was another possibility.

He also conceded there was a five-degree margin of error in his 45-degree angle of shot and that moving the rifle through an arc of 10 degrees while the tip is touching the temple area makes quite a difference to the ability of the left hand to reach the trigger — or, putting it another way, has quite an effect on the distance of the trigger from the point of the shoulder.

Michael Guest himself did a demonstration with the actual rifle in front of the jury and Dempster agreed it was at the correct angle. Guest said to him: 'I suggest to you it is not a difficult task to carry out the demonstration with the left-hand activating the trigger.'

'No, that is what I managed to achieve. It is not the most easy approach but it is possible,' Dempster replied.

Dempster expanded on his evidence in chief in respect to where Robin Bain might have been positioned at the time the shot was fired. 'I observed myself a fragment of bone on the floor and fragments of tissue and bone on the curtain. That suggests to me the deceased was probably facing the direction of the chair or the curtain.'

Guest turned to the question of the ageing of bruising and injuries. 'We heard evidence about the timing and dating of bruising,' he said to Dempster, referring to Pryde's evidence, and Dempster straightaway agreed that it is not always an easy matter. Guest showed the photo of David's face taken at the time he was examined by Dr Pryde at about 11 a.m. on the day of the killings and asked Dempster, 'Could you say with precision that the bruise had been caused 10 hours earlier?'

'I could not be so precise,' Dempster answered. 'I could not say any more than that it is a recent bruise consistent with possibly being caused in the last 24 hours.'

Dempster agreed with Guest in a generic sense that the ageing of bruises was a controversial and difficult area of medicine.

Bill Wright re-examined Dempster quite extensively, particularly in respect to his comments about the ageing of bruising. Dempster said that he could not age bruises in any circumstances at better than plus or minus six hours from any given point. He got Dempster to say that he did not think Robin Bain had very long arms; a judgment made by looking at photos to see where on his legs his hands reached.

The judge sought clarification on a number of matters, notably whether any insight could be obtained into the parameters of time within which the deaths occurred. Dempster answered that it was likely to have been five to eight hours before he was admitted to the house, which put the deaths between 4 a.m. and 7 a.m. that morning. He said this was confirmed by the stomach content observations he made at the time of the postmortems. Of course, that time frame left open both of the Crown's scenarios, but it also included the period David was out on the paper run.

Finally, Dempster confirmed to the judge that the literature did record right-handed people shooting themselves with rifles in the left temple, but said that of the four preferred methods that was the least popular.

CHAPTER 6

BACKGROUND ISSUES

FAMILY FRIEND

The jury and other observers at the trial would no doubt have been grateful that the very long and detailed expert testimony was now to be replaced by matters they could relate to much more easily. The next witness was Mrs Barbara Neasmith from Sydney, who told the jury she had lived in Papua New Guinea from 1975 until 1983 before moving to Sydney. She told the court she became very friendly with Robin and Margaret and their family while living in Papua New Guinea. In 1991 she had visited them in Dunedin and stayed for three weeks during the summer holidays. She slept in the room that had become known as Scene C, the room where Laniet was found. She said that while she was there she recalled on one occasion she looked in the front lounge and saw Robin in there and he was sitting with his head in his hands, which led her to think that he was praying. He was sitting on the beanbag facing the fireplace, which is on the opposite side of the room to the green curtains.

She also said the family used that front room where she saw Robin for family prayers. There was no special place anybody sat.

She told the court that Margaret slept in until about 11 a.m. or lunchtime.

The cross-examination of Barbara Neasmith provides possibly the most illuminating insight into the dynamics of the Bain family in the entire trial, and for that reason it is produced in its entirety, along with the re-examination by the Crown.

Q: You were good friends of the Bain family for quite a large number of years?

Neasmith: Yes.

Q: You knew them for many years in Papua New Guinea?

Neasmith: Yes, I stayed with them a lot in Port Moresby.

Q: And you were able to observe them there as a happy and close knit family?

Neasmith: Yes.

Q: A family bonded by quite deep religious beliefs?

Neasmith: Yes.

Q: And you observed close bonds between Robin and Margaret?

Neasmith: Yes.

Q: And the parents of the children?

Neasmith: Yes.

Q: And each of the children to one another?

Neasmith: Yes, just the normal but because you are in an area like that living alone I think you become much closer knit than you do in the city.

Q: There was a common love of music amongst the family?

Neasmith: Yes.

Q: Dad played keyboard and guitar.

Neasmith: Margaret was a very good pianist. Robin and I sung duets a lot and Margaret played.

Q: You were close to Robin emotionally?

Neasmith: Yes.

Q: You liked David?

Neasmith: Yes, very much.

Q: What was the relationship like between Robin and David?

Neasmith: I can remember many happy times, birthday parties with treasure hunts, going on wonderful picnics and having a lovely time.

Q: Did you come back to New Zealand to visit them twice?

Neasmith: No, I came once. I came for the funeral, that was the second time.

Q: You came in 1991?

Neasmith: Yes.

Q: Did you see the family exhibiting the same dynamics in 1991 as you have described in the last few questions to me?

Neasmith: No, I found there were lots of problems.

Q: I am going to suggest to you that what you saw was a quite seriously dysfunctional family in 1991.

Neasmith: I think so, yes.

Q: Margaret had embraced new-age beliefs.

Neasmith: Yes.

Q: And she was calling Robin Belial at that stage, wasn't she?

Neasmith: I heard arguments from Laniet's room when they were in the main room and she was saying he would have to change, he would have to let go.

Q: You heard arguments between Margaret and Robin.

Neasmith: Yes.

Q: And that was different from what you had observed when you were in PNG?

Neasmith: Yes, it was very different to how they sorted out problems previously.

Q: Did you observe that when Margaret needed to make a decision she generally had to consult some form of swinging ball?

Neasmith: Yes, very much so.

Q: Could you describe what happened?

Neasmith: She would take out the keyring or take off her necklace and she would dangle it, she would make her shopping decisions that way, whether we got peaches or apricots. She could tell by the way the pendulum was going. Can I tell you about an example?

Q: Yes.

Neasmith: We were down at Te Anau and I said I think we will go and have our tea in that restaurant, it looks good to me. She turned to me and said are you sure. I said I haven't asked God, I don't think he would mind, and she laughed. Most of the time we had to consult the pendulum.

Q: That was not the Margaret you knew in PNG.

Neasmith: No.

Q: Is it fair to suggest that the change in Margaret was such that it caused you concern?

Neasmith: Yes, it did.

Q: What was the relationship like between Margaret and Robin when you visited in 1991?

Neasmith: Strained.

Q: Strained perhaps being an understatement?

Neasmith: No, because at night-time Robin would come up and we would have a meal together, all the children there and we played games and everyone seemed to be almost normal. But they were not talking to each other very much around the house.

Q: Did they share the same room together?

Neasmith: No.

Q: Did you observe whether he was welcome in the house as far as Margaret was concerned?

Neasmith: I think that he was just put up with at times.

Q: Was he called the Devil by her on any occasion?

[Court does not allow question. Discussion in the absence of the jury.]

Q: Mrs Neasmith, you say that you recall in 1991 hearing arguments at night between Robin and Margaret?

Neasmith: Yes.

Q: Were they quite heated arguments?

Neasmith: Yes.

Q: Did they relate to the continuation of the relationship or less serious matters?

Neasmith: They related to the relationship.

Q: Were you able to observe whether one or the other wanted the relationship to end?

Neasmith: Yes, Margaret wanted it to end and Robin did not.

Q: Did Margaret call Robin by any particular term or phraseology at this stage?

Neasmith: No, she threatened him, that if he didn't change he would go to hell.

Q: Who appeared to make the adult decisions in the house when you were present?

Neasmith: Before Margaret got up Robin would do his best to keep the house running but Margaret seemed to think she should make most of the decisions.

Q: Did she appear to take over making most of the decisions?

Neasmith: Yes.

Q: In 1991 what was the relationship between Robin and David Bain like, in your own words?

Neasmith: I remember once going into David's room to try some homebrew and I was led to believe that David and his father had made it together and we sat there and made [sic] homebrew; it was under the bed.

Q: Did you accept from what you saw David was close to his father?

Neasmith: I always thought David was close to his father, yes. I was going to talk about Stephen's birthday. That was another time I spent with David. I remember being told about the shooting of the rabbits. I saw where Robin talked and David's dogs came too and Casey, a good family [sic].

Q: Do you know if Robin shot rabbits?

Neasmith: I can't remember, I assumed he did.

Q: Did you talk to David Bain in January of last year 1994?

Neasmith: Yes.

Q: Was that a friendly talk?

Neasmith: Yes.

Q: Did David appear happy and relaxed?

Neasmith: Yes.

Q: Was there anything about that phone call that caused you any concern?

Neasmith: Only at the end when I asked him about the relationship between his mother and father and he just gave a laugh and said, 'Oh, Dad still won't let go and I felt a bit sorry.'

Q: Did he laugh the matter off?

Neasmith: Yes.

Q: Did he tell you in that conversation that Laniet had left home?

Neasmith: Yes, he told me Laniet had run away but he told me not to worry because it was just typical of a rebellious teenager.

Q: In 1991 when you visited Every Street was the house in an extremely untidy condition?

Neasmith: No.

Q: You took some photos then did you?

Neasmith: Yes.

Q: Do you recognize four photos of Stephen, Margaret, Arawa and Robin taken by you in the house at Every Street in 1991?

Neasmith: That is Stephen, Margaret, Laniet — it is not Arawa — and Robin.

Q: On hearing of the deaths you came out to New Zealand?

Neasmith: Yes.

Q: Because of police lines quite properly you were not able to enter the house?

Neasmith: No, I went in the house. I was only taken into the front room to look at the position of a coffee table by the police.

Q: You were able to gain an impression of the house when you went in in June?

Neasmith: It was in such a mess from the police that I wouldn't like to say how the house was in.

This was the end of Michael Guest's questioning and then the Crown re-examined Mrs Neasmith.

Re-examination was short.

Q: You have described certain behaviour in Margaret in 1991 which caused you concern. Did you observe any behaviour in Robin which caused you concern?

Neasmith: I just felt he was being very passive and I just wished that he could stand up a bit more, but Margaret was very close to me and Robin knew that, and he was very pleased. He wanted me to come over to help Margaret. When I left he thanked me for what I had done. I tried to heal rifts in the relationship and I think I was able to do that in some ways.

SPECTACLES

Spectacles, the ownership thereof, and in particular the broken spectacles found in David's room and one lens in Stephen's room took on much importance in this trial. Margaret and David wore glasses all the time and Robin had recently acquired reading glasses. The background to the controversy was that on the Thursday before the tragedy, David had been at singing lessons with his teacher Mrs Dawson at her home on the other side of Dunedin. She lived in a house with a steep, slippery path running from the front door up to the road, something that would not be unfamiliar to many of Dunedin's residents in the hilly suburbs of the southern city. On this particular evening when David left it was raining and dark and as he was running up the path to get back into the car to drive home he slipped and fell over, his glasses fell off and were damaged. The following morning Arawa and David drove to the optometrist's and David took the glasses to be repaired. He was told they would be ready sometime the following week and that the optometrist would call when they were ready.

We know that on a chair just inside the doorway to David's bedroom the police found the frame of a pair of glasses and a right spectacle lens separate from the frame. This was first noticed by Constable Van Turnhout at about 9.30 a.m. while he was watching David Bain. We also know that at 8.46 p.m. on the Thursday night, 23 June, DSS Weir found a left lens in Stephen's bedroom. This was the lens that was shown to the jury in Photo 62, the 'new photo', in which it could be seen, according to Weir, lying on the floor a few inches from Stephen's body.

The next five witnesses were a series of optometrists and their staff, the first being the receptionist who had received the glasses from David and prepared a quote for him. She said he was not wearing glasses when he came in on that Friday morning to hand her the damaged glasses. Next was optometrist Peter Stewart Dick who had prescribed Robin's reading glasses in August 1993. He said Robin's glasses would be totally unsuitable for David or Margaret.

Then came Margaret's optometrist whose name was also Dick, but this time his name was Peter Leslie Dick. The second Mr Dick told the jury that he examined Margaret in December 1989 just after she had returned from Papua New Guinea. He said that her eyes were healthy but she was short-sighted and had astigmatism in both eyes. He prescribed a new set of glasses for her.

The third optometrist was Catherine ('Kate') Bridgman who told the jury that her records showed she had examined David Bain in October 1992, and during this examination he told her he had been wearing glasses since he was 13. She said David's eyesight would be somewhat blurred beyond about 33 cm. His eyes were healthy and his near vision was normal. She said that on this occasion she prescribed new lenses to go into David's old metal frames, and gave a little summary of the effect of short-sightedness on vision at night in the dark and how a person with David's eyesight would cope with and without glasses. These four witnesses' evidence was read to the jury by the consent of defence counsel.

It was now the afternoon of Thursday, 18 May, the ninth day of trial. The jury had heard from a number of experts. Expert witnesses are considered in a special category where they may offer opinions based on their expertise, and also give evidence of the factual findings upon which they form their opinion. The jury had heard from Dr Pryde, who opined with precision on the age of bruising; Chief Ambulance Officer Wombwell, who gave an estimate of the time of death based on his experience; Martin Cox was the computer expert from Otago University who testified that the computer was turned on at 6.44 a.m. on 20 June 1994; Mr Preston was the washing machine technician who gave evidence of water pressures and the mechanical state of the Bain washing machine; Ngamoki was the police armourer who gave evidence about tests on the rifle and got those measurements wrong; Kim Jones was the expert the police called in respect to fingerprints and his examination of various items, including the murder weapon, with the Polilight, which he had told the jury caused blood to fluoresce when it was activated using the violet waveband; Peter Hentschel was the first of the two ESR scientists who gave evidence of both his crime scene examination and his examination of various items in his laboratory in Christchurch, including the piece of skin which he said in his opinion was a match for the skin abrasion on David's knee; the other ESR scientist Dr Cropp gave evidence of the results of all the blood tests he had done and also expressed his opinion that two spots of blood on one of David's socks had fallen from above; Dr Stephen Gutowski was the DNA scientist who had tested two items and was able to say that the skin from Stephen's room could not have been from either of the Bain parents but could have been from any one of the four children; Dr Alec Dempster was the pathologist with some 25 years' experience who could not rule out that the skin had come from David, who believed that it was extremely unlikely that Robin had committed suicide but agreed that it was possible, and who reckoned that Laniet had been making audible gurgling noises as she was dying, among other things.

In this case another opinion was expressed quite strongly, although it was not from a recognized expert, and that was Constable Andrew's opinion that David had been faking a fit when he crashed down between the bed and the wall. This opinion was based on the fact that Andrew said that his eyes did not change. It was supported by an ambulance officer who said David's fit presented as being purposeful.

The final expert witness called for the Crown was about to take the stand and this was Dr Gordon Sanderson, a senior lecturer in the Department of Ophthalmology at Otago University. Like Martin Cox, Sanderson was not a forensic scientist and so he was not versed in the machinations of criminal proceedings. In fact this was the first time he had ever given expert evidence in a court and of course it was a very serious case. This is mentioned to contrast the situation that these two witnesses found themselves in when compared with other experts like Dr Cropp, Dr Dempster, Mr Hentschel, Dr Pryde, Dr Gukowski and Kim Jones whose work meant that they gave evidence in criminal cases as a routine part of their occupation. The word forensic actually means 'of or for the court' and is misused in the common lingo as referring to scientific findings in particular relating to such things as DNA. In fact, there are experts in many fields such as accountancy, for example, who provide evidence in court as a regular part of their work who are qualified to be recognized as forensic experts.

Dr Sanderson, then, was not a forensic specialist but rather a specialist optometrist consulted by the police in respect to the spectacles that formed part of the evidence in this case.

He began by telling the jury that on 13 September the previous year, about three months after the tragedy, he received from Detective Fitchett more than one spectacle frame and three separate lenses.

Essentially, his evidence related to David Bain's eyesight and the broken glasses found at the scene. Sanderson described the frame of the broken glasses as quite old and the appearance suggested to him that they had not been worn consistently for a very long time. He could not rule out that they may have been worn recently for a very short time. He said they were damaged on the left-hand side of the frames to such an extent that the left lens was unable to be fitted into the frames. The right lens, however, could be fitted perfectly and he noted that the frame for the right lens was only very slightly loose, but he said that he concluded they were not loose enough for the lens to have fallen out of its own accord. There was no damage to the frame on the right-hand side, the side of the face where David had those bruises above and below his eye.

He told the jury that he had been provided with the optometrist records which included the prescription given to David in October 1992. He said, 'The prescription for the two lenses [from the broken glasses] that fit this frame is similar to the prescription prescribed for the accused by Kate Bridgman in October 1992. It is similar but not identical. It is consistent with being an earlier prescription, and when I first saw the lens that is what I concluded.'

So what he was saying, when taken in context with all his evidence, was that the broken glasses were consistent with being an earlier prescription of the lens Kate Bridgman prescribed for David in 1992.

He estimated, and was at pains to point out that it was only an estimate, that the broken glasses would have given David about 90 per cent of his visual potential. Without glasses David operated at about 75 per cent of normal vision, according to Dr Sanderson. He told the jury that David suffered from myopia, which is short-sightedness in both eyes, and a little bit of astigmatism. In his view David would be unable to recognize a face at 2 m without his glasses on.

In cross-examination, Guest asked Sanderson if he had ever examined David himself, which of course he had not, and got him to agree that the only thing he was basing his opinions on was the October 1992 records.

He agreed that David could probably do his paper round without glasses but could not legally drive without glasses and that was about the extent of the cross-examination.

PAPER RUN

The next bunch of witnesses comprise the testimony about the paper round that David had been doing for some years for the *Otago Daily Times* (*ODT*) distributor Alistair McConnell. As well as McConnell there were a number of witnesses who saw something of interest about the time the newspaper was delivered which the police believed was relevant to their case, as well as the paper boy — not David — who delivered the newspaper to 65 Every Street itself.

It will be recalled that in his letter to the court just before the trial, Bill Wright made a list of those witnesses who did not need to be called in person if the consent of the defence was obtained. The only one of the 10 paper round witnesses on that list was the other paper boy who delivered the newspaper to 65 Every Street. However, as it transpired at the trial, and despite the fact that the other witnesses were present at court and ready to give evidence and be available for cross-examination, the Crown and Guest negotiated an arrangement on the day where all bar one of them would have their evidence admitted by consent, meaning their deposition statement was read to the jury by the court registrar.

It should be pointed out that the legal status of evidence read to the court by the registrar and admitted by consent is no different from that which is given in person, or as they say in legal terms, viva voce ('by word of mouth'). It is still the evidence of the witness in question and if it were deliberately false that witness could be charged for perjury in exactly the same way as if he or she had appeared personally on the stand.

And so in the late afternoon of this Thursday, the final half an hour or so of the day according to the records, the Crown raced through 10 paper round witnesses, nine of them having their testimony read to the court by the registrar.

McConnell the newspaper distributor said that he dropped three bundles of newspapers for David's paper round, each one containing about 50 papers. One was at the beginning of the paper round on the corner of Aytoun and Albion Streets, the second bunch was at 146 Somerville Street and the third was at number 66 Somerville Street.

His evidence did not take very long and included reference to the fact that David Bain would not have come across any other paper boys during his paper round and that David had been working for him for about six years. A map of the paper round was used to indicate the route that David would have taken.

McConnell's evidence then explained that in the course of his morning's work he drove past the various drop-off points at different times and on this particular day he didn't notice anything unusual. He did not see David himself and he told the jury that David normally starts at about 6 a.m. but occasionally starts later or sooner. As far as times were concerned he said that at 5.40 a.m. he drove past the first bundle and it was still there so David had not picked it up at that time. At about 6.15 a.m. he went past the second bundle of papers and noticed the yellow paper bag there which was David's normal procedure because he would just take a few papers to go up the very steep streets of Everton and Lauriston and then collect his paper bag on his way back. He went on to say that David must have started his paper round at around 5.50 a.m. and that if he did start at about that time he could finish about 6.30 to 6.45.

Then Mrs Rackley, an elderly woman on David's paper route, submitted very short evidence that she awoke at about 5.40 a.m. because of sleeping problems and went outside at six o'clock and the paper had been delivered. Her evidence read: 'I was surprised to find the newspaper had been delivered as it is normally delivered after 6 a.m. each morning.' Her address was not included in her evidence, but it was noted on the chart exhibited to the jury. One may think that it is rather strange that she went outside in the middle of winter to get the paper when it is never there at the time she went.

Then came Mr Stuart Warrington who lived at 2 Beverley Place, one of the streets in which David delivered newspapers. All he had to say was that at about 6.15 a.m. he saw the paper boy on Somerville Street a few doors up from Cawdor Place.

Mrs Mitchell's evidence was then read describing how she lived at 128 Somerville Street and had the *ODT* delivered every day. She knows the paper boy as David and said how on most days he had his dog with him. David would bring the paper right up to the balcony for her and when he did her dog would bark and on the Monday in question it barked between 6.10 and 6.15 a.m. She didn't see David but knew he had been because the dog barked. She said she seldom saw him in the winter because it was always dark, but when she did see him in the summertime he always wore shorts and gym shoes. She said he seemed very fit and he would normally be running.

The only one of the 10 paper round witnesses to actually take the stand was Douglas Richardson, a self-employed cleaner who lived on Everton Street, a little side street off Somerville Street. He said that he was pretty exact with his times because he runs a fairly tight schedule in regard to his work. On 20 June he said that he got down to the bottom of Everton Street at 6.18 to 6.22 a.m., with a rider, in his words, 'somewhere pretty close to that'. He saw the paper boy, he told the court: he had his dog with him and he was wearing an anorak and some washed-out shorts but he didn't notice his footwear. He admitted it was dark, but he would only have been about four metres away and he had his headlights on. He told the court he normally saw the paper boy two or three times a week over the past 12 months. In cross-examination Michael Guest showed the red sweatshirt that David had told police he had worn on the paper round that was found in the washing machine by the police and Mr Richardson agreed that that could have been what David was wearing. David also told the police that he had seen someone in a red station wagon and Richardson agreed that that was probably him because he did drive a red station wagon. He admitted to Guest that his times were an estimate based on routine as opposed to any direct evidence of looking at the clock or watch or hearing the time on the radio.

This witness was important to the police case because in their case it showed where David was at a particular point on the paper run, but also because they said he had *wanted to be seen* to establish his 'alibi' which was why he told them he had been seen by someone in a red station wagon. It is another example of their belief that he had planned the whole thing and was a consummate liar. But then it seems they believed him when it suited them and said he was lying when it did not.

Malcolm Parker was a police officer who lived at 47 Somerville Street. His evidence read to the jury is a good example of the bankrupt logic that seems to have pervaded much of Operation Every but somehow escaped the attention of the defence and the court. Parker's evidence read to the jury is very short and was as follows.

My full name is Malcolm Parker. I am a senior constable of police stationed at Dunedin. I reside at 47 Somerville Street, Dunedin. I was at home on Monday, 20 June 1994.

My normal pattern on an 8 a.m. shift is to awake on the alarm clock at 6.30 a.m. The electric jug goes on and then into the bathroom. I dress, pour coffee and then get the paper. This normally is between 6.50 and 7 a.m.

I only have time to read the front page and 'court news'.

I leave for work around 7.05 a.m.

That Monday, I awoke without the assistance of the alarm at 6.15 a.m. I carried out my normal ritual, that is jug, bathroom, dress. As I was running about 15 minutes ahead of the normal I looked out the rear window onto the driveway. The drive was dry so I took a chance that the paper was there. I went to the paper box and it had been delivered.

I went back inside, got my coffee and sat on the sofa. I remember looking at my watch and confirmed on the video unit that the time was 6.38 a.m.

I remember feeling pretty good as I would read most of the paper prior to heading to work. The paper is never delivered before 6.45 a.m. I think this is why I checked the time. On the odd occasion I have seen the paper boy coming along the street and this has always been after 6.45 a.m.

This statement is true to the best of my knowledge and belief. It has been made by me knowing that it may be admitted as evidence at a preliminary hearing and I could be prosecuted for making a statement known by me to be false and intended by me to mislead.

In standard fashion for the deposition statements, it was signed by two JPs and by Parker on 12 October 1994.

The two matters in the statement that appear to be striking and may have impressed the jury were that the witness was a police officer and that the paper was delivered quite a bit earlier than usual: 'The paper is never delivered before 6.45 a.m.,' stated the senior constable of police.

But when you read the statement carefully a number of anomalies present themselves. Parker's normal routine was to awake at 6.30 a.m. on the alarm clock. On this Monday he woke 15 minutes early without the need of his alarm clock, which is OK.

Because he was 15 minutes ahead of schedule he thought he would check to see if the paper was there and it was, at 6.38 a.m. But normally he never got ready before 6.50 a.m. at which time he would fetch the paper. How could he know when the paper is usually delivered, when he never looks before about 6.50?

Rather than saying, as he did, which of course suited the police theory that David was deliberately early, '*The paper is never delivered before 6.45 a.m.*' what he should have said was '*I never go out to get the paper before 6.45 a.m.*'

Put it another way; the paper could be delivered any time before 6.45 and he would be none the wiser.

But the reading of this statement in the two or three minutes it would have taken without any cross-examination would no doubt have left the jury with exactly the thought Bill Wright wanted to plant in their minds, namely that David was early — unusually early, in fact.

The court registrar continued with the readings, the next a short statement from a man called John Letts, who was a driver who lived nearby and drove to work down Every Street. He said his normal routine was to drive down the street a few minutes after seven o'clock when he would see the paper boy who he knew was David Bain, and his dog which he described as a husky with grey dark patches. However, he said that on 20 June 1994 he did not see the paper boy. He recalled that David first started the paper round in 1989 when his family returned from Papua New Guinea. His evidence included the fact that he knew the Bain family and also knew they lived at 65 Every Street.

This evidence was also intended to convey the impression that David was unusually early that day, but when taken in the context of the next two witnesses it is demonstrably nonsense.

The final two witnesses both worked at the rest home next door to the Bain house and their daily shift began at 6.45 a.m. Tania Clark was a caregiver and the second witness, Denise Laney, was a registered nurse. They both regularly saw the paper boy on their way to work at about 6.40 to 6.45 a.m. as he walked home up Every Street, which in itself makes a mockery of Parker's and Letts' evidence.

On Monday, 20 June Tania Clark told the court that she was getting ready to go to work at about 6 a.m. Her evidence went on to say that she guessed she would have left home at about 6.25 a.m. and she was concerned about icy roads that morning because it was very cold. It normally took about 15 minutes to get to work but 'a little longer if it is icy such as this morning'. She described her car and then said, 'I am fairly certain I arrived at work at 6.40 a.m.' Her evidence included the fact that she saw a man who looked about 50 years old walking down Every Street near the bottom of the street and he appeared to be carrying something like a torch. The defence agreed with the Crown that this man was not Robin Bain. It is hard to understand the basis on which this agreement was reached as the police never did make any attempts to find the man who must have walked right past David and Casey (the dog) as they were on their way home up the street.

Clark's evidence went on to record that at the intersection of Heath and Every Streets (about 280 m down the hill on the other side of the road from the Bains' house) she saw the paper boy. 'He was crossing the mouth of Heath Street *walking* up Every Street. I normally see the paper boy — he has always got the dog with him as he did on this occasion.'

The italicized word is to emphasize an interesting contradiction in the Crown case. They were advancing the theory that he was in a hurry to complete the paper round so that he would be home before his father got up in order to hide behind the curtains. Yet this witness says he was walking across Heath Street, and this was after he had delivered his last paper and was nearly home.

The chart of David's paper round showed that he delivered his last newspaper at 26 Every Street, which is about 20 or 30 m before the intersection of Heath Street where Tania Clark said that she saw him.

She described his dress as a black or navy sweatshirt with a hood which was on. 'It was not a parka/oilskin type. He had dark-coloured long trousers. I'm not sure if he had a newspaper bag on.' Her evidence went on to say, 'I did not see his face. He was walking and he had a dog with him.' She described the dog as a medium-sized fat dog which was tanned and cream colour.

She told the court she was travelling between 30 and 40 km/h when she passed the paper boy.

Denise Laney, the second witness from the rest home, had been working there for about six years. She was a registered nurse. Her evidence began by telling the jury that on that morning she was supposed to start work at 6.45 a.m. 'but I was a bit late'. The rest of her evidence is quoted in full.

As I drove to work I came up Every Street from Somerville Street, Dunedin. I drove past 65 Every Street, Dunedin. As I did so I noticed a person going past the partially open gate at 65 Every Street, Dunedin.

As I saw this person I thought I must be running late as I normally see him down by Heath Street, Dunedin.

I looked at the clock in my car and it read 6.50 a.m. I know the clock is four to five minutes fast as it was about 6.45 a.m. as I drove past him.

I think he had a lighter coloured top on and the bottom was darker. I couldn't see if he had shorts or trousers on as he was nearly in the gate. I didn't see the dog with him.

I have seen him before and he has had his dog with him. I can't remember what he normally wears.

The statement was sworn in the normal fashion.

The final evidence to do with newspaper deliveries came from the employee who delivered the paper to 65 Every Street. His name was Kieran Garbutt. His statement read to the court confirmed that he delivered the paper to the Bain house between 5.30 and 5.45 a.m. His evidence also told of one other interesting and relevant matter: 'When delivering the papers the ink from the newsprint comes off the papers onto my hands and by the end of the paper-run I always have black hands as a result.'

GENERAL BACKGROUND

The next witness was Mrs Geraldine Marsh who lived at 59 Every Street and her house was down a right-of-way and adjoined the Bain section. Her evidence was also read to the jury by consent and it was to the effect that on Monday, 20 June she was woken by the sound of the Bain dog barking at 7 a.m.

'The dog continued barking until I managed to go back to sleep at about 7.15 a.m.,' she said. 'This dog has never barked continuously like this before. The dog has woken me up before and when I have heard it before, it has only barked about three times — not continuously.'

Another very short brief was read to the court. Peter Sharplin was a supervisor at the Bob Shepherd Suit Hire shop. His evidence was to the effect that early in June 1994 a person came into the shop and bought a pair of white gloves for $9.90. He said: 'I have been shown a photograph of David Bain, I am sure that he is the person I served.'

The Crown were flying through their evidence at this stage because the next witness, Mr Alan Lowe, also had his evidence read by consent. He simply confirmed that he was a chartered accountant who administered an amount of money that the Cullen Bain family had lent on a personal arrangement to a Mr Hartley Meder in 1984 and that the balance owing by the Meders, as at 30 June 1994, was $65,109.83.

The trial by now was only a few days from completion, and it may well have been that the jury's interest was increasing as most of the remaining witnesses had evidence of a more human, personal interest nature than the mostly technical, scientific or medical evidence they had heard so far.

FEMALE FRIENDS

It was time for friends and acquaintances to take the stand. The first were two female music students who had met David Bain in February of 1994 during rehearsals for a production of Shakespeare's *The Tempest*. The girls had been friends before they met David Bain.

The first witness has permanent name suppression and shall be referred to simply as Miss X. She was a musician studying a Bachelor of Science degree at Otago University. She told the jury that she first met David in February during rehearsals for the show. They struck up a friendship during this time, particularly due to their common interest in music. She told the jury how one night David had dropped her home in the Bain family car, a white Toyota Corolla. She was performing in another musical at a different venue and due to their friendship David came along to watch the show and afterwards went backstage to meet her.

He told her he was going to be in a production called *The Gondoliers* and she decided to join up for that show as well. They began rehearsing on 4 May. She explained to the jury that she was very accurate with dates because her parents lived in the United Kingdom and she kept a daily diary so she could tell her mum and dad what she'd been doing.

She explained to the jury that as their friendship grew they talked about more personal details, which included David talking about his family. On 22 May she said they went for a coffee at the museum café where she met Arawa. She learned that they lived in Andersons Bay in a house that was about 140 years old. David told her of the plans to knock it down and build a new house and that he was going to help with building and planning. She said that he seemed quite pleased about being involved in the house plans. She went on to say that they went shopping together and maintained quite regular contact.

After the final production of *The Gondoliers* she and David and a girl-friend of hers went to a Chinese restaurant with the cast of the show. That was on 27 May, only about three weeks before the demise of the family, and after dinner David took both of the young women back to his place where they chatted. He showed her around the house and the three of them finished up talking in his bedroom. The two girls went home in the early hours of the morning. There was further contact and she told the court that she asked for his phone number and asked him to come to the theatre with her.

On 29 May they met again and went to the museum café. David asked her to go to the movie *Schindler's List* with him and she described to the jury the horrid nature of the film with the Jews being shot in concentration camps.

'During the film David reacted. He said, "I don't like it very much," and he asked me to hold his hand and he was crying during the course of the film … After the film was finished the accused gave me a hug. He said he had not cried that much in 10 years.'

They continued to make arrangements for further meetings. He watched her perform a solo and after that he invited her to go with him to a ball at Larnach Castle. She told of personal involvement with David's family. Arawa helped her with getting her hair done for the ball, and Mrs Bain provided her with some gloves in preparation for the ball. She described what David was wearing including that he wore white formal gloves and a top hat.

'It was a success,' she told the court. 'On the way home David took me to a lookout near his place and he described it as one of his favourite places. We went back to his house and then we went back to my place. David said that he wanted to get quite close to me. I didn't see it as a romantic relationship that we had at that stage. I took from what he said that he did not want to have a sexual relationship with me.'

She continued telling of the developing relationship between her and David and that he talked about the tension that existed at home when his father was there. He said Laniet was a bit of a rebel.

Miss X went on to explain that they went to the Symphonia with another person and at the end of the second half when everyone started clapping David didn't do anything. 'I sort of thought he was in some sort of trance,' she explained, saying that she had to give him a bit of a jab in the ribs to make him come to.

On Friday, 17 June she went with David to a restaurant and they talked about relationships and families. Miss X said that 'he felt that his father was his father. He knew of someone in Papua New Guinea who he saw as a father figure.'

On Sunday, 19 June Miss X and her friend went to meet David at St Clair Beach for the polar plunge activities during the morning. After festivities were finished, she and her friend walked back with David to their car and then they dropped him in town because he had rehearsals all afternoon at the university. They arranged to meet afterwards at the museum café where Arawa and Laniet were working. Miss X met David's other sister Laniet on the day before her death for the first and only time. After having coffee she left to go home, seeing David for the last time before the murders. He waited there to get a ride home with his sisters when they finished work.

Miss X's testimony then turned to post-tragedy events. She told the jury that on Tuesday afternoon about 2.30 p.m. as a result of a call she visited David at the Clarks' house in St Clair after dinner that night. She had to wait to see him because when she got there he was with a detective.

She was with David and the policeman Greg Dunne for a while and David was really upset because he had found out that two of the children were out of bed and he was very angry because he had not been told about it.

When Dunne left, she said, 'The accused said he had come in to the house and put some washing on, gone back upstairs and seen bullets on the floor so he went to see his mother.'

It would not be surprising if you, the reader, had at this point noted that this young woman, who was dating David at the time, seemed to have adopted a very distant and even accusatory attitude towards him. Apparently, she had distanced herself from him to the extent that she was now calling him 'the accused'. But in fact that was not the case; the transcript simply illustrates the way in which court stenographers used to record the evidence at trials at that time.

In 1994, and in fact until quite recently, the evidence during a trial was recorded by a court stenographer literally typing up the evidence as it was given. At that time and in this trial, evidence in chief was not recorded in question and answer form but rather the stenographer would combine the question and answer into a form that made it appear as though it was a statement. An easy way to illustrate this is the use of the word 'accused' as it appears in the evidence in chief to refer to the person charged.

Miss X's deposition statement, for example, was pretty much her information in narrative form and all references to David Bain were in the normal way by referring to him by name. But when the prosecutor led her through her evidence during evidence in chief, he used the word 'accused' to refer to David, and so when the stenographer typed up the statement it appeared, and in fact appears to the jury, as though the witness is one of the accusers, although that may not be the case at all.

Referring to Miss X's evidence in chief, the notes of evidence record her as stating: 'The accused said he had come into the house and put some washing on.' This is a direct quote from the notes of evidence of the trial. However, in her deposition statement she actually states on exactly the same matter: 'He told me how he had come in and put the jug on and prepared to do some washing and then went upstairs where his cupboard door was open.'

When it came to this part of the deposition statement the prosecutor would have asked her a question something like the following: 'And after Detective Dunne left did the accused say anything to you about what he had done when he got home?' Miss X would have answered: 'Yes, he said he had come into the house and put some washing on.' In combining the question and answer the court stenographer has recorded the evidence as: 'The accused said he had come into the house and put some washing on.'

A further example of this relates to what Miss X is recorded as saying in the notes of evidence: that 'David was angry with Mr Dunne because two of the children were out of bed'. The deposition statement records this incident in the following way: 'David told Greg Dunne that he was angry at Greg because he had said that all three were asleep.'

As is quite obvious, this is a far more reasonable and logical scenario. David was angry because he had not been told of the circumstances of the family's death and had found out about it in the newspaper.

This type of skewing of evidence is commonplace when comparing notes of evidence with the witness's actual statement in their own words. It is a common means by which there can be a subtle shift in the emphasis of a witness's evidence. The mere fact of a young woman who was dating David continually having referred to him as the accused gives the impression she is one of the accusers.

As a final point, by 2009 when the retrial commenced, more modern recording methods were being used which recorded in the notes of evidence both the counsel's questions and the response by the witness, thereby removing at least one ambiguity from the process.

Carrying on with the evidence of Miss X, she then recounted him telling her that there was a period of time that he was unable to account for. He said to her he had told the police about the trance he had when he was with her at the Symphonia and that they might want to talk to her about it.

On the evening following this conversation, Wednesday, 22 June, both Miss X and her friend visited David again at about 5.30 p.m. when they drove down to St Clair Beach and walked through the fields and along a path near the beach.

The other girl, Miss X told the jury, said something to David which caused him to fall to his knees and clutch his stomach. The other girl did not tell her what was said. She said that David was yelling and walked ahead by himself for a while, maybe for about 15 minutes.

On the way back she said she and David had a hug or two.

They then went back to the Clarks' house and remained there with David until about midnight. They talked about Arawa's birthday the following Sunday and David said he wanted to have a gathering for her, but he couldn't have it at the Clarks' house because they did not think it was appropriate.

The final words of her evidence in chief were describing what David was wearing when she was with him after the polar plunge on Sunday, 19 June.

'He had on running shoes, shorts and a red anorak and I think a cream jersey, sort of Arran knit. When he left me he was wearing his red jacket … I think he still had his red jacket on as we dropped him off at the lecture theatre. I thought he was wearing his red jacket. I thought he wore it when he went along the beach.'

However, the very last paragraph of her deposition statement says: 'At the polar plunge David was wearing white/creamy shorts, running shoes, a creamy Arran jumper and a scarf. He was not wearing a jacket. He also had a canvas army bag with him. David was not wearing glasses.'

This illustrates the difference between what a person may actually know, and what the jury might get to hear.

THE EVIDENCE PROCESS

This is a good point at which to pause and explain just how evidence is given at a criminal trial, as there are nuances that most ordinary people, inexperienced in that setting, will not pick up on.

In the case of a layperson — such as Miss X — giving evidence at trial there is normally a multi-step process. Generally speaking, the person will give a statement to a police officer in the first instance that very briefly outlines the information they have. That will be fed into the inquiry database of the inquiry team dealing with the case. The information may be highly relevant or it may have no relevance whatsoever as far as the inquiry is concerned. Or, it might be a double-edged sword, meaning that some aspects may ultimately suit the police theory of a case and some may not.

Naturally, when there is no relevance whatsoever, no follow-up would occur. However, the decision as to relevance is very much a subjective one made by the police officers in charge of the case and, depending upon their own theories of how the witness fits into the overall picture, highly relevant information may fall through the cracks. The officer doing the interviews and the witnesses themselves may not realize what will and what will not be considered relevant.

If the person's information is considered relevant to the inquiry, an officer will be sent back to re-interview the witness as soon as possible to get further details.

Once the police make an arrest the next stage is to prepare the prosecution case for the depositions hearing, which normally takes place a few months after an arrest has been made. This requires the police to submit all of the evidence on which their case is based in the form of sworn statements.

The police then, in conjunction with the prosecutor, will go through all the information and select the witnesses accordingly, and at this time the witnesses swear a statement called the deposition statement.

When the matter comes to trial most witnesses will be called to give evidence in person and be available for cross-examination, although if both the prosecution and defence consent, the deposition statement can be read to the jury by the court registrar or the judge.

Pertinent to this process is what is known in legal terminology as 'disclosure'. The Crown, or police in reality, have a legal obligation to disclose to any accused person, usually through his or her lawyer, all of the evidence gathered in the investigation regardless of whether or not it is being called by the prosecution in evidence at the trial.

Often, it is background documents — the original interview notes, deposition statement and so on — that provide the basis for cross-examination. However, as we have seen in this case already, important relevant evidence, normally unhelpful to the Crown case, is omitted from the evidence in chief of the witness at trial.

The deposition statement will often not include information that was contained in earlier statements, if it is to the advantage of the accused person. Sometimes a witness may have evidence that works for both sides and the Crown will not call the witness at all if they see the downside as being worse than the upside. Criminal trials are something of a cat and mouse game.

When the witness comes to actually give evidence at the trial, they do not read the evidence and nor do they simply recount their version of events.

Except in the case of experts, who may seek permission to refer to notes made at the time that they did examinations or testing, or police officers, who may be granted permission to refer to their notebook entries to refresh their memory, witnesses are not allowed to take any documentation with them onto the stand — nothing to remind them in that fraught environment of the key points they wish to make. The witness is led through their evidence by the prosecutor. The effect of this can be that their resulting testimony has an emphasis which the witness may not have intended. It also means that the prosecutor can skip aspects of the deposition statement that the witness will never get an opportunity to correct and, of course, in the nervous hurly-burly of the courtroom may not even realize has been omitted. It is also quite possible for counsel, when leading a witness through a brief, to subtly lead the witness in a particular direction, although leading questions, ones that carry with them a suggestion of the answer, are not permitted.

Obviously, witnesses when they take the stand in very serious cases are generally very nervous. They are focusing and concentrating on answering the questions put to them by counsel, and in consequence, if something is completely omitted, they may not have the presence of mind to realize at the time they are on the stand that the omission has occurred.

So it was that Miss X's observation that David was not wearing glasses on the Sunday before the murders was not made available to the jury, an omission that suited the police's case very well.

CROSS-EXAMINATION OF MISS X

Guest's cross-examination of Miss X began with the red anorak.

'The evidence will be that he had the red anorak on running down to the polar plunge but took it off when he into the water.'

Miss X answered: 'I didn't see him swim as we went to the wrong beach. I can't remember about the red anorak, I am sorry.'

He did not question her about David not wearing glasses, which, in the light of the Crown proposition that David had been wearing the broken glasses because his were in for repair, meant that the jury were never privy to this information, and caused an imbalance in this aspect of the evidence.

Miss X was then questioned in general terms about her impressions and knowledge of David. She agreed he struck her as a happy, active person and had a good studying and attendance record at the university, that singing was a common interest and he was very actively involved in a series of productions. She agreed the relationship was happy and pleasant and that there had been no arguments. He had interacted socially with friends and others in a normal way. She had asked him at the Larnach Castle ball why he was so good at ballroom dancing and he said it was because his father had taught him.

She told Michael Guest that David talked a lot about his family, and she used the words 'quite affectionately' to describe her impression of David's conversations about his family. The two little comments David had made about his father that she had mentioned in her evidence in chief 'were not at all' symptomatic of a negative attitude to his dad or his family.

She said David had a good sense of humour, was fun to be with and she didn't see him unhappy at any time. He loved all of his various pursuits and was looking forward to his future positively. Miss X agreed that many of the people in the theatre were crying during the screening of *Schindler's List*.

In regard to the meeting when she first saw David after his family's deaths on the Tuesday night she told Michael Guest that David was in a very bad way and was really cut up. On the Wednesday when he collapsed to his knees clutching his stomach and yelling, she had a more straightforward account: 'Well, I would describe it as a wailing. It was a very traumatic cry, it upset me a lot when I heard him like that.'

She told of seeing David again on Thursday and said: 'I spent the day at the police station.' She said that when she told David that, he said he was very sorry she had to go through that.

Guest then asked her: 'At any stage in the three times you talked to him on the Tuesday, Wednesday or Thursday, did any of his behaviour to you seem to be inappropriate, having regard to what had occurred?' She had nothing at all bad to say.

As regards David's trance at the Symphonia when she had to prod him to wake him up, she told Guest that was the only time she had witnessed such an incident.

MISS X'S FRIEND

The next witness was the friend of Miss X and she will be referred to as Jane. Jane confirmed meeting David over the months from February to the end of May with Miss X at the various productions he was involved in. But evidence quickly turned to the week before the tragedy when she said David asked if he could 'have a bit of a chat with me'.

So on 15 June he came to her place at about 11 a.m. and brought muffins for breakfast. 'He turned up in the first place because I was the one person that knew both him and Miss X,' she said. He wanted to talk about his friendship with Miss X. Jane said they talked in general and she described for some time the subjects which included friendship, trust, hurt, families and so on. She got onto what he was wearing: 'He invariably wore shorts even when it was really cold.'

She also said he had an anorak, pointing out the red one found in Robin's caravan.

She then told the court something that Miss X, either inadvertently or otherwise, omitted from her evidence — that Miss X had finally told him at the Symphonia that she actually had a boyfriend and he had not known of that at that point so he was a little confused and basically he went around to see Jane and sort things out in his head in terms of his relationship with Miss X.

What the jury did not know, and it was not brought out in cross-examination, was that in her deposition, this witness had said of that meeting: 'He started talking about a friend, Miss X, and her ex-boyfriend and how he felt silly not knowing about it. From this we got on to the concept of friendship.'

Once again the jury were getting a false picture. He was portrayed as a mixed-up person chasing a girl whom he had just found out after three months actually had a boyfriend. The picture they were getting was that this was a 'stressor' just a week before the tragedy, when in fact it was only that he felt a bit silly not knowing about the fact that she had an ex-boyfriend who had not long left the scene.

So the following evidence about a deep and meaningful discussion on friendship, trust and so on needs to be taken with a degree of caution as the entire foundation appears to be something of a beat-up.

Jane went on to discuss David's déjà vu and premonition experiences, putting them in terms that made it sound as though they were signs of a major mental illness.

She said that he was at her place for about three hours talking about lots of other things as well. 'Just before he left he said to me that he had this feeling that something really horrible was going to happen and he thought that it was something to do with Miss X ... I said how do you mean, and he said, "I don't know till it happens".'

She then quoted David as telling her, 'I always end up hurting the people I love and the things I love.' She told of an account he had given her, relating to some kittens, that apparently was supposed to support this pointed statement.

'He had a couple of kittens in PNG and they had been killed and I can't remember why or how but he had found these kittens and they were near death and he looked after them and they survived and then they got run over or something, I can't remember.'

Then Jane told of meeting David with Miss X at the polar plunge and she said that when they first met that day he thanked her for taking the time to talk with him earlier in the week.

Jane was then led on to the matters that happened after the tragedy in her contact with 'the accused'. She told of going to see him on the Wednesday night with Miss X when the three of them went for a walk at St Clair Beach: 'It was dark at this time but the street lights were on and it was a full moon.'

She went on to describe how they drove down to the beach and began walking through the park. 'Up to that point in time I hadn't told anybody of what David had said to me. He told me those things in confidence and I respected that and that was the first time I had seen him after the Sunday and with all the family being around and Miss X being around I hadn't had a chance to say anything — hey how are you going, kind of thing — and by the time we got three-quarters of the way along John Wilson Drive we were walking along, I was on the inside, David in the middle and Miss X on the side nearest the beach, and the wind was blowing from the sea. So I knew that Miss X couldn't hear what I wanted to ask him and it was the only chance that I could see that I would have to do it as discreetly as I could, and I said to him, 'Was [this the] something horrible you saw and told me about last Tuesday?' And he said yes and took another couple of steps and like threw his hands up in the air and turned around then dropped on his knees and I think he sort of cried himself out by then. He was dry sobbing, he couldn't cry physically, he had run out of tears but he was really hurting.'

Then Jane told the jury how he went ahead on his own for about 15 or 20 minutes, which seemed like a very long time, she said.

When walking back to the car she told the jury that they talked about the funeral and then Jane said to David: 'I said, "Was it your dad?" Because at that stage that is what it was portrayed as in the media, and he said, "If it was Dad I am going to be really angry with him. I don't know what I can say to the police to make them believe I didn't do it but I didn't do it." And he was really emphatic about it.'

This is another example of where the deposition statement is at some variance with the testimony in the trial. The deposition statement says: 'He said he was really angry that they were all gone and he said that he couldn't believe it was his dad and if it was he was going to be really angry with him. He said, I don't know what I can say to the police to make them believe me, that I didn't do it. He said "I didn't do it" with his fists clenched.'

She told the jury she asked how he was feeling. 'He said that everything was going round in circles in his head, why and how.'

She told them of going back to see David the following evening, the main reason being he had wanted Miss X to sit with him at the funeral. She said she explained to David that Miss X had never been to a funeral before and it would be difficult for her and it was for the aunts and uncles and the rest of the family to support David at the funeral.

She said that discussions took place between her and David about what to do with the house. She told the jury that David said he wanted to get clothes from there but the police had not released it.

She then recounted that David discussed with her whether she thought he or she should tell Greg Dunne the policeman about his déjà vu and premonition experiences. She said she didn't know what he should do because what he had told her was in confidence.

While talking about her meeting with him on Thursday night, she said: 'I had no idea he was going to be arrested or anything like that, and I said, "Well, I guess I will just make that decision when the time comes." Hindsight is a wonderful thing.'

This witness, Jane, should have faced a detailed cross-examination, bearing in mind how her evidence contained so many anomalies when compared with the deposition statement that she had made about nine months earlier.

In answer to questions from Michael Guest, she described David as a mate who normally seemed happy and he was excited about the plans for the new house that was to be built. She said that he had told her his mother did not want his father back in the house, but it was up to his father to come to the realization. The new house was for the family, but she got the impression Robin was not included, she told Michael Guest.

She agreed that David was very close to the rest of his family, particularly Stephen and Arawa. Guest questioned her about the incident on the beach when David collapsed to his knees and began wailing and clutching his stomach, and got her to make it clear that this happened when she asked him: 'Was it your dad?'

She said the times she saw him after the tragedy he 'was pretty much cried out. That was the impression I got and he hadn't been sleeping and all that.'

Under further questioning she said that after walking on the beach they had all gone back to the Clarks' house for tea. She admitted that during that meal David had a discussion with her about, in her words, 'why was he left' and 'what does it all mean'.

In re-examination by Bill Wright she reiterated that the 'falling to his knees' incident happened when she asked him if this 'was the something horrible you told me about on Tuesday and he said yes'. All in all Jane was a very verbose witness and there were many anomalies in her evidence.

On this Friday of the second week of the trial there were just two more witnesses to go.

SCHOOL TEACHER

The first was the only witness called from Taieri Beach School, apart from the fisherman that we have already heard from who went on a school camp with Robin Bain. This was Darlene Thomson, the other teacher at the school with Robin. She said she lived in Brighton, about halfway between Dunedin and Taieri Beach, and that when Robin was driving to school on Monday mornings he would often call and pick her up about 8 a.m., but sometimes it would be later as his van was very old and would break down. She said Robin was a very hard worker and she told the jury how at one stage he had slept in his van, but that he had moved into the schoolhouse with Laniet and a boy who was a friend of Laniet's called Kyle. Her evidence in chief concluded by saying that Robin Bain wrote with his right hand.

Cross-examination centred on whether the police had questioned her as to why Robin may have been trying to organize a relieving teacher to start work for a few weeks on 20 June, the day that everybody was killed. She admitted that the discussion with the police had come as a real surprise to her because she didn't know of any reason why a reliever would be needed for that time. She did say there were some courses that she and Robin may have attended at the end of June.

Then Guest made another assertion that fell flat. He said that the defence would say that on the Monday or Tuesday before these deaths Robin Bain was seeking a reliever for the school for the next three or four weeks. He never did call any evidence to that effect.

FAMILY

The Crown case was now moving to its end. The next witnesses were Jan and Bob Clark, David's aunt and uncle at whose house he had stayed for those few days in St Clair. They were then followed by his uncle John Boyd, one of the executors of the will, and John Boyd's wife Val Boyd. Jan Clark and Val Boyd were David's mother's sisters. Robin had two brothers and a sister, but none of them was called to give evidence in this trial.

The real thrust of both Jan and Bob Clark's evidence was that David's behaviour in the four days after the tragedy, in their view, did not seem appropriate in a number of ways.

Mrs Clark began by recounting a little bit of family history. Robin and Margaret went to Papua New Guinea essentially as missionaries, she told the jury. David was born in New Zealand, but the other three children were all born in PNG. The family returned to New Zealand in late 1988. She said that her two daughters Kim and Heidi were about the same age as Arawa and Laniet.

She went on to say that she went to the police station on Monday, 20 June and wanted to go to David straightaway but was held up because she spent a few hours talking to the police informing them about the bigger family picture in terms of relatives and names and addresses and so on. She said that she was very distraught and that when she finally met David, she put her arms around him and he broke down and cried. She promised to love him and look after him, she told the jury.

David was initially upset, but he calmed down very quickly. She said she was with David when the police fingerprinted and photographed him that afternoon and at night when they went home 'the accused did not display any emotion at all'. The next morning she went out to his room and there was a discussion about his dog Casey and that the previous dog, called Sasha, had died. 'He said that why does everything that I love and put time and energy into caring and nurturing die?'

She asked David what happened the previous week that could have caused such a tragedy and he said that the weekend was a bit tense but no more than usual when his dad was home on weekends.

They discussed the funerals and David told her that they would have to have a Quaker involvement. He wanted music to play a big part in the service and he told her the music he wanted for each member of the family. On the Tuesday night friends of her daughters came over and David was with them and they were talking and laughing, she told the jury.

That night David wanted to look at the newspapers. The police had told them to keep the news from him because of the stress that it could create, but he insisted on reading the paper. He became very distressed and had tears in his eyes, she said. Bob took him into the bedroom and when they didn't come back for a while she went up to check on them. David was sitting on the bed with his elbows on his knees and tears running down his face. He said, 'They lied to me. They knew what was going to happen and they knew they were going to die.' And then he said, 'He looked them in the eye and shot them.' She went on, 'He said, "If he did this I can never forgive him."'

She described what happened next. According to her, he closed his eyes, clenched his fists and started talking in a very stilted way. He had been quite relaxed but he became very tense, his eyes were screwed up and he started to speak slowly and deliberately. She said his manner of speech was slurred and spitty.

'He said black hands, they are taking them away and he couldn't stop them and he kept repeating this over and over [witness makes a screaming out sound] — it was like it was being pulled out of him, it was very deliberate, and I don't know how to explain it.' Then she said that after a time he said, 'If only I had run faster' and she said to him, 'No, it wouldn't have made any difference; it's not your fault. Then he kept saying, black hands, dying, everyone dying and can't stop them and taking them away and it was all jumbled and mixed.'

She then told the jury that she asked David a direct question. 'I said to him, "Did you see them dying, David?" He just stopped and opened his eyes and looked straight at me and said, "No, I only saw Mum and Dad and they were already dead."'

She then asked David if he wanted to speak to someone and so she called Greg Dunne and he came over to the house.

She said how Miss X came over and spent time alone with the accused and during this time she said that there was a lot of laughter and chatter. She then described discussions that took place regarding the funeral arrangements and then moved on to telling of Miss X and witness Jane coming over the following evening, and that she overheard a conversation between David and her daughters in which David said he felt happy in their home and comfortable and close to them.

She got back to the topic of the funerals and in particular the music that David wanted for each individual at the funeral. There was a requiem for Margaret and Bach's 'Air on the G String', the Queen song, 'Who Wants to Live Forever' for Laniet.

She told the jury that David wanted these songs because there had been a family discussion one day and those were the songs that his mother and Laniet had said they would want played at their funerals.

She listened to a tape of the Queen song 'Who Wants to Live Forever' and conceded that children would like it, but that she and the other elderly people found it really disturbing and after hearing it they were not any happier.

The week was over at this point. The jury would have been sent home with the customary, if somewhat pointless, admonition from the judge that they must not talk to anyone or read or watch anything about the case. They would no doubt have known that the Crown case was nearly finished and it is very likely their minds would have been nearly made up. They could have only one remaining question really, which was what evidence was Guest going to call to show that it was not David but Robin who was responsible for the deaths of the family?

At 10 a.m. on the following Monday, Jan Clark was re-sworn into the witness box and immediately took up the subject of the funeral arrangements again. She told the jury that David talked about what colour flowers he wanted for each person in the family.

There was further miscellaneous evidence before evidence in chief ended with a recounting of the incident that took place after David had read the newspaper seeing that Stephen and Arawa had been out of bed and awake when they were killed. She repeated what David had said: 'He had to look them in the eye and shoot them and he said he could never forgive him if he had done this.' The final words following on directly from this quote were, 'He never said who the "him" was.'

The only question that Guest asked Jan Clark was about the reference to the word 'him' which Guest put to Jan Clark was clearly a reference to his father. She answered, 'I don't know who he was referring to but I assumed that's who it was.'

Her husband Bob Clark was next on the stand and by and large his evidence mirrored that of his wife. He said that his limited contact with the family had left him with the impression that Robin and Margaret were not happy in their relationship.

He told the jury that he had been taken to identify the bodies at the crematorium. He described his meeting with David after David had seen the photos and depictions of Stephen and Arawa out of bed and he said that David had asked what injuries they had suffered. Bob told the jury that he explained to David what he had observed when he had been taken to identify the bodies. In the recording of the evidence he said, 'I couldn't answer how he reacted to that', which does not tell us much.

The deposition statement, however, says that after he told David about the injuries, 'he was visibly upset and withdrawn a bit. He spoke very quietly and almost went into a trancelike state. I couldn't pick up half of what he was saying. It became very disjointed.'

Bob said that he was asked on the Friday morning to take David to the police station and David seemed quite relaxed and made some comment like, 'I will be glad when this is all sorted out.'

Finally, he described how Greg Dunne had told David of the three possibilities being that either it was Robin, David or someone outside the family. 'David's statement back to Greg Dunne was "I will not forgive him for what he has done", referring to his father' — and these were the final words of Bob Clark's evidence in chief.

Guest had only two questions for Bob Clark. He asked whether his wife had been very upset in that week following the murders, and Bob agreed that she was extremely distraught. He then asked if he had seen David crying and he agreed he had on two occasions.

It was unclear who had phoned Dunne on the Tuesday night when David was upset and so the judge asked Bob Clark about it. He confirmed that he made the call while his wife Jan was with David.

Next up were the other two family members to give evidence: Margaret Bain's sister Val Boyd and her husband John. Val was first on the stand and she described how she lived in Wellington with her husband but they had shifted there from Dunedin in 1992, so were living in Dunedin when Robin and Margaret arrived back from Papua New Guinea in late 1988.

She said that Margaret wasn't much of a housekeeper but also explained that the reason the house was such a shambles was because it had been rented out for all those years from 1972 until late 1988 and that it deteriorated quite badly during that period. She said they hadn't spent money on it because they intended to demolish it and rebuild on the section.

She said as far as she could tell, David was very close to both of his parents. 'He was the apple of his mother's eye,' she said.

Her evidence then turned to her arrival at the Clarks' house on Tuesday, 21 June 1994. She said she never saw David crying. She described the discussions about the funeral arrangements in much the same way as her sister Jan had done. She related the conversation she had one night with David when he told her he hated his father; she said David said his father had become sneaky and listened to conversations he was not party to in recent times.

David told her, she went on, that Margaret had moved into the caravan six months after they returned from Papua New Guinea, but then she moved back inside and Robin moved out. That's how bad things had got, she said.

There was a little bit of evidence about Stephen being a happy, cheerful lad which was related to the fact that Val herself had a son called Stephen and she said that David had said to her that he thought his little brother would grow up to be just like her son.

Guest went in to more detail with Val Boyd than he had done with Jan and Bob Clark, which on the face of it seems a little odd, bearing in mind the extensive evidence from the Clarks about the week they had David living with them. He got Val Boyd to admit that the conversation between her and David when they were talking about Robin included the following passage: 'You say you recall him saying he hated his father?' 'Yes,' answered Mrs Boyd.

Guest continued: 'And did he say in the same part of the conversation, my father has done this I can never forgive him and that is a terrible burden to carry around for the rest of my life?' Val Boyd answered, 'He did.'

In regard to David's desire to organize the clothes and music for the funeral, she admitted that there had been a victim support officer working through all of this with David and she had been sorting these matters out with him: this certainly put a different perspective on things.

She conceded that the music David wanted was not what *he* wanted but what his family had said they would want played at their funerals, which again put her evidence in chief into a different perspective.

John Boyd did not mention whether he knew the family at all. He obviously would have met them, but it did not extend much past that, it would appear.

In one conversation he related that he had with David he said that David said to him, 'I haven't said this to anyone else but I wish I was dead.'

Apparently, this was said early on Wednesday morning when David had got up about five o'clock and John Boyd, hearing him get up, had gone to join him. Boyd said that everyone in the house at that time only thought of David as a survivor.

In relation to the three options put to David, which no doubt the police had discussed with the family as well, Boyd asked David if he had been under any particular strain the past week or so. Boyd said that David replied that he had been under no particular strain at all but he did have an exam coming up.

He told the jury that he visited David in prison on the Tuesday after his arrest with Robin's brothers Michael and Peter Bain. He told them Michael Bain asked David some questions. 'One of those questions was whether he, the accused, had done it, referring to the deaths,' John Boyd went on. 'The accused's reaction to this, he was very confident and very firm. He said no — words to the effect, "I have given my statement to the police and I am keeping to that." I don't recall if he said anything else.'

However, John Boyd's deposition statement records the matter slightly differently. According to that, David's reaction was as follows: 'Without getting upset or changing his composure, David replied, "No, it was just as I gave in my statement and I will be sticking to that." His composure is so unflappable that when talking to him he appears to have the confidence of an innocent person. He also said he did not understand why he was there. Michael asked if he knew what he had been charged with and he said yes.'

Guest quite aggressively put to Boyd that he and Michael Bain had gone to the prison 'with a preordained set of questions hoping to get some form of admission out of him you would take straight to the police'. Unsurprisingly, Boyd denied that this was the case, saying they were there solely as executors of the estate.

Boyd said they wanted to discuss with David the idea of having the house burnt down because 'he was potentially a beneficiary'. He went on to tell the jury that the executors had already decided that this was the best course of action.

As a final point Guest put to him again that David had told John Boyd that he did not carry out those murders. Boyd's answer to that proposition was, 'Yes, that was at the prison. We did not discuss it before then.'

PAPER RUN RECONSTRUCTION

The next two witnesses were both police officers who were involved in the timing re-evaluation that was carried out by the prosecutor and the police in late March and early April 1995, just six weeks before the trial. Detective Trevor Thompson was instructed by Detective Sergeant Weir to carry out some simulations of David's paper run, and to do this Thompson enlisted the services of Constable Laurie Peeters who would make the run while Thompson carried the stopwatch to time the various sections.

Peeter's evidence was read to the jury by consent and simply said that on 9, 10 and 11 April 1995, he re-enacted the paper round. He said Thompson instructed him to travel at a fast jog. On the third time he did this he carried a paper delivery bag with him.

Thompson then came on the stand and told the jury that he carried out this exercise on the instructions of DS Weir. This had nothing to do with the fact that Weir had been the officer in charge of the scene investigation the previous year, but was because he was now, along with Jim Doyle, in charge of preparing the case for trial. One might say that the re-enactments undertaken were in the nature of last-minute preparations.

It is irresistible to refrain from the observation that the evidence of this witness, including the cross-examination, represents nothing less than a complete farce. Thompson told the jury that the first run by Peeters was a test run, and that the second two runs were timed by him and that the whole exercise was assisted by the statements of the witnesses who had sighted the accused on 20 June. Thompson told the jury that the first run took Peeters

47 minutes and the second one took 50 minutes. Thompson used the map of a paper round with the identification points that various witnesses had seen David, this map being exhibit number 628.

Thompson said that it took Peeters three minutes at a *fast jog* to get from the intersection of Heath Street where David had been seen by Tania Clark to the gate at 65 Every Street on both of the timed runs.

Thompson then said: 'I myself also walked that route between Heath Street to 65 Every Street. On 28 March 1995 this was. To cover that distance at a *moderate walk* it took me two minutes and 15 seconds on the first test and the second took me two minutes and 16 seconds.'

It hardly needs pointing out that something is seriously wrong with Peeters' *fast jog* if it took him nearly a minute longer to cover the same distance of about 280 m than Thompson took at a *moderate walk*. Peeters was young and athletic into the bargain.

One would think that this was a real opportunity for Guest to show that perhaps the police were stretching credibility in these last-minute preparations to build their case against his client. He cross-examined Thompson but failed to give any attention whatsoever to this question and to how Thompson was able to walk the distance much quicker than Peeters was able to run it.

The rest of the cross-examination simply highlighted the fact that the bag Peeters carried was empty, he did not have to pick up the papers from each bundle and fold them and then put them in the letterboxes, he did not have a dog with him, nor was all this done in the dark. One would have to wonder at what the police thought they were proving with this evidence and whether the jury took any notice of it at all. It appears to have been a rather desperate attempt to show that David was early on his paper round.

INTERVIEWING OFFICERS

And so as the first day of the third week of David Bain's trial for the slaughter of his family was coming to an end, we in our journey through this prosecution return to the very beginning of the whole process with the evidence of the three detectives who conducted the interviews and arrest of David Bain almost exactly 11 months earlier: Greg Dunne, Neil Lowden and Kallum Croudis.

Greg Dunne was the first of the three to take the stand and he told the court that he held the rank of Detective Sergeant and had been appointed officer in charge of witnesses in Operation Every.

He arrived at 65 Every Street about 9.30 a.m. on Monday, 20 June 1994 and accompanied David as he was carried from the house to the ambulance and then in the ambulance to the CIB and was with him for most of the rest of the day.

Writing in his notebook, he recorded conversations with the accused, the first of which was during the ride in the back of the ambulance when David complained of a dry throat and asked about Casey the dog. Dunne told David that it was important to find out what had happened and David replied that he had lost his voice.

Dunne then read to the jury from the notes he had made at the time. It is not entirely clear whether this is a combination of a conversation which took place in the ambulance and then at the offices of the CIB or whether it is just at the CIB. The evidence he read to the court began with him asking David his name, address and date of birth, and then he asked: 'Can you tell me what happened last night?'

David: Starting at what time?

Q: Right at the beginning.

David: I have a rehearsal on Sunday for classics drama and waited for Arawa who finished at 5.45. We picked up some stuff from Laniet's flat, went to Countdown for some shopping and then went home. At that point we had, I went out to get chips with Laniet. Everybody watching TV. At 7.30 p.m. we watched a video movie, at 8.30 we switched it off so that my parents could watch a film. I went to bed at about 10 to 9. I do a paper run in the mornings. I set my alarm for 5.30 ... I read, finished off a book until 9.10. When I woke up at 5.30 I dozed until 20 to, that's my normal routine on weekdays. The paper run, left the house at 5.45, did my normal routine with Casey. Arrived back at about 20 to 7, took off my running shoes, Walkman, went downstairs, put on a wash. Washed printer's ink off my hands, is this the sort of stuff you want?

Q: Yes.

David: I feel like, [at that point I was unable to understand his next two words. He continued.] I think Mum's light was on, lounge door closed.

Bottom, no, I can't remember … I went back to my room and switched on my light. At that point I noticed the shells on the floor. I picked up the box and the plastic thing fell out. I went to Mum's room and she was dead. She didn't move. I went to the lounge and he was there. Then I called the police. I remember loud noises and lots of banging but I don't remember anything until the ambulance officer came in.

Q: Who else was home last night, this morning?

David: Everybody was there, my sister Laniet, him, usually flats down at the schoolhouse at Taieri Mouth. Laniet had work at the café. My father is it, can you tell me what has happened?

Dunne told the jury: 'I then advised him that he was correct and that his mum and dad were dead and advised that I would get him further information as it came to hand. David continued.

David: My closest relations are Jan and Bob Clark. He runs a job placement; I think she is teaching out at Mosgiel. My father's family is all up north. My father's mother lives at 38 Toy Street, Otaki.

Q: Do you know her name?

David: It's E M Bain. His sister is Colleen Trenworth. His brother is Paul, no, Colleen Trenworth is in Hamilton. She is my father's sister. Her address is in the flip thing at home. On my mother's side, Val and Andrea Cullen, Christchurch, mother's sister. My grandmother lives in Chapel Street, Alexandra.

Dunne then told the jury that at 11 a.m. Dr Pryde arrived. It will be remembered that Pryde had been through the house with DS Weir at about 10.30 a.m. to proclaim life extinct on the five bodies that were in the house.

'I was present when Dr Pryde made an explanation as to the examination he wished to perform and he asked the accused permission to do this,' Dunne said.

Dunne then arranged for Detective Ross to take David's clothes, and for photos and fingerprints to be obtained from David.

He then began taking a formal statement from the accused, he said, and he proceeded to read that statement to the jury and then it was produced as exhibit number 564.

He described David's demeanour during the interview as very deliberate, his eyes averted down as if he was recounting in his mind a scene. He spoke freely and was calm throughout.

He became upset and had tears in his eyes when Dunne told him that his mother and father were dead. Dunne then stated, 'He did not ask about his brother and two sisters.'

Dunne's evidence then turned to the following day when he took a second formal statement from the accused; he also read that statement to the jury. On this occasion he described David speaking freely and running through what he was saying without appearing to be visibly upset. He said that David would close his eyes when repeating information he had already told Dunne.

The court at that point adjourned for the evening and on Tuesday, 23 May, Detective Sergeant Dunne was re-sworn to the witness box. He began the day by telling the jury that he received a phone call on the night of Tuesday after the killings and that as a result of that call he went back to the Clarks' house where David was staying.

He told the jury, 'After speaking with family members I spoke with the accused, David, in a bedroom. He was physically upset and had been crying. He told me that he couldn't help it. That black hands were coming to get them. That he had not been able to stop them. He stated, 'If I had run home I may have saved them', that hands were pulling them away. He wanted to blame someone but didn't know who to blame.'

He then discussed the three possible scenarios with David — that it was David, his father, or a third party who had committed the murders — and also discussed stages of grieving and the release of information relating to the deaths.

Guest's cross-examination of Dunne was very brief. Dunne confirmed that he and David had developed a good and easy-going relationship but refused to comment when Guest put it to him that David had been cooperative.

He agreed that he had never warned David that his notes and the conversations between the two of them could be used in evidence.

Detective Lowden followed and he told the jury that he held the rank of Detective Sergeant and that at 10.30 a.m. DS Croudis cautioned David.

He explained that Croudis asked David a few questions relating to the positive bloody fingerprints on the gun, the palm print on the washing machine and whether bloodstained clothes had been washed. He said that Croudis then commenced a formal interview asking David if he wanted this to be recorded by video or by handwritten notes. David said that he was familiar with the handwritten form and so they proceeded with that.

Lowden went on to say that at 11.20 a.m. the accused asked for a lawyer. Michael Guest came in and as we know refused to allow David to answer any more questions or undergo a medical examination. Lowden then produced the statement in full, the contents of which were given in Chapter 2 and this became Exhibit 586. He told the jury that at 1.46 p.m. the accused was formally charged by DS Croudis and he said that when asked if he had anything to say David replied, 'No, I'm not guilty.' There were no questions from Michael Guest.

The penultimate Crown witness was DS Croudis himself, whose evidence mirrored that of Lowden. There was one little bit extra from Croudis that was not recorded in the statement or notebook entries when he stated that Guest had said: 'If I [Croudis] ask any more questions he would leave with the accused.'

In a very short cross-examination Croudis agreed that he did not have the benefit of any expert analysis of the various bloodstains, and in particular Guest put to him the fact that Peter Cropp had said that the bloodstain on the back of David's T-shirt was old. Guest also put to Croudis that he had questioned David about whether David owned the white gloves before he had told David that a pair of white bloodstained gloves had been found in Stephen Bain's bedroom. Finally, Croudis confirmed to the jury that until Guest arrived at the police station that morning David was fully cooperative.

Then followed some legal argument pertaining to the admissibility of evidence from potential defence witnesses, which was conducted in the absence of the jury. This related to psychiatric evidence that Michael Guest wished to call and also to the evidence of a person called Cottle. The legal jousting occupied the rest of the day and will be discussed in detail later as it fits into the defence case.

OFFICER IN CHARGE

And so the following day, Wednesday, 24 May, the Crown called their final witness. Jim Doyle, the officer mostly responsible for the Operation Every investigation, took the stand. His evidence in chief stated simply that he was a Detective Senior Sergeant at the CIB in Dunedin.

It may be thought that the defence would have a multitude of questions on a myriad of different subjects to put to the officer in charge of the case. But Guest had only two subjects that he traversed with Jim Doyle. The first related to Robin Bain's diaries. Guest produced one diary and Doyle confirmed that it was in fact a diary belonging to Robin Bain that the police had found. Doyle accepted the proposition that Robin as a school teacher would have had more diaries dealing with the day-to-day operation of the school but Doyle said 'they could not locate any others'. He confirmed that there were no entries in the diary that was produced after 20 June 1994 but that before then it contained lots of entries relating to Mr Bain's work as the school principal. The only entry subsequent to 20 June 1994 was on 22 August but nothing was said as to its content.

Doyle then confirmed to Guest that four transactions had taken place on Robin and Margaret Bain's joint bank account at the South Dunedin branch of the National Bank between 11.26 p.m. and 11.30 p.m. on Sunday, 19 June 1994, about seven hours before the deaths of the family.

Two transactions were balance inquiries; $385 was transferred to pay a credit card balance; and $200 cash was withdrawn. Doyle confirmed that $200 in cash was found in a bundle on Margaret Bain's bedside table in the form of nine $20 notes and two $10 notes.

Bill Wright re-examined Doyle very briefly to the effect that the diary shown to him by Guest had come into police possession sometime earlier in 1995; and that following the various transactions conducted at the bank on that Sunday night the balance of the bank account was $10 and some cents. Jim Doyle, the officer mostly responsible for the prosecution of David Bain for five counts of murder, had been on the stand for probably no more than 10 or 15 minutes by the time Bill Wright had finished with him.

The next line in Justice Williamson's notes of evidence reads in block capitals: CASE FOR THE CROWN.

CHAPTER 7
THE DEFENCE CASE

BACKGROUND

The jury in this first trial heard a vast amount of evidence from other people about what David had said or done in the period before and after the tragedy. Except for the few questions put to him by Lowden and Croudis on the day of his arrest, this evidence came about as a result of David believing that he was being treated as a victim and witness to the tragic event and trying to assist the police in every possible way; or alternatively from when he confided in his friends Miss X and Jane and his extended family comprising his uncles and aunts.

A full account of Dunne's record of the conversation and what took place on the morning of 20 June before, during and after Dr Pryde examined David Bain has been presented in this narrative. There is also a complete record of the evidence and questions put to David by Croudis and Lowden on the day of his arrest, including even those questions that Guest refused to allow David to answer that did not form part of the evidence in the trial. These final few questions were suppressed at the trial.

There is also the interview between David and Dunne at the Clarks' house on the Tuesday night. Of course, also included has been the evidence of the Clarks, Boyds, Miss X and Jane, the ambulance officers who spent time with David in the house before he was taken away to the CIB, Constable Andrew and Constable Van Turnhout who spent some time with David and made notes of the utterances and behaviour they observed.

This leaves only the two formal statements taken by Detective Dunne from David — the first on the Monday afternoon at the CIB, a very long statement which took nearly four hours; and the second the following day involving another two or three hours.

These statements have not been included in their entirety predominantly because the cross-examination of David by Bill Wright covers all of the contentious issues raised in these statements. In addition, much of the interviews cover details of a background nature which do not have any relevance to the case, and so the reproduction of these very long statements in their entirety would not add to the content of this book in any meaningful way.

The reader can thus be assured that these have not been deliberately avoided.

As a general rule under our adversarial process, people accused of serious crimes are advised against giving evidence even when they are innocent. It will be recalled that in the earlier case referred to of the police officers in Gisborne, John Haigh QC refused to allow his two innocent client detectives to take the stand at the depositions hearing because, as he said, even experienced police officers can get tied up in knots by a skilful cross-examination.

However, David wanted to give evidence and naively thought that he would simply be believed when he told his account of what had happened that day and said that he did not have anything to do with the deaths of his family. Guest, due at least in some instances such as the computer timing issue to an apparent lack of quality preparation, had very little else to offer in David's defence apart from his own demeanour, character and denial.

The case for the Crown ends on page 404 of the notes of evidence. Page 405 commences with the words: 'Defence witnesses. Mr Guest opens and calls David Cullen Bain.' Almost exactly 11 months after the tragic events of 20 June 1994 David takes the stand in his own defence.

And so at about 10.30 a.m. on 24 May, David began his evidence in chief by explaining that Cullen was his second name originally, but that about four years earlier because of the marriage difficulties between Margaret and Robin, his mother suggested that the children all introduced the name Cullen, her maiden name, to their names. The girls and Stephen altered their surname to Cullen-Bain. David simply put a hyphen between his second name and surname.

He explained to the jury that he had spent his childhood in Papua New Guinea until completing his sixth and seventh form years at Bayfield High School in Dunedin. He said that his parents' relationship began to deteriorate almost as soon as they got back to New Zealand, with first Margaret moving out to the caravan and then after about six months she came back to the house and banished Robin from the marital bed to the caravan.

He told of having a good relationship with his mother, and how she had been involved with him in all the shows that he had done in Papua New Guinea and New Zealand. He said that she was a very good pianist and helped with the singing and music studies.

He told how he and his father would go fishing and tramping together and that his father was very experienced with the use of firearms and a good shot and that he had taught David about the use of firearms. He said he had been shooting with his father at least a dozen times and they invariably came home with rabbits. He told the jury of how he came to buy the rifle and how his father helped to sight it in on a farm at Taieri. He talked about the piece of cardboard target that the police had found in his bedroom which they suggested had some sinister connotation because of the five circles on it. David said that his father actually drew up that target and put the rabbit ears on it when they went to the Taieri Beach farm to sight the rifle.

He said that last summer he had gone tramping with his father and Stephen in Silver Peaks Range behind Waitaki and of course he told how he was in the Dunedin male choir with his father.

He turned to evidence that had been given about saying to people that he hated his father. He said that he could not remember the events of the week of the tragedy before his arrest very clearly, but that if he had said that he hated his father he was just expressing the anger he was feeling — 'if he had done it. At that stage I didn't know what had happened, what the full story was and I was pretty confused.'

He said his father was very stoical and never discussed his relationship with his mother with David or the other children. He told the jury an argument he had with his father about the chainsaw on the Sunday night was just a war of words, not a heated argument at all. David said that his dad was a very proud person who kept his feelings to himself, 'so I very rarely knew what his true feelings were'. The notes of evidence then record him stating clearly, 'I did not kill either my mother or my father.'

He then went on to talk about his relationship with his brother and sisters and discussed lots of the things that they did together.

He told the jury of his study, singing lessons and sporting activities. 'I was involved in just about every sport that was around. I was a runner with the running club, ... triathlons, swimming clubs, orienteering. Actually, my father, Stephen and I were all involved in orienteering.'

He told of attending Outward Bound in July/August 1993 and said, 'I got quite a good certificate from the instructor.'

He talked about his friends: 'I had many friends prior to June last year.' He told the jury how lots of his friends would come to his house, and he talked about his relationship with Miss X, taking her to the ball and buying the white ball gloves as part of the outfit. 'I had a top hat, cane, and bought the gloves especially.' As has already been foreshadowed, the issue of spectacles had taken some prominence in the Crown case and David talked about his eyesight and how he had tripped over the previous Thursday before the tragedy when leaving the house of Mrs Dawson his singing teacher, and he described how the glasses fell off and were damaged. He told them that he did nearly all of the sports, including orienteering, without glasses.

He said that he had worn the glasses found broken by the police on occasions in the past, but that he could not wear them for extended periods of time.

'I know of the evidence of the optometrist [Dr Sanderson],' he said. 'There is a dispute with my evidence as to whether those glasses were mine or someone else's. I have no doubt they were my mother's glasses ... As to how those glasses got in my room I have no explanation. I had not used them or seen them that weekend or at least a year previous. I hadn't needed them. So unless my mother put them in my room because she had obviously — no I don't know.'

He talked about the night of 19 June — how he had driven with Laniet to get fish and chips for the family dinner, and that he did not wear any glasses while driving down to the fish and chip shop because it was only about a mile away from their house and he knew the route very well.

The next item of evidence that the police had against David that he talked about was the green jersey that they found in the washing machine and fibres from which had been detected under Stephen's fingernails.

He told the jury that the jersey was his father's but that Arawa wore it on occasions. He said that he had never worn that jersey that weekend or any other time because it was too small for him. The notes of evidence record that he stood up in the dock putting his arms out so that the jersey, which was on a mannequin nearby, could be compared as to whether or not it would be a reasonable fit for him. He said that his father had worn it the Saturday afternoon before the killings and went on to say that he thought his father had been wearing the same clothes over the weekend that he was found in when the police arrived on the Monday morning.

He told the jury that there was tension in the house on the Friday night and described it as just the same old tension that was always in the air when his mother and father were in the same room. In respect of the weekend prior to the killings he told the jury that it had been a very busy weekend for him with the polar plunge on Sunday morning and then rehearsals all afternoon.

He said on the Sunday evening before the killings he went to bed just before nine o'clock and finished reading a book for a while. 'It took me just a few minutes to get to sleep. I was quite tired after the long day.'

He said he had distinct memories of his mother's car going off at about 11 o'clock, and that it was quite unusual that someone would go out at that time of night. He also told the jury that he was woken sometime before the car went out by raised voices coming from the TV lounge at the far end of the house. He told the jury he could not hear what was being said.

His evidence then turned to the events of the Monday morning and he began by describing the paper round, telling the jury of the three bunches of newspapers with about 50 in each bundle that he had to pick up and pack into the *ODT* yellow delivery bag and how it was quite fiddly to rip the plastic straps off the bundles. The papers themselves were not folded up so each one had to be taken out of his bag and folded so that it could be placed in the letterbox at each address.

He was shown the red sweatshirt that was among the clothes that had been washed that morning. 'That is the red sweatshirt I was wearing on the paper run,' he said. Then he was shown the red anorak that was found in Robin's van on Friday, 24 June with the necklace in the pocket. David told the jury that it belonged to him; he had worn it to the polar plunge and left it in the van when he went into the water on the Sunday before the killings.

As far as the trigger lock was concerned, he told the jury that there were two keys to open it. David attached one of the keys to the string necklace along with some other keys and this, he said, was the key he normally used when he wanted to use the rifle. The other key was kept in a piece of pottery on a dressing table in his bedroom. It was the key from the pottery jar that was used to open the gun on that tragic morning. 'No one else in the family knew there were two keys,' he told the jury.

He was then taken through what he did when he returned from his paper round on that fateful Monday morning and it is repeated here in bullet point form.

The jury heard from David that:

- He walked in the front door and noticed a light shining out from his mother's bedroom because his mother's bedroom only had curtains across the door. He went directly into his bedroom — the first room on the left inside the front door — where he took off the yellow bag and hung it on a hook behind the door; took off his shoes and the Walkman that he had been wearing.
- He went to the bathroom and washed his hands to remove the printer's ink before sorting out the coloureds and jerseys from the whites and putting them into the washing machine, leaving the whites in the washing basket on the floor. He told the jury that he did the washing virtually every day when he got back from his paper round as a matter of routine.
- He took off the red sweatshirt that he had been wearing on the paper round and put that in the washing machine because he had worn it for the past week and it was quite sweaty.
- He did not notice whether there were already some clothes in the bowl of the washing machine before he started.
- He did not notice any blood in the laundry or on his hands.
- He took the blue container containing washing powder from the shelf and put washing powder in the machine before flicking the on/off switch around to the top, setting the machine in motion.
- The bathroom floor was very wet because apparently there had been a spill there the previous day when somebody had done the washing but forgotten to take a pile of towels from the tub. He could feel the wet floor because he was only wearing socks at this stage.
- He then went back upstairs to his bedroom and reached behind the door and turned the light on with the pull cord and it was then that he noticed the bullets and trigger lock on the floor behind the door in front of the wardrobe.
- He ran to his mother's room, calling her and asking what had happened. 'She did not respond. I went further, and saw the blood on her face and her eyes open and she didn't say anything at all.'

- Next, he said, 'I think I went into Stephen's room.' He told the jury that Stephen was covered in blood, his face was red and while in his room he could not remember seeing anything else, just Stephen. 'I touched him. I got down beside him and touched his shoulder to see if I could wake him but he didn't move at all.'
- He could not remember walking anywhere in the house but 'the next I remember is being in Laniet's room and I could hear her gurgling. I could see blood all over her face and on the pillow. I can't recall if I touched her. I went right up beside the bed.'
- His memory was very hazy and it was like a sort of a flashback of just seeing the bodies.
- He then said, 'I must have left the room at that stage, I don't recall it. I was — the next thing I remember is I was down in Arawa's room. I saw her face. She was on the floor. I can't recall how close I got to her. I didn't touch her, not that I can remember anywhere.' He said that Arawa appeared to be dead; she was white and pasty.
- He could not remember leaving Arawa's room or going anywhere else.
- He found his father in the lounge and stated, 'I went up beside him but he would — he wasn't awake either.'
- He could not recall seeing a rifle.

'I did not kill any of these people. I did not kill anybody,' was the final statement that he gave the jury in his evidence in chief about the events of that morning.

He then described how when he was interviewed by the police he made it clear that he did not go into any rooms except his mother's and father's. 'I said that to the detectives because I did not remember. At the time they asked me, all I could remember was being in Mum's room and going into the lounge. And that was all I could remember.'

He explained that it was during his sessions with Professor Mullen, the forensic psychiatrist from Australia who came to see him in December of 1994, that he was able to get back some partial extra memory, in the form of flashbacks of seeing the various bodies.

He told the jury that the 111 call seemed to go on forever: 'It seemed to take a long, long time.'

He talked of his father's dress habits, which were normally tracksuit pants and tops on the weekends and business clothes on days when he was going down to the school. David described the business clothes as a business shirt, trousers and a jersey of some type, and said that on days when his father was going to work, he would dress in his business attire before coming to the house.

Then it was the trances and black hands. He said that the evidence given about these trances made it sound much more serious than it really was. 'It only happened to me before when I find things really boring ... I would only describe it as being away with the fairies.'

He denied that he had used the word 'premonition' in his discussions with Miss X or Jane and that he only talked about déjà vu, which was a totally different thing. He said the 'something horrible is going to happen' comment was taken out of context. When they had been talking about people getting hurt it was in the context of having found out that Miss X had a boyfriend.

'I told the police about the sensation of black hands. As to what I remember about black hands, where they occurred was when I had been into the lounge to see my father but I didn't recall or remember that experience until I think it was the Tuesday night when I talked to Greg Dunne. It was the closest analogy that I could come to, to describe what I saw and the feelings that I was going through in that memory. I was very afraid. And it was like the whole world was closing in, in front of me and the image that I had was of my family set in the centre and these, what I described as black hands coming in from all sides and covering them and taking them away. It was almost as if I was getting tunnel vision and everything was receding away from me. The tunnel vision I refer to is everything on the outside of my peripheral vision was getting black, dark, inside was kind of speckly and I felt as if I was being drawn into that when I remembered — I remember all I could see this, all I could see in the centre was my family and these encroaching sorts of parts of blackness that covered them up.

'Prior to 20 June last I have never had such an image. I had never had a similar sensation prior to 20 June last, not as bad as that. But I had fainted once in a show that I was doing and it was that sort of speckly thing, start seeing stars and then the blackness, darkness, coming through and getting tunnel vision but it wasn't as bad as that. I fainted in the show in 1992 or 1993 when I was doing *Godspell*. That was the closest sensation I had had to the blackness experience, but that I can describe as a faint, the other was a lot worse.

'I recalled this experience first on the Tuesday when I spoke to Detective Dunne. In the presence of police officers or over the phone to the 111 caller I can't remember talking about black hands. The first time I mentioned it was to Greg Dunne that evening on the Tuesday and then again on the Friday. As to whether I can recall that sensation on 20 June, yes. That is when I remembered having, like when I first remember having it was on the Tuesday evening.'

In respect to the message on the computer, David stated: 'I did not type anything into the computer. I have not touched the computer since before the end of May.'

In reference to his statements to the police, which, of course, had been read out to the jury, David said that there was a discrepancy in those statements as to when he washed his hands, whether it was before or after he put the washing on. He told the jury that it was actually beforehand. He then stated: 'I understood I had a right to contact a lawyer if I wanted to through the Monday to Friday before you were phoned ['you' being a reference to Michael Guest who was leading his evidence]. I didn't see any need for it. No one had cautioned me. That was not the understanding. I was a witness, that was all.'

He went on to tell the jury that it was his decision to actually get some legal advice when he did. 'I had tried to explain that they had made a mistake, I was trying to answer some questions to get things cleared up, but it was obvious after a while that they were not considering any other option. That is when I called a lawyer.'

By now it was 1 p.m. — time for the luncheon adjournment and David had been giving evidence for about two and a half hours. After lunch he was led first to comment on a conversation with Greg Dunne when Dunne had put to him those three options about who may have been responsible for the killings. David stated: 'It was to help me cope with what I was going through and to help me understand what the police were doing.' When the subject of a third party possibly having been responsible came up he said, 'I couldn't think of anyone at all who had enough enmity towards us.' He told the jury that the subsequent discussions he had with members of his family were simply to let the family know what the police were thinking and what had taken place in the discussions between him and Greg.

As far as the funeral arrangements about which evidence had been given,

David explained how the victim support officer had asked him to discuss the funerals in detail. She asked him what clothing the people who had died would like to be buried in and suggested that he should choose the clothing each individual liked best. 'That was the stuff I chose,' he told the jury. He said there was nothing bizarre about it; he was simply following the victim support officer's advice and the same thing applied to the music that he had chosen.

He was coming to the end of his evidence in chief and according to all reports he came across as a very sound and eloquent person. He told the jury that he had never thought of himself as needing any psychiatric treatment and that he had never had any at any time in his life; nor had anyone else ever suggested to him that he did need it.

He said he became very depressed after the events of 20 June the previous year but before then he had never been depressed. He said that during the depression that took place after he was put into prison and after the loss of his family he had considered suicide a number of times but that had never happened before 20 June 1994.

He told the jury that he had terrible dreams and flashbacks about 20 June and of seeing his family dead. He had lost interest in music, and sleep patterns were now very different from what they used to be. He told the jury that he always slept very well but sometimes over the past year since the tragedy he was only getting two or three hours sleep a night for months at a time. Finally, he told the jury that he could remember very clearly all of the events on the morning of 20 June 1994 up to the time when he saw his mother dead, but after that, he told them: 'I can only catch snatches of memories and images of different things, places that I was in.'

When an accused person decides to take the stand the major factor at stake is credibility. Obviously, nobody would take the stand in their own defence if they were not going to deny the offence in question. It then becomes a question of whether the jury believes the denial or whether they believe that the evidence against him or her proves that he or she is in fact lying. Issues of credibility, therefore, are usually the focus of cross-examination, and David Bain's was about to be put to the sword in the hands of the wily, experienced prosecutor Bill Wright, who after a few preliminary questions wasted no time in going on the attack.

'Would you say that your memory is now better or worse than it was say on noon 20 June to say twenty-third of June?' asked Wright, to which David replied: 'It would be better, but parts are not as clear as before, leading up to June 20.'

Wright questioned David about doing the washing and in particular his memory about what setting he put the washing on. David answered that all he could do was tell what was his normal practice, which was to put it on 'after the very start of the super wash cycle'. That didn't take things any further than what he had already told the police and had been read to the jury in the statements.

He then had David confirm that he could not remember touching the rifle in the morning in question and that he had not used it since January or February of that year. 'Had it remained in your wardrobe since that time?'

To which David answered, 'As far as I knew, yes.'

When David was questioned on the subject by the police on the day after the deaths he told them he was not aware that anybody else had handled the gun.

At that time, Greg Dunne had asked him: 'You have told me earlier that Dad has been possum shooting with you, is that right?' David answered, 'No, he's been with me to sight the gun.' Then came the pertinent question from Dunne: 'Has he ever borrowed, or could he have without your knowledge?' David's answer was: 'It's difficult to say. He could have borrowed it if he knew where the key was and I was away long enough.'

Now, at the trial, Wright moved onto the black hands that various witnesses said David had talked about. David confirmed that the description given by his auntie of the conversation they had about black hands was accurate. Although David had given a long description of what he meant when he was talking about the black hands taking his family away, Wright wanted more. And so David answered in the following way: 'The vision, the impression I got when I recalled that memory was of seeing the family in the closed off, closing in of the black around them, and the impression of the black hands over them. And it was as if everything was moving away from me at that time.'

'Where were they being taken away from?' Wright wanted to know. To which David answered, 'From me.'

Then it was déjà vu. 'Just so that we are clear, could you define what you regard as déjà vu?'

David's definition off the cuff was not too bad really: 'It is where a certain event starts off a chain reaction of other events and the feeling; it is more than a feeling than anything, of having been there before.' The *Oxford Dictionary* says 'an illusory feeling of having already experienced a present situation'. David had talked about the fact that Laniet could see black auras and Wright questioned David about that but it did not go far.

There was some discussion about the incident in the evening when David was walking along the beach with Miss X and Jane, and fell to his knees wailing. David confirmed that basically what the girls had described was roughly what happened that night to the best of his memory.

Then without warning or introductory questions Wright simply said: 'How would you describe your relationship with your father?'

The answer came back very directly. 'It was a close relationship, we got on well. We had very similar interests and therefore did things together.'

David went on to mention singing, music, sports, fishing, cricket, tennis and swimming and all the shows that David did. 'I loved him a great deal; I mean he was my father.'

Wright tried to get David to agree that David wanted Robin out of the house, but David insisted that he was telling people about his parents' relationship and that it was what his mother wanted, not what he wanted.

'Did you tell Val Boyd that you hated your father?'

'I think I did but I can't remember exactly, clearly.'

The adversarial process was in full swing now. Both sides reinforcing the interpretation that suits them best, the witness struggling to maintain his equilibrium and the jury wondering where in the spectrum the truth really lies.

David explained about the chainsaw argument that David told the police about between him and his father on the Friday night of the fateful weekend: 'He was off down to the school every week and there was a bundle of firewood down there that he used to chop, so only having the one chainsaw we were constantly at it to see who could get the chainsaw for that time.'

David confirmed his father would assert his authority over him, but he did not resent it. 'No I think it was natural,' he explained, 'because he had been going through a very tough time with Mum pushing him out and his feeling of loss of his family. I know he would try anything to get back into the family.' It may be that this comment will be seen as extremely relevant as this narrative comes to an end.

David agreed that he told Miss X there was a man in Papua New Guinea he saw as a father figure. Funnily enough, one may think he was not pressed on who this person was or why that was the case.

He was then asked to confirm that he had told Val Boyd that Laniet was a sweet girl and that his father had 'got her' and asked David what did he mean by the words 'got her'.

'That he got that control, being able to assert his authority, being the father sort of thing. Arawa stood up for herself and she was her own person — that would be the other end of the spectrum I suppose. As for myself, I was somewhere in the middle. I was more concerned with Mum and Dad splitting up.'

There was a particularly acute piece of cross-examination founded on the notes that Greg Dunne had made of his very initial conversation with David on the morning of 20 June before he started taking a formal statement: 'Do you recall asking or his [Greg Dunne] confirming that your mother and father were in fact dead?'

David answered 'Yes.' Wright then pointed out that Dunne's records showed David referred to individuals, even the dog by name, whereas in respect to his father David used the words 'he' or 'him'. Why was that, Wright wanted to know. David said he didn't know.

David confirmed that on Saturday, 18 June his mum and dad were arguing about spouting repairs and then it turned to the plans for the new house. Yes, David agreed it was to be a large house with six bedrooms.

'It was intended that your father would reside at the new house?' Wright wanted to know.

'No, my mother had basically made her plans on what she discussed with us and they did not include my father … She felt the marriage was completely over and I don't think she would have settled with Dad living at the same address.'

He wanted to know if David was angry that his father, in David's view, had not provided well financially for the future of the family.

David told the court that he was not worried for himself. 'I was quite capable of looking after myself.' But he said his mother had no super-annuation or whatever.

He pressed David on his use of the terms sanctuary or retreat to describe the new house. David explained in Papua New Guinea they had lived in very natural surroundings but back in New Zealand it was very urban and concrete and they wanted to create a very natural haven at 65 Every Street.

The large trees were there and they had done a lot of gardening; a rock garden, native trees and a waterfall had been created and planted. 'A place that you could sit and be at peace from the outside world' was how David forlornly described it.

Wright wanted to know how it was to be financed.

David explained that his mother was going to get the money back from the loan they had made to family friends, and also she planned to sell land they owned up north and in Australia.

Wright went on: Was David worried that Arawa would go flatting? Did he consider going flatting himself? Was he worried that if he left home the house would never be built?

David's answers were pretty simple. Laniet was cut up about the marriage split and it was hoped that the new house would bring them all back together again. David said that Arawa and Stephen were just as much involved in the new house as he was. He admitted that things could change but 'at that stage everybody was involved'.

The afternoon tea break came and went; David had now been in the witness box for about four hours.

At the resumption Wright addressed David's assertion to Greg Dunne on 20 and 21 June that he had only gone into Margaret and Robin's rooms. David had told Greg Dunne that he had not gone into Arawa, Laniet or Stephen's bedrooms. Having confirmed with David that the partial recall of memory had occurred when Professor Mullen interviewed him in December 1994, Wright put to David that this was after David had become aware, through the depositions hearing, of the evidence about blood on his clothing belonging to other members of his family. 'In particular, you were aware ... the droplets of blood on your socks had been identified as coming from Stephen,' Wright said.

Presumably, Wright was alleging that David's partial memory recovery was faked to try to explain the evidence against him. An alternative view could be that if he was such a cunning killer that he did the washing to get rid of bloody clothes, he would surely have put his white socks in as well, as according to Wright he had been wearing them in the violent bloody struggle.

The next subject was David's purchase of the rifle, and particular emphasis was placed by Bill Wright on the home-made target with five rabbit ears found in David's bedroom. 'Was your father's only involvement with this rifle when he took you to Taieri Mouth to sight the rifle in?'

'That is correct, yes.'

'And you say that Exhibit 212 [the target] was used for this purpose?'

Again David answered, 'Yes, that is correct.' He explained that he only acquired the rifle during August 1993 and he had not used it very much.

Prior to that, he told the court he had the use of a borrowed rifle from his uncle. His dad taught him how to use rifles including things like safety, loading, cleaning and sighting them.

Wright said to David that quite a large amount of ammunition was found in David's wardrobe to which David agreed and said that some of that had been a Christmas present from his mother. Wright wanted to know if the rifle was prone to misfeeding and suggested that it was a difficult task to clear when it did. David agreed that the rifle did jam on occasions but said it was not that difficult because sometimes it could be freed just by giving it a shake.

At this stage Wright was jumping from one subject to the other very abruptly, presumably trying to catch David out. David agreed that his father worked very hard, and then next that his mother had begun to act in a very strange way. 'I suppose to people on the outside they would call it strange. I did find the pendulum weird,' was the apparently frank answer.

Mrs Neasmith described the family as dysfunctional, the prosecutor persisted, to which David replied, 'That is a perspective of someone from the outside. I mean I love my family and I am sure there were, everybody had friction. There was friction in the family but there was nothing I could see that I would term abnormal. I felt that my family was close, and a lot closer than your average normal family.'

David agreed that the house was dilapidated, smelly and unhygienic. 'Things were going downhill a bit,' he stated or, some may say, understated.

'You have said the green jersey on the dummy, Exhibit 98, was your father's jersey,' Wright said, jumping subjects again; and David agreed that yes, it was his father's jersey. Wright made the point to David that when he was being interviewed by the police he had said he had put a green jersey in the washing machine, but it was Arawa's jersey, and David agreed he had said that. The point being made by Wright was that once the green jersey was shown to have been worn by the murderer, David's evidence about whose it was had changed; Wright was putting this in the same category as David's recalled memory about having gone into the bedrooms. Wright wanted to know where his father would have kept that green jersey and David said that he would probably have kept it out in the caravan but that Arawa borrowed it quite frequently because it was large and baggy. 'You say that jersey Exhibit 98 would not fit you,' Wright said. 'No, it would not,' replied David. Wright put the denial to the test; the jersey was removed from the dummy and put on the witness at this point.

A number of photographs of Robin Bain wearing a green jersey were pointed out to David who thought one of those was the jersey in question, Exhibit 98. He was wrong.

'Could you be confused about Exhibit 98 being your father's jersey?' Wright wanted to know, after having shown that David had identified the wrong jersey in the photo. David said, 'Yes, that would be possible, but I have seen him wearing that jersey.'

From clothes it was now to the polar plunge evidence. David agreed he took off the string necklace and put it in the pocket of the red anorak and left it in the Commer van.

Where did David keep the dress gloves?

David pointed in a photo to a set of drawers in his bedroom: 'The third drawer up,' he said.

'Did your father go through your drawers to your knowledge?' Wright asked, to which David said, 'No, not to my knowledge.'

'Do you have any explanation for the presence of the gloves in Stephen's room on the morning of June 20?'

'No, I don't.'

Then it was on to the broken glasses.

'You say they are not yours but an older pair of your mothers?' Wright asked, accusingly. 'That is right,' David replied.

'The ophthalmologist, Mr Sanderson, from the hospital was of the opinion that they were an earlier prescription of your existing optometry prescription,' Wright persisted.

It would seem David would not be bullied, by doctors from the hospital or anyone else. 'That is incorrect,' he said. 'One of those lenses I would not be able to see out of clearly to give me full vision.'

In this passage Wright rams home the dispute about whose glasses they actually were and he continued on in that vein. He reminded David of Sanderson's evidence that both lenses were similar to David's prescription. David agreed that one of the lenses was but the other one was not.

'You say he is wrong?' came the challenge.

'Yes,' replied the accused, just as positively. But who would the jury believe? And if he told one lie, why not others?

Wright then asked David if he had used those glasses on the Friday or over the weekend. David denied that he had, saying he had forgotten all about them.

'Were the glasses in your room, or the frame and the lens, on the Sunday night'?

'No.'

'Can you account for their presence as found in your room by the police on the Monday morning?'

'No, I cannot account for that,' David said.

Then without any ado, a barrage of direct questions came straight at David, who by this time had been in the witness box nearly all day. Due to the harrowing questioning of the last hour in particular, Wright may have thought he had him on the ropes.

Q: Can you account for your fingerprints on the rifle found in the front room A?

A: No, I cannot account for that because I don't remember touching the gun at all that morning. All I can say is that I must have picked it up at some stage, but I do not recall touching the gun at all or seeing it.

Q: Can you account for the injuries to your face as documented by Dr Pryde when he examined you at 11.20 a.m. on the morning of June 20?

A: No I can't. I cannot remember how I got them, but I do know I did not have the bruise or the scrape on my knee while doing the paper run or immediately after it on entering the house.

Q: How do you know you did not have those bruises?

A: Because my memory is clear up until seeing my mother.

Q: In the course of the night say between midnight and 4.30 to five o'clock do you recall anything happening?

A: No.

Q: Do you recall getting up during the night?

A: No. I slept right through until 5.30 a.m.

Q: You do not recall getting up at all during the night?

A: That is correct.

Q: Have you had any flashbacks or pictures of getting up in the middle of the night?

A: No.

Could David account for the blood spots on the duvet on his bed? David didn't know but he did remember the cat sitting on his bed.

What about the blood on the light switch in his room? David had no idea about that either.

Then it turned to the washing in the laundry. Could David account for his palm print in blood on the washing machine?

A: Only if I touched some blood at some stage. But I did put on the wash so if I touched some blood I would expect it to find at least some sort of print there.

Q: Are you certain that you washed your hands prior to commencing the wash?

A: Yes.

Q: Could you account for blood spots in the hand-basin?

A: No I cannot.

Q: Did you see any blood spots on that porcelain basin when you washed your hands, before commencing the washing?

A: No, I did not.

David next confirmed that when he came home and went to his bedroom he did not turn the light on immediately.

The time was now 10 to 5 in the evening and, no doubt at the suggestion of Wright, the court adjourned for the day. It is always an advantage for a lawyer cross-examining a witness to get an overnight adjournment in the middle of the cross-examination. It gives the opportunity of reviewing the questions that he has put so far to see if any further exploration of those subjects is required, and also to see what else is remaining. It also means that the accused person on the stand has to sweat overnight wondering just what is going to be coming the next day. Bill Wright and his junior lawyers, along with Jim Doyle and Milton Weir, undoubtedly did some serious study on that final Wednesday night of the trial.

First thing on Thursday morning proceedings began with David being questioned about his choice of the song by Queen, 'Who Wants to Live Forever', to be played at the funerals. David said that Laniet loved the song so much she played it over and over and over again until it nearly drove everybody crazy.

He queried David again about the sequence of events in the laundry but nothing more came from that.

David was probed further about his account of having found his mother dead. It will be remembered that David said he went to her room in panic after finding the bullets on the floor in his bedroom, and he had said he knew she was dead 'because her eyes were open'.

But when the police arrived, according to their evidence, her eyes were shut.

Q: Are you certain you saw her eyes open?
A: Yes, because I called her and asked what the story was and she did not respond.

Some innocuous questions about seeing his father dead on the floor in the lounge were followed by what David had to say about the *Gondoliers* sweatshirt found in the wash basket with diluted bloodstains on the right arm and shoulder area.

David confirmed that it was his and that he had worn it on the Sunday and put it in the wash basket that night. He did not notice any blood then, he told the jury, and confirmed that he could not offer any explanation for the bloodstains on its shoulder or cuff.

Some general questions about the various productions David had been in did not add anything significant to the general knowledge of the case or evidence against David. Wright then tried to make something of the alleged comment by David that he always ended up losing the things and people he loved.

David said that was taken out of a much larger conversation and related to pets that he had that had died, friends who had betrayed him and particularly in the context of the conversation about his relationship with Miss X, 'because of the relationship she had with someone else'.

Then came another attack on David's credibility relating to the fact that he had said he heard raised voices from the lounge on the Sunday night. He had not told this to the police in the interviews in the week of the murders. Bill Wright wanted to know why he hadn't told the police this. David said that he simply had not remembered at that time. 'I was under a lot of pressure and he was asking me to remember a lot of things,' he said.

Immediately following this question, Wright asked: 'Have you put on weight since 20 June?' David answered: 'Some weight but not markedly.'

This question was an attempt to rebut the visual effect of David putting on the green jersey earlier, because when he did, according to eyewitnesses at the trial, it was quite clear that the jersey was far too small for him.

The intensive questioning over many hours drifted to a conclusion with questions about clearing misfeeds from the rifle, aimed at trying to show that was why David had put his fingerprints on the gun in the reverse position they were found. David disagreed entirely with this line of questioning.

As a result of these questions Judge Williamson asked David what action would have caused him to put his hand over the rifle rather than under it in the normal way. David told the judge that the only time he ever held the rifle like that was if he was getting over or under a fence.

'What about if the front of the rifle were pushed up?' the judge wanted to know, firmly planting in the jury's mind his view that the fingerprints got there when the first shot to Stephen was diverted by Stephen's hand pushing the rifle away.

David agreed that if it was pushed up that would be a possibility, but that it would not be necessary because he could hold the rifle the full way round. It is doubtful David comprehended the thrust of Justice Williamson's intrusion.

David was now discharged from the stand and the young man who would soon be convicted as one of the most callous, cold-blooded murderers in New Zealand's history resumed his seat in the court.

PSYCHIATRIC TESTIMONY

Michael Guest had two other witnesses who did not occupy the stand very long and neither of whom was of much benefit to David's defence.

Professor Paul Mullen is one of the pre-eminent forensic psychiatrists of his age. He told the jury that he had over 25 years' experience in dealing with a wide variety of offenders and that in June of 1995 he was a director of the Victorian forensic psychiatry services in Melbourne. He was also the Professor of Forensic Psychiatry at Monash University in Melbourne.

He went on to say that he had been instructed by Michael Guest to interview David between 13 and 19 December 1994. The depositions hearings had concluded by early December and so he had prepared himself by reading all of David's statements to the police, listening to the 111 tape recording, and familiarizing himself with the evidence against David.

He interviewed David on five separate occasions for about seven hours in total. He also organized EEG tests to be carried out on David. This is an electrical recording done by electrodes being placed on the skull, recording activities of the brain.

On the basis of his own observations and EEG results, he said: 'One can virtually exclude a significant pathology.' The déjà vu and trance experiences, which formed part of the Crown case against David, Mullen described as quite normal experiences for many people, particularly young adults.

He then went on to describe the condition known as dissociative amnesia, as being 'a disturbance of memory and of consciousness produced by intense arousal in those involved in tragedy or disaster'.

Perfectly normal people exposed to horrifying or frightening situations can respond by cutting off to a greater or lesser extent from the reality of the situation they are confronted by, he explained. If the situation they have been involved in is one of great horror, their memories of those events become patchy and incomplete. They may totally fail to recall some of the events, push some out of awareness altogether, and they may retain an incomplete, very partial recall of what happened, due to the state of intense arousal, fear or distress.

He went on to say that in a situation of dreadful crimes this can happen with the perpetrators as well as the onlookers or victims.

He then made a very simple but powerful point, one easy to overlook: that you can't know what you don't know. In other words, people can be aware that their memory is incomplete because their memory stops at one point and then starts again at another. They have no idea how they got from point A to point B and how long it took or what they did during that period. They simply do not know.

Mullen explained to the jury that David Bain was fully aware there was a period of time between finding his mother and calling 111 that was a blur in his memory — the famous 'missing 20 minutes', so highly incriminating at the Croudis interview. He said he helped David to explore his memory to see if he could fill in any of those gaps.

He went on to comment on David's reaction and behaviour at the movie *Schindler's List*. He could see nothing sinister at all and described as fanciful any view that the movie and the Bain tragedy could be causally connected.

The cross-examination was succinct but effective. Wright got Mullen to confirm that dissociated amnesia is memory loss, not mental illness. He then went on with the following line of questioning:

Q: It can arise by the person being either a witness to an act or by being
the perpetrator of the act?
A: It can.

And then later:

Q: Recovered memory may be genuine or self-serving?
A: Indeed.

Mullen was then referred to a report conducted by English psychiatrist Pamela Taylor where, in a study of amnesia, she found that 70 per cent of the murderers she examined had some form of amnesia relating to the event. Mullen agreed that was the finding of the report.

The problem with Mullen's evidence from David's point of view was that he had never had the opportunity to consider the psychology of the case based upon the new Crown case of David being a psychopath — killing four people and then doing the paper round before coming home and killing the fifth after laying in wait behind the curtains.

THE FINAL WITNESS

Just before lunch on Thursday, 25 May, the final evidence that the jury would need to consider was called and it came from Kyle Cunningham, who had been boarding at the schoolhouse with Robin and Laniet for a few weeks prior to the tragedies. Michael Guest had to subpoena the 18-year-old

Cunningham from Auckland, where he had moved after the death of Robin Bain.

Cunningham told the jury of having known Laniet for about three to four months and went on to say that he had lived at the schoolhouse with Robin and Laniet.

The main reason Guest called Cunningham was that in a statement he had given to the police just days after the incident, he told them about a conversation he'd had with Robin in the week prior to the murders. Robin talked about getting a firearms licence and asked how much noise various types of rifles would make. Cunningham told the jury that he told Robin a .22 would make less noise than a shotgun.

He said that David seemed to be the most popular in the family with Robin. 'He kept going on about David whenever I inquired about family members.'

Cunningham said that when Robin drove down to school from Every Street on Monday mornings he would come dressed ready for work and go straight from the van to the school without going inside the schoolhouse.

In cross-examination Wright had a field day, because Guest had not briefed his witness in the normal way as he was a reluctant witness and so much of what he had to say was not included in his evidence in chief, leaving the omissions and anomalies open to exposure by Wright. They discussed the gun conversation in much more detail. What was actually discussed was that they were both going to shoot rabbits and possums and that Cunningham was going to sell the skins to earn some money.

However, when Wright tried to get Cunningham to say that Robin wore a brown jersey to school (he was wearing a brown jersey when found by the police) Cunningham said he had never seen him in that jersey at all, only ever a green jersey. He then confirmed by looking at some photos that it was a round-necked green jersey that he normally saw Robin in. The one worn by the killer was V-neck.

The final question in the trial of David Bain was: 'What was the last thing he said to you on the Friday when he left?' Cunningham responded: 'That he would see me on Monday.' Not a bad line for the Crown to end on. It might be said that the prosecution had the final say — and in fact they did, because Guest did not re-examine this final witness.

CHAPTER 8

JUDGE'S RULINGS

There were eight formal rulings made by the judge during the course of the trial.

1. TIMING OF MURDERS

The first was before evidence commenced and was discussed earlier. The judge ruled that the prosecution could leave open the actual allegation of when David Bain was said to have performed the killings until the end of the trial.

2. ADMISSIBILITY OF RECONSTRUCTION EVIDENCE

The second ruling on 9 May related to the admissibility of reconstruction evidence. It appears a consensus or compromise was reached as the Crown agreed not to call evidence relating to reconstructions done by the police of the various killings and in particular the death of Robin Bain. Of note in the bigger picture are the opening words in this ruling, which were: 'In this case one of the essential issues is whether Robin Bain committed suicide or was shot by the accused.'

3. BLOOD SPATTER EVIDENCE

Ruling three came in the second week on 15 May when Guest protested that additional blood spatter evidence the Crown wished to call was so late that it would be unfair to allow it to be admitted. The judge upheld the protest.

4. HENTSCHEL AND THE PIECE OF SKIN

In ruling four the judge ruled against Michael Guest who argued that Hentschel was not qualified to give opinion evidence about whether the piece of skin matched the graze on Stephen's knee.

5. VICTIM SUPPORT OFFICER'S EVIDENCE

Ruling five came on 23 May and related to the woman who worked as the victim support officer who assisted David during the week following the killings. She did not want to give evidence on the principle that her discussions with David were confidential and it would be an abuse of trust between a person doing her job to testify against a person who had trusted and confided in her in the way that David did. The Crown wanted to call her to reinforce the belief that David was an actor, feigning drama and shock. The judge agreed that the evidence could not be called, in part because he said it added very little to the case.

6. EXTENT OF MULLEN'S EVIDENCE

Ruling six related to the extent of Professor Mullen's evidence. Michael Guest's submissions relate to the Crown having changed its theory about when the killings happened and therefore the type of personality David would need to be. He submitted a brief of evidence that he proposed Mullen would deliver to the court which included Mullen describing and giving evidence about the déjà vu and trance matters raised and evidence by the Crown. He also wanted to give evidence about post-traumatic stress disorder and the effect that can have on memory. It is the final two paragraphs of Michael Guest's submissions that are of interest:

'Finally, I believe this is an appropriate time to raise a psychiatric matter which might be relevant to Your Honour's summing up. *The defence is not raising insanity or automatism.* The defence explains the trance evidence as an idiosyncrasy not related to the potential to commit multiple homicide and the defence explains subsequent memory loss on the basis of dissociative amnesia. However, I suggest that the Crown has raised evidence, and presumably intends to either comment upon that evidence in closing, or leave a pregnant inference for the jury, that the accused was insane or was acting in an automatic state. I suggest that the Crown must take extreme care in making such suggestions or leaving such suggestions open to the jury.'

In the final clause of his submissions he went on to say: 'The defence evidence from Professor Mullen, and the defence *not* raising the issue of insanity, must lead a jury *not* to make some finding of *insanity*. I assume you will direct on this point. But the question of *non-insane automatism* has at least been raised in the evidence by the Crown. Will the jury now have to be directed on the non-insane automatism? The defence does not wish to go down that track because it is a mutually exclusive defence.'

This comment by Michael Guest that it is 'a mutually exclusive defence' means David was claiming that he did not do it at all and so did not wish to rely upon mitigating circumstances such as non-insane automatism. The submission went on to raise the point that is at the crux of this book:

'This aspect of automatism is all the more difficult in this case because the Crown advances the picture of the accused as being cold-blooded and calculating, both planning these killings and making attempts to clean up and lay false trails after the event. The defence does not wish the jury to determine this matter on the basis of automatism but the Crown comes close to suggesting just that. It is my submission that the Crown must make it crystal clear what is the relevance of the trance and of the déjà vu premonition experiences of the accused.'

In other words, the Crown was confused and was trying to have a bob each way, as it were, leaving Guest in an almost impossible position. Indeed, it will be seen from Wright's closing address that he continued with the two-pronged approach.

The Crown objected to much of the evidence but the judge ruled that Mullen was able to give expert explanations for the déjà vu experiences, the trances and the possible effect of the movie *Schindler's List*, as well as the effects of dissociative amnesia. There is no specific mention in the ruling of what should not be allowed, nevertheless the following assessments in Professor Mullen's brief of evidence supplied to Guest were not part of his evidence as heard by the jury:

- David Bain gave no history suggestive of significant mood disorder prior to the killings.
- There was nothing in the history he provided to suggest persecutory beliefs or abnormal phenomena such as ideas of reference.
- There was no evidence for any grandiose notions or abnormal preoccupations.
- David Bain's intelligence would appear to be within the normal range.
- In my opinion David Bain shows no evidence of having a major mental disorder. There is nothing in his history suggesting that he has ever suffered from significant psychiatric disorder.

- There are elements of a depressive reaction and of a post-traumatic stress disorder.
- David Bain consistently denied any involvement in the deaths of his family. He acknowledged uncertainties as to the extent and accuracy of any recall following being confronted by the body of his mother. He was adamant, however, that he had no difficulty recalling the events up until that time and no sense of any lapses or distortions in his memory.
- Mr Bain shows no evidence of any current mental illness nor does he appear to have had a mental illness prior to or at the time of the killings.
- From my experience grief manifests itself in so many varied ways, ranging from normality to the other end of the spectrum, that there are no valid grounds for drawing any adverse inference from such observations either way.
- *Those who kill others, particularly when the victims are family members, are prone to amnesia for the actual killing. They do not, however, 'forget' they have committed the killings and are aware and acknowledge their responsibility even though they do not recall the details of the fatal act.* This is not the situation with Mr Bain, who both denies guilt and provides a clear account up to the time of discovering his mother's body.

The passage in italics above was highlighted in the brief of evidence of Professor Mullen.

7. AND 8. DEAN COTTLE — THE POTENTIAL 'SILVER BULLET'

Rulings seven and eight both relate to the admissibility of evidence from a potential witness called Dean Cottle. Michael Guest regarded Cottle as the silver bullet in the defence case and had placed great reliance on getting it before the jury. Cottle's evidence was in fact to have been the *coup de grâce* of Guest's defence — and not without reason.

So let us consider the situation as it existed in 1995 as Michael Guest was preparing a defence for his client. He had been floundering to know what to do. The evidence against David appeared compelling and yet at the same time David appeared to Guest and everyone else, except his uncles and aunts and the police, as being a genuinely honest, decent and caring young man. As far as Guest could see, there was no evidence that seriously implicated Robin. David was adamant, though, that despite not being able to account for the missing 20 minutes — the period in which Guest understood it was alleged the killings occurred (until day one of the trial, that is) — that he came home and found his mother dead. That was either a lie, or he was innocent.

Then one day out of the blue, among the thousands of pages of statements and job sheets disclosed to him by the police, a statement from Dean Cottle appeared, taken by the police on 23 June 1994, the day before David's arrest. The essential thrust of the statement was that Laniet had been a prostitute. Cottle had known Laniet for about a year and had been acting as her 'pimp' so to speak. He had lent her a cellphone to help her conduct her business (cellphones were very much the latest gadget in 1994). They had become quite friendly and she had discussed various personal issues and told him that her father had been having sex with her since they had been in PNG when she was only 11 or 12 years old.

He went on to say that he had run into her in the street on the Thursday before the murders and they had chatted for five or 10 minutes. She told him she was sick of everybody 'getting up her' and she was going home to tell her mother everything that weekend. Cottle said that by 'everything' he took it to mean the incest and the fact that she had been a prostitute.

The gravitas of this evidence as it related to the trial can be gleaned from a *New Zealand Listener* article written by Bruce Ansley following the verdicts. He wrote: 'At the end [of the trial], it was clear that this monstrous killing lacked a monster. David Bain was just a normal young man and, after tens of thousands of words of evidence, there is still one question no one can answer: why?'

Guest believed Cottle's evidence may have given the jury the clue they needed.

But back to the events that unfolded in highly dramatic circumstances in Dunedin in May of 1995. The jury had heard from nearly 100 witnesses and there had not been one mention of prostitution, let alone allegations of incest. There had been nothing in the evidence to give any indication or clue why this tragedy happened or what triggered it off. Even Wright, as we shall see in his closing address, said he had no idea. As far as the jury knew from the evidence, Robin was a perfectly normal man going through a marriage separation with a rather weird wife, but nothing had been reported that set that weekend apart.

Michael Guest viewed Dean Cottle as his trump card and it is that which makes his handling of Cottle difficult to understand. He realized that this evidence could serve to throw the spotlight on Robin in such a way as to give the jury a genuine concern that there might be more to the case than the police were letting on. They may have viewed much of the other evidence in a different light with this new shadow cast over proceedings.

Dean Cottle's family are well established in Dunedin. His father owned a successful car sales business. Dean was engaged to be married, had a permanent local address and worked in the family business.

So bearing all that in mind, one might think that as he was Guest's 'silver bullet', he would have been nurtured carefully all the way into and out of the witness box. But, for reasons of his own, Guest never made direct contact with him prior to the trial. Instead, in April 1995 not long before the trial, he arranged for a private investigator to serve him with a subpoena which required him to attend the court to give evidence as a defence witness on 22 May 1995.

However, Cottle did not show up and so a warrant was issued for his arrest. In his absence Guest made an application to the judge to have his police statement of 23 June 1994 read to the jury.

The seventh ruling of Judge Williamson declined this application, despite conceding the relevance of the contents of his evidence. 'A motive for Robin Bain is certainly relevant to the primary issue in this case,' wrote the judge. He declined it because: 'The real stumbling block is the question of reliability. If he had been present I would have required him to be called to enable a judgment to be made as to whether what he said was reasonably safe or reliable, but that assessment is just not possible.'

So the jury continued to have no idea of those significant issues lurking beneath the surface of the case.

Cottle, though, would resurface before the end of the trial, and become the subject of yet another ruling by Justice Williamson.

CHAPTER 9

THE END

CROWN CLOSING ADDRESS

We now turn to Friday, 26 May and Bill Wright's closing address to the jury, which lasted about three hours. It has been described as powerful, well-constructed, strongly delivered and convincing. A précis below is from his own handwritten notes that were tendered to the Court of Appeal in his affidavit of 2002. He said in the affidavit that he did not deviate in any material way from the notes. The italicized sections are actual quotes from his notes.

The Crown case is:

Firstly: There is a mass of evidence that proves the accused was responsible for these killings.

Secondly: There is no evidence that Robin Bain committed the murders and in addition there is evidence he didn't do it.

Thirdly: The evidence makes it clear that this was not suicide by Robin Bain.

He then raced past the question of why David did it by telling the jury that '*it is beyond our comprehension. We can't understand it.*'

'*Your job,*' he told the jury, '*was to work out who did it, not to worry about why it happened. We will probably never know why it occurred much less understand it.*'

He told them it was '*not a contest between barristers or a points scoring exercise*'. Indeed, he said, '*If you regard it as such … Then the only ultimate casualty is truth.*'

Relevant points from the balance of the three-hour address are listed.

What went wrong for the accused involved two things. Firstly, he didn't kill Stephen with the first shot and, secondly, '*he is not quite as clever as he thinks*'. He did not count on the fact that the police and experts involved carried out such a careful, detailed and thorough investigation.

The accused's behaviour was bizarre: '*This horrible thing was going to happen so he made it happen'* — a reference to what he said to witness 'Jane'.

On the crucial issue of how David is supposed to have gone about the killings, Wright by now was explicit.

David was lying when he said he got up at about 5.45 a.m: *'His statement that he never got up until quarter to six or thereabouts for his paper run is untrue.'*

In fact, Wright said, he got up and killed the four in the house between 4 a.m. and 5 a.m. He didn't put shoes on because it would be quieter in socks.

He shot Laniet first and then when he heard her gurgling he shot her two more times in the head. Then he shot his mother and then Stephen and that is when things began to go wrong. *'He had a misfeed'* and couldn't get off the second shot. He had to take the gloves off, which he was wearing to *'protect against fingerprints'*, to clear the misfeed.

A fight developed — and *'the accused suffers facial bruising and an injury to his leg. His glasses are knocked off — he finds the frames and one lens, can't find the other.'* He gets blood on his jersey, his shorts and socks in the fight.

'He leaves these right stockinged prints which the luminol reveals.' He goes downstairs and shoots Arawa, but now he has no glasses so can't see properly, which is why the first shot missed.

He then cleans himself up — washes hands. *'Dries them on the green towel — diluted blood on it. Puts the green jersey in the wash. Doesn't notice the drop of blood in the hand-basin or the two drops of blood on his sock, or the blood on his shorts.'*

But he does notice blood on the *Gondoliers* sweatshirt and so he sponges it off and puts it in the washing basket because *'he can't put whites with coloureds'*.

He *'puts on another sweatshirt and top'*.

There are spots of blood on the duvet cover and light switch in his room — *'Cold — may have even got back into bed'*.

'Fundamental to his plan is to shoot Dad in the front room', because it would *'be no use shooting Dad in the caravan, putting the gun beside him'*. That proposition was based on the next statement in his handwritten notes: *'Gone back to bed and killed himself'*, meaning it would be an unrealistic suicide if Robin had shot himself in bed in the caravan.

Doing the paper run *'was essential to his plan'* for three reasons, according to the prosecutor. Firstly, it was *'his normal activity'*. Secondly, it provided *'the apparent opportunity'* for the father to have done it, and, thirdly, *'he had to have his father up, dressed and in this house'*.

David knew according to Wright that his father regularly went into the front room to pray each morning about 7 a.m.

David did the paper run early, as shown by the evidence of Rackley and Parker, and he ran it so that he could be home before his father got up and so he could take the paper in himself, the narrative continued.

Tania Clark saw David at Heath Street at 6.40 a.m.

David said 6.40 just above Heath Street and said it would take *'two or three minutes to get home'* from there. *'Suggest one to two minutes'*, Wright wrote.

In regard to Mrs Laney he wrote:

'Mrs Laney — she passed at speed. Did not identify accused. Saw someone at the gate.'

'Imp — He was back in the house before the computer was turned on.'

David's scheme did not allow for the fact that a computer expert would get into the innards of the machine and work out when it was switched on, he said. *'People know about fingerprints but how many know that?'* the prosecutor posited to the jury.

'Timings will be close', so the first thing David did, the story continued, was to put the paper in the hall and then he *'went straight to the alcove (where the computer was) with the rifle to wait'*. It was dark, but David could see close up so he typed on the computer. Then he waited. *'It's 7.44 [sic] [6.44 a.m.]. The father eventually comes in about 7 o'clock and sits or kneels in prayer and is shot.'*

It is this waiting that accounts for the 'missing 20 minutes'. David, having killed them all between about 4 a.m. and 7 a.m., and been out on a paper round for an hour as well, made two final mistakes according to Wright.

The first is described as a *'nice little touch'*. It is the placing of the 10-shot magazine on edge beside his father's right hand. (It might be asked why he did not place it in his father's pocket if he wanted to incriminate him.) After this 'touch' he probably washed his hands again, which maybe accounts for the spot in the basin.

Finally, at 7.09 he rings 111, *'a very distressed voice'*. The giveaway was that he *'corrects the street number immediately'* and he was very clear on giving out his phone number.

'Not the hallmark of the irrational distressed person.'

Based on Mr Anderson of the ambulance staff, David's shivering and quivering was put on. There was an *'absence of psychological symptoms — all* normal. *When he fell back he hit the back of his head, not where the injuries were.'*

Mr Anderson had said: *'I experience sometimes in the job people who display a similar fit, which has always been put on, always been purposeful.'*

Wright told the jury, *'You can put it the other way round. If Robin didn't kill the wife and the three children — then who did?'*

So the die was cast. David pre-planned the entire affair with the essential elements being the doing of the paper round and shooting his father afterwards, having provided an *'apparent'* opportunity for his father in the process, as Robin customarily came to the room to *'sit or kneel'* in prayer.

He described 'reasonable doubt' to the jury, saying that although it was a high standard it was not impossible.

'If after you have considered all the evidence against the accused, the lack of any evidence against Robin and that his death was not suicide you can honestly say "I have reasonable doubt" then you must acquit. If you can't honestly say this then no matter how distasteful, you must convict.'

No doubt the last statement was a parry to the appearance of David being a normal caring son and brother and yet inexplicably executing his family with cunning premeditation and deception.

He lists what he calls *'facts — not speculation'*, proving it was David:

- It was his rifle and ammo — *'don't overlook the obvious'*.
- His *'positive fingerprints in blood'* on the rifle — *'can't be explained'*.
- His bloodied gloves — *'can't explain'*.
- *'Unexplained injuries to the accused.'*
- *'The lens from the glasses in Stephen's room.'*
- *'Two droplets of blood on his socks.'*
- *'Computer time — 6.44 a.m. — straight into that alcove.'*
- The trigger lock keys — *'no one else knew where they were'*.
- *Gondoliers* sweatshirt with diluted blood on it.
- The washing machine cycle was too long.

These, wrote Bill Wright in his notes for his closing address, were *'facts — not interpretation, memories or theories'*.

He lists a lot of other evidence and implicating matters, some referred to as *'curious'*, including the luminol footprints — *'too big to be his father's'*.

David's injuries, which he couldn't explain — *'he certainly didn't get them after 6.45 a.m. this morning,*' Bill Wright wrote.

Notably, he recorded that the other four bodies were '**cold** *as compared to Robin Bain — they were killed sometime earlier*'.

Accused home when computer was turned on. '*He made a beeline straight for the computer alcove to wait for his father.*'

Then on to Robin. '*No one else's blood on him. No blood on his shoes or socks. No unexplained injuries.*'

'*One important piece of evidence — Robin Bain's bladder was full — it was his overnight collection of urine — he hadn't been to toilet. If not bursting — at least uncomfortable.*'

The message was clear — no one could shoot four people and themselves as well as typing a message on the computer with a full bladder.

He goes on to Robin not having committed suicide, '*On the evidence of the pathologist alone you could eliminate suicide.*'

He then moved on to the defence, stating that it opened its case by asserting the Crown had two theories. There was an answer for that. '*The Crown does not present theories to you. The Crown has presented to you facts which on my submission proves this beyond any doubt.*'

About David's evidence, he wrote: '*When an accused gives evidence we may do one of three things: Believe; Reasonable; Reject.*' Presumably this means he can either be believed, he is reasonable, or you can reject his explanations and claims of innocence.

But it was not so simple in this case, Wright wrote, because '*the accused may even believe he is not the murderer*'. He may have amnesia and have forgotten that he killed everyone. '*He doesn't know that he doesn't know.*'

In the next breath he described David's evidence of loving his family and having considered suicide since being arrested as contrived — designed to '*tug at the heartstrings*'. It would appear he was still trying to have a bob each way.

He listed anomalies in the accused's evidence. The green jersey was his father's, but he told the police it was Arawa's. David had been vague about timing but precise in his statement to the police when he said he was at Heath Street at 6.40 a.m. and it took him two to three minutes to get home.

His recalled memory helped him, like explaining the blood on the duvet by saying '*the cat was there*'.

So whether his memory recall was genuine or feigned — '*whichever way he is still the murderer. You can't acquit him because he murdered and then had a memory loss of the killings.'*

It is said '*that loss of memory is the first refuge of the guilty mind*', wrote Wright.

'*The accused is an intelligent young man and whatever else he may be he is no fool.*

'*Don't have the wool pulled over your eyes.'*

He saved what many considered to be the best for last. He argued that David Bain had made a *slip* in his evidence when he said he heard Laniet making gurgling noises and this slip identified him as the killer. It is noteworthy that Wright did not cross-examine him at all on this so-called *slip*. Only the killer could have heard Laniet gurgling was Bill Wright's final message to the jury.

COTTLE

Guest was expected to complete his closing address that afternoon. But during the lunch break Cottle unexpectedly turned up at the court under rather dubious circumstances. He was arrested by the police for not having responded to the subpoena and thrown into the holding cells. Guest applied to have him give evidence even though the case was closed and the Crown had completed its final address. The judge's eighth and final ruling relates to that application.

Cottle was called into court in the absence of the jury and questioned by Wright, Guest and the judge. Perhaps understandably, he prevaricated and was generally unhelpful and evasive when questioned, because he was very unsure of what was going on, having just been arrested and not being legally represented.

The upshot was that the judge ruled against the admission of Cottle as a witness based on his own judgment of Cottle's 'appearance, demeanour, background and general conduct'. He concluded, 'Weighing all the matters I have mentioned I conclude that his evidence would not be reasonably safe or reliable.'

DEFENCE CLOSING ADDRESS

Guest summed up after the Cottle drama was over. Features recounted are taken from the judge's summing up, and the following matters were of note.

He emphasized very powerfully that there was no motive put forward at all against David. Neither was there any mental disorder that could explain him being the killer. He told the jury that *if* they accepted Mrs Laney's evidence that it was David she saw and it was 6.45 a.m. that she saw him, then he could not have been the person who turned on the computer. It must have been turned on by someone else, and that person was the killer.

Guest accepted that it must have been David who made the five luminol footprints, but said they could have been put there innocently when David walked about the house finding his family dead.

He did a demonstration with the gun showing it was quite easy for Robin to have shot himself. The judge, however, warned the jury to be wary of that demo as Guest was not an expert and he might not have had the various angles and trajectory matched up correctly. A big point was also made that if David wore the red sweatshirt found in the washing machine on his paper round then he must have done the washing as he said upon returning, not before the run, as the Crown case relied upon.

Guest argued that Bill Wright's claim about the gurgling went much further than Dr Dempster's evidence allowed for. The pathologist did not say that the gurgling must have finished when the final fatal shots were administered.

One would think Guest must have made mention of the bruising and skin injuries to David but if he did, it is not mentioned by the judge in his summing up to the jury.

So the jury went home for the weekend, having heard both sides' closing addresses but totally ignorant of Cottle and what he claimed Laniet had told him.

JURY DELIBERATIONS AND QUESTIONS

On Monday, 29 May Justice Williamson summed up and the jury retired at 11.45 a.m. At 5.23 p.m. they came back to court with four questions. The judge consulted with counsel to ascertain the appropriate extent of the answers.

The first was: '*The glasses found in David's/Stephen's room. Whose were they according to the optometrist?*' In answer the judge read to the jury the relevant extract from Gordon Sanderson's evidence: 'The prescription of the two lenses that fit this frame is similar to the prescription prescribed for the accused by Kate Bridgman in October 1992. It is similar but not identical. It is consistent with being an earlier prescription. When I first saw the lenses that is what I concluded.'

He then read David's evidence in chief and answers under cross-examination where David denied they were his, said they were his mother's and that although they were of assistance to him that was only in one eye and finally that he had not seen or worn them for about a year. The cross-examination passage included the question from Wright: 'You say he [Sanderson] is wrong?', to which David answered, 'Yes.'

The second question was: '*Did the police close any of the deceased's eyes?*' This was obviously a reference to David's evidence that his mother's eyes were open when he found her dead.

The judge answered the question by telling the jury that he was unable to answer the question except to say that none of the police who had given evidence had said that they did.

The third question was a request for the judge to read them Denise Laney's testimony.

The judge went out on quite a limb on this one. He reminded them that in his summing up he had read extracts from the evidence of Mr McConnell the paper distributor, Denise Laney but only as it related to times, Detective Thompson (who it will be recalled walked from Heath Street to 65 Every Street in a shade over two minutes according to his evidence) and from David's evidence about timing.

He said he had omitted to mention Tania Clark's evidence in his summing up so he proceeded to read her entire statement which is twice as long as Laney's. Only after all that did he read what the jury had actually asked for — Laney's statement.

The fourth question was a request to listen to the 111 tape again, which was they played to them twice.

THE VERDICTS

The 12 men and women retired again at 5.42 p.m. and it was eventually all over at 9.10 p.m. on that same day, 29 May 1995, when they came back with five guilty verdicts.

David fainted in the dock: Bruce Ansley wrote in the *Listener*, 'He paled, swayed, collapsed.'

In that article — from the *Listener*, 17 June 1995 — Ansley described the children, David, Arawa and Stephen, as 'happy, well adjusted ... They were the best tribute to the parents,' he wrote.

'The only unusual child in this family was Laniet,' Ansley went on. He wrote that he had learnt that she was 'on the game ... Was it something about Laniet that triggered the events of 20 June 1994? There is possibly yet another twist to the family's story. But Guest, who wanted to pursue this in David's defence, was prevented from doing so by the judge's rulings. The *Listener* can publish no details.'

The article went on to say that something must have happened that night to trigger the events. 'Money was withdrawn from the parents' cash point account at about 11 p.m. — the money was found beside Margaret's bed,' he wrote, 'which is one of the known abnormalities of the evening in question, the other being that Laniet was sleeping over.'

The final paragraph of this article reads:

'Something traumatic happened that night to trigger the killings. Perhaps Laniet was both catalyst and — *if it's true* that only the killer could have heard her gurgling — nemesis' (author's emphasis).

The jury, of course, knew nothing of prostitution; there was not one mention in the entire trial. Neither did they know that Laniet had told at least one person that her father had been committing incest with her for years, and that, if Cottle's evidence was correct, she was going home that weekend to tell her mother 'everything'.

SENTENCING

David was sentenced on 21 June 1995, one year and one day after he called 111, to life in prison with a minimum parole period of 16 years.

In sentencing him the judge confirmed the gravity of the jury's verdicts and the allegations that had now been proven.

'In the absence of any evidence of insanity, or of interference with mental functioning, the jury's verdicts in this case lead inevitably to the conclusion that David Bain killed the other members of his family deliberately, and with a significant degree of cunning and premeditation.'

In the space of 366 days he had gone from being a happy, productive and active young man to being one of the most reviled people in New Zealand's history.

PART THREE

FIGHT FOR FREEDOM

CHAPTER 10

POST-TRIAL DEVELOPMENTS

APPEAL

Guest announced almost immediately after the verdicts that he would appeal. On the day of sentencing — 21 June 1995 — David signed a Notice of Appeal and Guest filed it with the New Zealand Court of Appeal where it became Number CA 253/95.

The primary ground of appeal was the judge's refusal to admit Dean Cottle as a witness. In a letter to the Court of Appeal seeking confirmation that legal aid would be granted for the appeal, Guest argued the matter very forcefully.

> The accused argues that Cottle's evidence was so relevant and cogent that it ought to have been admitted, and that a miscarriage of justice has occurred as a result ... Such evidence could well have influenced the jury in his favour because motive was very much at issue at the trial in relation to either himself or his father being the killer in these homicides.
>
> There is a substantive matter to argue in the Court and the appellant should be entitled to be legally aided.

Legal aid was declined and Guest funded the cost of the appeal from his own resources.

There were three ancillary grounds of appeal that Guest accepted were in themselves insufficient to warrant the granting of a retrial, so in essence the appeal was founded on the Cottle issue.

Although the appeal was unsuccessful, there were a couple of matters of interest that eventuated from the hearing that bear on the future of the case.

Oral arguments were heard by the Court. Representing the Crown on appeal were John Pike and Bill Wright. Pike was a lawyer at Crown Law in Wellington who specialized in handling appeals on criminal matters.

Pike's submissions to the court included the proposition that if Laniet had said to Cottle that she was going home that weekend to tell her family about the incest with her father, 'Then that may have tipped the scales.' One cannot help but think that the Crown could not have been that convinced of their forensic evidence on the basis of that statement.

Bill Wright presented the Court with written submissions that included a bullet point summary of the Crown case. It reiterated the three planks on which the case was built and then dealt with each matter of evidence that it said proved the case.

Clause 4.2 of Wright's written submissions focused on the timing issues and were as follows:

4.2 The timings as given by witnesses who observed the accused on his paper run allowed for him to shoot his mother, two sisters and brother, complete his paper round and be home at 6.44 a.m. to switch on the computer and then shoot his father after he had entered the house:

(a) The papers were delivered earlier than usual that morning. Rackley had the paper at 6 a.m.; [it was] normally after that.

(b) Parker had his paper at 6.30 a.m. and was surprised by the early delivery and checked his watch. He had never had the paper before 6.45 a.m. in the past.

(c) The appellant gave evidence that he was at the intersection of Heath Street at 6.40 a.m. when he checked his watch and that it took two to three minutes to get home from there.

(d) Clark observed a witness [sic — the appellant] at the Heath Street intersection at 6.40 a.m.

(e) Thompson covered the distance from the intersection at Heath Street to the appellant's house in two minutes 15 seconds on one occasion and two minutes 16 seconds on the other.

(f) Laney observed some person at the gate of the house (whom she was unable to identify) at around 6.45 a.m.

(g) That the computer was switched on at 6.44 a.m.

You may recall that some passages were highlighted, pointing to contradictions in some of this evidence, in particular relating to Parker and Thompson's evidence. For present purposes, however, the matter of importance is point (f) of the submission.

The assertion that Laney '*saw some person ... whom she was unable to identify at around 6.45 a.m.*' seems to have taken Guest by complete surprise, because in his written response to the Court of Appeal in 1995 he wrote the following:

> There was nothing in the evidence of the paper run witnesses which clearly and directly put the appellant back in the house prior to 6.44 a.m. which was when the computer was turned on. Mrs Laney's evidence, read in full by the trial Judge in answer to one of the questions by the jury, clearly put the accused outside the gate at either 6.45 a.m. or 6.46 a.m. This evidence was unchallenged because *it was Crown evidence read to the jury. The defence does not accept for one minute that Laney had not been able to identify the appellant.* It was always accepted by the Crown that the person she referred to in her statement was the appellant and the Crown cannot now in submissions to this court attempt to fudge the issue by suggesting that Laney's evidence did not contain an identification of the accused.

Now this is rather interesting, for when one looks back to Wright's closing address notes, he specifically wrote that Laney could not identify the accused. He wrote: 'Mrs Laney — she passed at speed. Did not identify accused. Saw someone at the gate. Imp — He was back in the house before the computer was turned on.'

In his summing up the judge said that Guest himself had said: '*If* you [the jury] accept that it was the accused Mrs Laney saw', then he could not have turned on the computer and therefore could not have been the killer. This would seem to indicate that at trial it was not as clear as Guest would have the Court of Appeal believe. The alternative is that the judge put a question mark on Guest's submission which was not in fact a part of it. Due to the fact that the counsel's addresses were not recorded, it is not possible to resolve the matter.

It would seem, being as generous as possible to each of them, that

Bill Wright and Michael Guest had been operating on some kind of misunderstanding about witness Laney.

On 19 December 1995, the Court of Appeal declined David's appeal.

EVIDENCE DESTROYED

It did not take long for the various parties to swing into action. Just three days later, on 22 December, DSS Jim Doyle ordered that the slide containing a smear of blood from Robin Bain's left little finger (Exhibit 97) and his fingernail scrapings (Exhibit 51) were to be destroyed. These were the only samples collected from Robin Bain's hands and neither of them had been tested. He ordered that the destruction must occur before 26 January 1996.

APPEAL TO THE PRIVY COUNCIL

Guest resolved to go to the Privy Council and he enlisted the assistance of his law lecturer brother who resided in London. Official notice of this appeal was provided to the Crown on 31 January 1996, by Michael Guest's office.

DAVID'S FRIENDS

David became even more depressed and downcast than he was after the verdicts. Incarcerated as he was in the high security section of Christchurch Prison with the most vicious of offenders, he was barely coping.

David's friends, people who actually knew him, were incredulous that he was capable of the evil premeditation required to kill anyone, let alone his own family. They had witnessed first-hand the caring and loving relationship he had with his family. They could not accept the case as it had been presented.

It was one thing for a person to have some sort of psychological mental breakdown and 'snap', which then could not be remembered for reasons unknown (the missing 20 minutes scenario), but it was entirely another, they thought quite rightly, to plan to kill your family and have the cruelty and hardness of heart to intersperse a paper round in the middle of it for the purpose of normality, then to implicate your own father. On top of all that, they found it utterly preposterous that he could then carry off the pretence of being traumatized and innocent to all and sundry for the next 18 months. They could not reconcile all that with the mate they knew.

One of this group of friends was Kathleen Dawson, an elderly woman well known and respected in Dunedin who had been David's singing teacher for the past few years. Her husband John was a lecturer at Otago University and he had got to know David as well. The group was an eclectic bunch, young and old, male and female, single and married, but with a common view, very strongly held, that the young man they knew could not have done what was alleged. And they had the guts to follow through on their belief.

The group called themselves Friends of David Bain and set about working under Michael Guest's directions to raise the money for him to take the case to the Privy Council. Were it not for this group of people having the guts to stand up and be counted in the face of public ridicule, David Bain would almost certainly still be in prison today.

THE ESTATE

Also very busy since the trial were David's uncles Michael Bain and John Boyd, the executors of the Bain family estate. Most of the property had been realized. There was a sizeable amount available for distribution, however once David was convicted of the killings he was legally disentitled to the proceeds, which then fell to the next of kin.

However, distribution of the estate was delayed because of Guest's expressed intention to seek leave to appeal to the Privy Council in London. On 29 April 1996, the Privy Council declined an application for leave to appeal. This application was based solely on the Cottle admissibility issue. So even if the jury sitting in judgment of David Bain along with other observers (like Bruce Ansley of the *Listener*) may have been slightly bewildered by the fact that this seemingly decent young man was guilty of such an atrocity, guilty he surely was, according even to the highest court in the Commonwealth.

At the retrial in 2009, John Boyd gave evidence about the estate and its distribution, however the financial details were suppressed by order of the court. Subsequently David, through his lawyer, made a request to the trustees Michael Bain and John Boyd, that he be provided with the documents relating to the realization and winding up of the estate. The trustees replied through their lawyer that they had no difficulty in making the material available but they refused to revisit the issue of David's entitlement to the estate after his acquittal. Those documents indicate that a sizeable amount at today's values was available for distribution and that final distribution of the estates of Robin and Margaret was made on 31 October 1996. There was nothing of value retained.

CHAPTER 11

NEW DEFENCE TEAMS

1996

In early January 1996 I read an article printed in the *New Zealand Herald* featuring the efforts of the group known as the Friends of David Bain to which I have already referred. There was a photo of the group accompanying the article which explained their belief in David Bain's innocence and their campaign to raise money to have his case taken to the Privy Council in London.

At the time I knew nothing about the case. What struck me about the article was that a group of people would be so fired up as to get out on the street and publicly proclaim their belief for a friend. It was not as though this was a mother overwhelmed with emotion standing by her son. They could have no possible ulterior motive that I could think of and so I made contact with the intention of donating a few hundred dollars to their cause.

I contacted Michael Guest to ensure that the campaign was bona fide. He assured me it was and further piqued my curiosity by sending through a copy of the submissions made to the Court of Appeal by Bill Wright, along with his own response. In a covering letter with this material, written in his own handwriting and on his letterhead dated 17 January 1996, he wrote: 'I believe in his innocence or, at the very least, that a miscarriage of justice has occurred.'

Guest was anxious that I should meet David himself. This was something that had not even occurred to me. However, it so happened that I was visiting Christchurch later that month on unrelated business, and when Michael Guest found out about this he arranged a meeting for me with him and David Bain at Paparua Prison. We visited David together and then spent the evening and late into the small hours discussing the case and the reason he wanted to go to the Privy Council. The following day I visited David again.

GUEST/KARAM DEFENCE TEAM

Following those meetings I agreed to provide the funds for the Privy Council appeal to take place. It wasn't that I was convinced about anything on the case at that stage. I was relying mostly on Michael Guest's legal assertion and passionately expressed belief that there had been a miscarriage of justice. I was also by this stage intrigued to learn more and so the only condition I placed on this arrangement was that Guest would provide me with his complete file relating to the prosecution, conviction and subsequent appeal in 1995 at the Court of Appeal. Guest was not only quite happy with this but he also made me a member of his defence team and invited me to go to London with him to attend the hearing. He advised the prison that I was a member of the defence team so that I could visit David in that capacity. He wrote to David telling him that he was finding my input very helpful. He also invited me to Dunedin where I spent a few days with him and his staff discussing the case. I went to a meeting with the Friends of David Bain and learnt more about their strongly held beliefs.

It was at this time in February or March of 1996 that Guest packaged up all of the documents and witness statements disclosed to him by the police as well as the official court documents, photos and relevant correspondence relating to the depositions hearing, trial and appeal, and sent them to me in Auckland. There were about six boxes of documents.

By the time I set off to London to join him towards the end of April I had completed an initial analysis of these files and so I had become quite well versed in the case. Michael Guest and I spent a few days together in London and I felt that he was very defensive on a number of questions that I put to him as a result of my initial study.

The Privy Council declined the application for leave to appeal and Guest and his wife stayed on in Europe for a holiday afterwards.

Upon my return to New Zealand I went to Christchurch and over a period of three or four days had some extremely intensive meetings with David in prison. I interrogated him mercilessly, far more ruthlessly than the police could, due to Bill of Rights restrictions. I needed to make a decision whether to pursue the case any further, and I would not do so if I could not rely on David's word. I had enough information in my grasp by this time to lay traps for him. I wanted to satisfy myself as far as possible that David was telling the truth, as far as he could remember it at least. My sessions with him were so intense that at times he collapsed to the floor in tearful anguish.

MY DECISION

By this time I had serious concerns about aspects of the case and also that some matters of evidence had not been fairly represented during the trial before the jury. I had become particularly concerned about the accuracy of the timing evidence to do with when David got home and when the computer was turned on, aspects of the evidence about the glasses and also the allegation upon which the convictions were founded that David had planned and premeditated the executions. It also had struck me from information on the file but not in evidence that Robin's general state of well-being may have been much worse than the jury was led to believe. It seemed to me that as the proposition was that it was either one or the other, it must be important that all relevant admissible material about each possibility should have been before the jury.

You will recall that no evidence of an adverse nature about Robin's character was heard by the jury. And yet on the file there were a number of statements taken by the police themselves suggesting Robin was not in the best of health. For example, there was a statement from a friend of Robin's, Orphen Matches, taken just days after the tragedy. This man was a psychologist and he had said that the last time he saw Robin was a few months before his death. He described him then as gaunt, haggard and depressed. I could not understand why this evidence would not be relevant to a jury making a decision in such an important defended hearing.

The next step I took was to have long-lasting consequences. I made an appointment with the head of police in Dunedin, Athol Soper, and expressed my concerns to him. I presented him with a list of some 30-odd anomalies that I had gleaned from my reading of the file. The meeting itself was very cordial, but the outcome was not so pleasant. I had expected to be taken seriously. I had never been involved in the criminal adversarial process and naively thought that justice would be the overriding principle of all concerned.

A few days after this meeting Guest phoned me, back home in Auckland by then, and said he had just been advised that the police were intending to destroy all the remaining exhibits in the case. He wrote a letter of protest and so did I. I sent mine to the Commissioner of Police in Wellington as well as the Minister of Police. The legal equivalent, it seemed, of World War Three was set in motion.

At the same time, I was well aware of my own limitations in that I had no legal training or background in criminal investigation or procedure. I was out of my depth you might say. I was coming at the case from the point of view of a thirteenth juror and it seemed to me that a lot of relevant evidence had not been shown to the actual 12. But what to do about that was another question altogether. Obviously, seeking the police's cooperation was not going to get me far.

I also resolved that harping on about and relying on Cottle's evidence was futile. It was the hard physical evidence that needed to be examined. I have mentioned Guest's comment on the TV programme about having a 'quick flick' through documents. At this time I had not seen that programme, but it had already struck me that he was much stronger on rhetoric than he was on detail. He did not even know how the computer expert Cox had gone about calculating the turn-on time of the computer. So it seemed to me the case needed a fresh look from a legal and evidential point of view. David agreed with my reasoning.

I told him I would attempt to advance his case but there was one irrevocable condition to my continued support. That was that if I ever found that he lied to me on any matter whatsoever, that would be it. As far as I can establish to date, he never has.

WITHNALL/O'DRISCOLL/KARAM
1996

So, around June of 1996, I approached Colin Withnall, a long-standing QC in Dunedin. The outcome was that the Dunedin law firm of O'Driscoll and Marks replaced Guest as David's lawyers and they instructed Colin Withnall QC to act as counsel. Withnall had agreed to evaluate the concerns I had identified and provide an opinion as to whether, in his view, there had been a miscarriage of justice. The Withnall/Karam team began work. Our efforts were made very difficult because the police remained steadfastly uncooperative. In early December 1996, I was in Dunedin meeting with Colin Withnall for the last time that year. As I was about to leave his office I expressed concern that at the rate things were going in our dealings with the police, we were going to take years to unravel the case and I did not want to spend the rest of my life on this matter! What can we do to speed things up? I surreptitiously asked him, and, shrugging his shoulders whimsically in typical Withnall style, he coyly replied to the effect of why don't I write a book about it.

That was the first time any mention was made of a book and then one of those strange happenstances of life occurred: fate wielded its magic wand. I left Withnall's office and went back to my hotel to collect my baggage and head to the airport to fly back to Auckland, and while I was waiting for the taxi in the lobby a young lady approached me and introduced herself as the publicist for Reed Publishing. She indicated across the lobby to an elderly woman in a wheelchair and told me that this lady would like to meet me.

The woman in the wheelchair was one of the most amazing people I have ever met in any walk of life. June Opie is a New Zealander who is far better known overseas than she is in her own country. She had written a book titled *Over My Dead Body* in the 1950s, which had been a worldwide success and was translated into many languages. It recounted her experience as a young New Zealander on an OE who contracted polio while travelling in Egypt in 1957. She almost died, and then spent a considerable period of time in a steel box known as an 'iron lung' because it was the contraption that kept her lungs going and allowed her to breathe. For about two years she was able to move no more than one eyelid. The hospital gave consideration to letting her go, so bad was her condition.

But with incredible determination and an amazing spirit, she not only recovered and wrote this very moving account of her experience but also travelled the world, climbing mountains and traversing great rivers in the process. She became an inspiration for disabled people everywhere, but much to her chagrin was largely shunned in her country of birth. She lived in Australia and visited New Zealand once a year to see family and friends.

On the occasion I met her she had written further chapters to her original book, which was published by Reed Publishing under the title *Over My Dead Body: 40 Years On,* and was travelling with the Reed publicist promoting the book from her wheelchair. It is with great pride that I can say she befriended me. We became dear friends; she came to my home for dinner and another memorable outing was when I took her for a picnic at what she always said was her favourite spot in New Zealand: Piha beach. June died a few years later.

Anyway, the upshot of this chance meeting in December 1996 was that I had a meeting with Reed Publishers and came to an agreement with them to write a book about the Bain case. I can recall driving down to the stationery shop in Papakura and buying a number of pads and pens and settling down to commence writing in the week before Christmas of 1996. I did not own a computer in those days.

1997

In January 1997, as a result of Withnall's evaluation of my concerns as well as further evidence that had come to hand, Stephen O'Driscoll issued a public statement to the effect that Colin Withnall believed there had indeed been a grave miscarriage of justice due to anomalies and contradictions in the Crown case. The statement advised that a petition would be prepared and filed with the Governor General seeking the exercise of the Royal Prerogative of Mercy.

1997 was a tumultuous year. My first book on the case, *David and Goliath*, was published in April 1997. In that book I called into question a significant proportion of the evidence against David. The allegations in the book resulted in a joint investigation by the police and the Police Complaints Authority. Their report was released in November 1997 and it exonerated the police of any wrong-doing. Upon its release the Police Commissioner made a special award to Milton Weir for his role in the investigation and prosecution. The investigation was referred to by police authorities as a 'copybook' inquiry.

1998

On the strength of the findings of that report, in April 1998 defamation proceedings were filed against me by Milton Weir and Kevin Anderson in which they claimed about $500,000 in damages. Their claims arose out of allegations I had made in the book that aspects of the evidence they gave at David's trial were wrong. Their legal costs and other costs associated with the proceedings were met by the Police Association to the tune of about one million dollars.

In June 1998, a petition was filed with the Governor General seeking the exercise of the Royal Prerogative of Mercy. It comprised about 500 pages of submissions and attachments. It was very comprehensive and contained evidence which Withnall and I considered undermined virtually every aspect of the Crown's case.

2000

The defamation case finally got under way in June 2000 when a two-week jury trial took place in the Auckland High Court with Justice Noel Anderson presiding. I was represented by Julian Miles QC. At the end of the trial the judge presented the jury with a list of 19 questions they were required to answer in writing. They dismissed one of Weir's allegations and all three of Anderson's allegations on the basis that the words complained of in their natural and ordinary meaning and in the context of the book as a whole did not carry the meanings alleged by the two plaintiffs.

In respect to whether the book carried a meaning that Weir committed perjury at David's trial, they found that it did. They found that that meaning was an expression of opinion in a legal sense. They were then asked whether that opinion was based on facts alleged in the book, to which they also answered yes. Then came the critical question: 'Are such facts proved to be true or not materially different from the truth?' They answered yes to that question, which meant in effect that I was justified, by the facts contained in the book in expressing an opinion that Weir had committed perjury. The disastrous outcome of the case for the police had the effect of creating a maelstrom of support for me and my belief that David had been wrongly convicted. Weir and Anderson appealed the jury verdicts but lost the appeal as well.

Following the defamation trial, new evidence adduced during the trial relevant to the case against David was supplied to the Ministry of Justice in support of the application to the Governor General which was still ongoing more than two years after it had been lodged. By way of example, it was during cross-examination evidence at the defamation trial that Anderson said, 'If I had have been asked whether my watch was found to be approximately two minutes fast I would have answered it.' In the same passage he accepted that he prepared his brief of evidence and it was checked by Jim Doyle himself. Weir admitted under oath for the first time that he misled the jury about his finding of the lens and that his evidence about Photo 62 was wrong. (Julian Miles: 'Putting aside for one moment whether there was any intention by you to mislead the jury, can I suggest there is little doubt that on that issue the jury was misled?' Weir: 'The jury was misled as to where the lens was, yes.') He admitted to be 'shocked' to find out that Anderson's watch was checked and found to be fast and that he did not know of this until after the trial. Miles put to him further erroneous evidence about the paper run and asked, 'Just another police mistake?' To which Weir answered yes. Weir also admitted that a private investigator was hired on his and Anderson's behalf, with his agreement, to investigate into my personal life.

In December 2000 the Minister of Justice, Phil Goff, announced that the Governor General had ordered a hearing of certain issues in the case, under section 406(b) of the Crimes Act. The Orders were that the Court of Appeal should advise His Excellency as to whether the new evidence on four matters raised the reasonable possibility of a miscarriage of justice. They were: David's bloody fingerprints on the gun; David's whereabouts when the computer was turned on; Bill Wright's submission that only the killer could have heard Laniet gurgling; and the broken spectacles and lens found in Stephen's room.

2002

That hearing took place over five days in September 2002 at the Court of Appeal in Wellington where many Crown and defence witnesses were called for cross-examination. Colin Withnall QC and Stephen O'Driscoll acted for David at the hearing. I was involved in the preparation work for the hearing and I provided very substantial affidavit evidence but was not cross-examined. In December that year, the Court answered positively on the four issues and accordingly advised the Governor General that their inquiry led them to the view that a full appeal against the convictions was warranted. The petition to the Governor General had ultimately been successful.

2003

The Order in Council for a full appeal was made in February 2003. The appeal was heard, again over five days, at the Court of Appeal during September of that year. Justice Andrew Tipping was the presiding judge along with Justices Noel Anderson and Susan Glazebrook. By this time O'Driscoll had become a judge and so David was represented by Colin Withnall QC and Kelvin Marks, O'Driscoll's former partner.

On 15 December 2003, in the most unusual circumstances of a live television broadcast from the Court of Appeal, Justice Tipping announced the decision declining the appeal. The 60-page decision concluded that there were three points of evidence of such cogency that they proved David's guilt on their own. They were: David's statement to the police that only he knew where the key to the trigger lock was; the bloodstained condition of the rifle; and the fact that the 10-shot magazine was found on its edge beside Robin Bain's hand on the floor.

I was with David in the prison with my son Richard at the time of this announcement. David was totally distraught. I was simply incredulous and felt as though I had let David down. It was the worst moment in the whole case. Colin Withnall was shocked. We had worked so hard for nearly eight years together and after the previous hearing where witnesses' evidence had been exposed as misleading on a number of critical matters of evidence central to the case it was believed that David would at least be awarded a retrial. A reading of the decision left us feeling bewildered that some evidence that we considered vital was not even mentioned in the decision rejecting the appeal.

CHAPTER 12

APPEAL TO THE PRIVY COUNCIL AND RETRIAL

REED/MORTEN/KARAM

2004

In January 2004, about a month after the decision declining the appeal, Michael Reed QC called me. He had acted for me on a personal matter that arose when *North and South* magazine featured me on the front page of their March 2002 issue in a feature entitled 'Joe Karam's Magnificent Obsession'. I believed the article was defamatory of me and contained gross inaccuracies. I issued a defamation claim, which was settled prior to trial following a judicial settlement conference in 2004.

In the course of working with me Michael naturally became interested in the broader case itself. He read the 60-page decision handed down by Justice Tipping and was disturbed by it. He offered to take the case to the Privy Council if Colin Withnall and David were in agreement. They were both delighted, although David, understandably, had had enough of the justice system by that time.

The major problem for him was that with every effort sprang new hope and he had exhausted his capacity to cope with having that hope extinguished. But in time his strength recovered.

Paul Morten was, and still is, a barrister practising in Wellington. Reed and Morten work very closely and Paul had assisted Michael on the *North and South* case. Morten and I, under Reed's direction, began preparing submissions for a petition to the Privy Council in London.

And so another Bain defence team was born: Michael Reed QC, Paul Morten and me.

REED AND MORTEN TO THE PRIVY COUNCIL
2006

On 6 June 2006, this latest defence team presented a case to the Privy Council in London seeking special leave to appeal the decision of the New Zealand Court of Appeal delivered by Justice Tipping in December 2003. The Crown was represented at this hearing by John Pike who had also represented the Crown on appeal in 1995, at the Privy Council in 1996 and on appeal in 2003. As well as working with Michael and Paul on the submissions, I prepared a specific document (see Appendix B) for the Privy Council that identified factual inaccuracies and inconsistencies in the Court of Appeal decision. There was nearly one for each of the 60 pages. In a historical landmark decision, leave to appeal was granted.

PRIVY COUNCIL APPEAL
2007

The appeal itself was set down for a week in March 2007. Precisely the same evidence that had been before the Court of Appeal in 2003 was now before the Privy Council, with the exception of a minor additional affidavit regarding the luminol footprints. This was in order to clarify an ambiguity that had become evident from the Court of Appeal decision.

The same team — Reed and Morten — represented David. This time the Crown was represented by the Solicitor General himself, Dr David Collins QC. John Pike was his assistant. Kallum Croudis was there for the police. I had worked almost full-time helping Paul Morten prepare for the hearing and most nights during the hearing the team were hard at it till the small hours of the morning.

The Privy Council decision was delivered by Lord Bingham of Cornhill on 10 May 2007. The panel of the Board that conducted the appeal under Lord Bingham was Lord Rodger of Earlsferry, Baroness Hale of Richmond, Lord Brown of Eaton-under-Heywood and Sir Paul Kennedy.

The Lords of the Judicial Committee of the Privy Council granted the appeal, ruling there had been a 'substantial' miscarriage of justice. In respect to the three matters identified by the Court of Appeal as so compelling, the Privy Council was terse in its appraisal. In regard to the first point about the trigger lock they pointed out that 'the force of the point depends on three assumptions'. In dealing with the assumptions it noted that the court did not mention important evidence that might contradict the assumption. On the second point the Board pointed out that it was an argument that was not relied upon by the Crown at the trial or by the judge in his summing up and so the Board stated it was hardly likely to have been relied on by the jury. They concluded on this point: 'Whatever the merits of the point may be, it can hardly be fair to rely on it for the first time on appeal eight and a half years after the trial. On the third point they dismissed it almost with disdain. 'It must be very questionable whether the jury attached significance to this point.'

They summarized the three points thought so overwhelming by Justices Tipping, Anderson and Glazebrook with the single sentence: 'Neither singly nor cumulatively can these points fairly bear the weight which the third [Tipping] Court of Appeal gave to them.' I would draw your attention to the use of the word 'fairly'.

It had been a long road, and remarkably it still would have many twists and turns to go. But at the time it was euphoric for David, all his friends and legal teams who had worked so hard for him.

DAVID BAILED

Less than a week later, on 15 May 2007, in the Christchurch High Court, Justice Fogarty granted bail for David before a very large crowd of delighted supporters. By this time he had spent almost exactly 13 years in prison as a result of the miscarriage of justice. On that occasion, he was represented by a poignant coalition of Colin Withnall QC, Michael Reed QC and Paul Morten. As a result of the New Zealand Court of Appeal's decision in 2003, in my opinion his incarceration was more than three years longer than it should have been. Nevertheless, this too was a joyous moment.

RETRIAL ORDERED

The Privy Council had quashed David's convictions and ordered a retrial. They did not order David be released from prison as that application was not before them. However, in the same passage as ordering a retrial they stated: 'The order of the Board for a retrial does not of course restrict the duty of the Crown to decide whether a retrial now would be in the public interest. As to that the Board has heard no submissions and expresses no opinion.' The duty for this decision fell with the Solicitor General, David Collins, who had represented the Crown at the hearing and lost. He called for submissions from the defence and the police. In what the defence believed was a hasty decision he decided to press ahead with a retrial.

During this period I wrote a letter to Helen Clark, the then Prime Minister, and copied it to the Attorney General Michael Cullen and the Solicitor General. I exhorted them to consider other options that would serve the public interest much better than a costly, time-consuming retrial. I suggested a public inquiry similar to that which took place with Arthur Thomas, which would have the effect of putting the matter to rest once and for all, as a better option. One of the main reasons I gave in support of this was expressed in the following terms: 'The Crown has no reasonable hope of [obtaining] a conviction against David Bain.' I set out some of the evidential grounds on which I based that statement and concluded: 'The best they could hope for would be a couple of diehards hanging out and creating a hung jury. And then what?' I asked the Prime Minister.

I also pointed out in the letter that the trial was likely to last about 12 weeks and cost millions of dollars including millions in legal aid, which would be better spent on other deserving citizens. I also warned that many Crown witnesses and agencies would have their reputations indelibly tarnished. I did not receive a meaningful reply.

NEW POLICE INQUIRY

On 22 June 2007, about six weeks after the Privy Council decision and 13 years and two days since David came home and reported his family dead, the Solicitor General announced there would be a retrial. The police launched a new inquiry team led by the head of the Dunedin CIB, Ross Pinkham. His second in charge was Kallum Croudis, who had been continually associated with the case since the day he arrested David. The operation for the retrial was code-named Operation Huia and had up to 25 detectives working in it. Their first course of action was to set up and publicly promote an 0800 number calling for new witnesses. It may be thought that this was a desperate measure considering they had been investigating the case for 14 years. They also began a fresh series of further scientific tests.

DEFENCE COUNSEL: M. REED QC, H. CULL QC, P. MORTEN, M. KARAM

For the defence, Michael Reed QC was of course lead counsel. He invited Wellington QC Helen Cull to join the team. Apart from her vast experience in criminal law she was a leading authority on the new evidence act which had just come into force, and she assumed the major responsibility for arguing evidential admissibility issues in the pre-trial phase. These ranged from a number of pre-trial hearings before the trial judge, right through to the Court of Appeal and the Supreme Court. Her powerful advocacy in these forums along with her skill and acumen in cross-examination at trial proved invaluable.

Paul Morten was an indispensable member of the team. At the Privy Council he had been mostly responsible for the detailed written submissions at both hearings and he also shared oral submissions to the Board with Michael Reed QC. His detailed knowledge of the case, extraordinary capacity for quality work and skilled advocacy made up a formidable front bench.

There was a vast amount of behind-the-scenes work involved and so my son Matthew Karam, who was practising as a barrister in Auckland, became the fourth member of the legal team for the retrial, with responsibility for the background slog. In particular he assisted in the preparation of the cross-examination files for senior counsel Michael Reed and Helen Cull.

The huge volume of documents and electronic communications posed a logistical problem. The Auckland Branch of Duncan Cotterill Lawyers became the instructing solicitors and managed this problem with precision. Duncan McGill was the partner responsible and a member of his team, Richard Griffin, undertook most of the work. A meeting room at their Auckland offices became the dedicated war-room and by the time of the trial its floor-to-ceiling book shelves were overflowing with hundreds of Eastlight folders full of documents relating to the case.

CROWN LEGAL TEAM AND JUDGE

The Crown legal team for the retrial was led by the very experienced Auckland prosecutor Kieran Raftery. He was backed up by the Deputy Solicitor General Cameron Mander from the Crown Law Office in Wellington and Bill Wright's successor in Dunedin, Robin Bates. They had very significant horsepower in the back room of their respective employers, and of course the expert support of the New Zealand Police with all its resources.

Justice Pankhurst was the appointed judge for the new trial. The trial was shifted from Dunedin to the Christchurch High Court. Between September 2007 and the commencement of the retrial in March 2009 there were numerous pre-trial or interlocutory hearings at which he presided, as well as hearings before the Court of Appeal and the Supreme Court mainly to do with evidential matters. A complicating factor was that the law regarding evidence had been rewritten in 2006 in what is called the Evidence Act 2006 and many of the new provisions were being seriously tested for the first time in this trial.

THE RETRIAL
2009

Due to the highly public nature of the case, extra efforts were made in the jury selection process. About 2000 writs were sent out. The Christchurch Town Hall was engaged to accommodate the numbers for the first step in reducing them to the final 12. Hundreds of people turned up and a ballot was conducted. The number was reduced to 60 people. They were required to attend the court at the commencement of the trial for the final selection. Justice Pankhurst told them that if they had exposure to the case such as being associated with the police or connected to any party from either side and their name was called, they should advise him and he would rule whether or not the matter required them to stand aside. He also told them that the trial would last three months and they had to be sure they could put that time aside. The names were balloted again. Some challenges were made by both sides.

Finally, 12 people were selected comprising seven women and five men. One juror was retired. There were no jurors listed as unemployed and there were a range of occupations including managers and tertiary-qualified individuals and all had English as a first language. It is not an uncommon criticism of the jury system that juries comprise the unemployed and uneducated and so do not properly represent the community. But regardless of one's stance on this issue, this was clearly not the case with the jury empanelled to listen to the three months of evidence about to unfold.

David was required to enter his plea to each charge before the 12 people who would decide his fate. The television network cameras were rolling. He forthrightly stated, as he had done to Croudis almost 15 years earlier, 'Not guilty' to each of the five counts of murder as they were read out by the court registrar.

The Crown opened its case on 6 March 2009. Almost exactly three months later, after having heard from about 180 witnesses and listening to closing addresses of about four hours each from the Crown prosecutor and the defence, as well as the judge's summing up, also about four hours long, the jury retired to consider their verdicts.

THE VERDICTS

The announcement of the verdicts was screened live on television on the evening of 5 June 2009. The host of New Zealand's leading current affairs programme stood next to me in the hushed silence of the packed courtroom while we were all waiting for the jury to return. You could have heard a pin drop. He made a comment to me in a reasonably loud voice that I did not appear nervous like most others in the court. I responded to the effect that I had nothing to be nervous about. I had told the nation 13 years ago what the outcome would be if ever David had a fair trial.

A few moments later, a friend of mine was disembarking a flight on the other side of the world. The airport lounge television was broadcasting the *BBC World News* programme. A 'breaking news' flash hit the screen telling the world that David Bain had been found not guilty on all five counts of murder at his historic retrial.

The jury deliberations had lasted only about five hours and the verdicts were unanimous. The courtroom erupted into cheering and displays of emotion.

For Michael Reed QC special acknowledgement is due. Firstly, and possibly most significantly, he was disturbed by aspects of the Court of Appeal's decision and volunteered his services. Secondly, he personally proved more than a match for everything the might of the Crown could throw at him, whether it was in the pressure-cooker role of leading a team in such a demanding case or when he was on his feet as an advocate before judges and the jury. At a stage in life when he was becoming more selective in the quantity and type of work he would undertake, he took up the cudgel in the toughest battle of all that lasted nearly six years from when he picked up the phone and called me in January 1994. He and I worked together with Paul Morten and others throughout that entire time as intimately as two people ever could. The not guilty verdicts completed one of the greatest legal trifectas in New Zealand's history.

And so, at about 5 p.m. on 5 June 2009, just a couple of weeks short of 15 years since his family had been killed, David Bain was a free man without any record of criminal behaviour and in the eyes of the law as innocent as any other citizen of New Zealand and the British Commonwealth.

So now, surely, questions must be asked. Perhaps the main one being: what happened to Operation Every's 'copybook inquiry' and Bill Wright's proclaimed mountain of evidence built on three planks as he described? Could it be that rather than a fortress built on planks it was really just like the flimsy old proverbial house of cards?

PART FOUR

NEW EVIDENCE

CHAPTER 13

EVIDENCE ISSUES FOR THE RETRIAL

None of the new Bain defence teams had a problem with the first jury's verdicts on the basis of what they heard at the trial. The problem was with what they did not hear.

New evidence that impinged on the guilty verdicts was uncovered periodically over the years from 1996 right through until the retrial in 2009. Time and space do not permit an analysis of each stage of proceedings.

Just to put into perspective the volume of material generated over the years, consider the fact that the three main appeals, being the Court of Appeal hearings in 2002 and 2003 and the Privy Council appeal in March 2007, each occupied about a week of argument and dealt with a vast amount of evidence. Many lawyers would spend their entire career without spending a day in Appeal courts, let alone three weeks on one case alone. The appeal process was titanic in both the ferocity of the contest and the volume of new evidence considered.

The notes of evidence of the retrial comprise almost 4000 pages of typewritten transcript made up of about 1.2 million words compiled over a 12-week duration. This compares to 440 pages and three weeks for the first trial. There were about 100,000 pages of files disclosed to the defence under the discovery provisions for the retrial. There were about 50 decisions made in the lead-up to the retrial in pre-trial hearings relating to admissibility issues and other matters. The judge made over 20 formal rulings and many more off-the-cuff determinations during the trial itself.

With this volume of material in mind, it is easier to follow and appreciate the impact of the findings by dealing with the evidence on an issue-by-issue basis.

The Crown theory of the case for the retrial was pretty much the same as it was in 1995, but the evidence was markedly different, a major point that seemed to have escaped the attention of the police and prosecution when the decision to have a second trial was made.

Indeed, if one remembers that the Crown case at the first trial was predicated on three points of a triangle, to use Bill Wright's analogy, then unless they turned a blind eye to the evidence that had been submitted over the years and to the Privy Council, they must have known that each of those propositions had at the very best a tenuous hold on reality. But reality was never much a part of the Crown case against David Bain.

Rather, as will be demonstrated in the following chapters, that case which succeeded in 1995 and managed to hold on until 2007 while David languished behind bars was arguably predicated upon concealment rather than disclosure, arguments unsupported by the evidence, incomplete and defective scientific analysis, and in some instances, totally bankrupt logic.

RETRIAL EVIDENCE: PHOTOGRAPHERS

The evidence at the retrial began with a series of police photographers, which in itself was interesting because, as you may recall, in the first trial no photographers were called. However, now five police photographers took the stand and a sparkling array of booklets, video productions, animated graphics, a computerized display system, and about 3000 individual photos (compared to only 300 or 400 in the first trial) were introduced into evidence. No doubt this show of arms was intended to impress the jury by indicating to them that no stone had been unturned, no expense spared and there was nothing to hide for the Crown in the presentation of the case. Unfortunately for them, the superficial nature of the case was exposed right away once these witnesses were cross-examined. Disagreement arose between the photographers themselves about which photographer had taken which photos, when they were taken, in which order they were taken and even what they were intended to depict. Photographs apparently evidencing bloodstains became confused with those taken during police reconstructions using tomato sauce. The fact that for the most part no one had kept a record of the evidential basis for any photographs, and that the photographs were not time or date-stamped, meant that no one really knew what they were looking at.

Normally, in a case like this, the calling of photographers, draughtsmen and other technical people, who have not been involved in the investigation itself but rather are called to produce a specialist piece of evidence, is a matter of routine. Often, there would be almost no cross-examination of such witnesses and on many occasions their evidence would be admitted by consent for the record. However, on the opening day of the new Bain trial in respect of these five police photographers their evidence in chief occupied about 20 per cent of the time, the rest being subjected to cross-examination.

Some of the photographers insisted that they only took photos when they were instructed to by a police officer at the scene and it was the police officer's duty to record the taking of the photo. Those photographers said they had kept no records whatsoever of what they did or when they did it. Other photographers said that it was the duty of the photographer to keep a record in a notebook of what they were doing. In any event no records were found from anybody. At the time, the cameras used by the police did not have a date-time recording facility, which I'm sure must seem strange to anybody who owned a reasonable camera in 1994.

One of the police photographers had taken all of the video footage at the scene, amounting to just over one hour in total. An edited version of this footage had been produced at the first trial by Detective Sergeant Weir and shown to the jury. This edited footage contained a description at the end that it had been edited and produced by the photographer who took it. However, when this was put to him under cross-examination he denied having had anything to do with the editing. He said that it must have been one of the other photographers who did that. The other photographers could not remember having done it, though, so at the end of the day it was impossible to know how the one hour of footage became reduced and altered in sequence or by whom it was done.

The significance of this for the jury no doubt lay in the fact that the Crown placed great store on items that they found, when they found them, the condition they were in and their specific location when they were located. However, a close examination of the photos showed that the same item could be seen in a number of different places and positions. At times it was impossible to be sure where it actually was or what condition it was in when the police first arrived at the scene.

Then of course it will be recalled that when Weir and Hentschel did the luminol testing and found the bloody footprints, photographs were taken, but at the first trial Weir gave evidence that these photos did not come out.

One of the photographers questioned admitted to taking the photos and said that they did come out but they did not reproduce what could be seen in the dark glowing where the luminol had been sprayed. So evidence that they did not come out was not the entire truth and this aspect of Weir's evidence was brought to the attention of the jury at this point.

Weir's role in the proceedings as officer in charge of the scene investigation and one of the officers in charge of presenting the Crown case at the first trial will come under some scrutiny as the evidence at the second trial unfolds. It may be worth mentioning at this point that Weir was portrayed by the defence at the second trial as an untrustworthy witness. Some excerpts from Michael Reed's closing address will indicate the point. 'Then we come to Detective Weir. We know, and he's admitted, that he misled the first jury.' Then again: 'To assess Weir, you have to take into account a number of matters.' These matters will arise in due course, but having mentioned them Mr Reed then said to the jury, 'But do you believe him when he does that?' He also referred to exhibit number 1012 produced by the Crown which was the psychological report done for Weir when he left the police. Reed quoted from the report itself: 'Detective Sergeant Weir feels that he continues to be viewed with suspicion by his superiors ...' Reed made the point that Weir himself stated that his own superiors did not trust him.

Perhaps the most debated photographs in the entire trial were the fingerprint evidential photographs referred to by the fingerprint expert Kim Jones during presentation of his evidence about what he called David Bain's positive fingerprints in blood on the rifle. It struck the defence team that none of the photographers called by the Crown in this opening day of the trial had been responsible for taking these fingerprint photos. If the situation wasn't already enough of a shambles for the Crown, then it became much worse later on when the specialist fingerprint photographer was called, not by the Crown but by the defence, and his evidence contradicted that of Kim Jones.

The defence used the services of Peter Durrant, a forensic photographic analyst who lives near Christchurch, to help analyse the photographic record. He came to the attention of the defence in 1997 when his name was mentioned in the police/Police Complaints Authority report. The police had commissioned him to try to sort out the shambolic state of the photos and to look at specific matters that had been raised in *David and Goliath*. He had given evidence for the police in a number of cases and was highly regarded by them. However, they did not like what he found in 1997. They wrote: 'In the circumstances we are not persuaded by Mr Durrant's advice as it relates to shoe impressions.' Mr Durrant was less than impressed by that comment and eventually provided his expertise to the defence. His unstinting and highly professional work over the years and during the trial was of great service.

SURVEYOR

Next up, the Crown called the surveyor who had drawn up a plan of the house, Reece Gardner, whose evidence was admitted by consent at the 1995 trial. He was obviously very proficient at his work, yet he also was closely cross-examined. In fact his evidence in chief occupied just two or three pages whereas there were about 20 pages of cross-examination, because certain items throughout various rooms in the house appeared to be missing from the survey plans for no obvious reason. When questioned, the surveyor said that the plans were done according to instructions from the officer in charge of the scene, DS Weir. Almost without fail, the items that were missing were important to the defence, one particular example being a set of drawers in David Bain's bedroom with very sharp edges right beside the corner of the bed where David crashed down in front of Constable Andrew and had to be dragged past by Andrew afterwards. Another was a table in the computer alcove.

This opening barrage exposing the fundamental record as shambolic and inaccurate not only had the impact of undermining various matters of evidence, but also left the indelible impression that the Crown case might not be the open and shut proposition that Robin Bates had described in his opening address on the previous day.

If Kieran Raftery, Cameron Mander and Robin Bates were at all flummoxed by the turn of events with their first few witnesses, then what came next should have shaken them to the core.

JIM DOYLE GIVES EVIDENCE

On Tuesday, 10 March, the second day of the trial, just after midday, the former DSS who had been second in charge of Operation Every was called to the stand. It was only a few weeks before the trial that the defence was notified Doyle would be giving evidence at all, let alone at this early stage. It is quite unusual for the officer in charge of a case to give evidence at the beginning of a trial.

Interestingly, just before Doyle took the stand the Crown informed the judge that they might run out of witnesses to fill in this particular day because, they said, Doyle would only be on the stand for a few minutes.

Indeed, his evidence in chief took just a few minutes. However, he did not leave the stand until after 12 o'clock the following day and he was hammered by the defence on almost every aspect of the investigation and on many of the points of evidence from trial one.

Doyle had by this stage been retired from the police for some time, although he had maintained a close association with the officers responsible for the continued work on the Bain case. His brief of evidence was about half a page long and simply attested to the fact that he had transferred a few exhibits from Dunedin to the ESR in Christchurch sometime before the first trial.

You will recall that at the first trial his evidence in chief entailed him simply stating his position as a detective senior sergeant at the CIB. He was cross-examined very briefly by Michael Guest on two matters which the police had not called in evidence: the bank transactions at 11.30 p.m. on Sunday, 19 June, and Robin's diary.

This time, though, the defence had put a great deal of work into preparing the cross-examination, which incorporated a vast number of documents supporting its propositions — propositions which revolved around the allegation that rather than being a copybook inquiry the investigation was sloppy, incomplete and did not follow procedure as set out in the *Manual*, which resulted in a premature arrest.

Doyle had the good sense for the most part to 'fess up', as it were, when he realized that he was skating on thin ice. The cross-examination occupies approximately 100 pages of notes of evidence and by the time he left the stand on the third day of the trial the defence were confident that the case for the Crown was irretrievable.

As we traverse the cross-examination of Doyle, many matters of new evidence will arise that the reader will find difficult to follow. It was the same for the jury listening to the evidence, but, as with the jury, you the reader will gain a full appreciation as the new evidence unfolds through the following chapters. In particular, the references to the computer timing, Denise Laney's second statement, the footprints and incest allegations were raised with Doyle, and as you read them they will appear incomplete. Fear not, for the full picture follows later.

DESTRUCTION OF EVIDENCE

The first subject put to Doyle was the destruction of evidence. It was Doyle himself who personally ordered the destruction of exhibits just days after David's appeal had been turned down in 1995, before all avenues of appeal had been exhausted. At the time these exhibits were destroyed David still had available the well-worn path to the Privy Council as well as other avenues such as petitioning the Governor General. Doyle admitted that he gave the order to destroy evidence, and that the destruction was to be done before 26 January 1996. The date is fascinating, because it pre-dates by just a few days when Michael Guest filed documents and notified the Crown of his application to the Privy Council. The fact that he was going to do that would, of course, have been out there on the legal grapevine well before then and anyway was signalled by the public recognition of the fundraising efforts of David's friends. Doyle was unable to explain the significance of this instruction to complete the destruction of exhibits by 26 January 1996.

Among the samples destroyed on his orders were fingernail scrapings taken from Robin Bain (Exhibit 51) and a slide of blood from the left hand of Robin Bain (Exhibit 97). Furthermore, the records show that the computer had been given to Michael Bain on 19 January 1996. The computer was not produced as an exhibit for the first trial and by the time of the retrial it was no longer in working condition.

Doyle began to agree with the defence propositions on a regular basis.

Q: Your case has always been that Robin came into the house, knelt in front of a curtain and was shot by David Bain, that's been your case, hasn't it?

Doyle: That's the Crown case, yes.

Q: That means he can't have gone into any of those rooms and got blood on him, it means that, doesn't it?

Doyle: Correct.

He accepted that Exhibit 97 was a slide containing a smear of blood removed from the left little finger of Robin Bain. He agreed that there was a smear of blood on the heel of the thumb of Robin Bain's left hand that had never even been collected in the first place. He accepted that neither of these smears of blood was photographed. He conceded that if any of the blood on Robin Bain's hands had come from Stephen Bain then 'big questions would have to be asked'. He agreed that samples and exhibits such as those under discussion should not be destroyed until after the appeal process is complete. He accepted it was very important to know where the blood had come from and that now, despite all the advances in DNA technology, it is impossible to test this blood because it was either not collected in the first place or it had been destroyed at the soonest possible opportunity on the instructions of Doyle himself.

Michael Reed pressed Doyle about the source of the blood. Doyle hedged, ducked and dived as best he could. Eventually, it came down to this:

Q: Put into common sense terms, you didn't know where it had come from, did you?

Doyle: That's correct.

Q: Unexplained, another way.

Doyle: Unexplained.

Still Michael Reed persisted, wanting to know what Doyle would say if the blood had been saved, had been tested and was found to be Stephen Bain's blood. After a verbal tussle, Doyle agreed it could mean Robin had been involved in the homicides, but then he lamely added: 'It could have got there by someone else putting it there.'

POLICE PROCEDURES

Reed moved on to the *Manual* and the roles and responsibilities that are designated to various officers involved in a murder investigation. Doyle agreed that in many important respects the procedures laid down in the *Manual* were not followed. The crime scene was not original by the time the officer in charge of the crime scene got to the scene. Gunpowder residue tests were affected because the hands and clothes were not protected as they should have been.

Doyle acknowledged that from a very early stage the police were well aware that timing was a very significant and important feature in investigating this case. Reed, in questioning Doyle about the police understanding of timings on the first day of the inquiry, said: 'It was important very early on, wasn't it, as to the timing of David's return to the house and the timing of the computer switch-on?' Answer: 'Correct.' A few more details followed and then Reed said: 'So the point is that both Weir and you knew from an early time the importance of the switch-on time and the arrival home time, correct?' Doyle: 'Correct.' He said that 'Probably sadly', no time base was established so that detectives' watches were set to the correct time. On this point it will be remembered that Wright had relied on David's statement that he was at Heath Street intersection at 6.40 a.m. That was according to David's watch. The police admitted in the retrial that his watch was never checked for accuracy either.

He agreed that the *Manual* states that skin from around a bullet wound should be cut out and preserved. This is more especially so when the shot is possibly self-inflicted. He did not know if this was done for Robin Bain and accepted that the carpet where the footprints were found should have been retained but it was not; it went up in flames with the house. The photographic record should have shown all the blood on Robin's hands; he agreed that it did not. More on this later.

All of these matters and more were accepted by Doyle as standard procedures that were not followed; that these procedures were set out in the *Manual* of the day. Even if they weren't, common sense would tell you that they should have been done.

As a matter of interest, the much hailed police/Police Complaints Authority report of 1997 which proclaimed Operation Every to be 'copybook' stated in its introduction: 'The basic investigative procedure is laid out in the Detective Manual and is invariably closely followed in every instance.'

On and on it went. Nearly every important aspect of the inquiry was admitted to have been defective in some way or another.

Doyle agreed that once David had been arrested the focus of the inquiry shifted away from Robin and on to David, a significant understatement.

When questioned about the turn-on time of the computer, he claimed that the significance of this had bypassed him at the time of the first trial. He was well aware of the new evidence put before the Privy Council about the timing and admitted that the fact that Anderson's watch was two minutes fast but that Cox was never told 'was shocking'. He agreed that the turn-on time should have been 6.42 a.m., not 6.44 a.m. as put to the jury in the first trial.

He agreed that a second statement confirming it was David at the gate was taken from Mrs Laney on the instruction of the Crown prosecutor Bill Wright. He agreed it was not given to the defence but that it should have been.

Both these matters (the timing and the statement) are explained in a later chapter.

This was not a trite, nit-picking cross-examination aimed at merely sowing seeds of doubt. The questioning and answers actually dissolved the integrity of the police case and exposed the inquiry as one-sided. Reed, with screeds of notes in front of him including manuals, job sheets, statements and excerpts from previous evidence piled on his desk, was well prepared and relentless.

Doyle confirmed that when Dr Pryde examined David Bain on the first day of the inquiry at the CIB he strip-searched him as a standard procedure. This was relevant due to the police having located a new witness who claimed to have seen scratch marks on David's chest on the day of his arrest. This witness, like so many other new ones that the police found for the retrial, seemed to materialize out of thin air after the Privy Council decision quashed the convictions.

But back to the witness stand, with Jim Doyle working hard to maintain his equanimity.

Q: The detective manual provides that before the bodies go to the morgue hands and feet are to be covered with plastic bags, and place the body in a plastic sheet to avoid losing evidence, correct?

Doyle: Correct.

Q: Not done, was it? Not done.

Doyle: Not done on all the bodies but done on some.

Q: Which ones was it done on?

Doyle: I'm not sure.

Q: On arrival at the mortuary it is a requirement that the plastic sheet is taken possession of in which the body is conveyed to the mortuary so residue can be tested. Correct?

Doyle: Correct.

Q: Not done.

Doyle: I'm not aware of it.

To illustrate the appalling quality of the investigation and the resulting disadvantage to David, consider this: in the case of Robin Bain no protection was afforded his hands, feet or clothing, even though at the time his body was removed he was the prime suspect.

In the case of Arawa, the initial procedures were done correctly, but then the plastic bags and body container were discarded without ever being sent to the ESR for examination. It defies belief. To make matters worse in the case of Arawa, Dr Dempster collected scrapings from her fingernails but these were destroyed without ever being examined. Arawa was up out of bed and may have confronted her assailant! There may have been debris or material under her nails confirming the identity of that assailant.

But back to Doyle on the stand on 10 March 2009.

Q: None of these measures were done for Robin Bain, are you aware of that?

Doyle: I am aware of it now, yes.

Q: Once again you see when it comes to Robin and the ability of the police or the defence for that matter to evaluate whether Robin was the killer, each time either the evidence is thrown away, it is lost, destroyed, that's what happened, isn't it? Why is it always with Robin this happens? Because you just didn't bother, did you?

Doyle: I didn't deal with Robin. You have to ask the detective himself.

Questioning then moved on to the carpet where the footprints were found.

Q: Attempts were made to photograph them but not very successfully, correct?

Doyle: Correct.

Q: But what you didn't do was cut out those parts of the carpet and keep those bloodied sock print parts, you never did that, did you? Well, we know you didn't, Mr Doyle.

Doyle: Mr Weir would have to comment on that, I am, I don't recall them no.

Q: But being the officer in charge and, looking back on it, that certainly should've been done for such an important bit of evidence?

Doyle: That's why I'm hesitant, I thought it had been done.

Q: You thought it had been done?

Doyle: Yes.

Q: Well, that's the answer, isn't it? It should have been done.

Doyle: I agree.

Q: But now we are left with arguments, photographs that didn't come out, measurements and so on as to whose sock prints these are, that's where we're left now?

Doyle: Correct.

For the record, the carpet went up in smoke when the house was burnt down on 7 July 1994, 17 days after the tragic events.

ROBIN BAIN'S MOTIVES

Next Reed moved on to possible motives for Robin Bain, particularly as they may have been known to the police on the day they arrested David. Doyle claimed he knew of no motive for Robin, but then in the next breath admitted to knowing of Laniet's background as a prostitute and to the fact that she had been telling people that her father had been having sex with her for years.

Doyle's answer: 'This was a homicide investigation, Mr Reed, not an incest investigation, and that was our focus.'

To which Michael Reed responded: 'Exactly, there's the problem, Mr Doyle, throughout. You weren't prepared and didn't want to investigate Robin, did you? That's the problem.'

Doyle: 'If I can just clarify this. Detective Chief Inspector Robinson was the one who was directing inquiries at that point in time. Now if he had felt he wanted to take it down that line then that was up to him.'

Regardless of whose job it was, the propriety of deciding that the allegation of incest was unworthy of follow-up may be commented on by drawing a comparison. If an armed robbery took place and a person got shot and killed in the process, would the police say that it was a murder inquiry, not a robbery? The murder happened because a robbery was planned.

During the evidence submitted by the Crown at the retrial, whenever a particular person got themselves into difficulty they would frequently blame someone else involved in the inquiry. Doyle's statement fairly and squarely puts the decision not to investigate background matters relating to Robin Bain or the family dynamics and Laniet's involvement in prostitution at the feet of Detective Chief Inspector Peter Robinson. But then Robinson would be relying on information from below, and we do not know what got to him and what did not.

Michael Reed continued to press on this issue, questioning Doyle about what inquiries had been made regarding Laniet's allegations that her father had been having sex with her. Doyle told the court that nothing was done because it 'wasn't appropriate' at that time.

Incredulous, Reed asked: 'How could you possibly say that Mr Doyle?'

The response was revealing.

Doyle: On the second day of the inquiry it wasn't clear if it was a homicide per se or a homicide/suicide.

Q: Exactly, thank you, so it wasn't clear?

Doyle: Correct.

Earlier in the cross-examination Jim Doyle had confirmed that not long after the trial he had made a public statement that 'not one iota' of evidence existed against Robin Bain. Michael Reed went on the attack, pointing out to Doyle that surely the fact that Laniet was a practising prostitute should have raised a red flag with the police sufficient to cause them to investigate the reasons for these domestic homicides. Doyle tried hard to skirt around the issue.

Q: So there was at least a red flag to be pursued?

Doyle: It was just another factor concerning the tragedy of the victim, I guess.

Q: You also knew there was blood on Robin's hands, which we have spent some time on, you knew that?

Doyle: Correct.

Q: You also knew that Robin had injuries to his hands?

Doyle: Correct.

Q: You also knew that 20 spent rifle shells had been found in the caravan that Robin was living in?

Doyle: Correct.

Q: Sorry — yes in the caravan, yes, and five of them were of the same subsonic bullets used in the killings, you knew that didn't you, fairly [early] on?

Doyle: Correct.

Some further questions followed and then Reed said: 'Right, you also found blood on a hair in the Commer van, we have discussed that and you didn't know what happened about that, correct?'

Doyle replied: 'Correct.'

Michael Reed made the point that all of this information was collected and relayed to Doyle as the effective officer directing inquiries in the investigation. It was he who decided to arrest David.

Doyle agreed that it was, but said: 'A lot of this documentation that you are talking about would not have come and been in my possession necessarily at the time that the decision was made for the arrest.'

That statement in itself is an admission of what was expressed as the primary contention of *David and Goliath* in 1997 that the arrest was made in haste, based on untested and unproven assumptions and therefore prematurely; that is, as Doyle just said, before the pertinent evidence had been reviewed.

In response Reed asked: 'And if you found evidence that contradicted your decision to arrest you have a duty to change your mind?'

Doyle replied: 'Most certainly.'

Reed recounted the evidence — the time of David arriving home, the time the computer was turned on, the bloody footprints — and challenged Doyle that no follow-up was done whenever anything pointed to Robin.

Q: They obviously had to be followed up, didn't they? Or did you just cast him out of the equation early on? Which is it?

Doyle: I think that the thrust of the inquiry moved away from Robin towards David. That's fair to say.

TIMING ISSUES

It was then back to examining the timing evidence and the evidence of Denise Laney in more detail. In stark contrast to Doyle's earlier claim that at the time of the first trial he was not aware of the significance of timing issues, he agreed that both he and DS Weir knew from early on (in fact on the second day) the importance of the switch-on time of the computer and David's arrival home time. In answer to this proposition, Jim Doyle gave his by now standard answer: 'Correct'.

Doyle agreed that he was jointly involved with prosecutor Bill Wright in deciding to re-interview Denise Laney. He agreed that he read the statement at the time and he agreed that the statement firmed up the identity of the person and also that the time was set as 6.45 a.m. The relevance of this admission and the following one about the turn-on time of the computer will become apparent in the following chapter.

He agreed he knew of the error in Detective Anderson's watch, but claimed that he didn't realize its significance. Doyle was on the ropes. Reed probed further.

Q: And the jury were told that the time difference between 6.44 and 6.45 when he was seen — and remember the second statement was not given to the jury — meant that the police were able to fudge that timing of David's return home and the computer going on. That's what happened by not telling the jury that, of both matters. Correct?

Doyle: There was certainly some confusion for the jury on that occasion.

Q: Well, it wasn't confusion. They didn't know of the confusion, Mr Doyle, that's the point. They were not told of it, were they?

Doyle (very hesitantly): Agreed.

Q: So don't talk about confusion of the jury; it was your confusion, wasn't it?

Doyle: That … the significance of it did not … was not apparent to us at that stage. Otherwise I would have taken the matter further.

The point was made. The veracity of Doyle's assertion that the significance was not apparent, based on his testimony cited earlier, must at the least have a question mark hanging over it.

ROBIN BAIN'S STATE OF MIND

The questioning moved on to the issue of Robin Bain's emotional and mental state leading up to and at the time of the tragedy. Doyle was presented with an affidavit sworn by Mr Cyril Wilden, a specialist psychologist working for the Department of Education who had been attending the school in the months leading up to the tragedy and who spent the entire week of 20 June 1994 at the school. Among other things, this affidavit claimed that he had been interviewed by the police during that week. Doyle said that he had never seen a copy of the statement given to the police by Wilden in the days after the killings. In fact, the defence had never seen a copy of it either.

FOOT SIZE ISSUE

Doyle was then questioned as to why the police allowed the false impression about the size of Robin's foot to go before the jury. You may remember from evidence given at the first trial that the jury did not hear evidence of the size of his foot. Rather than evidence of Robin's foot length they produced evidence of his sock length and then Bill Wright made submissions that Robin's foot was too small to have made the footprints based on the sock size. Doyle's response was to say that he would have been relying on advice from the ESR scientists in relation to the best evidence on the matter. This is another explanation that defies belief, as we shall see.

DAVID'S INJURIES

Next, it was David's injuries. After some searching questions Doyle reluctantly agreed that it would have been very likely that a person in David's asserted position, finding his family dead, may well have fainted at some point and in doing so banged his head or scraped his knee. He also agreed that it was quite possible that stumbling about the dark house, going up and down stairs, could have been a likely explanation for the very minor bruising and minor graze that David had sustained to his knee.

Jim Doyle also accepted that the very light smears of blood on David's shorts and T-shirt could have got there while stumbling about the house finding his dead family or when he was in the laundry.

LENS

Michael Reed then addressed the lens found by Milton Weir in Stephen's room that was shown to the jury in the first trial in Photograph 62.

> *Q:* It was discovered by Mr Karam after consulting photographic experts that what was in the photo was not a lens at all. It was a reflection, remember?
> *Doyle:* Correct.

A few more questions followed and then:

Q: And I think you were shocked later to find, weren't you, that the photo
   that had been produced was actually not a photo of a lens at all?
Doyle: That is correct. It was a specular effect.

Jim Doyle agreed that the Crown theory relating to Robin's death was that
David came home and hid behind the curtains, lying in wait to shoot his
father when he came in to kneel and pray.

Q: And the case put forward by you was that Robin was kneeling down
   near the curtains when he was shot.
Doyle: Correct.
Q: That evidence depended upon some scientific testing and measure-
   ments.
Doyle: Correct.
Q: To establish whether you thought he was kneeling or not?
Doyle: Correct.
Q: If evidence is given showing that could not have been the case
   scientifically, what would your reaction be to that?

Justice Pankhurst intervened and did not require Jim Doyle to answer
this question. However, the point had been made in front of the jury. The
jury were then on alert to look out for evidence about how and in what
circumstances Robin Bain actually died.

It was getting close to the end now. Any thoughts that the Crown had a
strong case had been seriously shaken over the past 24 hours, in the first few
days of a three-month trial.

CHERRY-PICKING

Another matter of concern to the defence at the second trial regarding the
prosecution case was that they had cherry-picked the evidence to suit their
own case. This proposition was based on the fact that many of the witnesses,
about one third in total, called by the defence at the retrial, who contradicted
police and Crown witnesses and the Crown case theory, had originally been
interviewed by the police themselves.

As an example of this manifest cherry-picking, a couple of statements
were put to Jim Doyle. The first was from a local Dunedin resident who gave

a statement to the police on 21 June 1994. The witness described himself to the police as a good friend of Robin's who had known him for a very long time, and he said that when he saw him recently he appeared 'cadaverous, white and gaunt, and seemed depressed'.

The second witness statement put to Doyle was also made to the police on 21 June 1994, and the witness in this case was a registered psychologist. He had also known Robin for quite some time and told the police on that Tuesday after the killings that he had seen Robin quite recently and that he had been dishevelled and looked terrible. He described him as looking 'haggard, grey and depressed, much older than his age'.

Jim Doyle accepted that these statements had been taken by the police and that he did not know of any follow-up action that resulted. In this retrial, the Crown case was that it was a defence fiction that Robin was depressed. At the first trial, depression never even got a mention. Did they remain in hope that the defence would not call these witnesses?

Jim Doyle confirmed that he had been aware that Robin Bain had lived in an old van in a paddock near the school for about three years. A photo of the van was put up on the computer screens for counsel, the jury and judge to view. It was derelict and had no ablution facilities.

The Crown case had always been that Robin was a proud man who was in good spirits, a teacher highly regarded by all of the children and the Board of Trustees at Taieri Beach School, and this had been confirmed in Robin Bates' opening address. The picture presented of Robin Bain by the time Jim Doyle's testimony was finished on just day three of the trial starkly contrasted with that image.

The cross-examination concluded by making the point that the police simply did nothing whatsoever to investigate the allegations that Laniet had been making about her father relating to criminal sexual behaviour with her since she had been a child.

Q: With regard to the allegations that Robin was in an incestuous relationship at least with Laniet, you really didn't follow up those allegations at all?

Doyle: No I didn't. The thrust of that inquiry or the total direction of the inquiry in respect of that matter is a matter for the officer in charge, Mr Robinson.

Q: But you did make a comment I believe, didn't you, from memory on a TV interview you gave that it really wasn't for you to go knocking on doors everywhere, words to that effect, didn't you?

Doyle: That's correct.

Q: But you knew where Laniet had been living in Russell Street, Dunedin. You knew she'd been there?

Doyle: Correct.

Q: Isn't it normal to make some inquiries in the area where someone had been living?

Doyle: She had moved out of that area sometime prior, I can't recall exactly when but I know inquiries were made at the flat. I don't recall how extended they were around the area.

Q: But you see the local dairy owner from where Laniet bought groceries and so did Robin Bain; he was never interviewed, was he?

Doyle: No.

Q: And yet when Mr Karam spoke to him he gave evidence of what Laniet had said about incest and a relationship with the father quite openly, didn't he?

Doyle: I don't know the circumstances of Mr Karam's introduction to Mr [name suppressed] or the dairy owner, but he certainly did speak to Mr Karam, yes.

Q: That dairy owner has even gone so far as to be interviewed on TV … you've seen that interview?

Doyle: I may have, I can't recall it.

Q: I'm told it's connected with the same interview that you gave on the same sort of programme. Did you not see that programme?

Doyle: I may well have done but I can't recall it.

These were the final words of this cross-examination.

Re-examination was something of an anti-climax, a rather forlorn effort at trying to save face over the destruction of samples and nondisclosure of the exculpatory evidence contained in Denise Laney's second statement.

PETER ROBINSON

Later that day, after a couple of neighbours of the Bains had given evidence, Peter Robinson himself was called to the stand by Raftery. At the time of the murders he was head of the Dunedin CIB, and officer in charge of Operation Every. After nearly 15 years, he would give evidence for the first time, as he did not take the stand at the first trial.

His evidence was a very brief statement attesting to the movement of exhibits in the same fashion as Doyle's. Robinson told the jury that on 9 March 1995, just two months before the first trial, he took items of clothing from David, along with the heavily bloodstained green towel from the bathroom and two pieces of skin found in Stephen's room, to a Melbourne laboratory for DNA testing.

He also told the jury that he had not attended the first trial at all, and that he retired from the police on 7 June 1995, just a few days after the verdicts.

He appeared rather uneasy on the stand, no doubt wondering what he might face after the grilling his second in charge Jim Doyle had received. The Bain defence team could have kept him on the stand for a very long series of questions as well, but decided it was largely unnecessary. So much harm had been done to the Crown case through Doyle that another assault on Robinson — who by now had been retired for 14 years and was looking suitably like an elderly statesman — may have been seen as vindictive overkill.

It was decided to simply reinforce the defence contention that this was a one-sided investigation that lacked integrity. Robinson confirmed that the reason he had taken the samples to Melbourne was that the laboratory there had more advanced DNA technology than was available in New Zealand at the time. It was then put to Robinson that he did not take to Melbourne the two samples taken from Robin Bain's hands, Exhibit 51 the fingernail scraping and Exhibit 97 the smear of blood from his little finger.

Robinson agreed that these were not taken.

Michael Reed wanted to know why. 'But the fingernail scrapings in a homicide case where the fingernail scrapings show a red substance might alert a detective, mightn't it, to the fact that it ought to be tested for blood?'

Robinson: Ah yes, yes it could.

Q: Well, why wasn't that done?

Robinson: I don't know.

Q: Then we had blood from the hand of Robin Bain that's unexplained.
Wouldn't it have been wise to test that blood to see whose it was?'

Robinson: In hindsight, yes.

Robinson was probably fearing the worst at this stage, but with that Reed sat down and so, no doubt to his great relief, after just a couple of simple questions from Raftery in re-examination, he was free to distance himself once again from the Bain case.

With the benefit of hindsight, it would have been interesting to have explored with Robinson two matters which Doyle had passed off as being his decisions: firstly that the inquiry would not investigate the incest allegations and also that Robinson was ultimately responsible for the decision to charge and arrest.

And so, with the number one and two officers responsible for the investigation that led to the miscarriage of justice suffered by David Bain all those years ago having confirmed nearly every allegation made against the Crown case, the scene was set and it never got any better for them. The officers in court from Operation Huia must have rued the day they ever set about trying to uphold the efforts of their predecessors in Operation Every.

It was a real bonus for the defence to have these two witnesses available at such an early stage. They confirmed the defence's long-held, publicly expressed view that the investigation was bungled, one-sided, incomplete and did not follow procedure, the combination of which caused aspects of the evidence to be presented to the first jury in a distorted or otherwise incorrect manner.

CHAPTER 14

TIMINGS AND ALIBI ISSUES

TROUBLE WITH TIMINGS

In Bill Wright's notes from the first trial, he had written that 'the timings were tight'. He was referring to his ultimate theory that four were killed before the paper round and Robin afterwards. Scrutiny over the years revealed just how tight they were. By the time the retrial was over it was shown they were not just tight, they did not fit any better for that theory than they did the original scenario of all the deaths happening during the 'missing 20 minutes'.

The reason the first theory was dropped was because on the Crown's own evidence it did not fit. There were a number of facts that could not be reconciled. The first was that the washing could not be done until after the killings of Margaret, Arawa, Laniet and Stephen. On the original belief that they were killed by David after the paper round, the wash could not have been put on before about seven o'clock, leaving insufficient time for it to be finished by the time the police came in at 7.35 a.m. Secondly, it meant that David would have had to turn on the computer to write the message before he began the killing spree, a proposition inconsistent with someone snapping or going troppo so to speak. Thirdly, it meant that Robin would almost certainly have been up and about inside the house during the killings and when the clean-up was going on. David remained on the phone the entire time from 7.09 when he called 111 until the police made entry, meaning he could not have been downstairs fiddling with the machine or cleaning up during that time. An unknown in all of this was the size of the gap between when the first four were killed in relation to Robin.

Timing-related evidence therefore relates to the following questions:

1. The time of death of the five deceased and, just as importantly, the sequence of deaths and whether or not there was any evidence to

suggest significant gaps between the deaths of various individuals.

2. The time David left home to start his paper round and, more importantly, the time he returned from his paper round.

3. The time the computer was turned on.

4. The age of bruises and abrasions found on David Bain's forehead and knee and on Robin Bain's hands.

5. The time it took for the washing machine to complete a cycle.

Items 2 and 3 above represent what has become known as 'the alibi' evidence.

It was discovered over the years and brought out by the defence at the retrial that the evidence at the first trial to get these timings to fit the scenario that David began his killing spree at about 4 a.m. was not a complete version of the evidence at all.

TIME OF DEATHS

The first significant omission from the first trial evidence came in regard to when the individuals may have died or, putting it in other terms, the time and sequence of deaths. Remember that the expert in this field, with the correct equipment to conduct tests aimed at establishing a time of death, was Dr Dempster, but because he was not admitted to the house until after noon that day, he said there was no useful purpose in carrying out those tests by that time because rigor mortis had set in.

However, Chief Ambulance Officer Craig Wombwell checked all the bodies at about 7.45 that morning and his evidence at the first trial was that Robin's body was warmer than he expected and that the other four bodies were all the same — cooler than Robin. 'Cool but not cold' was how he described them in evidence.

For the retrial, the defence had very thoroughly reviewed and analysed the documents relating to the case, and so was not susceptible to being ambushed as Guest was in 1995. Wombwell was witness number 10 in the Crown's case. They had barely recovered from Doyle's admissions and Robinson's concession. A statement Wombwell had made to police on 30 June 1994 was put to him by Michael Reed. He agreed in evidence at the retrial that he had told the police that the other four bodies were 'still relatively warm' but not as warm as Robin's and that in his view the deaths had all occurred in the last hour and a half. He also said in regards to the fatal bullet wounds: 'My thoughts were that the wounds were relatively fresh'. He also agreed that the other four bodies were the same warmth as each other. Notably, Cameron Mander in re-examination for the Crown did not venture into the realm of the time of deaths or warmth of bodies. Bill Wright's notes from his closing address stated the other four bodies were 'cold as compared to Robin — they were killed sometime earlier'.

On the basis of Wombwell's evidence, the deaths had occurred sometime between 6.20 a.m. and when David called 111 at 7.09 a.m. David was out on his paper round from 5.45 a.m. until 6.45 a.m. and as he can't have done it after he got home then the deaths must have occurred while he was away.

However, at the time of David's arrest, Wombwell's evidence would have supported the theory that David had been the killer during the 'missing 20 minutes'. One can only presume that if the Crown had run with this theory at trial, then Wombwell's evidence would have been along the lines of his original assessment, that all had died in the past hour and a half and were still warm.

It is accepted that pinpointing the precise time of death is a difficult area even for highly trained experts. However, in this case there are some inferences that are very compelling, based simply on common sense and the circumstances of the day.

The temperature on 20 June 1994 was approximately at freezing point, and inside the Bain house that morning it was probably even colder than it was outside as it was a very old, cold, draughty house with no insulation and no heating.

The bodies of Margaret and Laniet were tucked up in bed under blankets and duvets. Robin Bain was very heavily clad with multiple layers of clothing on his upper body and tracksuit pants, shoes and socks. Although Arawa was out of bed she was dressed in warm attire that covered her entire body except for her hands and feet.

Stephen, however, was found on the floor of his bedroom wearing only underpants and a T-shirt that was wrapped around his neck. To all intents and purposes he was lying naked on the floor. Stephen was a lean and lanky teenager who carried no extra body weight whatsoever and weighed only 52 kg.

On the Crown's ultimate scenario, Stephen had been killed at about

4 a.m. or earlier, which meant that by the time Wombwell checked his pulse he would have been lying almost naked on the floor for over three hours. Wombwell did not do any scientific core body temperature tests, but he did touch the skin of each of the deceased and he said that Stephen's body was 'warm to touch' and that the temperature of the skin felt very much the same as that of Margaret, Laniet and Arawa. Common sense would tell us that even an unharmed and fully alive 52 kg 14-year-old boy lying practically naked on the floor for over three hours in a freezing house would not be 'warm to touch'. This was confirmed at the retrial by Dempster and also by Dr Thomson in an interview conducted by the PCA in 1997, where they agreed that Stephen's skin in those circumstances would have cooled rapidly and much faster than the other bodies lying covered up in bed or fully clad in warm clothing.

Extrapolating further and considering that Stephen's body felt the same as the other three, then all four of them could only have been dead for a short time before Wombwell felt their skin, which is exactly what he said to the police when he made his statement at the time.

So to recapitulate on the time of death, three points are worthy of mention.

Firstly, Wombwell's language at the first trial regarding the relative warmth of the bodies altered the nuance of his evidence from that which was contained in the statement he gave to the police at the time. The words 'cool' and 'cold' were not contained in his initial statements. In those, he said they were still relatively warm, and warm but not as warm as Robin's. He also said that all five had died within the last 90 minutes or so. The use of the words 'cool' and 'cold' suggested a longer time gap, which provided the basis for Bill Wright to submit in closing that the other four were killed some four or five hours before Robin.

The second point is that this inconsistency escaped the attention of Michael Guest or, if it did not escape his attention, he for some reason failed to bring it to the attention of the jury. In his defence it might be said that he did not know what to do because he did not know what the Crown case actually was.

The third and the most critical point in the final analysis is that the best evidence of time of death is from the Crown's own witness, Chief Ambulance Officer Craig Wombwell. At the retrial, when his original statement to the police taken at the time of the tragedy was put to him, he agreed with it, from which it can be extrapolated that the deaths occurred while David was out on his paper round.

Finally, it is worthy of reiteration that all of the evidence recounted above is from Crown witnesses.

TIME OF INJURIES

Timing was also important as it related to the injuries to both Robin and David, relatively insignificant as they were. A brouhaha had erupted when Dr Pryde ambushed Michael Guest in the first trial with his claim that he could pinpoint David's injuries to between 1 a.m. and 6 a.m. that morning. He actually said that David's injuries could absolutely be ruled out as having happened after about 6 a.m. In his deposition statement, Dr Pryde had merely described the injuries as recent.

The evidence of Dr Pryde had been tweaked to support the new theory that David was involved in a fight with Stephen in the early hours of the morning, rather than after he returned home on 20 June 1994.

By the time of the retrial in 2009, Dr Pryde had died. The Crown wished to put his evidence from the first trial in as evidence for the second trial; however, his evidence relating to the age of injuries was ruled inadmissible. All experts had agreed in the intervening years that his assessment was outrageously over-precise. In fact, generic medico-legal literature makes it very clear that it is virtually impossible to age bruises or small abrasions any more specifically than having occurred within a 12-hour period, more particularly so when relying solely on visual assessment.

Turning now to Robin Bain's injuries, you will recall that at the first trial Dr Dempster had noted a number of bruises and abrasions on his hands and fingers. Dr Dempster's evidence was that they showed healing and other characteristics indicating they had occurred at least 24 hours before his death.

However, before the second trial a very interesting thing happened. It related to an injury on the back of Robin Bain's right hand between his wrist joint and knuckle which Dr Dempster had described as a 3 mm abrasion surrounded by bruising 20 mm in diameter. The first trial evidence did not include any specific reference to the age of this injury and the photograph produced by the police of the back of Robin Bain's right hand was taken at a very oblique angle under poor lighting, so the injury was virtually impossible to see. This is another example where an omission by the police worked to David's disadvantage.

Dempster discovered a bunch of photographs taken by his assistants during the postmortem examinations that had not been produced previously. One of these was a very high definition close-up photo of this particular wound on the back of Robin Bain's right hand and it was produced for the retrial. Even to the uneducated and inexpert eye it is obvious that there is no sign of healing around the quite noticeable abrasion in the middle of the bruising.

At the retrial, Dempster described this wound as having occurred between the time of Robin Bain's death and 12 hours before. This assessment was put to the other Crown pathologist Dr Thomson, who agreed with Dr Dempster. So here we have two Crown pathologists giving evidence at the retrial that Robin Bain suffered a significant injury on the fist of his right hand, after nightfall, between about 6.30 p.m. on the Sunday night and his death on the Monday morning. Imagine what the Crown would have made of such an injury had one been found on the back of David's right fist!

At the first trial, when the Crown said there was not one scrap of evidence indicating a link between Robin Bain and any of the killings, they were able to make such a claim only on the basis that this evidence and photograph were not before the jury.

It may well be that the Crown would argue that the differences in evidence between the first trial and the retrial, as they relate to the times of death of the deceased and the injuries to Robin and David, could have been exposed by thorough cross-examination by Michael Guest at the first trial. But even if that is right, is it really the point? Surely the onus should not be on the defence to fill in holes in the prosecution's evidence. Certainly any lawyer will seek to examine the credibility of a witness and to see whether a different interpretation of the circumstances may be agreed. But one might have some sympathy for Guest if he believed that the basic facts in the Crown's evidence were accurate.

DAVID'S ALIBI

The next matter relating to timing issues is David's whereabouts when the computer was turned on. It became known over the years as the 'alibi' issue. It was the Crown case that the killer turned on the computer and that when

David got home he made a beeline for the alcove in which the computer was kept and did exactly that.

The history of the evidence relating to when David got home and when the computer was turned on illustrates two of the causes of the *substantial* miscarriage of justice. The first is that David was arrested prematurely because at the time of his arrest the collection, collation and verification of information (as agreed by Doyle) was in its very early stages and as a result the decision was based on many untested assumptions. The second is that when the police obtained further evidence after the arrest that impacted adversely on the Crown case, it was not dealt with fairly and objectively. We now turn to each of those matters.

THE LANEY SIGHTING

On the issue of David's whereabouts, it was a simple mistake that set up the train of events. As we know Denise Laney worked in the rest home next door to the Bain house. A Constable Darling had been sent there to conduct inquiries at about lunchtime on the day of the killings. He recorded the results of his interviews in his notebook and found two people who had information bearing on the investigation: Denise Laney and Tania Clark. This information led to Tania Clark being re-interviewed twice more over the following few days on the direction of 2IC Jim Doyle. However, when Darling's notebook entries were typed out for referral to Operation Every headquarters, Denise Laney's name and information was omitted in what might be called a 'typo'.

The consequence of this was that when David was arrested four days later no one in the police except for Darling had any knowledge of Laney's existence or, therefore, what information she had.

On the following Monday, 27 June, when David was spending his third day on remand in prison and exactly seven days after he had reported the tragic deaths of his family, the police conducted a roadblock on Every Street early in the morning to see if this would locate any regular users of Every Street who may have seen or heard anything the previous Monday at the relevant time.

Denise Laney was as usual on her way to work driving up Every Street when she got to the roadblock. She told the police how she had seen the paper boy leaning over the gate of 65 Every Street the previous Monday. At

1.52 p.m. that Monday afternoon, a statement was taken from Laney at the rest home by Detective Lowe, in which she said that when she saw the paper boy she looked at her car clock and it read 6.50, which meant it was actually 6.45 as her digital car clock was four to five minutes fast. This prompted Detective Lowe to go to Laney's car and check the car clock. On the bottom of the statement signed by Laney and the Detective, Lowe recorded that the car clock was five minutes fast, thereby verifying Laney's evidence.

Whereas the information received from Tania Clark the previous Monday had prompted Jim Doyle to seek clarification of a number of matters which resulted in her being re-interviewed and drawings being made by the detectives of precisely what she saw and where she saw it, Laney's information, which actually placed a person at the gate of the crime scene, was apparently ignored for there was no evidence that any more detailed clarifications were undertaken. The statement taken that afternoon became Laney's deposition statement and as we know it was read to the jury twice at the first trial: the first time with Guest's agreement during the trial, and the second when the jury asked to hear it again during their deliberations.

If the police thought it was David she saw then surely some more detail about the exact circumstances of the sighting would be relevant. After all if it was him then she was the last person to see him before he began his killing spree, as they then thought. If, on the other hand, they thought that the person seen by Laney was not David then one would think even greater alarm bells would have been ringing. What is someone doing at the gate of 65 Every Street at exactly the time the police believed the killings occurred? On this point Doyle sought clarification of the identity of the old man down the bottom of Heath Street seen by Tania Clark. Surely a person at the gate of the crime scene might be important!

MARTIN COX'S COMPUTER EXAMINATION

Martin Cox had examined the computer at the Bain house on Tuesday, 21 June at about 2.15 p.m. During his examination of the computer Detective Kevin Anderson had recorded the times at which Cox carried out certain functions, including saving the message on the computer, which had not already been saved. When Cox got back to his office he realized that the time he did that was crucial to his calculations and so at 3.10 p.m. he called the CIB with a request to have Anderson's watch checked for accuracy. On the following morning Detective Chris Robinson visited Cox at the university to get a statement from him regarding his findings. In this statement Cox said that the computer was turned on at 6.44 a.m. He could not say when the message was typed except, of course, that it had to be after that. This calculation was based on the fact that Anderson, using his own watch, had recorded that Cox saved the message at 2.16 p.m. the previous day. No mention was made of Cox's request to have Anderson's watch checked. Although the significance would have escaped your attention, you may recall that at the first trial Anderson said in evidence on this point that 'At *approximately* 2.16' Cox had undertaken particular tests.

So when David was arrested on Friday, 24 June, the police were relying on this statement from Cox, that the computer had been turned on at 6.44 a.m. They did not even know of Laney's existence. Tania Clark was 'fairly certain' she had seen the paper boy at Heath Street at 6.40 a.m. and David himself had told them he was at Heath Street at 6.40. Obviously, on the theory at that time, David had made it home before 6.44 and turned on the computer.

But then on the Monday *after* David's arrest the Laney information came to hand in the form of the statement taken by Detective Lowe. Anderson's watch had still not been checked. However, Detective Chris Robinson was finally detailed to undertake the task the following day. It can only be presumed that this delay was an oversight as no other explanation has ever been given, but it is interesting that it finally came about immediately after Denise Laney's evidence was received. When Robinson checked Anderson's watch against Telecom real-time it was found to be two minutes fast.

The effect of this on Cox's calculations would have been to change his conclusion of the time the computer was turned on to 6.42 a.m. — if he had been informed by the police, which of course, as we shall see, he never was.

ALIBI INACCURACIES AND OMISSIONS

Evidence given over the years shows that the police officers responsible for preparing the deposition statements of witnesses in 1994 were Jim Doyle, Milton Weir and Kallum Croudis.

The information in the sworn deposition statements in relation to the 'alibi' issues that were prepared for the preliminary hearing included the following inaccuracies or omissions:

- Laney's statement was in exactly the form in which it was given to Detective Lowe, with the omission of the fact that her digital car clock had been checked by Detective Lowe and found to be five minutes fast.
- Anderson's statement did not include any reference to the fact that his watch had been checked.
- Martin Cox's statement was that the computer had been turned on at 6.44 a.m. and some seconds when it should have been 6.42 a.m.

Additionally:

- Detective Lowe, who took the statement from Denise Laney, did not provide evidence at all.
- Constable Darling, who first interviewed Denise Laney at the rest home, did not give evidence so the initial typographic failure went unnotified.
- Detective Chris Robinson did not give evidence that he checked Anderson's watch.

The next event after depositions was the jury trial in the High Court in May 1995. As we have already seen, Bill Wright in his opening and closing address for the Crown played down Laney as a witness, saying that her time was only an approximation and that she was unable to identify the person that she had seen going past the gate at Every Street. The map of the paper round produced by the police as an exhibit said Laney saw 'a person', whereas references to the other witnesses who saw the paper boy say they saw 'the accused'.

Cox's evidence at trial remained the same as his deposition statement and he was not cross-examined. Detective Chris Robinson did not give evidence in person at the trial but a very short brief of evidence was read to the court by consent, simply attesting to the fact that he had issued a search warrant on Telecom for the records of a phone number. There was nothing in his brief of evidence regarding his time check on Anderson's watch or his interview with Martin Cox.

Detective Kevin Anderson took the stand on a number of occasions at the first trial and, although he mentioned in his evidence that he arranged for

Martin Cox to examine the computer, he was totally silent on the fact that his watch had been checked for accuracy by Robinson and that it had been found to be two minutes fast.

In response to the jury's request to hear Denise Laney's evidence, the Crown argued successfully that Tania Clark's evidence should also be read to provide proper balance.

The next stage takes us to the Court of Appeal hearing a few months later when Bill Wright made written submissions to the court and repeated his claim that Laney 'could not identify the person' and that it was 'around' 6.45 a.m. that she had seen this unidentified person. Guest responded disbelievingly, claiming it was agreed at trial that the person Laney saw (on page 187) was David. The evidence does not seem to bear that out, though.

The police/Police Complaints Authority (PCA) report was released in November 1997 following publication of *David and Goliath*, in which an entire chapter ('The Phantom Murderer') was devoted to this issue. The PCA accepted that Cox had *never* been informed of the time check on Anderson's watch but made no reference to the handling of Denise Laney's evidence, which had also been criticized in the book. In 1998 the Bain defence made strident complaints to the PCA judge Neville Jaine about this apparent omission. He arranged for a detective to go back to Dunedin to investigate the matter who in a search of the archives at the Dunedin CIB uncovered a statement from Denise Laney taken by Detective Trevor Thompson on 28 March 1995. This was just a few weeks before the trial, during the same period Thompson had done the paper round reconstructions with Detective Laurie Peeters.

It was a rather apologetic PCA who supplied the freshly discovered statement to the defence in the early months of 1998. The police, Judge Jaine said, claimed the non-disclosure was an unfortunate oversight! The evidence heard by the jury was in the form of the original deposition statement. This undisclosed second statement was never seen by Michael Guest, the jury or the judge. Laney's statement on 28 March 1995 made it very clear that it was the paper boy she saw because the yellow *ODT* delivery bag was on his shoulder. She also said he was actually halfway in the gate to 65 Every Street. She also explained how she knew the precise time. This was because her car clock read five minutes past the hour when the news came on. She looked at it and it said 6.50 in digital form.

On 14 May 1998 Trevor Thompson who took the second statement from Laney was interviewed by Detective Superintendent I. E. Lines who had been involved in the police/PCA review team. Lines' Job Sheet is headed up BAIN: LANEY DISCLOSURE. The interview was conducted at the South Dunedin CIB. Lines records that Thompson can recall being present at a meeting with Weir, Doyle, Bill Wright and perhaps Wright's assistant prosecutor Marie Grylls, where it was decided Laney should be re-interviewed. He believes that meeting was at the premises of the Crown Prosecutor in their library. That decision, according to Thompson, was made the day or night before the interview took place (28 March 1995).

The interview with Laney was definitely at the request of Bill Wright, Lines further records and goes on to say that Thompson has no doubt he told Doyle and Weir about the significant point being that 'it was quite clear she had seen David Bain going through the gate'.

Lines goes on to record that Thompson said, 'Everyone from the Crown and police inquiry team would have known because of the significance of her having firmed up on her identity.' At that time the job sheet says the Crown and police were having regular meetings and Thompson attended quite a few of those because he had made the inquiries.

It may be recalled that Doyle said in his evidence that the significance of timing issues was not clear at the time of trial!

Then another unusual thing happened which threw even more light on the matter. In about July of 2000 the Dunedin CIB decided to sell off a number of its computers in a public auction. A purchaser of one of them discovered a large number of files relating to the Bain case on the hard drive which was copied and supplied to the Bain defence. One of these files was written by Detective Trevor Thompson who took the statement from Denise Laney on 28 March 1995 that was never disclosed.

The file was headed up 'Note to Prosecutor — Denise Laney' and it was dated 7 April 1995, about a week after Thompson had interviewed Laney and a month before the trial began. The subheading states: '28 March 1995 Denise May Laney a witness in the Bain homicides was interviewed in regard to her statement to *clarify any ambiguities*.' He wrote to the prosecutor: 'She now says the person was going through the gate sideways and that she saw the yellow bag on the left shoulder. This was the thing that caught her attention.'

How many people would be likely to be walking through the gate to 65 Every Street at 6.45 in the morning with a yellow bag on the left shoulder?

The document finishes with the words: 'Confirms when it would be 7 o'clock the time in her car would be 7.05.'

At the retrial Doyle confirmed in his evidence that the decision to review the timing evidence involving the paper run and Denise Laney was taken jointly by senior officers on the case in consultation with Crown Prosecutor Bill Wright.

On this issue of the alibi, all the evidence so far recounted was before the Court of Appeal in 2003. The written 61-page decision delivered by Justice Tipping states: 'Mrs Laney *claimed* to have seen David *outside* the gate to 65 Every Street at 6.45 a.m. [author's emphasis].' As is clear, she made no such claim. She didn't even know what the paper boy's name was. She saw a tall, lanky guy in his twenties who she saw most days on her way to work and he was wearing a yellow bag over his left shoulder. Her statement does not say 'outside the gate', but 'squeezing between the partially opened gate and the hedge at 65 Every Street. He was definitely more inside the property than out in front of the gate.' Yet the reference to 'outside the gate' is repeated twice in the decision.

The New Zealand Court of Appeal decision goes on to say in respect to the time she saw the person that 'the circumstances she came to that view are such that her suggested time cannot be regarded as anywhere near precise'.

Not unsurprisingly, given the previous example, the decision fails to mention the fact that Detective Lowe had checked the car clock and found it to be exactly five minutes fast, thereby corroborating the accuracy of Laney's statement. Alas, this was not the only subject where such omissions or inaccuracies on matters crucial to the case formed part of the judgment.

The next step in proceedings was the Privy Council decision delivered in May 2007. The Board of the Privy Council viewed the identical alibi evidence seen by the Court of Appeal but summarized the content of Denise Laney's undisclosed statement as follows:

'The jury [at the 1995 trial] were invited to treat Mrs Laney's identification of David as problematical and her estimate of time as at best approximate. The fresh evidence might lead a reasonable jury to infer that her identification was not in doubt and her estimate of time reliable.'

COMPUTER TURN-ON TIME

We turn now to the other side of the alibi evidence, the computer turn-on time. The background is that in late 1996 the Bain defence, after discovering that the two-minute time deficit in Anderson's watch had not been factored in to the time of 6.44 a.m., wrote to the police wanting access to the computer to conduct its own tests to see whether Cox's calculations were accurate or not. The Bain defence was advised by the police that the computer had been given to Michael Bain, Robin Bain's brother, who was one of the executors of the will. Eventually, Michael Bain agreed that the Bain defence with its expert could examine the computer at the offices of the police in Wellington. The Bain defence engaged a technical expert from Philips, the manufacturers of the computer, to assist in its evaluation. Colin Withnall QC and the technician conducted that examination in the presence of police officers in Wellington and concluded that the computer had in fact been turned on between the time of 6.40.07 a.m. and 6.42.05 a.m. on 20 June 1994 as recounted in *David and Goliath*.

In 1997 as part of the police/PCA review into the allegations in the book, the police arranged for the police electronic crime laboratory in Wellington to conduct tests on the computer. The expert who did this work was Mr Martin Kleintjes. He came up with a completely new theory, which, although apparently helpful to their case, was not, as he would eventually admit, based on reality.

The Kleintjes findings were published in the police/PCA report and it involved cloning the computer hard drive and other highly sophisticated techniques. He agreed within 18 seconds to the defence's earliest possible turn-on time of 6.40.07 with his *earliest* time being 6.39.49 a.m. However, adopting logic that the Court of Appeal suggested defied the laws of physics and gravity, Kleintjes said that the *latest* time was 6.49.11 and further, that by using what Kleintjes referred to as medium logic (halfway between the two) the *most likely* time the computer was turned on was 6.44.30, almost exactly the same time that Cox said it was turned on at the trial in 1995. It should be noted that the dispute about Kleintjes' theory relates to the data he assumed relative to the latest time but that data is not relevant to the earliest time calculations which were agreed.

So on the earliest time, the door was well and truly open to the likelihood that it was switched on five or six minutes before David arrived home.

However, with this new theory came a window of three or four minutes at the other end, which the Crown would say was the time David had to turn it on after being seen by Laney at 6.45, for by now having been exposed to the contents of her hidden statement they could no longer claim that the person she saw was 'unidentified'. In addition, they could now say that the most likely time is nearly the same as the jury heard, so what's the problem? How did Kleintjes arrive at this theory? He gave evidence at the retrial and soon it shall be recounted.

But, in the meantime, there was Justice Tipping's judgment which analysed at great length the computer evidence and stated in its conclusion: 'We find ourselves unable to conclude with any confidence or precision exactly when the computer was switched on.'

This of course was not their job but the job of a jury. The very fact that the computer could have been turned on nearly five minutes earlier than what the jury at David Bain's trial had been told, and long before Mrs Laney saw David getting home, should have been sufficient for the Court of Appeal to at the very least express grave concern.

The Privy Council examined exactly the same evidence that was put before the Court of Appeal and its summary on the matter was:

'It is now clear that the jury should not have been told as a fact that the computer was switched on at 6.44 a.m. It may have been switched on nearly five minutes earlier; it may perchance have been switched on at 6.44; it may theoretically have been switched on later. A prosecutor alert to the fresh evidence now before the court would have had to approach the switch-on time with a degree of tentativeness.'

RETRIAL CROSS-EXAMINATION OF COX AND KLEINTJES

The final evidence in the saga that began between 6.40 a.m. and 6.42 a.m. on 20 June 1994 when David Bain was walking home up Every Street with his dog Casey and probably thinking about his next move with Miss X, and when someone else hit the 'power-on' switch of the computer, was heard at the retrial in Christchurch when for the very first time Martin Cox and Denise Laney would be cross-examined.

In 1995 Cox was led through his one-page statement and not cross-examined at all. He spent about five or ten minutes on the stand. However, at the retrial his evidence occupied 48 pages of typewritten notes. The total evidence at the retrial in relation to just the computer turn-on time went for over a day. Cox was on the stand for almost three hours and Martin Kleintjes for even longer.

The reason for this was that at trial one, the turn-on time was an exact minute, 6.44 a.m., and that time was not disputed by Guest. At the retrial the Crown knew, because the true evidence was known to the defence, that the best they could do would be to keep open a window of time for David to have got there after Laney saw him.

For over a decade the Bain defence had engaged a mathematician, Philip Tomlinson, and an English computer expert who resided in Christchurch, Brian Thomas, to help analyse the computer evidence and in particular the methodology of Martin Kleintjes. Brian Thomas had a BSc and a PhD in physics from Leeds University in England. Both provided evidence during the appeal process.

These two left no stone unturned in the lead-up to the retrial in Christchurch and as a consequence the defence were very well briefed on the whole matter. The cross-examination of Martin Cox was arduous, requiring a multitude of skills over and above just having a detailed understanding of what was quite technical evidence regarding the computer, because Cox was so defensive in the beginning. But as time went by and he understood that the defence complaint with his evidence was not to do with what he personally had done but that the police had kept him in the dark about Anderson's watch check, the dialogue became much less argumentative and some frank admissions were forthcoming. He told the court that he had never been told by the police before the trial in 1995 that Anderson's watch was two minutes fast. He agreed that if he had been told, it would have changed his conclusion from 6.44 a.m. to 6.42 a.m. He also agreed with another factor that had escaped his attention (in common parlance 'boot time', before Word initialized) which was agreed by Kleintjes and the defence experts at 54 seconds. He also agreed that it may have taken only 15 seconds to perform the 12 keystrokes associated with saving the message but that it could have been a minute. In the final washup, he agreed that it meant that as a result of factoring in these matters, the computer was turned on at 6.41 and some seconds, matching precisely the times calculated by Colin Withnall and the Philips' expert way back in 1996.

It is not unusual in the adversarial system of justice to which we subscribe that in controversial cases on appeal, the state will often resort to secondary experts to overcome defects exposed in the original case. It is often seen as a telltale sign of a very weak case by people accustomed to dealing with such matters. Kleintjes was such an expert in this instance, but then as will be seen it applied to a number of situations at the retrial.

He had come up with a set of tables involving some theoretical possibilities suggesting that the turn-on time may have been as late as 6.49 a.m., which of course gave the Crown the window it needed as discussed earlier. It also put the median time at 6.44.30. This theory was founded on the proposition that it took Cox six minutes to save the message which Cox himself said took 15 seconds to a minute as just recounted. Klientjes was questioned on this theory in cross-examination by Michael Reed:

Q: But I want to put to you this, is the theory, is an impossibility, isn't it?
Kleintjes: It's a — in theory—
Q: No, just could you answer it? Isn't it an impossibility, that theory?
Kleintjes: In reality it is, yes.
Q: Well, aren't we dealing in reality?
Kleintjes: Yes, but you have to take those extremes into account to arrive at reality.

After some interesting Q & A it finally fell upon Kleintjes having to concede.

Q: No, no Mr Kleintjes, your midpoint is based upon the one extreme being an impossibility, you've agreed with that? Yes? Can you answer yes to that or no?
Kleintjes: Yes, it is.

So Klientjes agreed that his latest possible time (and therefore the most likely time which was derived from that time) was based upon an impossibility.

LANEY CROSS-EXAMINATION

Then, on 22 April 2009, at about 10.30 a.m., almost 15 years after she saw the lanky boy with the yellow bag squeezing in the gate at 65 Every Street, Mrs Laney finally took the stand before a jury. She was led through her evidence by Dunedin Crown prosecutor Robin Bates and as expected the tenor of her evidence was to make it appear as though she was completely uncertain about everything that had happened on that morning.

However, when cross-examined by Michael Reed she confirmed that she looked at her digital car clock when she went past the Bain gateway and it said 6.50 a.m. and that it was four or five minutes fast. Her workplace was just around the corner and so she would have been just a couple of minutes late for work. She did not deny that. She also confirmed that the police officer had checked her car clock and it was found to be five minutes fast.

It was pretty obvious where David was when the killer turned on the computer.

EVIDENCE CONSIDERATIONS

The evidence listed above had been before every authority since 1998 and the police and the Crown were fully versed in it before the retrial began. The most important evidence was from their own witnesses. However, when all the chickens had come home to roost by the end of the second trial they finally had to face up to the reality of it. In his closing address Crown prosecutor Kieran Raftery made the astonishing admission that 'it doesn't actually matter who turned on the computer'. Apart from all the other ramifications of this statement which will be summarized, it certainly puts rather a chill cloak on the Court of Appeal assessment delivered in 2003 recorded above.

However, to really appreciate the gravity of what happened in regard to evidence about the 'alibi' one might consider the legal responsibilities of a defendant who wishes to call alibi evidence. This was not the case here as the alibi was established by the Crown's own witnesses. But if an accused person wishes to call evidence that is intended to establish an alibi they are required to notify the prosecution of that evidence. This enables the prosecution to have the opportunity of rebutting or confirming the evidence prior to trial.

The Crown, in explanation, call the failure to disclose the re-interview of Laney an unfortunate oversight! In this case the very least that should have been done was for either the prosecutor or the police to have made a special point of supplying the second statement taken from Laney to Michael Guest. He should have been phoned and told that fresh important evidence was being delivered. It should have been high priority and urgent. It could even be said that in an ideal world where justice was not a competition, when Wright and Doyle decided to re-interview her they should have invited Michael Guest to be present.

In regard to the two-minute inaccuracy in Kevin Anderson's watch there are a number of considerations. It is well known that when a person gives evidence they swear 'to tell the whole truth and nothing but the truth'. Police officers would be even more familiar with this requirement than the average person in the street.

- Detective Chris Robinson checked Anderson's watch for accuracy. He could and should have included this fact in his deposition statement.
- Kevin Anderson could and should have insisted it was in his deposition statement. At the defamation trial he said on oath that he would have told of it 'if I had been asked'.
- The job sheet completed by Robinson of the result of his check must have been seen by the officers in charge of the investigation. That they did not recognize the significance of it would be incredibly negligent. It will be recalled that Cox's statement specifically describes that he ascertained the time the computer was turned on as 6.44 a.m. by utilizing the time he saved the message, which was recorded by Detective Anderson as 2.16 p.m. It defies belief that the hierarchy, having before them Cox's request to check the watch and his calculations showing why the time on the watch was so important, did not immediately realize that it would bring the turn-on time back to 6.42 a.m. when David could not have been home on anyone's evidence.
- The fact that the time check was not done when it was requested on 21 June but was done immediately after Laney's statement was received on the afternoon of 27 June makes it seem likely that the one led to the other meaning that 'timing' issues were on the minds of the said hierarchy at the time.
- There is no evidence that the prosecutor was aware of this matter, which, if that is the case, is a further indictment on the police because according to Doyle's evidence as we have seen, the decision to revisit the timing issues just before trial was a joint decision involving the police and the prosecutor. Those discussions should surely have raised the question of the turn-on time of the computer, and therefore it can

only be that the police did not inform the prosecutor of the discrepancy despite the fact that the issue of timings was under the spotlight.

If all of this were not enough, having failed to disclose the evidence of an 'actual alibi' from the defendant and his lawyer, submissions were made to the jury that David 'wanted to be seen' on his paper round in order to create a 'false' one.

The admission or concession by Raftery, call it what you will, that it was no longer the Crown case that the person who turned on the computer was the killer meant the Crown had to advance the theory that Robin Bain turned it on that morning but David wrote the message sometime later. This amounted to a complete capitulation by the Crown and a back-down from the case it had run in every forum since 1994. The reason it had always run that case is that it is the only one that makes sense.

The scenario that Robin turned it on and then went walkabout with four dead people in the house while David somehow sneaked inside, washed his hands and got in behind the curtains with the gun stretches credibility to farcical proportions. It was the tragic end to a saga of deception and incompetence that all began when the police jumped to a false conclusion about the 'missing 20 minutes' all those years ago.

THE WASH CYCLE

David arrived home from the paper run at 6.45 a.m. After hanging up his bag and kicking his shoes off, he went directly to the laundry, washed his hands and put the wash on, according to his evidence. It is safe to say the washing machine on that scenario would have been activated by 6.50 a.m. The Telecom woman gave evidence that she hung up the phone when she heard the police enter the house. That time was 7.36 a.m. By the time Sergeant Stapp had checked on the upstairs rooms and made his way downstairs to the laundry it would have been about 7.38 a.m., which is 48 minutes after the wash would have been started.

The two tests done on the wash cycle took almost exactly one hour, which if they were accurate meant that the machine should have been still going when Sergeant Stapp got to the laundry. It was not, according to his evidence.

At the retrial the washing machine expert Mr Preston gave evidence again.

Preston's evidence confirms that those tests could not be relied upon as any sort of accurate guide. Firstly, in regards to the cycle, he said: 'It took a lot longer than I expected, to be honest … The normal sequence of events, that would have taken, the time, the machine would have taken about 40 minutes.'

He confirmed that the timer on the machine was faulty, which could cause it to jump or skip cycles and also that at the start it could activate on a different cycle than the one where it appeared to be set.

At the top of the machine was the 'superwash' and immediately adjacent to it was 'normal wash'. Preston said the normal wash would take about four minutes less than the superwash. David's evidence was that he flicked the switch to the top where the two cycles were labelled. The gap between those two cycles is very tiny and as Preston said even when it appeared to be on one it could start on the other. Of course it cannot be known exactly where David put it, or which cycle it started on.

Preston agreed that on the Saturday and Sunday when the tests were done the 'water pressure was unusually low'. Both tests involved about 30 minutes of filling time, whereas he said the normal time was between 10 and 14 minutes. Tests were never done at the relevant time of 6.45 on a Monday morning. The tests done are tantamount to calculating how long it would take to make a trip on Auckland's motorway during peak hour traffic by doing driving tests at midnight.

In addition to that the taps had been replaced so it is not known what effect the different taps had on the filling time.

So, collating all of these factors, if at 6.50 on a Monday morning the pressure was normal, and if it started on 'normal wash' then the whole cycle could have been finished in 36 minutes. Even on the 'superwash' cycle of 40 minutes the machine would still have been finished by the time Sergeant Stapp got to the laundry.

There are two further points about this matter which are not of a technical nature. It may not surprise that they relate to the 'missing 20 minutes' false assumption made by the police. David could not have put on the washing machine until after he had fought with Stephen and become bloodied, which on that scenario would have been about 7 a.m., in which case, on any reconstruction, it would still have been going when Stapp arrived. So it was that 'guilty mindset' of the police which caused them to over-emphasize the significance of the washing machine cycle. This is another example illustrating the necessity of doing reconstructions and collating evidence before acting on personal beliefs of guilt or innocence.

The second point is that when David rang 111 he did not know the police would take 26 minutes to make entry to the house. The ambulance, after all, arrived after only 10 minutes or so, but they had to wait outside for the police to arrive. If he was lying about when he did the washing as the police believed he was, it would have been a hopeless lie, immediately revealed if the police had arrived sooner because it could not have been going (on the basis he had done it before the paper run); or, under the other scenario, it had to be still going if the police had arrived at, say, 7.20 a.m.

Finally, this is another example where failing to follow procedure led to problems. Reconstructions, as with the tests done by Preston and Lodge, should be done before conclusions are reached in order to assist the validity of the conclusion, not afterwards to try to validate an existing belief.

CHAPTER 15

BLOOD EVIDENCE

THE RELEVANCE OF BLOOD EVIDENCE

Some of the blood in the house gave rise to very powerful inferences, while much of it was no help in determining who was responsible. Indeed, much of the blood evidence was actually a distraction from the real issue: who did it — Robin or David? The factor with the most bearing on that central issue related to Robin's death. Was it suicide or was he murdered? There was plenty of evidence bearing on that question as we shall see, even though the Crown were very silent on it.

This point was made to the jury over and over again by the defence at the retrial. Much of the evidence called by the Crown was only evidence of the existence of blood and was not capable of indicating who may or may not be guilty. By way of example, we can consider the laborious and painstaking evidence by the Crown, indicating bloodstains on door jambs and stairway posts in various places throughout the house. It is very obvious that these bloodstains did not assist at all in ascertaining who put them there. Obviously, it was somebody who was walking about the house with a bloodstained garment on, and that person was very likely to be the person involved in trying to kill Stephen but failing with the first shot. It was also very likely that it was the green jersey found in the washing machine that was the transporter of this blood. The best evidence on that was that it was too small for David when he was asked to put it on at the first trial. Apart from that there was no evidence whatsoever to say who had been wearing it or indeed who might have deposited these various blood smears in different parts of the house.

A similar argument can be advanced about the white gloves covered in blood found under the bed in Stephen's bedroom. There was not one scrap of evidence to suggest who wore them. The Crown advanced the argument that because they were David's gloves he must have been the wearer of them, but that was no more than speculation.

Equally compelling, an impartial observer may think, is that if David meticulously planned these killings as alleged, he might have worn his father's gloves rather than his own, if he was on a premeditated course to implicate his father. A vast amount of time in the Crown's presentation of evidence was spent on such matters.

The two separate categories of bloodstains that could directly put one person or the other in the frame were the bloody footprints that were found by the use of luminol, and the smears of blood on Robin's hands. But both of these were either destroyed or never collected in the first place, and for the most part were not even captured on camera. There were no permanent markers put on the floor to indicate the position of the footprints, and in possibly the most basic blunder of all, the carpet on which these footprints were found was not retained. It was burnt with the house. And yet they secured as an exhibit the piece of carpet into which blood from Robin's head wound had flowed. It was of no benefit at all in assisting as a piece of evidence that could discriminate between the two possible perpetrators, and was not even produced as an exhibit.

Then, of course, in regard to David's claim that he was the finder of the dead family, not the killer of them, the Crown say that Stephen's blood on his socks, shorts and shirt proves that he was the killer. But the little bit of blood on his shirt and shorts was smearing caused by the lightest contact with a bloodstained object, such as the blood on one of the bodies, the blood on the bed and bedding in Stephen's bedroom, the blood in the laundry where he had been or the blood on the door jambs throughout the house. It certainly did not establish that these were the clothes worn during a fight with Stephen. Surely it would be likely that anyone stumbling into the scene, as David claims to have done, would have such traces on their person. Indeed, it would be most suspicious, one may think, if David had absolutely no blood of his family on him, after claiming to be the finder of them in the very bloody circumstances of parts of the house.

Indeed, on this point a very telling question was asked by the jury, which Justice Pankhurst put to the Crown's DNA and blood expert from the ESR, SallyAnn Harbison, for response.

The question was: 'Could the blood staining on David's T-shirt have been caused by blood soaking or leaking through a jersey overlay, or is it more consistent with direct contact staining?'

The scientist answered: 'I think it is more consistent with direct contact staining' because 'for example, the stain on the mid-back of the T-shirt is sort of discrete lines of smearing, which I have described in my notes as lines of contact smearing as opposed to a more diffuse stain with edges that are not clearly defined.'

On the other hand, if David had any blood on him which had been deposited as a result of airborne blood splatter, then that would have been very incriminating. But neither on the top of David's socks, where one would certainly have expected blood to drop if he had been involved in a fight with Stephen, nor on his shorts or any of his other clothing was there any blood splatter of an airborne nature. The only two spots of blood found on David were the two spots on the sole of the sock, which in the first trial the ESR scientist Peter Cropp advanced had fallen from above. That evidence, virtually uncontested as it was, formed very powerful evidence against David because if the jury accepted it — and as there was no contrary expert opinion on it they had no reason not to — then it could only have got there, they probably thought, in the fight with Stephen.

At the retrial, however, Dr Cropp from the ESR recanted on this evidence when he was cross-examined on a proper evidential basis and agreed that the blood spots could have got there in the logical way by David walking in blood. So with those two little spots of blood innocently explained and the couple of light smears on David's clothes actually supportive of his account of events rather than the Crown case, the blood evidence was not helpful to the police at all. A totally different bloodstain profile on David would be necessary to tie him to the killings.

There is another point about the blood on the socks which contradicts the Crown theory. They said he got the blood on his socks from the fight with Stephen and then went out on his paper round. However, there was no blood on the inside soles of the running shoes he wore that morning as there should have been according to that theory. In other words, this supports his story that those spots got there when he got home, not during the alleged fight with Stephen at 4 a.m.

All of this returns to the proposition that a determination of whether Robin Bain's death was self-inflicted or not would throw more light on the case than debating the merits of a spot of blood in the hand-basin, for example. After 15 years of forensic analysis and investigation the police have not produced one scrap of evidence capable of incriminating either party in relation to the deaths of Margaret or Arawa.

In respect to Laniet, as we saw in the first trial, David's frank disclosure that when he went into her room he heard gurgling noises was very much used against him by the Crown, suggesting that he was the killer of Laniet. That was the only evidence against either party in relation to that death and it will be dealt with in due course.

In regard to Stephen, there was the skin suggested as coming from David's knee and the spectacle lens found by Weir, which go against David along with the 'bloody' fingerprints on the murder weapon. We will get to those in due course; suffice to say now that neither lens nor the frame had anything on them, such as blood or other matter, to link them to the events that led to Stephen's death.

What can be said with a degree of certainty is that whoever was responsible for killing those four members of the family was wearing the green V-neck jersey found in the washing machine. That green jersey got blood on the right arm or shoulder region during the shooting of Stephen. The killer was wearing socks during the fight with Stephen; the sock on his right foot got enough blood over the sole to leave footprints for the first four or five steps that he took as he left Stephen's room. It can also be said with reasonable certainty that the killer wore white gloves and that for reasons unknown and by means unknown these were removed in Stephen's room where they were found. The police advanced the theory in the first trial that the killer removed these gloves in order to clear a misfeed from the rifle, but there was no evidence of a misfed bullet in that room. This was another submission bereft of evidential foundation. We can also say with certainty that the killer must at some stage have removed at least his socks and the green jersey.

SUICIDE OR NOT

The lack of direct evidence involving Margaret, Arawa, Laniet and Stephen means that the key to solving the Bain case, from a forensic science or physical and trace evidence point of view, lies in ascertaining whether Robin's death was self-inflicted or not. If he was murdered, then his murderer is the person who also killed the rest of the family; equally as certain is that if his death was self-inflicted then that act of suicide followed after he killed his family.

This was why at both trials the Crown went to great lengths to try to disprove suicide by Robin Bain. The key figure, of course, in the first trial relating to whether or not Robin Bain committed suicide was Dr Dempster, the Crown pathologist.

A very notable feature of the retrial was that the Crown called multiple experts on the same subject in a number of instances, who in many cases contradicted each other. This was particularly so in respect to the three pathologists they called: Dr Dempster, the original pathologist, Dr Thomson, and Dr Ferris. Dempster had said from day one that the wound to Robin Bain was a contact shot. By 'contact' it is meant that the tip of the rifle, or in this case the silencer on the end of the rifle, was in contact with the skin when the shot was fired. Ferris and Thomson disagreed completely with Dempster.

Thomson first became involved in the case when he was consulted by the police/PCA in 1997, and it was at that time that he came up with the theory that the wound had the characteristics of an intermediate shot from a distance of about 20 cm. Ferris was brought in by the Crown at the last minute for the Court of Appeal hearing in 2002, to deal with the gurgling issue. He then moved on to the shot that killed Robin. It was his opinion that the wound was an intermediate shot from a distance of 30 to 40 cm. This new evidence from the two subsequent pathologists was extremely important for the Crown because if they were correct it would have been impossible for Robin Bain to have reached the trigger, thereby ruling out suicide completely. On the other hand, international forensic data shows that over 95 per cent of fatal contact rifle shots to the head are self-inflicted.

During the cross-examination of these witnesses it came out that they had met with Dr Dempster to try to pressure him into changing his mind about the fact that it was a contact wound. But Dempster knew what he had seen: a 4 mm entry wound surrounded by a ring of soot about 10 mm in diameter. He would not succumb.

DETERMINING RANGE OF SHOT

As this issue assumed so much importance in the retrial, a brief explanation about how experts are able to determine the range (distance from which fired) of gunshot wounds and some of the terminology involved is warranted.

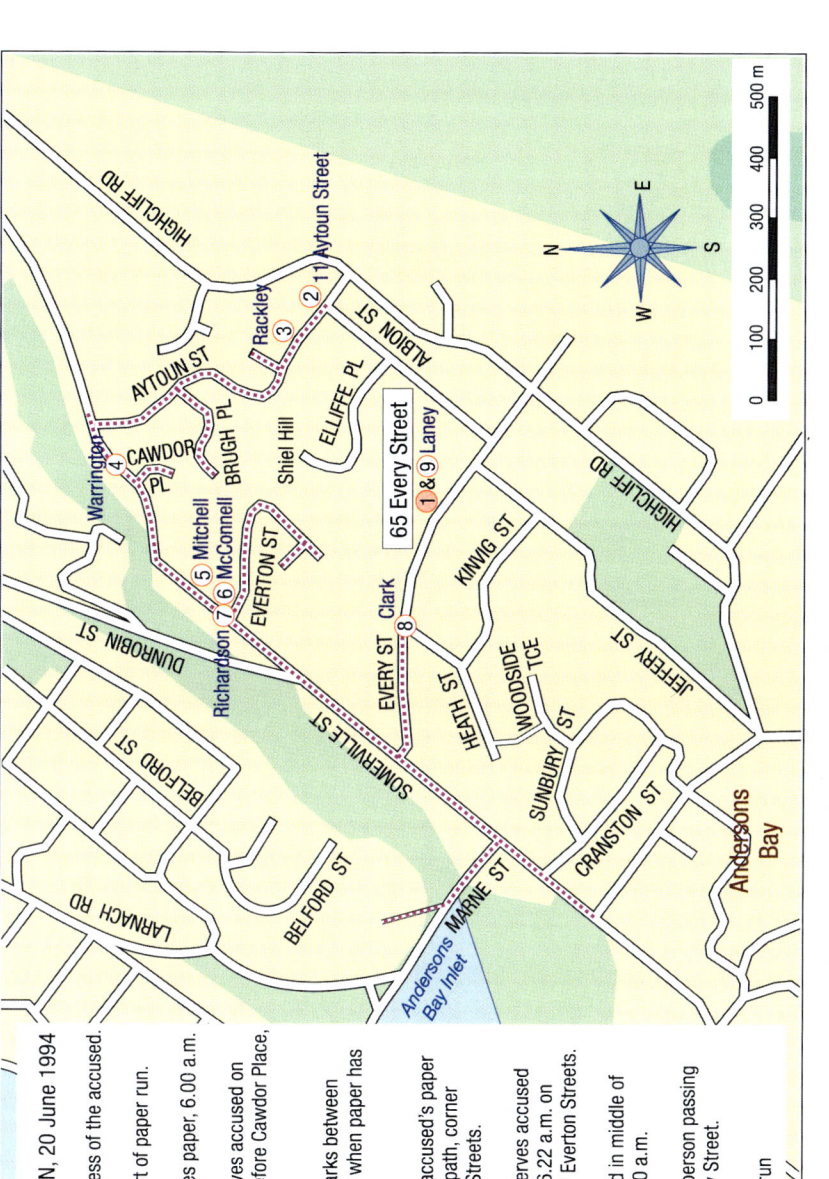

DAVID BAIN'S PAPER RUN, 20 June 1994

1. 65 Every Street — address of the accused.

2. 11 Aytoun Street — start of paper run.

3. Deborah Rackley receives paper, 6.00 a.m.

4. Stuart Warrington observes accused on Somerville Street just before Cawdor Place, at about 6.10 a.m.

5. Yvonne Mitchell's dog barks between 6.10 a.m. and 6.15 a.m. when paper has been delivered.

6. Alistair McConnell sees accused's paper bag at 6.15 a.m. on footpath, corner Somerville and Everton Streets.

7. Douglas Richardson observes accused between 6.18 a.m. and 6.22 a.m. on corner of Somerville and Everton Streets.

8. Tania Clark sees accused in middle of Heath Street prior to 6.40 a.m.

9. Denise Laney observes person passing through gate at 65 Every Street.

········· Paper run

The legend was a police exhibit at the first trial. Note all references are to the 'accused' except Denise Laney sighting, number 9.

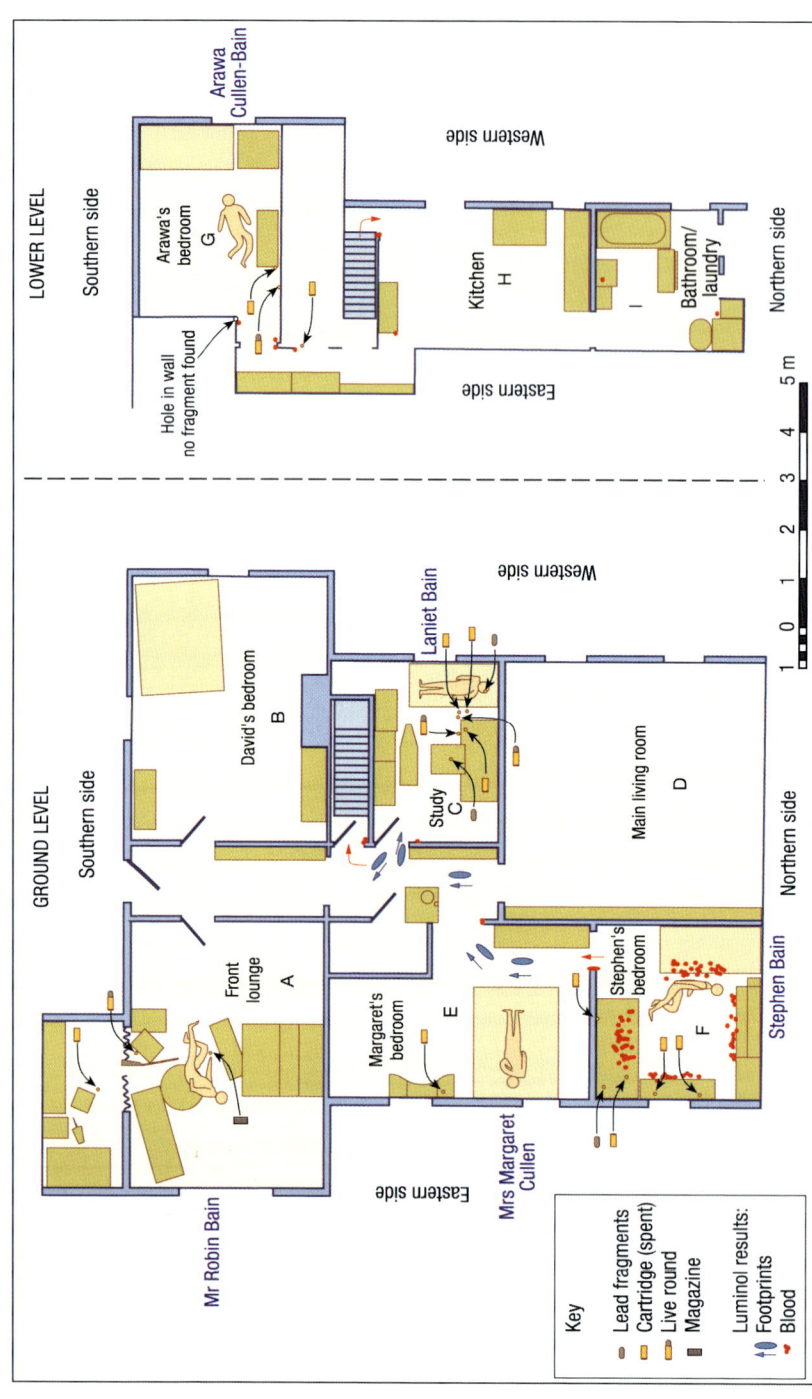

Scene plan.

The front of the house looking from Every Street. On the left is the window to room B (see opposite page). In the centre is the front door, and on the right the large windows in the computer alcove off room A.

Room B, David's room: note the very small gap between the blue case, the set of drawers and the bed where David crashed down when he fainted and was dragged out by Constable Andrew.

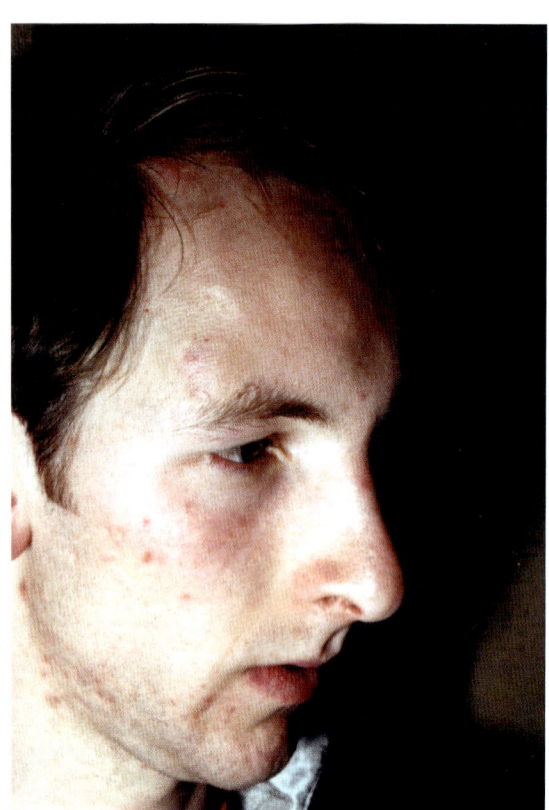

Police photo of David taken 20 June 1994 showing the 'injuries' to the right side of his face.

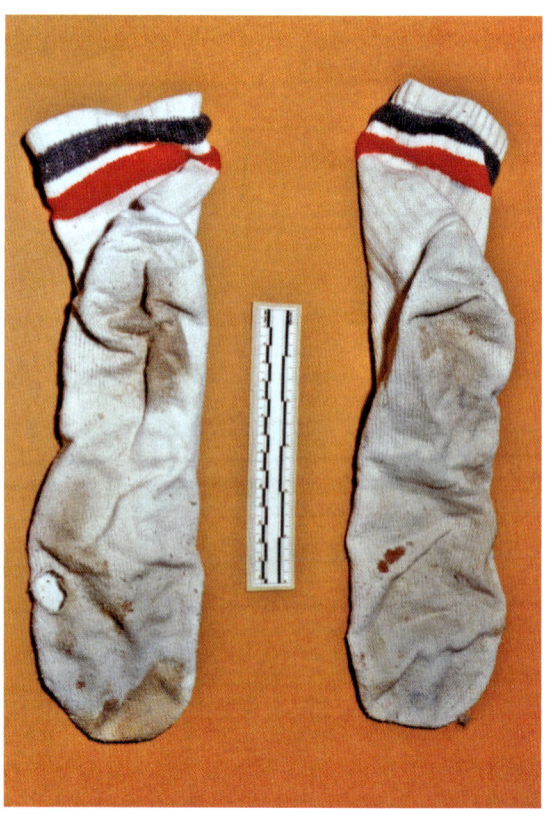

The soles of David's socks. There was no blood at all on the top of either sock.

The T-shirt (front and back) David was found in, said to have been worn under the green jersey during the fight with Stephen.

Photo 62.

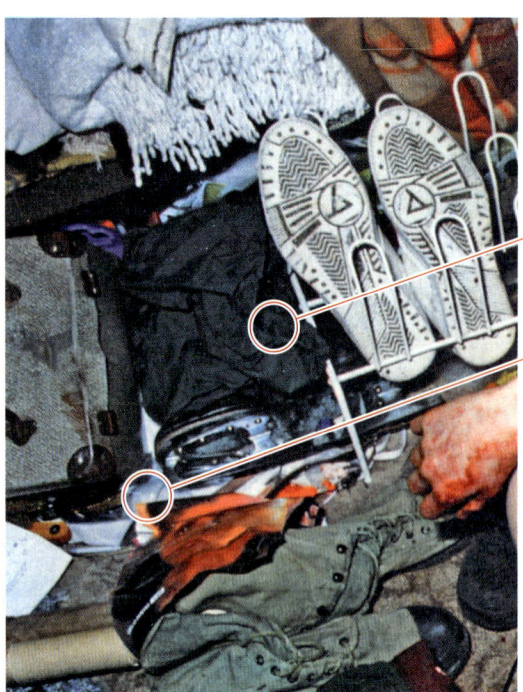

The lens was actually on the floor under the raincoat and leather ankle part of the ice-skate boot.

The specular reflection said to be the lens.

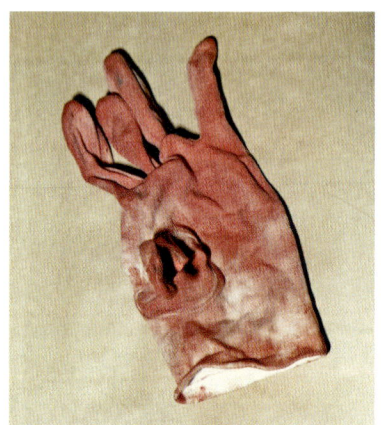

One of the bloody gloves found in Stephen's room.

Room F: Stephen's blood-drenched room.

The 'whites' in the laundry basket, which were dry and unwashed.

The dial on the washing machine.

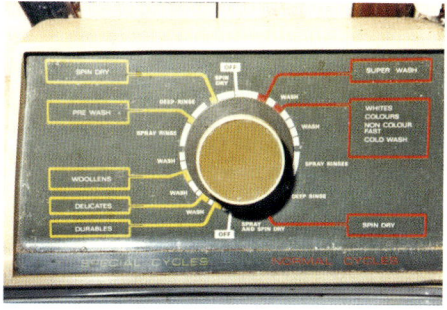

The clothes David had washed hung out to dry by the police. Note green jersey in foreground.

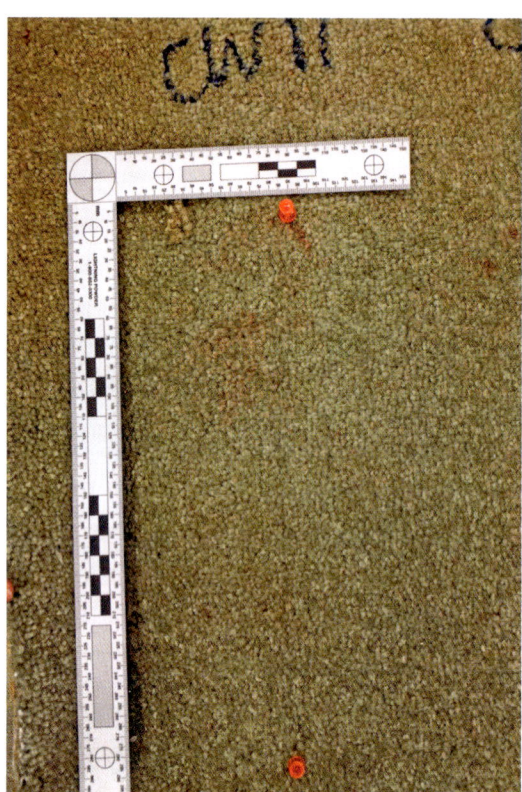

Photo 1

These are photos of the same footprint from tests done by Kevan Walsh in 2008 on a foot measuring 270 mm, the same size as Robin Bain's. Note that no print can be seen under full light (Photo 1) but after being treated with luminol and photographed in the dark (Photo 2), a complete print 'from the top of the toe to the heel' becomes visible and was measured by Walsh at 276 mm, almost exactly the same as the two 280 mm complete prints found at the scene.

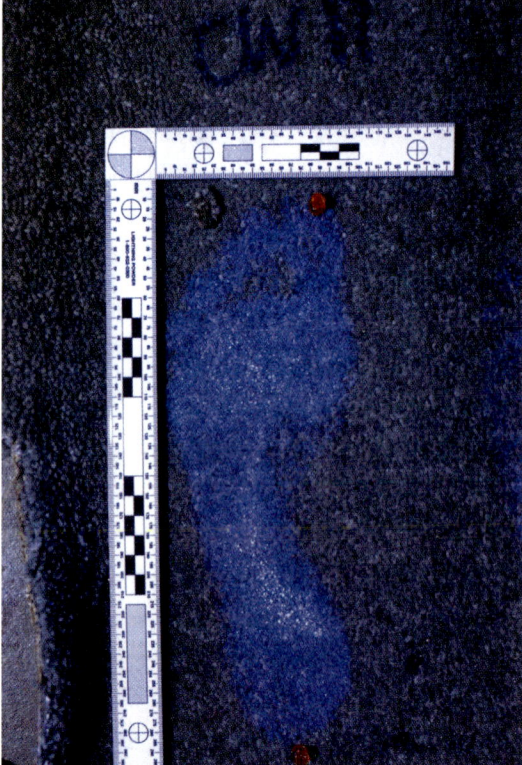

Photo 2

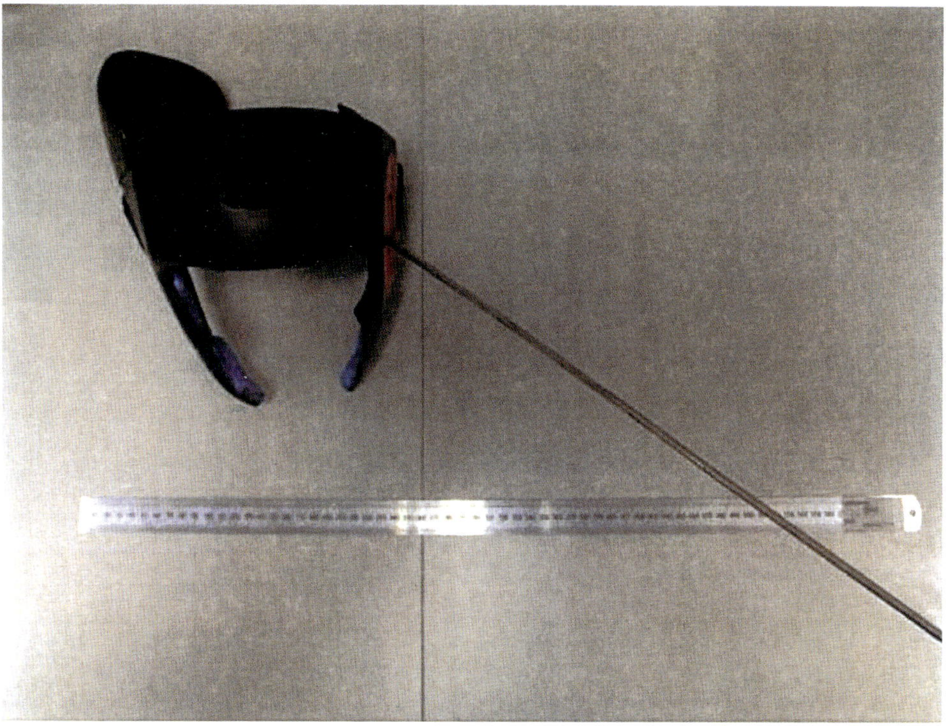

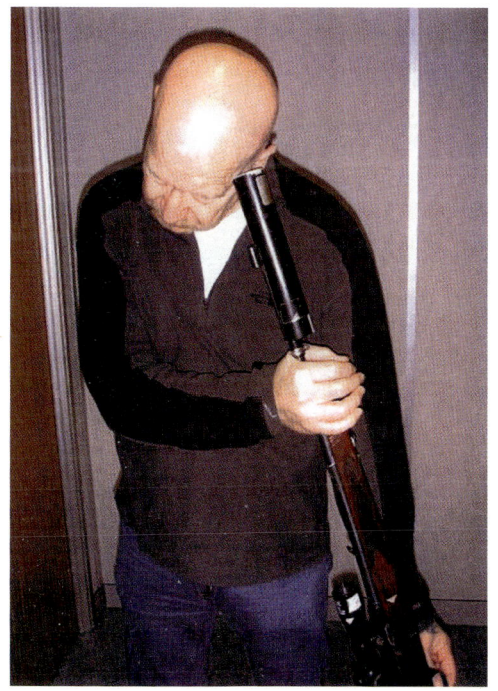

The helmet with rod produced by police under direction of Dr Dempster for the second trial.

One of the many positions shown to the jury, which Dr Dempster agreed was compatible with suicide.

Robin in the jacket used by police to determine his arm span.

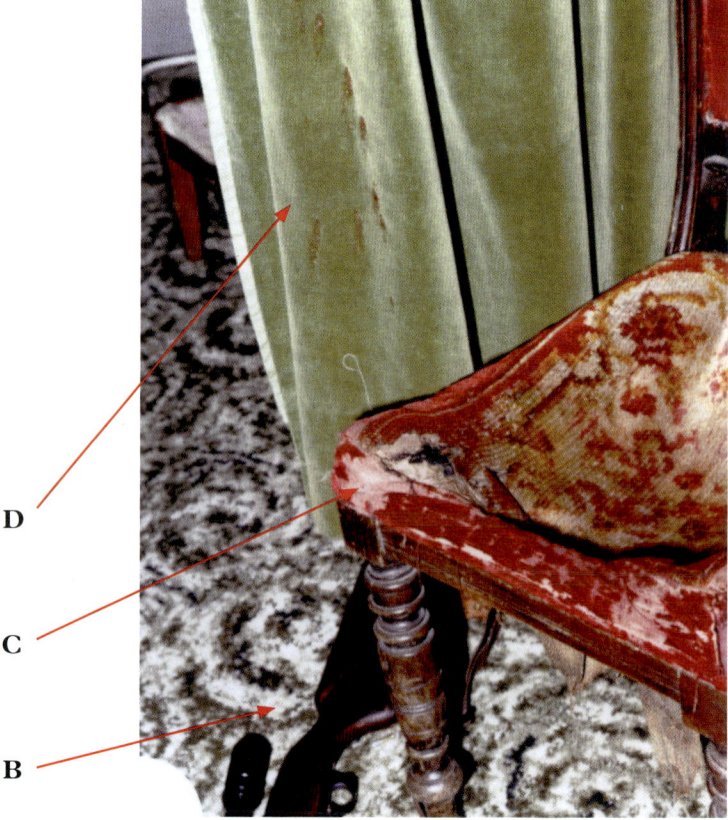

The scene in room A when the police arrived. Note: A, right leg bent; B, rifle; C, red chair; D, blood drops on green curtain.

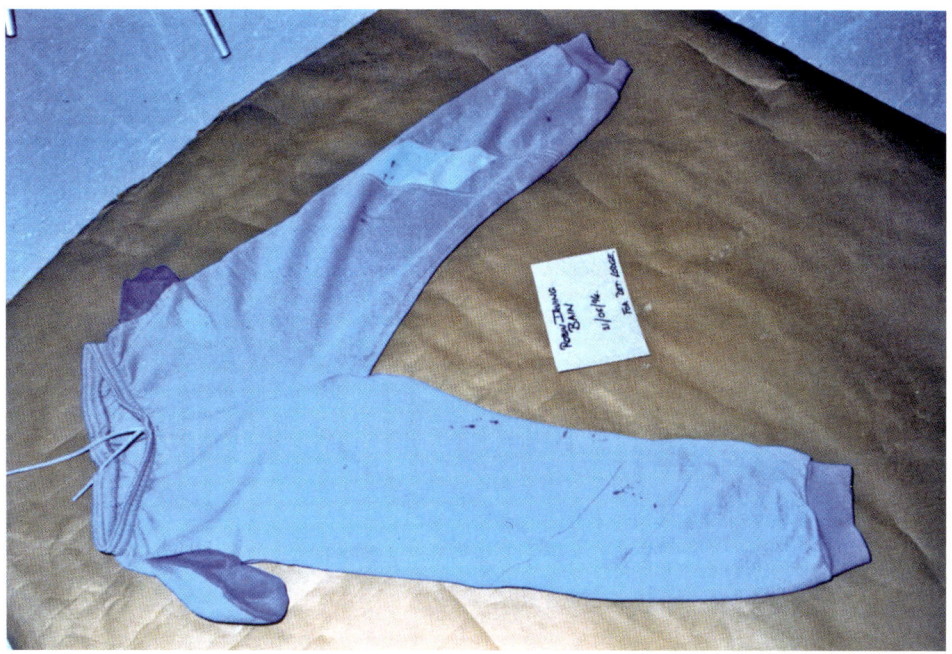

Drops of blood going up on inside of thigh, and down below the knee.

Blood splash on top of Robin's boat shoe coming in direction from his left.

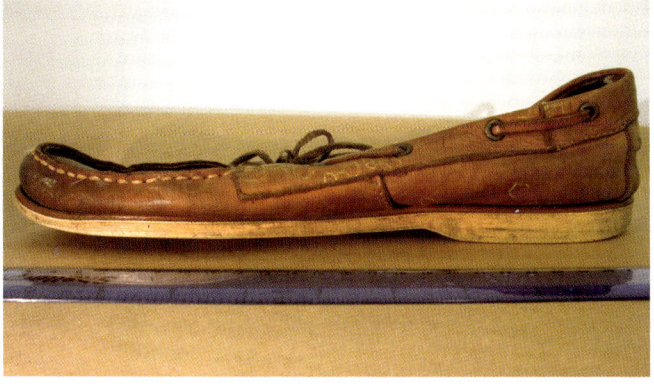

Pinpoint spots on the left upper region of the same shoe that are compatible with blood spatter from close range.

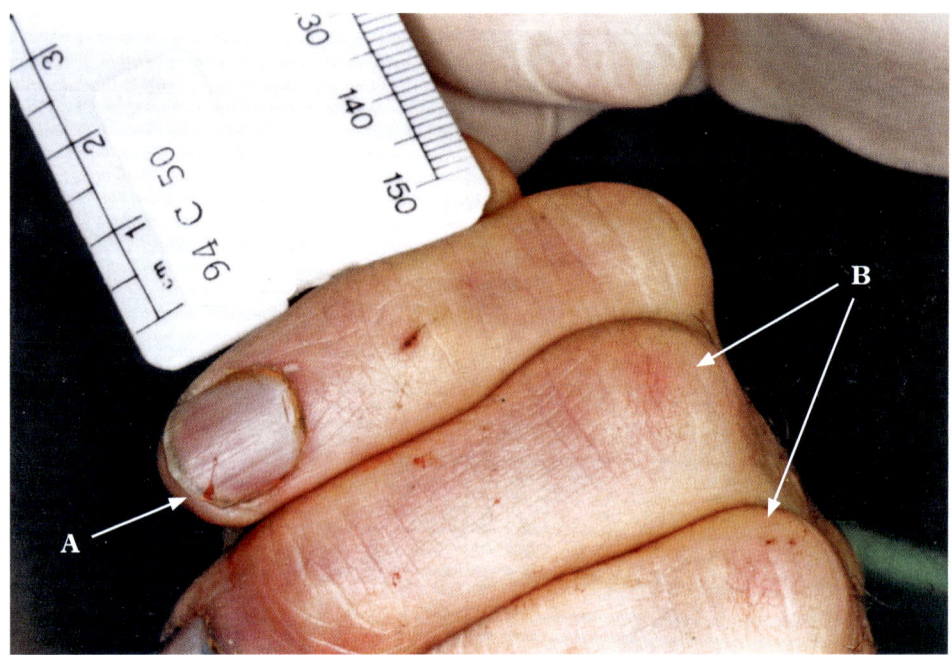

Robin Bain's left hand: A, the splash of blood heading towards the body that Guest spent so much time on; B, residual blood staining on both these fingers remarked on by Dr Dempster.

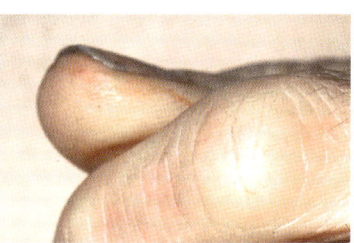

Residual red smear around the top of Robin's left thumb — the photo supplied by Dr Dempster in 2009 for the first time.

Wound to Robin's right fist.

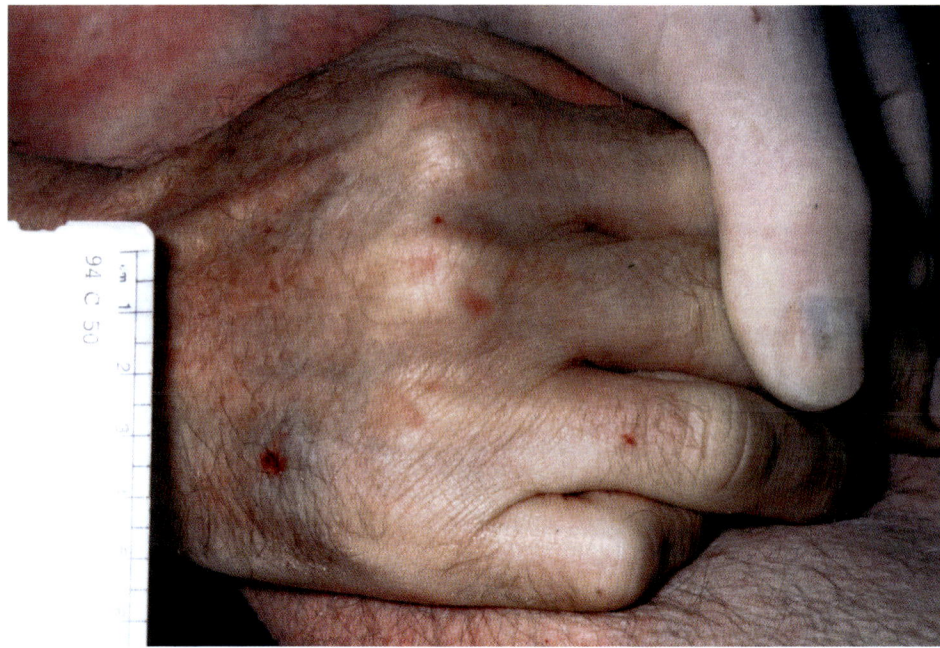

The scene in room C — Laniet as found by police.

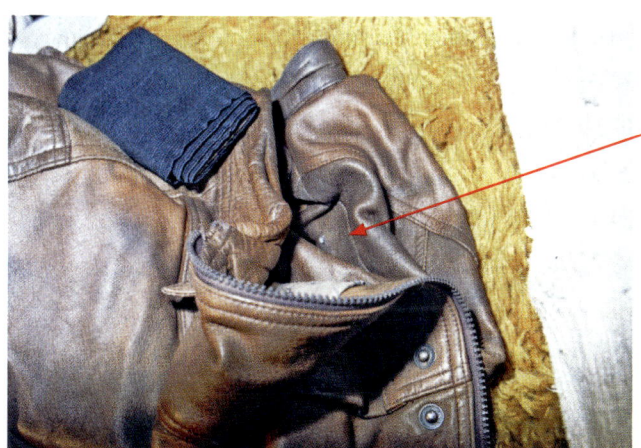

Bullet fragment on leather jacket on chair.

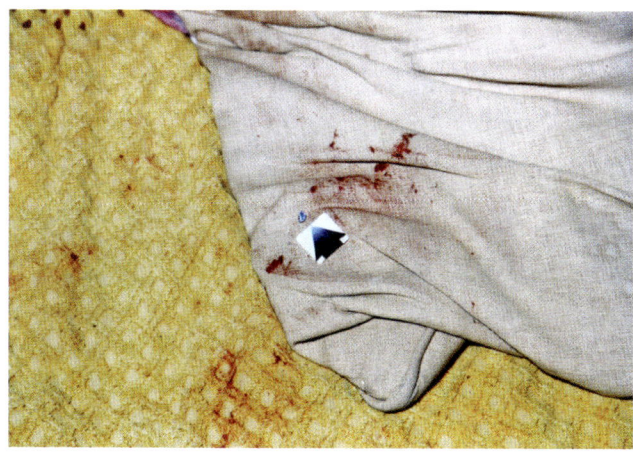

Bullet fragment on pillow underneath Laniet.

Piece of skin in Stephen's room that Hentschel said in the first trial, in 1995, matched the abrasion on David's knee but which DNA tests in 2008 proved was Stephen's skin.

Robin's Commer van in which he lived at the school for about three years.

Robin's bed in the caravan. Note reading material: *Death at the Dolphin* and the Agatha Christie book open at a novel called *Death Comes as the End*.

The 20 bullet shells in Robin's caravan.

Jones exhibit at the first trial showing the left forefinger print (1) from the rifle and (2) of David Bain. Note in 1 the ridges are the wrong colour if it was blood, and the notation states 'chemically enhanced' which in 2009 Jones claimed was wrong.

1

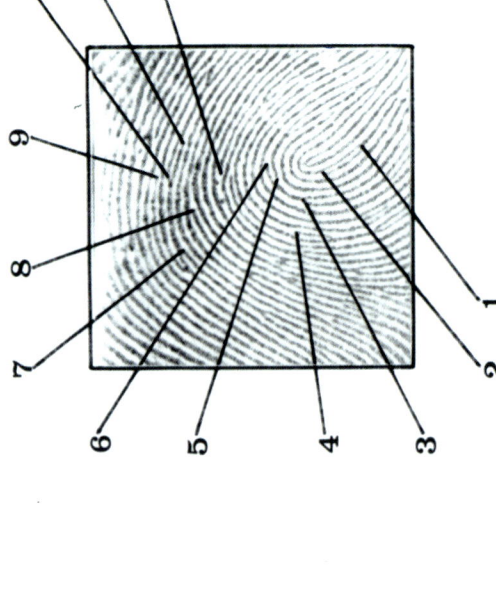

Left fore finger chemically enhanced on the right side of .22 Calibre Winchester Rifle

2

Left fore finger as recorded on the fingerprint/palmprint form bearing the name David Cullen BAIN

There is a vast amount of literature on the subject, which has been extremely well researched by forensic scientists from all over the world.

GUNPOWDER RESIDUE

The starting point of this science relates to the fact that when a bullet is fired from a firearm it is followed out of the end of the barrel by a body of burnt and unburnt residue from the gunpowder. If the tip of the rifle is in touch with the target at the time the bullet is fired then this is referred to as a contact or near-contact wound. In such wounds the gunpowder residue discharged from the end of the rifle barrel has no opportunity to dissipate because the tip of the rifle is against the skin and so it deposits itself in a ring around the outside of the entry wound and in some cases, if the contact is particularly hard, a quantity of it will also find its way into the wound itself.

The term 'intermediate range' is used to describe a situation where the gun is at a distance from the target and so the residue discharge has begun to disperse as it travels through the air but still has enough velocity and concentration to make an impression on the target. The resulting impression is called 'stippling' or 'tattooing'. As the distance increases away from the target, two things happen: the first is that the residue spreads further and further in diameter and, secondly, it loses velocity. An intermediate range wound is regarded as a wound that is any distance between contact and the point where the residue no longer makes an impression on the target. The distance from the target at which this will occur varies according to the weapon and ammunition used in each particular instance.

If there is no evidence of a 'ring of soot' or 'stippling' on the target it is called a 'distant' wound. It may be as close as a couple of metres or even less, but it has not left any stippling or tattooing effect on the target.

With distant wounds, there is no way of ascertaining the distance it has been fired from except for the physical characteristics of where the shot was fired. That is, if a person was shot in the open the distance could be anywhere from a metre or two to hundreds of metres; whereas if the shot was fired inside the same room as the target then, obviously, distance would be determined by the size of the room.

BULLET WIPE

There is another factor that is called 'bullet wipe'. When a bullet passes down the barrel of a gun various particles attach themselves to the projectile and as it passes through the target the matter on the bullet will be wiped onto the edges of the hole created by the bullet. This usually appears as a greyish impression on the very peripheral edges of the entry wound itself. Bullet wipe can be distinguished from the ring of soot that is seen around a contact wound in two ways. The soot is burnt gunpowder and appears as a black deposit, whereas bullet wipe is distinctively grey. Also, bullet wipe appears only on the very edge of the wound whereas soot deposits are not only on the edge of the wound but also on the surface surrounding the edges of the wound.

It will therefore be obvious that bullet wipe will occur on a wound from any distance because it is the bullet that is the carrier of the matter that is wiped onto the edges of the wound as it passes through the target.

So in summary: the soot discharged from the end of the rifle displays a very distinctive impression of a black ring like a collar immediately around the wound when it is a contact shot. In an intermediate range shot there is no ring of soot but rather minute impressions scattered around a greater diameter of the target by individual particles of gunpowder discharge, known as stippling or tattooing. When there is no ring of soot or tattooing this is described as a distant shot.

Dempster's postmortem reports showed that he recognized the difference between the bullet wipe and a ring of soot. He said the bullet entry wound on Robin Bain was 4 mm in diameter, exactly what would be expected with a .22 bullet, and that this wound was surrounded by a ring of soot up to 10 mm in diameter. Specific photos were taken to show this ring of soot. In addition, he noted that there were no gunpowder marks any distance from the wound. What he saw and documented fitted perfectly with what one would expect to see in a contact wound.

MISLEADING NATURE OF PHOTOGRAPHS

Another point to consider in determining firing distances is that photographs of skin surfaces involving gunshot wounds can be very misleading. Kevan Walsh, ESR scientist, in his 1997 report described it in the following words: 'The determination of firing distance by viewing photographs in this manner has a large potential for error. There is no effective alternative to being able to personally examine the wound entry, skin surface and wound interior.'

This is because residual blood remaining in the skins pores after cleaning the skin around the wound or natural defects such as blackheads can, in a photo, look like stippling or tattoo marks. It is internationally accepted that the use of photographs to determine firing distance is fraught with danger and an unacceptable practice. Whereas the initial examiner, in this case Dr Dempster, had the benefit of first-hand observation, nobody else looking at a mere photo, regardless of their expertise, could be sure of what they were seeing.

In addition, clear evidence of stippling on the skin any distance from the wound can only be evidence of an intermediate range wound. Putting it another way, the terms 'contact wound' and 'intermediate wound' are mutually exclusive.

What is usually done as a final check in such cases, and which was done in this case, is that the murder weapon will be subjected to test firing by a ballistics expert to ascertain the characteristics of the particular weapon and ammunition. A white cardboard target is set up or sometimes pig skin is used, and the rifle is fired into it starting from a contact shot and gradually edging out usually in 5 cm increments until the powder no longer makes a mark, which will determine the cut-off distance between intermediate and distant. The resultant pattern of discharge residue can then be compared with that which was found on the body.

Tests done with the Bain rifle for the police with the same ammunition on two separate occasions showed that contact wounds with this rifle indeed produced a 4 mm entry hole surrounded by a ring of soot 10 mm in diameter, exactly what was seen and recorded by Dempster in respect to the entry wound in Robin Bain's left temple.

After Dempster had cleaned the skin area surrounding the wound and photos were taken there were a number of spots and marks ranging 3 to 4 cm out from the edge of the wound itself which Dempster looked at and specifically determined were not tattoo marks from gunshot residue. There was one mark on the left eyelid which Ferris and Thomson brought to his attention that he said he could not rule out as a tattoo, but being so far removed from the wound he would have expected there to be others if it was a stippling mark.

However, doctors Ferris and Thomson, looking only at photos of course, asserted that those spots were powder stippling marks, indicating an intermediate range wound. They compared the distribution of these marks with the test firing cards done by the police ballistics people and came to the view that the wound was an intermediate range shot at some 20 to 40 cm distant from the target. This meant that the trigger would have been too far away for Robin Bain to have reached it to have fired the shot. Thomson's and Ferris's evidence then, if accepted by the jury, would have precluded Robin Bain shooting himself.

In evidence at the retrial, Dempster remained adamant that this was a contact wound and that he had taken into account all of the matters put up by Ferris and Thomson to say that he was wrong. Ferris and Thomson, for their part, stuck to their opinion while at the same time admitting that the use of photos to determine gunshot range was 'unreliable', so in a sense their argument was defeated by their own evidence.

It should be pointed out that the defence pathologists Dr Chapman and Professor Cordner said that the photos of the wound showed the characteristics of a contact wound while at the same time agreeing that certain other marks could have been stippling. As they had not inspected the marks but only seen photos, they deferred to Dempster's opinion because he had inspected them and discounted the possibility outright.

BLOOD IN THE BARREL

By the end of the retrial the issue became moot anyway with the emergence of another piece of evidence proving beyond any doubt that this was a contact shot. This evidence emerged very late in the trial when Hentschel's working notes showing he had found blood in the barrel were put in evidence to defence scientist Peter Ross from Melbourne. Hentschel, in one of many omissions by him, had not included this finding in his evidence. Ross explained that this blood could only have got inside the barrel of the rifle by what is known as 'drawback' resulting from a contact wound. He explained that in those circumstances blood from the wound is sucked back into the barrel of the rifle.

A question from Justice Pankhurst to Peter Ross followed: 'I take it that if there's blood in the barrel it would have to be from the last firing of the rifle that it was vacuumed in?' Peter Ross explained that when the next shot is fired that bullet would remove the blood in the barrel as it passed through. This means that this blood seen by Hentschel could only have got there from the last shot fired that morning. On the Crown's own case, the shot to Robin was the final shot.

Interestingly, and in a further illustration of the way the police conducted the case, Hentschel was questioned about this during the police/PCA inquiry. In this interview Hentschel confirmed that he got a 'reaction for blood inside the barrel'. He also confirmed that it would have got there by 'the firearm being very close to someone being shot'. So, here was evidence of a contact shot to Robin Bain confirming Dempster's evidence, but it was not called in evidence; rather they found two pathologists to give contrary opinions.

What is so important about this is that, as Dempster volunteered at the retrial, contact wounds to the front of the head are *almost exclusively determinative of suicide*.

And so it was that the attack by the Crown on their own first-hand expert Dr Dempster collapsed and backfired.

A note here about the *Manual* in order to illustrate just how vital it is to follow procedure carefully. The *Manual* states that the skin around a wound should be cut out and preserved during the autopsy; you may recall that this was put to Jim Doyle. If it had been done in this case, the enormous amount of money and time expended on doctors Thomson and Ferris, and on the defence pathologists, would have been unnecessary and the trial would have been reduced in time by some days. In fact, there may never have been a trial at all.

PRACTICALITY OF SUICIDE

It had always been a remarkable aspect of the case that suicide by Robin Bain was said to be virtually impossible. The reasons that were advanced by Dr Dempster at the first trial were: the site of the entry wound on the left temple, the angle of the shot at approximately 45 degrees from the left front to the right back of the head and the trajectory of the shot at approximately 10 degrees upwards from the horizontal plane. Dempster went on to say that his attempts to emulate a shot with these characteristics were very difficult if not actually impossible and that there were much easier ways for someone to kill themselves with this weapon. He also said it will be recalled that although he could reach the trigger with his left hand fully extended it was marginal and also very difficult.

In the first trial Michael Guest had demonstrated in front of the jury using a similar weapon with the same measurements that it was quite simple to place the tip of the weapon against the temple with the butt of the rifle on the floor or on a chair to reach down and push the trigger with a finger of the left hand while holding the rifle either around the barrel or the silencer with the right hand. The judge in that trial very sternly warned the jury to beware of Guest's demonstration because he was not an expert and the angle and trajectory were very important factors in Dempster's reasoning and that nothing in Guest's demonstration indicated that these very precise angles and trajectory had been taken properly into account.

Over the years on a number of occasions, defence members including myself had the opportunity of handling the rifle and found no difficulty in reaching the trigger, irrespective of the angle and trajectory at which the rifle was held to the temple. It was noticeable that holding the rifle out at a horizontal plane while standing upright was much more awkward than when the butt of the rifle was placed resting on the floor or a chair and the top of the body was stooped over with the left temple placed against the tip of the silencer.

For the retrial, the police arranged for Detective John Gallivan from the Dunedin CIB, in conjunction with Dr Dempster, to produce a helmet with a rod fixed to it at exactly the spot on the temple where the bullet entered Robin's head. When this helmet was in position the rod was on exactly the angle and trajectory at which the rifle was held when the bullet was fired. This was done to ensure there could be no argument about the exact angle and trajectory and site of the shot when this helmet was used.

Normally speaking, such aids are not admissible in criminal trials for similar reasons that reconstructions are often not admissible. Initially, the Bain defence team intended to have the helmet ruled as inadmissible but instead decided it could be put to good use. The Crown wanted to use it because they chose to believe the opinions of Dr Ferris and Dr Thomson that the distance from the tip of the rifle to the head was at least 20 cm. The rod attached to the helmet had distance markings on it which they thought they could use to prove that when the rifle was held at the correct angle and trajectory in relation to the head, Robin Bain could not possibly have reached the trigger.

Of course, the first thing that went wrong for the police was that Dempster's evidence that this was a contact wound prevailed over the two later pathologists who had adopted the frowned-upon practice of using photos to ascertain firing range in formulating their theories in contradiction of Dempster's evidence.

ARM LENGTH

The second piece of new evidence that the police thought would sustain Ferris and Thomson's 'intermediate' range shot evidence came in the form of a photograph of Robin Bain wearing a dinner jacket and the dinner jacket itself. The police took this photograph and dinner jacket to a bespoke tailor in Dunedin named Ivan Coward. Based upon its measurements he was able to take from the jacket itself and the photograph showing where the cuffs of the jacket's arms fell in relation to Robin Bain's hands and wrists, he was able to determine Robin Bain's arm span and arm length.

Coward determined that Robin Bain had a full arm span of approximately 185 to 190 cm. The police believed that this measurement in conjunction with the helmet and rod attachment, along with the evidence from Ferris and Thomson that the wound was an intermediate range of at least 20 cm, would prove that Robin Bain could not have killed himself.

In fact what happened was that, first, the intermediate range wound evidence did not stand up to scrutiny; and, second, the defence were able to use the helmet and arm span evidence to demonstrate the various positions in which Robin Bain could very easily have shot himself. Tests were carried out by forensic scientists and ballistic experts in the United Kingdom and a series of photographs were taken.

The upshot was that a person with an arm span similar to Robin Bain's could easily reach the trigger in a variety of positions even with the thumb of his left hand. By using the middle finger there was about 12 to 14 cm over-reach. When these photos were put to Dr Dempster during cross-examination he agreed that they showed the ease with which Mr Bain could have killed himself with the rifle, taking into account the site of the entry wound, as well as the angle and trajectory of the shot.

The defence agreed to have the evidence of Gallivan and Coward read to the court by consent before Dempster began giving evidence. This ensured that their evidence attesting to Robin Bain's arm length and the accuracy of the helmet/rod exhibit was in the evidence before Dempster himself took the stand.

In his evidence in chief at the retrial Dempster, sitting in the witness box, had held the rifle at arm's length on a horizontal plane out against his head to show how difficult it was to shoot yourself on the correct angle in that position. In cross-examination he was questioned on this demonstration.

> *Q:* Doctor, yesterday when you gave your various demonstrations about holding the gun up to your head in various positions I assume that was intended to show how difficult you thought it might be to commit suicide holding the gun as you demonstrated?
>
> *Dempster:* That was the intention.

Then, a little later:

> *Q:* I am saying to you if you are giving a fair demonstration to the jury, why would you give a demonstration that really is just totally unrealistic, why would you do that?
>
> *Dempster:* Because I was not asked to step down and show it in other positions.

That answer gave the impression that the Crown deliberately led him to demonstrate the most awkward and unlikely means possible.

Michael Reed had taken Dempster through the series of eight or nine photographs depicting the various positions showing how Robin Bain could have held the gun. In these photographs the helmet was on the model with the rod inserted into the barrel. The model's arm had been measured as being less than the police evidence of Robin Bain's arm length. Dempster agreed that there was no argument whatsoever that the demonstrations absolutely mirrored the site of the wound and the angle and trajectory of the shot. He agreed that all of the positions were perfectly feasible. Each of the following passages is Dr Dempster's reaction to a particular position as demonstrated in the photographs.

> *Q:* I'm giving you an opportunity to criticize that if you so wish.
>
> *Dempster:* Well, the — the rifle and the mask has been used and it is — I think replicated the situation reasonably accurately, as accurately as possible with this arrangement.

Q: Yes that's better, you can't replicate it any more accurately?

Dempster: Not more exactly than that no, that's correct.

Then in regard to another photo, Dempster answered: 'Well, I'm surprised that he is able to use his thumb in that position, but it certainly seems that he's got the rifle oriented appropriately.'

Q: But there's the proof of it.

Dempster: It seems to be.

Moving on to other photos, Michael Reed asked: 'Once again, it seems that it is perfectly feasible in this position to shoot yourself, should you so wish.'

Dempster: It would seem so.

Q: Those are a combination of positions, aren't they?

Dempster: Yes.

Q: And you agree that in each of them it is quite possible to shoot yourself?

Dempster: To activate the firearm, yes, at that particular angle.

Q: And you don't have to contort yourself in any particular, with any particular difficulty, do you?

Dempster: No.

Once it had been demonstrated to the jury in the retrial, by using the Crown's evidence of arm length and its helmet contraption, and with the complete agreement of the examining pathologist, that suicide by Robin Bain was far more likely than just a mere outside possibility, any chance of the Crown proving David guilty had all but disappeared.

On the matter of suicide a passage from the Court of Appeal decision of 2003 is worthy of inclusion. The defence submitted evidence from two Australian forensic pathologists, which was dismissed by the Court of Appeal because they were not persuaded by it and believed that other physical evidence was more important. Paragraph 150 of the Court's decision is as follows:

In summing up [at the first trial], [Justice Williamson] referred to the overwhelming evidence that Robin Bain did not commit suicide. David

[Bain] has produced further evidence on this topic from Professor Cordner and Dr Gwynne. We accept that this evidence demonstrates a case for saying that it would not have been as physically difficult for Robin to have committed suicide as the evidence at trial might have suggested. Indeed Dr Gwynne considers the case was one of suicide. We are not, however, persuaded on an appraisal of all the relevant evidence, which of course goes far beyond matters of pathology, that the jury could reasonably have found it was suicide. Nor are we persuaded that the jury could have found there was a reasonable possibility that it was suicide. We do not think it necessary to go into the physical intricacies of how the suicide could or might have been performed in a manner which was consistent with the known features of the case. The most important of these are the location and state of the entry and *exit* wounds on Robin's head and the angle and plane of the path of the bullet.

You may be surprised, or then bearing in mind other passages quoted from the decision, not surprised, to know that one of the most important factors relied on by the Court to not be persuaded by the two forensic pathologists was wrong. 'There was no exit wound.'

NEW EVIDENCE FROM DR DEMPSTER

As it turned out, additional evidence from Dr Dempster detracted even further from the Crown case. A little background will illustrate that it would appear Dr Dempster had some misgivings about the Crown case even before the retrial had been ordered. It will be recalled that for the retrial he produced a photo from his own collection of a wound on the back of Robin Bain's right hand. He aged this injury as happening between just minutes before death up to a maximum of 12 hours. This bruise and abrasion on the right fist of Robin Bain happened sometime during the night or in the early hours of the morning of the tragedy. At the first trial he said that all the injuries on Robin's hands were at least 24 hours old.

He also produced two photos showing what appeared to be bloodstains on Robin Bain's left hand. Apart from the spatter of blood on the index fingernail the police did not take photographs of other reported smears of blood on Robin's hands, which are dealt with in detail later. The photos produced by Dempster from his mortuary collection show what experts agreed appeared to be residual blood smearing around the tip of the left thumb and also between the knuckle at the base of the thumb and the wrist joint. The general appearance was that it was ingrained into the pores of the skin as though it had been heavily stained then rinsed but not scrubbed thoroughly — it could be described as residual blood staining. This general description was agreed to by Dempster and other Crown forensic scientists as well as defence experts.

Of course it can be argued that whatever this red substance was it had never been tested and therefore even if it was blood it could not be said whose blood it was. However, that is not an argument the police are likely to advance because they are to blame for not having collected it in the first place. The appearance of it as ingrained residual blood staining means that it could not be blood spatter from the wound or smearing that somehow could have got there at the time of his death. The defence argued, and with very good cause based upon its appearance, that it was the residue of blood from the bloody gloves found in Stephen's room; Robin Bain was the wearer and had rinsed but not thoroughly cleaned his hands.

But this was not all. There was the Crown proposition at the first trial, relied on again in opening at the retrial, that Robin Bain's full bladder meant that he could not have been the person responsible for these killings. The logic behind this argument was ridiculous for a number of reasons and will be dealt with in due course. However, for some reason it captured the imagination of the public at large, some sections of the media and, believe it or not, a lot of people in the legal profession.

Dempster was asked in cross-examination whether he could draw any inference from the fact that there were 400 ml of urine in Robin Bain's bladder. He very promptly said he could not. He said that all he had done was report what he found in the bladder and that he personally did not place much store on that argument. It was put to him that the defence would call a urologist to provide expert opinion, and Dempster agreed that urology was a specialist area of medicine and he would defer to the opinion of a urologist on the matter.

He also agreed that the blood spatter on the left index fingernail of Robin Bain, the subject of protracted discussion with Michael Guest in the first trial, you will recall, was perfectly compatible with having got there as back spatter from one of the other deceased if Robin Bain had been the firer of the weapon. In talking about this splash of blood on the left index fingernail in cross-examination it was put to Dempster:

Q: Has it ever occurred to you, Doctor, that the direction that it's coming from indicates that it might have come from someone else?

Dempster: It certainly could have.

Q: And if it has come from someone else, obviously all your surmising and theorizing about the position when someone's holding the gun just falls to the ground, doesn't it?

Dempster: That's right.

Q: In fact it would just be a waste of time that evidence.

Dempster: Yes.

However, perhaps the most poignant indication of the concerns which Dempster clearly had about the Crown case, even to the extent of whether or not there should be another trial at all, is gleaned from a letter he emailed to Robin Bates, the Crown prosecutor, in Dunedin on 16 May 2007, just a few days after the Privy Council had quashed the convictions and ruled that there had been a substantial miscarriage of justice.

The email to Robin Bates from Dr Dempster is produced in full as follows:

Dear Robin,

Before any decision is made with respect to a retrial or otherwise for David Bain I feel that I should raise with you, a component of my evidence in the original trial, on which events subsequent to the trial have influenced my opinion.

It is as to whether Laniet could have continued to have respiratory activity at the time when David returned from his paper round. Assuming the alternative proposition that Robin was the killer, one would have to allow 15 min or so for him to have cleaned up after the shooting.

Subsequent to the first trial, I was the pathologist in the case of a motor vehicle crash in Kaikorai Valley Road. In that case the driver of the vehicle suffered an injury which almost completely transected the lower brain at a point below where Laniet suffered, what I believe, was the fatal gunshot injury. The victim in the crash was reported by the ambulance officers who attended the case, about 15 minutes after it occurred, to be making a few gasping respirations when they arrived at the scene.

As a result of this case, I do not feel that I can now express a firm opinion that Laniet could not have been heard to have been making gurgling noises at the time David returned from his paper round. It is impossible to determine conclusively, the precise effect on the nervous system of any single gunshot wound unless it completely destroys the medulla or hindbrain.

At the time of the trial I felt that prosecuting counsel, as reported, placed a greater emphasis on this point than I would have preferred on the basis of my evidence. I did expect, however, that my evidence, which I assume was scrutinized by the defence pathologist from the Victorian Forensic Institute, would have been challenged, if he saw any issues in it to which he took exception. Similarly other pathologists who had scrutinized my evidence in reviews of the case have not, to my knowledge, raised specific concerns.

For what it is worth it is my opinion that a lot of the scientific evidence which was presented, not permitted to be presented (such as the ESR report on the splatter pattern on the curtain) or subsequently raised as issues by the defence (such as the length of Robin Bain's arms), should also be critically reviewed prior to any decision concerning a retrial.

Sincerely,

Alex Dempster.

The issue of gurgling and whether or not it is incriminating as far as David is concerned will be dealt with later. Suffice to say at this point that Dr Dempster, before the decision was made to hold a second trial, was expressing his serious doubts about the claims made by the Crown 'that only the killer could have heard Laniet Bain gurgling'. In addition, he is telling the Crown prosecutor that Bill Wright in the first trial made more of this matter than Dempster would have liked. This allegation and his evidence above about the 'full bladder' proposition illustrate the view expressed in this book that one of the reasons for the substantial miscarriage of justice was that the Crown drew conclusions and made submissions far beyond the factual basis provided for them.

What may seem even more remarkable, and certainly did to the defence team in the light of this email from Dempster to the Crown, was that Dempster's brief of evidence submitted to the court and defence for the retrial contained no reference whatsoever to the opinion expressed in it about gurgling noises.

This raises the interesting question as to whether or not the Crown were aware that this email had been disclosed to the defence. If they did know it would seem very strange that it was not included in his evidence in chief, thereby not exposing them to looking foolish and deceitful in the event that the defence would raise the email with Dempster in cross-examination. On the other hand, if it was disclosed inadvertently, it raises the question as to whether this was another example of the sort of non-disclosure that happened in the first trial with a number of matters, most particularly the knowledge regarding Mrs Laney's evidence and the true ownership of the broken glasses.

If they did know that the defence were aware of this email, then it can only be said to be a further example of how little understanding they apparently had about the weakness of their case. They opened the case at the retrial with the gurgling as one of the most significant aspects of their case and they had obtained opinions from both Dr Thomson and Dr Ferris that were very emphatic that David's evidence that he heard Laniet make a gurgling noise was extremely incriminating.

The email letter was addressed to prosecutor Robin Bates who actually led Dempster through his evidence in chief. When cross-examination got round to the subject of gurgling the email to Bates was raised, and it caused some embarrassment. An objection was raised by the Crown and the email was shown to Bates before the judge allowed Michael Reed to continue. Even Dempster appeared a little sheepish, as the way it came out, paragraph by paragraph, and being actually addressed to Bates himself it gave the impression that this was a case of deliberate concealment. By this time, Doyle and others had been exposed for the similar tactics they got away with at the first trial. It seemed they were at it again, only this time against a defence team who had given the disclosed documents more than a quick flick.

This may be a useful point to explain what confronted the defence for this trial. Approximately 100,000 pages of documents were disclosed to it by the police in the months leading up to the trial. This email, and other sensitive information, is just a few pages among screeds of paper, in many cases completely randomly filed. Every single document has to be read and analysed to find out what is there, and also to see whether things that should be there are not. This can only be done by a person with a thorough knowledge and appreciation of the case. It was incredibly time-consuming for the defence team members responsible.

THREE PLANKS OF CROWN EVIDENCE AGAINST DAVID DISCREDITED

And so at the retrial, Dr Dempster, one of the most important Crown witnesses, virtually single-handedly showed some of the most important arguments of the Crown case to be of little or no substance. If we take the three planks of the Crown's triangle and call the mass of evidence against David *Plank A*, evidence that Robin Bain did not commit suicide *Plank B* and that there was no evidence whatsoever to link Robin Bain to any of the other killings *Plank C*, we can get some idea of the effect Dr Dempster's evidence had on the Crown case. In no particular order of importance, Dempster confirmed the following points:

PLANK A

- That Laniet Bain could have been making gurgling noises when David arrived home from his paper round if Robin had shot her three times in the head 15 or more minutes before David got home, and that the Crown had overstated matters in the first trial as far as his evidence was concerned on this issue.
- In a further matter that will be discussed in relation to the death of Laniet and the gurgling evidence, Dempster agreed that he did not examine the bullet fragments from her head or the bullet fragments found external to her body. He accepted that if these bullet fragments contained white fibres, it meant that the bullet must have been fired through an intermediate target of white fabric and that when that happens this can cause unusual entry wounds like the one in the top of her head.
- That if Stephen Bain, lying almost naked on the floor in the freezing house, had been killed by David at about 4 a.m. as the Crown postulated, his body would have got cold much quicker than Margaret, Arawa and Laniet.

PLANK B

- Dempster was aware of reports that showed that right-handed people sometimes shot themselves in the left temple when committing suicide. One report indicated that this occurred one in every eight times and that it was perfectly feasible that Robin Bain was one of those eight.
- That the wound to Robin Bain was a contact wound.
- That contact wounds to the head are in 90 per cent of cases the result of suicide. Putting it another way, fewer than 10 per cent of contact wounds are the result of homicide.
- That suicide by Robin Bain in any or all of the positions demonstrated by the defence was perfectly feasible and did not require any contortions of the body.
- That when he first entered room A where Robin Bain's body was found, he could hear the whirr of the computer fan, making untenable the proposition that Robin came in and knelt down to pray unaware that someone was behind the curtains where the computer was located.
- Based upon the new evidence that he had put to him from defence pathologists Professor Cordner and Dr Chapman, he accepted that the site of entry and the angle and trajectory of the shot were in fact quite normal and did not exclude suicide at all.
- He agreed that the test firing results done with the rifle matched his original measurements of the wound to Robin Bain.
- That when he examined Robin Bain's gunshot wound he noticed a number of skin defects including blackheads and that those sorts of things are hard to distinguish when just looking at photos.
- That if the live bullet found on the floor beside the rifle had got there as a result of a misfeed, that was hardly compatible with homicide because a person, Robin Bain, would be very unlikely to just stand there while a killer cleared the bullet and reloaded.
- There was nothing in the way Robin's body was lying when he was discovered that contradicts the photographs showing the various positions in which he may have shot himself.

PLANK C

- That the blood splash on the index fingernail of Robin Bain could have got there as a result of Robin Bain shooting someone else.

- That none of the blood on Robin Bain's hands had been tested and that if any of that was the blood of anyone other than Robin, it would have dramatically changed his view of what happened.
- He was very concerned that two samples collected from Robin Bain's hands had been destroyed.
- The bruise/abrasion on the back of Robin Bain's hand happened sometime in the 12 hours between nightfall the previous day and his death.
- He accepted that the red staining running around the top of the left thumb of Robin Bain was likely to be blood and similarly with the red smear on the base of the thumb, and that neither of these was collected as a sample.
- He said that the Crown thesis relating to the 400 ml of urine in Robin's bladder missed the point. He accepted that he was not a urologist and it was a complex area of medicine. He accepted that the important point as put to him was the way the bladder functioned rather than the amount or quality of liquid retained and also that the urge to urinate can be overridden by external events.

The list of 19 points from their primary expert made a serious impact on all three planks of the Crown case. It all but destroyed any support for the suggestion that Robin's death was not suicide.

CHAPTER 16

NEW FORENSIC EVIDENCE: BLOOD AND SKIN

EXTENSIVE ANALYSIS

Reference has already been made to the fact that the word forensic is loosely used in popular vernacular to refer to scientific evidence; in fact 'forensic' really means *of the court* and so it refers to any evidence given in court.

There has been a wave of publicity since the retrial claiming that there was 'no forensic evidence incriminating Robin Bain' at the retrial. However, very little has been offered in support of this proposition.

Dr Dempster's evidence alone shows the fallacy of it. When various commentators, for example David Bain's uncle, Michael Bain, in a major feature published by the *New Zealand Listener*, make this claim, they do not venture into details about the actual forensic evidence, but rather make the statement as though it is an accepted fact.

The first trial evidence was recounted in detail and all the forensic evidence adduced by the Crown was included. It is true that at the first trial no forensic evidence was put before the jury suggesting that Robin may have been involved in the killings or that he in fact killed himself, and it is also true that at the first trial the forensic evidence against David appeared overwhelming.

In the 14 years between the first trial and the retrial a vast amount of scientific analysis was done by both the Crown and the defence and this resulted in exposing the evidence in the first trial for what it was, and for the misleading picture that it created for the jury.

The first lot of post-trial analysis took place during the police/PCA investigation in 1997. ESR scientists Douglas Elliot, Kevan Walsh and SallyAnn Harbison were involved in this series of tests, which included the examination of a vast number of exhibits by Elliot, DNA analysis by Harbison and various ballistics and other tests, including luminol tests relating to bloody footprints, by Walsh. Obviously, the rifle involved in the killings was one of the most scrutinized exhibits. In particular, the police wished to prove that David's fingerprints found on the gun had been made in Stephen's blood. This involved DNA testing by SallyAnn Harbison.

Subsequent to that the Bain defence arranged with the police to have a considerable number of those exhibits delivered to a forensic science centre in Melbourne (the Victoria Forensic Science Centre, VFSC). This took place during August and September of 1997. The work done in the Melbourne laboratory was done on written instructions from the David Bain defence. I attended the laboratory on a number of occasions and personally viewed most of the exhibits that were sent there, including the rifle.

When the case was ordered back to the Court of Appeal at the end of 2001 by the Governor General, another series of tests took place on instructions from the police at the ESR in Auckland on a variety of exhibits. This included further DNA testing on the rifle and on other exhibits, including the heavily bloodstained green towel from the laundry referred to by Croudis on the day of David's arrest. The examinations and testing conducted by the ESR at this time were also attended by me, with the reluctant agreement of the Crown.

After the order of the retrial the Crown again indulged in a significant amount of further DNA analysis, testing and examination of exhibits. After the retrial was ordered, the police uplifted defence documents from the VFSC which related to work done by that institution on instructions from the Bain defence in 1997.

This conduct resulted in a dispute between the Bain defence team and the Crown. The defence alleged that this was a serious breach of proper practice and it was a major factor in the defence application to have the trial stopped, or in legal terms, to have the Court 'stay the proceedings'. Although the Court did not stay the proceedings they did rule that the actions of the police were improper. Anyway, apart from the inconvenience and distraction that it caused the defence, it also resulted in the VFSC refusing to do any further work on the case. This meant the defence had to go elsewhere for scientific and other expert advice. Suitable facilities were found in the UK.

The defence team prepared copies of a vast amount of documents relating to the pathology and scientific analysis done for the Crown over the years and sent this to Britain, along with a considerable number of exhibits. In particular the issues under scrutiny related to the fingerprint evidence of Kim Jones, especially his evidence about 'bloody positive fingerprints' on the rifle; analysis of blood patterns; ballistics and scientific demonstrations as to how Robin Bain may have killed himself with a rifle taking into account the arm span evidence produced by the police, along with the helmet and rod device and pathological findings, including histological slides.

The combined effect of all this testing by both sides dramatically affected the forensic evidence that had been produced in the first trial, first of all by negating matters that had been held up as highly incriminating of David; secondly, by showing that Crown theories relating to the death of Robin were totally unsound; and, thirdly, by showing that there was indeed a strong body of 'forensic' evidence pointing directly at Robin and excluding David.

FINGERPRINTS NOT IN BLOOD

At the trial in 1995 ESR scientist Peter Hentschel gave evidence that he removed five samples of blood from the murder weapon, including one sample 'from the area where those fingerprints were found', a reference to David's fingerprints on the wooden fore-stock of the rifle. He said that he gave these five samples to ESR scientist and blood analyst Dr Peter Cropp, who said that when he tested them they all proved to be human blood. The natural inference, which no doubt the jury in the first trial accepted, was that David's hands got covered in blood during the fight with Stephen, resulting in these bloody fingerprints being found on the murder weapon. The Court of Appeal in 2003 emphatically endorsed that view, listing it as one of the three points of evidence that in their view would cause any jury to convict David Bain.

DNA TESTS 1997

Assistant Commissioner Brian Duncan was the head of the police side of the review conducted in 1997 and when he met the defence, his opening gambit was to ask what the defence would say if David's fingerprints were found to be made in Stephen's blood. He said DNA tests were being conducted and he expected that would be the result. The report of over 100 pages published by the police/PCA review team and signed off by the Police Complaints Authority, Judge Jaine and Brian Duncan, contained no reference to these tests. If it had not been for Duncan's smug comment the defence may never have known of the tests. The defence obtained the scientific case notes relating to the tests which were conducted by SallyAnn Harbison from the ESR in Auckland. She had removed 10 samples of blood from the rifle including two from the fingerprints. The only one of the 10 that did not contain human DNA was the sample taken from the fingerprints. All other samples taken from various points on the rifle proved to be human blood and in most cases were able to be profiled as the blood of Stephen Bain. No doubt as a result of the failure of the sample from the fingerprints to yield human DNA the test was repeated. However, the second test resulted in some kind of human contamination during the test and so was scientifically invalid and therefore unreportable.

The case notes relating to Harbison's tests revealed another unusual fact, which was that when the gun was examined by Elliot and Harbison they found two fingerprints remaining of the four left-hand prints of David Bain and also two large smears between the fingerprints. The smears and prints were sampled and tested as one sample, and it was this sample from which not even a trace of human DNA could be detected, nor anything to suggest that it was even blood. It will be recalled that the evidence of Kim Jones and Peter Hentschel at the first trial was that this area was clear of any contamination except for the four fingerprints. This raised the question: what were these smears found between the fingerprints by Elliot and Harbison? Whatever it was, according to the DNA test, it was not human material, and nor were the two fingerprints they sampled.

ESR CONTAMINATION CLAIM

When this information became available from Harbison's case notes the Bain defence team inquired as to whether any of the sample from the fingerprint area remained and was informed that a very small amount had been left over. This was obtained and tests were conducted on it for the defence. A very large quantity of mammalian DNA was detected, which included the possibility that it could be either rabbit or possum blood. This result was included in the petition to the Governor General. The response from the ESR to inquiries made by the Ministry of Justice was that they had supplied the defence with a 'contaminated sample' from the second test and therefore the defence results were valueless. This claim, that a forensic laboratory would supply a sample to another laboratory for testing knowing that it was contaminated but not telling them, left the defence speechless, but appears to have been found to be perfectly acceptable by the Ministry of Justice.

It was on the basis of the 'mammalian' DNA result that the Bain defence advanced the proposition to the Court of Appeal in 2003 that, although this test had a shadow cast over it by the belated claim of the ESR, it still provided evidence that the fingerprints may have been made by David in rabbit or possum blood when he was using the rifle long before the killings of 20 June 1994.

ORIGINAL HENTSCHEL SAMPLE NOT FROM PRINTS

Meanwhile, in 1999 during the Ministry of Justice investigation resulting from the petition to the Governor General, there had been another issue identified with the prints. Peter Hentschel had told them that the sample he took, which he labelled 'fingerprints', and in the first trial had told the jury it had come from 'the area where those fingerprints were found', was not, in fact, taken from the fingerprints at all, but from an area somewhere adjacent to those fingerprints.

At the Court of Appeal in 2003, Hentschel's evidence was that he took the sample from an area towards the trigger from where the fingerprints were found: about 10 mm from the first print (the forefinger). This was not based on any contemporary notes or diagram, and at best seemed to be guesswork. It was contradicted by the fact that where he said he had taken this sample from was an area which had a Sellotape strip wrapped around the rifle to hold a label put on there by Kim Jones when he found the fingerprints. Hentschel said he took the sample on 4 August, some weeks after Jones had attached the label with this Sellotape. So by 2003, the Crown evidence, particularly that involving Hentschel and Harbison, was what the defence scientist described, and the Court of Appeal endorsed, as an 'unspeakable mess'.

DNA TESTS 2003

Yet more DNA tests were conducted for the police in the lead-up to the 2003 Court of Appeal hearing, this time by Dr Sue Vintiner from the ESR in Auckland. On instructions from Colin Withnall, I attended the preliminary examination of the rifle, and also present were Kim Jones, Kallum Croudis and other scientists from the ESR. The thoroughness of the police to try to find Stephen's DNA, or at least human DNA, in the area of the gun where David's fingerprints had been, was evident when they pulled the gun apart and swabbed for samples in the area where the barrel sits on the stock of the rifle, and any obscure spot they could find that looked like it may have concealed a smidgen of blood. All of the samples removed from this area again failed to show any human DNA. At the same time, samples removed from the silencer and other parts of the rifle were also tested and human DNA was found, from which they were able to obtain profiles. Interestingly, one of the samples yielded two DNA profiles that did not belong to any of the Bain family.

JONES: BLOOD FLUORESCES

The genesis of the idea that these fingerprints were in blood, it will be recalled, came from Kim Jones's evidence in the first trial. He said that under the violet light band of the Polilight, he saw what appeared to be blood all over the gun, including where those fingerprints were, because 'it fluoresced' when he put the Polilight on it. Jones also, you will recall, produced an evidential photo of the fingerprint as an exhibit, under which was the notation that the fingerprint had been 'chemically enhanced'. This is a reference to a standard fingerprint enhancement technique where the area of the print is set in a special glue or other similar substance.

WHEN AND WHERE WAS SAMPLE TAKEN? CROWN EXPERTS DISPUTE

At the retrial Hentschel's evidence was that the sample from adjacent to the fingerprints was removed by him in his laboratory when he examined the rifle on 4 August 1994. However, Jones told the jury that Hentschel took the sample 'under his [Jones's] direction' on 22 June 1994 in the offices of the Dunedin CIB, and that it was taken not from where Hentschel said but from the tip of the middle-finger print, which is in the opposite direction from Hentschel's evidence dating back to the letter he wrote to the Ministry of Justice in 1999.

Jones's evidence in the case has been extensive. There were his initial reports, his deposition statement, evidence at the first trial, lengthy interviews during the police/PCA review, sworn affidavits and cross-examination before the Court of Appeal hearings in 2002 and 2003. This, in the retrial, was the first time that he ever made the claim that he actually directed Hentschel in the taking of the sample, that it was taken from the tip of the middle finger and that it occurred in the Dunedin CIB just two days after the killings on Wednesday, 22 June 1994. In addition to that, this evidence was not included in his brief of evidence submitted to the court for the retrial. He just suddenly blurted it out during his evidence in chief.

No record from Jones or Hentschel, nor the police exhibits register nor any other job sheet or document exists to record the obtaining of a blood sample from the rifle in Dunedin on 22 June 1994. It is common sense and generally common knowledge that the sanctity of forensic samples is vital, and that records of their movements are also vital. This record is so important that, as we have seen, the police called evidence from Jim Doyle and Peter Robinson in the second trial simply to attest to the fact that they had uplifted samples or exhibits from the exhibits officer and taken them to a Christchurch laboratory and a Melbourne laboratory respectively. However, although these fingerprints, in blood according to Jones because 'it fluoresced', was the single most important discovery made by the police about the case as at 22 June 1994, here we are being told in evidence for the first time 15 years later that blood was removed without any record whatsoever.

Not only is there no record of it being removed, but neither is there anything to indicate how it was removed (swabbing or scraping are the normal means), what it was put into, and how it got from Dunedin to Christchurch. Adding to that of course, the person, Hentschel, said to have removed it denied that he did. In contrast, as has been described, the one swab that was taken from Robin's hand, recorded in the exhibit register as Exhibit 97, and every movement of it, including its destruction in 1995, is noted.

This would not be the only contentious claim made by Kim Jones, the police fingerprint technician, at the second trial.

PRIME EVIDENCE — NO PHOTOGRAPH

Another point on this most vital of police evidence is that no photograph was produced to show these four fingerprints together on the rifle. Nor is there a colour photograph showing the fingerprints as 'red', which would support the contention that it might have been blood. It will be recalled that in the first trial, in answer to direct questions from Justice Williamson and Michael

Guest, Jones could not confirm seeing any red colouring in the fingerprints. His assessment that they appeared to be in blood was made on the basis that they fluoresced under the violet band of the Polilight.

BLOOD DOES NOT FLUORESCE

The fingerprint evidence was submitted by the defence team to the United Kingdom in 2008 in preparation for the new trial. The fingerprint expert consulted was Carl Lloyd who had been involved in fingerprint work for the British police and forensic science services for about 40 years. He had done work for Scotland Yard and was a man of vast experience in the field. When Lloyd examined Jones's evidence and other statements he had made, the first thing that raised his eyebrows was the claim that the fingerprints appeared to be in blood because they fluoresced when he shone the Polilight on them. Lloyd told the Bain defence that *blood does not fluoresce*. Blood absorbs the light and shows up as a dark area. What would fluoresce is the gun oil and lacquer on the wooden surface of the rifle. Lloyd's expert opinion is confirmed by the manufacturers of the Polilight, who say in their manual: 'Although blood has a broad absorption spectrum, it only exhibits a single absorption maximum of around 415 nm and does not display any photo-luminescence properties.' They cite grease, oily substances and varnish as examples of materials that naturally fluoresce.

RIDGES THE WRONG COLOUR

The second matter that caused Mr Lloyd concern related to the black and white photograph evidencing the forefinger print of David on the exhibit produced by Jones to the court, which included reference that it had been 'chemically enhanced'. The ridges of the fingerprint in that photo were white, whereas Lloyd said if the fingerprint was made in blood the ridges should be black and the gap between the ridges should be white. Lloyd's opinion is confirmed by the manufacturers of the Polilight, whose manual states that when viewed under a Polilight, 'blood marks look dark against a lighter background'.

BLOOD POOLS

It will also be recalled that Jones had given evidence that these fingerprints were very well defined, meaning that there was no smudging or deterioration.

He said this was evidence that the prints were placed there when the gun was gripped very firmly. Lloyd pointed out that a natural property of blood is that it coagulates and pools. The effect of this is that fingerprints made in blood are not well defined at all because the blood tends to 'pool', thereby smudging the ridge detail. There was no evidence of pooling in the evidential photo of the fingerprints.

Carl Lloyd obtained a rifle with a similar surface to the murder weapon and made some fingerprints in blood which he photographed and produced in evidence at the retrial to demonstrate this point.

These three factors caused Lloyd to believe that David's fingerprints on the rifle were not made in blood at all but rather that they were latent finger-prints, that is, they were normal fingerprints, made without any contaminant except the natural moisture in the skin, which had been chemically treated to enhance their appearance. Note that if they were in blood there would be no need to chemically treat them because the blood would be visible without any enhancement application.

These assertions and opinions advanced by Lloyd at last suggested some explanation for the fact that no human DNA had been found in the so-called 'positive bloody fingerprints' and had further ramifications in that Jones had claimed the entire rifle appeared to be covered in blood when he examined it with his Polilight and it fluoresced. This claim had always confused the defence because photos of the rifle did not indicate blood all over it. In fact large areas of it appeared to be clean, and when it was examined for the defence in 1997, the scientists could not locate any blood on it at all.

If Lloyd was right, as the Polilight manufacturers' manual indicated he was, then Jones's entire evidence could not be relied upon. What did Jones have to say?

JONES'S EVIDENCE AT RETRIAL

When Jones gave evidence at the retrial, he told the jury that he agreed with Lloyd that blood does not fluoresce. He said he told the first jury that it did because he thought that it would be easier for them to understand. He admitted that the ridges in the exhibit photo of the fingerprint should indeed be black. He claimed that the notation that this fingerprint had been enhanced by chemical treatment was a mistake and that the fingerprint had never been enhanced at all except to have a light shone upon it.

Excerpts from Jones's cross-examination:

Q: Mr Jones, are you a police officer?

Jones: Non-sworn police officer, sir.

Q: Yes, you are familiar, though, with giving disclosure of evidence before a criminal trial, aren't you?

Jones: I am.

Q: You are familiar with giving a signed brief of evidence so the defence knows what you will say?

Jones: I am.

This line of questioning went on, establishing that Jones had given evidence on a number of occasions about his involvement in the Bain case including at the Court of Appeal and that he had signed a brief of evidence for this trial.

Q: In all those years you have never mentioned to anyone except at the end of your evidence to Mr Raftery, as to where you now say you took a blood sample from, being at, under or near a fingerprint, correct?

Jones: I have never been asked before.

Q: It is not a question of being asked, Mr Jones; it's a question of giving fair information as to where you have relied upon for your evidence.

You never divulged that to anyone in the course of 15 years, did you?

Jones: I have never been asked, sir.

Jones's only explanation for suddenly blurting out that the sample from the fingerprints taken by Hentschel was taken in the Dunedin CIB on Wednesday, 22 June under his direction was that he had never been asked. He maintained that Hentschel was mistaken, but was not able to produce any records to support his claim.

Moving on to the next subject of blood fluorescing under the Polilight:

Q: You've also said in the first trial, and this is page 209 of the first trial evidence, 'blood actually fluoresces' and this is in relation to the use of a Polilight. That's not correct, is it?

Jones: That's not correct, no.

Q: Well, why did you tell the High Court judge and jury that back then? Was that your own experience at the time?

Jones: No, it wasn't, sir. I was trying to put that in layman's terms so that the jury would understand.

Q: You actually said, 'The blood is actually fluorescing when I carry out my investigation with the Polilight. I am looking for blood, I will turn it on to the violet waveband.' And then you go on to say, 'And hence any fingerprints that may be in blood will fluoresce black.' Nothing fluoresces, does it, Mr Jones?

Jones: You are correct, blood does not fluoresce, but I was trying to put that in layman's terms so the jury would understand.

...

Q: But you did tell the first jury that it did, 'The blood is actually fluorescing when I carry out my investigation using the Polilight', that was false, wasn't it?

Jones: As I said, I tried to put it in layman's terms so the jury, at the time, would understand.

Q: You didn't have to put it in layman's terms, all you had to say is, when I used the Polilight, blood may indicate a black area. That's all you had to say, wasn't it? That was the accurate way to do it.

Jones: I was trying to tell the jury how the Polilight behaves.

Q: But it's completely the opposite [of] what you told the jury, because the blood doesn't fluoresce, it simply goes in a dark patch, that's all. It's, the opposite, Mr Jones.

Jones: Blood doesn't fluoresce, the background fluoresces but once again, as I say, I was trying to talk in layman's terms to the jury so they would understand.

Q: But you're asking them to understand something that wasn't right, why would you do that?

Jones: I was hoping the jury might be able to follow it better, if I put it in layman's terms.

Q: But what you put in layman's terms was false, Mr Jones, it does not fluoresce under a Polilight?

Jones: We both agree with that, it doesn't fluoresce, but the background fluoresces.

The questioning went on seeking an explanation from Jones as to why he had given evidence he knew was untrue to the jury, and that he now disputed the evidence of the other Crown witnesses Hentschel and Cropp. He also admitted that the lacquer on the gun does fluoresce. Then further evidence of misinformation given to the first trial jury was put to him regarding other substances that can react with the Polilight.

Q: Well, how could you give that evidence on oath to a jury on a murder case if you didn't know it at the time? Why would you give false evidence, Mr Jones? I'm waiting.

Jones: I haven't got a comment to make on that, sir.

Then followed a series of questions relating to the photograph evidence of the fingerprints, during which Jones accepted that the ridges should show up black if the fingerprint had been made in blood, but that on his photograph they were white. His explanation was that the photograph was a negative and therefore that explained why they were the wrong colour.

But it was put to him that the photographer who took the photo disagreed. He was asked, 'Who is right, you or him?' Jones replied, 'I am right.' So now he was not only in dispute with the ESR scientist Peter Hentschel but also with his specialist photographer and the defence's fingerprint expert from the UK, Carl Lloyd.

Then it got on to the question of the chemical enhancement.

Q: Do you remember telling the first jury that photograph number one there in front of you was chemically enhanced?

Jones: As we said the other day, that should be 'visually enhanced'.

Q: And in fact written on this sheet at the bottom for the jury to read, it says, 'left forefinger chemically enhanced', yes?

Jones: And we all can see that should read 'visually enhanced'.

Jones accepted that all of the other material that he said was blood on the rifle, he could not see with the naked eye but only when he used the Polilight.

He was re-examined quite extensively by Raftery and continued to maintain that the fingerprints he saw on the rifle were made in blood and tried to explain all of the other discrepancies in his evidence, but his credibility had been so seriously undermined that it is doubtful that anybody in the court, regardless of which side they were on, would have staked ten dollars, let alone their house, on Mr Kim Jones.

The defence duly called both Carl Lloyd and the police photographer who actually took the evidential photographs of the fingerprints at the fingerprint offices of the New Zealand Police in Wellington in 1994. Lloyd's evidence had in effect been confirmed as accurate by Jones. All Jones had to cling to in his assertion that the fingerprints were made in blood was that the evidential photograph showing white ridges was a negative. If that claim were untrue, it meant that everything that Jones thought was blood on the rifle — because in 1994 he thought blood fluoresced — was not, in fact, blood. It also meant, of course, that the explanation he was giving to the retrial jury that he was simply trying to help the last jury by telling them that blood did fluoresce was a straight out untruth. The same may be said of his claim that the exhibit of the fingerprint stating that the print was 'chemically' enhanced when it should have said 'visually' was a mistake. It is incomprehensible that in the biggest case of his career, on such a basic matter, a mistake of that nature would be made, for it could hardly be said that there is any commonality in either the functions described by the two words or the words themselves.

Paul Morten led the evidence of the police photographer. He confirmed that he took all the photos of the fingerprints, including the one in the exhibit produced by Jones. He was adamant Jones was wrong in his claim that the ridges appeared white when they should have been black because the photograph was a negative. Not only that, but he kept very good records of all the photographs that were taken, and these should have been retained with the fingerprint file by Kim Jones. However, according to Jones and the police, these records could not be located.

One might think this would have been the end for Jones, with such damage having been done to his credibility, most of it self-inflicted. But the Crown sought leave to have him recalled, and as it turned out he was the last witness to give evidence at the retrial. In the meantime he had done some hurried tests to try to show that he was right and his photographer and Lloyd were wrong about the colour of the ridges in the exhibit photo. However, these tests were off the cuff and highly controversial, especially considering that his conclusions from them also contradict the information in the Polilight manual. The main point of his evidence when he was recalled came right at the end when he stated: 'When I first examined the rifle on 21 June 1994, I was alerted to the fact that they were prints in blood by the mere fact they were red in colour, the red pigment, and that alerted me to the fact, as I say, they were bloody fingerprints.'

So in the last line of his evidence, which was not even his main evidence at the trial but on recall when his credibility had been demolished by the contradictions in his evidence and by the testimony of the photographer who worked with him, he states that it was the fact that the fingerprints *looked red in colour when he first saw them* that made him think they were blood. Contrast this with his own evidence at the first trial, where the judge had sought clarification from him about the rifle being 'covered' with blood. Then, he said that 'most of its entirety fluoresced when I applied the Polilight'. When the judge pressed him about whether he could see the blood with the naked eye, he hedged, saying: 'The strap appeared to have blood on it, and visibly blood type material on the scope and barrel which did not require the assistance of the Polilight.' No mention of the fingerprints, but as we know, they were not on the strap, scope or barrel.

IN SUMMARY

Repeated fastidious sampling and testing by the police has failed to detect even a trace of blood or human DNA on any substance removed from the area of the rifle where David's fingerprints were located. Jones was forced to confess that very crucial aspects of his evidence were patently false. When all else failed he blurted out that he had seen 'red pigment', in yet another contradiction of the evidence he gave to the first jury. The best evidence, then, is that these fingerprints were not made in blood at all. When they were put there no one knows. David owned the rifle; it should not be a surprise that his fingerprints were on it. They were not in a firing position and under all the circumstances are entirely capable of innocent explanation. Did David touch the gun when he found his father and then in shock can't remember having done so? Or were the prints there all the time from when he had previously handled it?

The lack of proper evidential photographs and the contradictory testimony mean we can never know.

SKIN FOUND IN STEPHEN'S ROOM: DNA TESTS 2008

You will recall that the two pieces of skin found in Stephen Bain's bedroom had been taken to Melbourne for DNA testing by DCI Peter Robinson just before the trial in 1995, and that the result was that these pieces of skin could have come from any of the Bain children but not from either of the parents. Records supplied to the defence in 1996 by the police stated that the two pieces of skin had been destroyed during testing. After the retrial was ordered in 2007, the Bain defence became aware from disclosure documents that the police had contacted the laboratory where the tests were conducted in 1995 and found that the test tubes in which the skin had been dissolved in 1995 had been located in a storage freezer. The police uplifted these test tubes, and although the original solution had dried over the years in the bottom of the glass containers it was believed there was sufficient material for modern DNA testing to get a result. The ESR in Auckland subjected the remains of the skin to DNA testing in 2008. The result was that both pieces of skin gave an unequivocal DNA profile belonging to Stephen Bain.

The Crown's shaky assertion posited by Hentschel that this skin could have been the piece of skin from the abrasion on David's knee was put to bed once and for all.

The fact that a result was obtained after 13 years also graphically demonstrates why the defence and David himself are so angry that other vital samples like the fingernail scrapings and blood smears from Robin's hands were either destroyed or never collected.

BLOOD ON ROBIN BAIN'S HANDS

At the first trial the major discussion to do with blood on Robin's hands focused on the splash of blood on his left index fingernail. Although there was mention in that trial that some other blood had been noticed, it was not the focus of any attention by the defence and no photos of it were produced.

At the retrial the following evidence was given about blood or likely blood-stains on Robin Bain's hands; in any sense of the word it is forensic evidence, and it is incriminating of Robin Bain. Just by way of example there are the following quotes from Crown experts and witnesses: Jim Doyle accepted that it was 'unexplained'. Dr Dempster said that if any of the blood was someone else's it would be 'incredibly material' and 'dramatically change' his view of what happened. He also agreed that the splash of blood on the index fingernail, item 3 below, was travelling in a direction that meant it could have been from somebody else. Peter Robinson said that the two samples that were collected should have been taken to Melbourne for DNA testing before the first trial. Douglas Elliot, the ESR scientist called by the Crown, said that the smear on the top of the thumb, item 5 below, 'looks like a smeared blood-stain or something similar'. The bloodstaining on Robin's hands took centre stage more than once as a topic in the retrial.

When it came to the closing addresses, Mr Raftery for the Crown did not make one specific mention to any of this evidence. He made the claim that there was no forensic evidence to link Robin to the murders, seemingly hoping that not mentioning it would lead to the conclusion it did not exist! Michael Reed, on the other hand, addressed the matter very early in his address where it occupied five pages of the record. His opening words on the subject were: 'Then Mr Raftery makes this statement to you that there's not a shred of forensic evidence connecting Robin to any of the scenes let alone Robin's. But I want you to look please at the situation of Robin. Just look at the blood on Robin's hand for a start.'

The following list describes the evidence of this blood.

1. The fingernail scrapings were Exhibit 51. They were taken from under Robin Bain's fingernails by Dr Dempster and contained what appeared to be traces of blood. This finding was found by the defence when it made a request for and received Peter Hentschel's case notes in 1997. These scrapings were examined by Hentschel in his laboratory on 29 September 1994. He did not include this finding in his report to the police, nor did he include it when he gave evidence at the first trial. The scrapings were never tested or photographed. They were destroyed on the instructions of Jim Doyle given in December 1995.

2. There was a smear of blood on the base of the left-hand little finger of Robin Bain. This was sampled and became Exhibit 97. It was

the only bloodstain from his hands that was collected by the police and provided to the ESR for examination. It was confirmed to be blood by Hentschel, but he recorded in his notes that there was insufficient for further testing. He omitted this finding in his report and from his evidence at the first trial. The fact that this sample had been tested and found to be blood became known to the defence in 1997 on discovery of Hentschel's case notes. The sample was also destroyed on Jim Doyle's instructions in December 1995.

3. The splash of blood on Robin Bain's left index fingernail was photographed but never collected as a sample.

4. Detective Lodge, OC body for Robin, recorded in his notes that there was a smear of blood on the heel of the left thumb inside the hand. This was not sampled or photographed.

5. A smear of blood around the top of the left thumb was not photographed, recorded or collected and was disclosed for the first time when Dr Dempster introduced some new photos from his collection at the retrial in 2009.

6. Traces of smears of blood on the skin at the base of the thumb between the thumb knuckle and the wrist on the left hand were also not recorded, photographed or collected. Again this was disclosed for the first time at the retrial by Dr Dempster.

7. Blood on the back of the right index finger was not recorded, photographed or collected and was revealed for the first time in the evidence of Detective Lodge at the retrial.

8. Spots and smears of blood on the back of the middle finger of the left hand were never collected and are vaguely discernible in a general photo of the hand but were not photographed for evidential purposes.

9. Spots and smears of blood on the back of the ring finger of the left hand were noted but not collected and of which there are no photos.

The mere fact that Hentschel did not inform the first jury of his examination of Exhibits 51 and 97 is of grave concern. In his evidence at the first trial he systematically went through all the exhibits he examined, but omitted any reference to either of these samples. If the jury at the first trial had known that there appeared to be blood under Robin's fingernails and that testing had confirmed a smear of blood on the base of his little finger, that alone would have required some explaining. This is yet another example of omissions or failures always being to David's disadvantage.

No photos have ever been produced showing the palms of Robin Bain's hands. As we know from the record above, there are no tests to show whose blood was on Robin Bain's hands because none of it was tested, and it has not been preserved so none remains that can be tested using modern DNA profiling techniques.

The stain running around the top of Robin's thumb has the characteristics of a residual bloodstain. One way in which such a stain might be left is if the hand had been covered in blood which had dried or partially dried and then been rinsed without being properly scrubbed all over. The same applies to the other residual bloodstains. It points very strongly in a forensic sense and in the circumstances of the case to a link with the bloodstained gloves.

The smears of blood on various parts of the hands cannot possibly have got there as a result of the wound from Robin himself. The traces of 'possible' blood in the fingernail scrapings cannot have got there from his own wound. It will be recalled that Dr Dempster agreed that the spot of blood on the index finger was perfectly compatible with being someone else's blood because of the direction in which it was travelling towards his body. Various experts during the retrial, including Dr Manlove for the defence, and Dr Cropp and Dr Elliot for the Crown, agreed that the smearing that could be seen in the few photos available appeared to be blood of a residual nature.

Perhaps not surprisingly, Mr Raftery in his closing address was silent on the existence of these bloodstains. Various Crown experts and Jim Doyle had agreed that if any one of these bloodstains belonged to any member of the Bain family other than Robin or David then it would completely change the whole perspective of the case. Putting it more simply and directly, the Crown case fails completely on the basis of the extensive unexplained blood staining on Robin Bain's hands.

The defence's contention is that these stains prove who wore the bloody gloves. The killer wore bloody gloves up to the point when some kind of fight took place with Stephen, when those gloves were removed. At the same time the killer got blood on at least one of the garments that he was wearing and this was probably the green jersey that was found in the washing machine. It is an accepted fact that the killer was wearing socks, not shoes; and that the killer left five footprints, all from his right foot, in blood from the sole of the sock. The blood got on the sole of the sock while the killer was in Stephen's room.

It is obvious the killer then removed the bloodstained clothing in the laundry. The only explanation that fits the facts that have been presented in evidence is that Robin Bain was this person and that he rinsed his hands without scrubbing them, and hence we have the ingrained staining around the peripheral areas of his hand.

In any criminal investigation, let alone one where right from the outset the police believed there were only two suspects, the failure to treat blood staining on one of those suspects in the proper way is inexplicable.

Leaving aside the question of what inferences may be drawn from the bloodstains, and the absence of any explanation from the Crown for how they got there, what can be said about the negligence of the police? It is so difficult to understand and so utterly reprehensible that it leaves one speechless. The subsequent destruction of the only two samples that were collected, without them ever having been tested, and in such haste, cannot help but cause speculation and give rise to sinister inferences.

FURTHER EVIDENCE ANALYSIS
EXHIBIT 18: BULLET — DAMAGED AND NOT REPORTED
A live bullet was found lying next to the trigger guard of the rifle which was on the floor next to Robin Bain's body. This bullet had been examined by Hentschel prior to the first trial, but he did not refer to it in his report and gave no evidence at the trial relating to his examination. Before the retrial the bullet was sent to the UK where it was examined by Philip Boyce, the defence ballistics expert. This bullet was found to have indentations and striations caused by the lip of the five-shot magazine that was in the rifle when the rifle was found. The expert conclusion was that this bullet had not been properly in the breech. There was some debate about whether the striations occurred as the bullet was going into the magazine or coming out, but either way it is more evidence that casts serious doubt on the theory that David was hiding behind the curtain with the gun. He would hardly be standing in there loading a magazine in the dark while waiting for his father, and equally

Robin would hardly have waited calmly beside the curtain after hearing the click of the trigger and the noise associated with removing the bullet and discarding it before reloading, a suggestion with which Dr Dempster agreed.

EXHIBIT 246: ROBIN'S BROWN BOAT SHOES

The brown boat shoes that Robin Bain was wearing at the time of his death had been examined by Hentschel prior to the first trial. As will be recalled, in 1995 he gave evidence that he found no blood on the soles of those shoes. When his case notes were obtained by the defence, it was noticed that they said the right shoe gave a reaction to luminol on the upper surface. Hentschel did not put this in his report or tell this to the jury in the first trial and Guest did not know because he had not seen the case notes. The shoes were then examined by Douglas Elliot in 1997 during the police/PCA investigation and Elliot reported that he found no blood on the shoes. They were not examined by the defence before the appeal process.

However, in preparation for the retrial the defence had the shoes sent to Manlove Forensics in the UK in 2008 for examination. They detected three spots of blood on the top of the right shoe almost in the centre. The spots were very close together and had impacted the shoe at high velocity according to the expert evidence, coming at an angle from left to right across the shoe. This blood was subjected to DNA testing and found to be the blood of Robin Bain.

In addition, on the upper side of the instep area of the same shoe covering an area about 5 or 6 cm long by 2 cm wide was a pattern of pinprick-sized spots typical of those found from high-impact blood splatter. Testing of these minute spots, however, could not prove that they were blood, something that did not surprise the scientists considering they were so tiny and had been on the shoe for at least 14 years. Although it cannot be proven scientifically, it is very likely that they were blood associated with the same incident and happened simultaneously to when the three blood spots found nearby on the top of the shoe were deposited.

On the assumption that this blood got there at the time of the shot, which was not disputed by the Crown at the retrial for obvious reasons, it proves firstly that Robin cannot have been kneeling down when he was shot, because, with him in a kneeling position, the top of the shoe would be occluded as it would be facing the floor. Secondly, the expert opinion was that the nature of the spatter indicated the foot was within a metre of the head at the time of impact, strongly supporting the contention that Robin was stooped over at the moment the shot was fired, which is consistent with suicide but not homicide as will be discussed.

EXHIBIT 56: ROBIN BAIN'S TRACKSUIT PANTS — NEW BLOOD SPATTER EVIDENCE

The tracksuit trousers that Robin Bain was wearing when he was found were also examined at Manlove Forensics in the UK. Nearly all of the blood-stained areas had been cut out for testing over the years. Nevertheless, after 14 years more blood staining was found, although most of it was of the pinprick variety and was not big enough for further testing. However, it was another example where trace evidence had been overlooked by previous examinations.

A study of the photographs of these track pants taken before any of the bloodstains had been cut out revealed a surprising result. The evidence from Hentschel at the first trial was that all of the blood on Robin Bain's track pants had fallen from above, the inference being that it had dropped from the wound to his head. But there was one blood splatter pattern on the inside upper region of the right thigh area which indicated that this blood splatter was travelling up towards the top of the pants rather than falling downwards. This blood had been tested and it was Robin's blood, although traces of Arawa's DNA were also detected as well.

At the retrial in 2009, Dr Manlove gave evidence to this effect, and Crown witnesses Dr Cropp and Dr Elliot confirmed that in their opinion it also looked to be travelling up the leg of the trousers. When this was put to Dr Hentschel, he said that he thought it could still be travelling downwards.

If Manlove, Elliot and Cropp are correct, however, it proves Robin must have had his leg raised and bent at the knee at the time the blood spurted from the bullet wound, which when considered in conjunction with the blood on the top of the shoe is very powerful evidence that his right foot was on the red chair in front of the curtain at the time he was shot.

EXHIBIT 2: DAVID'S WHITE SOCKS — SPOTS DID NOT DROP FROM ABOVE

Dr Cropp's evidence in the first trial that the two spots of blood on the sole of David's sock had fallen from above was scrutinized by Dr Manlove, who did some laboratory trials to test the theory. He found that these two spots of blood were perfectly compatible with having got there by the wearer of the socks standing in blood, which of course David would necessarily have done when he went into Stephen's room after he found his mother dead. Dr Manlove gave evidence to this effect at the second trial and when the test results were put to Dr Cropp at the second trial he agreed that it was entirely likely that the two spots of blood could have got there from walking in blood as opposed to having fallen from above.

The two spots of blood on the sole of David's sock, so incriminating at the first trial, were found to have a simple and innocent explanation.

Exhibit 14: Rifle — blood in barrel not reported

Hentschel's case notes also revealed that he detected blood in the barrel of the rifle when he examined it, but this was omitted from his report and from his evidence at the first and second trials. This fact, however, was brought out by the defence at the retrial in 2009. This provided very powerful confirmation that the shot to Robin Bain was a contact shot and therefore diagnostic of suicide.

Exhibit 51: Fingernail scrapings — traces of blood not reported

As noted above, Hentschel's case notes also revealed that when he examined the fingernail scrapings taken from Robin Bain he detected traces of possible blood. He did not put this in his report and did not include this fact in his evidence at the first trial. This was of course brought out in the second trial.

What would blood be doing under the fingernails unless the hands had been immersed in blood? This provides an obvious link to the wearing of the bloody gloves.

Exhibit 97: Smear and slide — blood not reported, no printer's ink, no photo

Hentschel's case notes also revealed that the smear sampled from Robin Bain's little finger, Exhibit 97, contained blood, but this was not put in his report and nor did he give evidence of that at the first trial. This sample was destroyed with the fingernail scrapings above. There was also a blackish substance originally speculated to be printer's ink which would indicate Robin had brought the paper in from the letter box. However, the case notes reveal that this was not printer's ink, another matter Hentschel did not include in his report or in evidence at the first trial.

EXHIBIT 25: 10-SHOT MAGAZINE — BLOOD LOST, NEVER TESTED

Hentschel's case notes also show that he found blood on the 10-shot magazine that was found on the floor beside Robin Bain's hand. The case notes record that he removed this blood and sent it to Peter Cropp for further analysis. However, the blood was never received by Cropp. There is no record of what happened to it. It will never be known what it may have revealed. The fact that this blood sample was lost in transit was brought out at the second trial by the defence.

EXHIBITS 19, 24, 66–69: LEAD FRAGMENTS — WHITE FIBRES NOT REPORTED

Bullet fragments removed from the head of Laniet Bain (Exhibits 66–69) relating to the entry shot that went down into the top of her head were examined by Hentschel in his laboratory. He made no reference to them in his report or evidence at the 1995 trial. The two bullet fragments found external to her body, one on the pillow underneath her left shoulder (Exhibit 19) and the other one on a chair about five or six feet towards the doorway from her head (Exhibit 24) were also examined by Hentschel. He recorded nothing unusual about these bullet fragments. These were sent to Melbourne by the Bain defence team in 1997 because there was no explanation as to why the entry wound of the shot into the top of the head was 1.5 cm in diameter or how bullet fragments could be outside her body when there was no exit wound.

The reason this shot to the top of the head had taken on some significance was that it was the Crown case that this was the last shot of the three fired into Laniet's head. They suggested that the first shot was the one to the cheek, which did not kill her and after which she made gurgling noises, causing David to shoot her twice more in the head. The size of the wound from the top-of-the-head shot was perplexing because a .22 bullet normally leaves an entry hole of about 4 mm, which it did in all other instances in this case.

This was the first of three inconsistencies the defence had identified with this theory. The second was that it was impossible to fit the rifle between her head and the wall to effect the shot as would have been necessary if it was the last shot.

The third was that, bearing in mind that there was no exit wound, two lead fragments were found external to the wound (one some distance from her body), which needed explanation that had not been provided by the detectives or by the forensic analysis.

Under inspection with the naked eye, white fibres were clearly visible in both of the fragments that were found outside the body and in some of the fragments found inside the head. Under the microscope these fibres were very prominently apparent embedded in the lead fragments. It was also easy to see an impression of the weave pattern of some kind of fabric on the lead fragments. These unusual features were not mentioned in Hentschel's case notes.

These findings completely undermine the police theory of what happened in Laniet's room in relation to the gurgling submission made so powerfully by Bill Wright in his closing address, as we shall see …

CHAPTER 17

GURGLING, FULL BLADDER, FOOTPRINTS ...

IMPORTANCE OF THE GURGLING EVIDENCE

The final words of Bill Wright's closing address to the jury in 1995 were to the effect that 'only the killer could have heard Laniet gurgling'. This assertion was based on Dr Dempster's evidence relating to the autopsy he did on Laniet. We have seen from Dr Dempster's retrial evidence and the email he sent to the Crown explaining that as a result of a car accident he attended he could not discount the possibility that David would have heard her gurgling when he got home if she had been shot by Robin sometime earlier while David was on the paper round.

The Privy Council, who of course did not know of Dempster's new opinion, included this as one of the nine factors that contributed to the substantial miscarriage of justice and summarized the matter in the following way:

> The trial jury was encouraged to regard David's evidence of Laniet gurgling as a clear indication of his guilt. The second Court of Appeal heard oral evidence from Professor Ferris, but concluded that the issue was not so straightforward. The evidence before the third Court of Appeal [the Tipping decision] revealed a sharp conflict of opinion as to the order in which the shots were fired at Laniet's head (arguably relevant to the congestion of the airways and the likelihood of gurgling) and the phenomenon of postmortem gurgling. Without hearing any of these witnesses, and without giving any reason for discounting the evidence of the witnesses relied on by David, the court found it possible to regard the issue as concluded in the Crown's favour by its

further evidence. But the evidence of Professor Ferris is the subject of sharp expert criticism. The Board feels bound to rule that the court assumed a decision-making role well outside its function as a reviewing body concerned to assess the impact which the fresh evidence might reasonably have made on the mind of the trial jury.

In essence, the Crown argument went like this: Laniet suffered a shot to the cheek which would not have been immediately fatal. Continued respiratory efforts would have caused blood from the cheek wound to be inhaled into her lungs and airways. This would have caused gurgling noises. These would have been audible in the still quiet of night in the house. David said in his evidence in chief that he had heard her gurgling. There were two further shots to Laniet, each of which would have been immediately fatal, one above the ear into the side of her head and one directly down into the top of her head. The Crown submission was that David could only have heard her gurgling after the first shot because she could not have been making gurgling noises after either of the two second shots because both of those would have been immediately fatal, causing respiratory effort to cease. So, said the Crown, the second two shots were fired by David to finish her off when he realized that she was still alive after the first shot to the cheek.

This theory depended on a number of things, the first of which was that David was lying about when he heard her gurgling. David said this happened after he got home from the paper round in the course of finding his family dead. The Crown theory meant that David actually heard the gurgling when he was killing her and the rest of his family in the house at about 4 a.m: three hours or so before he got home from his paper round.

The second thing the theory depended upon was that Dr Dempster's order of shots was correct. If either of the two shots that would have been immediately fatal had been the first shot then this theory fell to pieces. Putting it another way, the theory depended upon the shot to the cheek being the first shot.

The third thing it depended upon was that dead bodies do not make gurgling noises, because if they did, then regardless of the order of shots, David could have heard gurgling noises after all three shots had been fired when he got home (as Dempster said in his email to the Crown prosecutor Bates).

We know that the police found two bullet fragments external to her body, but there was no exit wound; and we also know that the police and forensic scientists involved made no efforts whatsoever to explain this obvious anomaly. We have also seen that the shot to the top of her head caused an entry wound of about 1.5 cm, which is about four times larger than one would expect from a .22 calibre bullet. Indeed, all of the other fatal wounds observed by Dr Dempster in each of the deceased were about 4 mm in diameter. No effort was made to investigate why this wound was as large as it was. In fact, both these very obvious anomalies completely escaped the attention of the police and Hentschel.

However, in 1997, these two matters attracted the attention of the Bain defence team and as a result, the pathological findings of the bullet wound together with the bullet fragments from inside the wound to the top of the head and those that were found external to her body were sent to experts at the VFSC. There it was found that the bullet fragments in her head as well as those external to her body had white cotton fibres attached to them as explained in the previous section. In addition to that, scientists were able to identify the weave pattern of a fabric on some of these bullet fragments.

The experts concluded from this evidence that this bullet must have passed through an intermediate target between when it left the end of the barrel and when it entered the top of her head. This finding was subsequently accepted by scientists and pathologists instructed by the Crown. The bullets that were used in these killings were soft-nosed lead bullets; and although it may seem odd to the layperson, as it did to the defence at the time, it was not unknown in forensic circles that when this type of bullet impacts even a relatively soft target like a towel or a cushion, it is prone to disintegrate.

It was also found that the two fragments external to the body had no blood or brain matter on them, showing that they had not entered the head. This meant that when the bullet came in contact with the intermediate target, these two pieces must have flown off and landed where they were found, while the main body of the bullet continued on to the top of her head. The large wound was caused by the fact that on impact with the intermediate target the bullet had expanded and deformed, what is called 'mushroomed', making it much wider in diameter, and/or had been on an angle as it made contact with the skull.

The position of the two lead fragments external to the body also provided evidence from which powerful inferences could be drawn, as will be shown. The one found on the chair was nearly 2 m from where she was lying, and back towards the entrance to the room. The other fragment on the pillow was underneath her body.

The original investigators had also failed to notice a significant pattern of blood spatter high up on the top of a wardrobe at the foot of her bed, however fortunately it was photographed. It was generally accepted at the retrial that this blood spatter could not have got there as a result of the two shots to the left-hand side of her face and head.

Another point that contradicted the Crown theory was, as already stated, there was insufficient room between the top of her head and the wall or the head of the bed to fit the gun into a position to effect the shot to the top of the head.

And so, taking all these factors into account, the conclusion of the defence expert Peter Ross from the VFSC was that the shot into the top of the head was the *first* in time, not the last as the Crown's gurgling theory demanded. The fact that there was a fragment under Laniet's body meant she must have been sitting up when the shot to the top of her head was fired, which also explained the blood on the wardrobe.

DR FERRIS AND THE CROWN CASE

Dr Ferris, the pathologist hired by the Crown in 2002, was vehemently of the opinion that Laniet could only have gurgled after the shot to the cheek, which would have proved that David Bain must have been in the room between the time of that shot and the following two shots. He advanced theoretical medical explanations for his opinion, but none of these took account of or could account for the undeniable physical evidence outlined above.

Professor Cordner, a forensic pathologist from Melbourne who had been engaged by the Withnall/Karam defence team in 1997, made the observation in his evidence that due to the variables associated with medical matters, the physical evidence in this circumstance must trump the medical evidence. Another point forcefully made by Professor Cordner was that pathologists seldom witness bodies soon after they have died. It is normally many hours later that they become involved. For that reason he said frontline staff such as ambulance officers and mortuary assistants would be in a much better position to comment. Dr Dempster agreed with this proposition. Dr Ferris did not. However, his attempt to explain the two bullet fragments located external to the body demonstrated how incomplete his knowledge was of the physical evidence.

His theory was that the shot to the top of Laniet's head was second and the one above her ear was third. The third, he proposed, had caused the two fragments from the second to pop back out of the entry wound. He said they could possibly have moved a few centimetres on exiting. This fanciful proposition was put to the test under cross-examination, when he admitted that he did not know that one of the fragments was found on a chair two metres away and the other was found under Laniet's body. Nor did he know that the fragments had no human material attached to them, showing that they had not entered her head at all, which of itself dispensed with his theory. He also knew nothing about the white cotton fibres found on the bullets.

By the time of the retrial, Ferris had been involved with the police on this case for about six years and yet he claimed not to be aware of the new evidence discovered by the defence experts and tabled before the Court of Appeal in 2002 and 2003. Reed question: 'What about the white fibres, please?' Ferris: 'Sorry, what white fibres?' And then a bit later: 'Do you not know of any white fibres on any bullet fragments?' Ferris: 'No.'

Ferris had failed to notice or take account of evidence that was visible to the naked eye. So at the retrial, in its closing address the Crown tried a new tack. The police, they said, did not find any white cotton object or material in Laniet's room or anywhere else in the house that had a hole in it the size of a tiny bullet, therefore it must have been disposed of, and as there was no evidence that Robin Bain left the house it must have been David who disposed of it somewhere during the paper round.

It did not seem to occur to them that as the initial investigators and experts had not realized the significance of the bullet fragments found on the chair and the pillow, and did not notice the cotton fibres embedded in them, they did not know that this bullet had passed through some cotton object and therefore nobody would have been looking for it.

It also did not seem to occur to them that in advancing this argument, they were highlighting just how inadequate Operation Every and the experts it engaged really were. If the investigators would send the carpet with the bloody footprints up in flames with the house, and not be troubled by stray hunks of bullet lying around the room, or an entry wound triple the size that it should be; then, people may think, there would be little chance that they would find a minute hole in a piece of white cotton that they were not even looking for. It seems likely that whatever it was went the same way as the carpet.

GURGLING AFTER DEATH

Then there was the second aspect of the Crown theory: that Laniet could not have made gurgling noises after she died. The first answer to that had been submitted by the defence in the petition to the Governor General in 1998, which enclosed an affidavit from a mortuary assistant, Mr Pritchard, who worked in the mortuary in Dunedin for many years. He said that in his personal experience of dealing with dead bodies he had experienced many instances of postmortem gurgling. He said that it was more likely to happen when a body was moved, but that it could spontaneously occur even when a body was lying unattended. This was not opinion evidence. This was first-hand observation by a person whose job involved the handling of dead bodies at a mortuary. This was one part of the defence evidence rejected by the Court of Appeal as being inferior to that of Dr Ferris. Support for Pritchard's observations was given to the Crown itself by Dempster in the email already referred to, that the victim of a car accident was making gurgling noises some 15 minutes after suffering the apparently lethal brain damage, and where the injuries to the brain were at least as bad if not worse than those suffered by Laniet. This was direct first-hand evidence, as opposed to mere theory such as that advanced by Ferris.

At the retrial, Dr Chapman, the pathologist from London called by the defence, gave evidence of a case reported in England where a person had permanently survived brain damage much worse than that suffered by Laniet. Dr Chapman said that this case illustrated very clearly that it was impossible to be definitive about how long after sustaining such injuries a person who, to all intents and purposes, appears to be dead and on medical grounds should be dead, may still continue to have some respiratory function.

Perhaps even more telling was another witness called by the defence, Mr Cooper, a very senior ambulance officer and advanced paramedic from Dunedin. He was the operations supervisor for St John Ambulance in

Dunedin in 1994. He called at the Bain house for about 10 minutes early on the morning of 20 June 1994 at about 7.45 a.m. to ensure that everything was under control. His name did not appear in the Operation Every files, but he was interviewed by a detective from Operation Huia for the retrial, which is how he came to the attention of the defence. That interview was disclosed to the defence, but the Crown were not calling him as a witness. When interviewed he told the detective that he spent about 10 minutes in the room with David and two other ambulance officers. The defence called him as a witness and he gave evidence that he personally had experienced the phenomenon of dead bodies making gurgling noises up to an hour after death.

Q: With the recent dead, have you had any experience of bodies making noises after they're dead?

Cooper: In my experience, there are times where gases in the body, the bowel may make noises, yes.

Q: How long after death can that occur in your experience? From what you've seen and observed yourself?

Cooper: Those that I've observed is probably within half an hour to an hour after death.

Q: Is this when the body is moved or when the body is still stationary?

Cooper: It can certainly happen when the body is moved, but it can certainly happen when the body is stationary.

He went on to say: 'Occasionally you know, if there is a noise from the body such as this, the body, the family may interpret that as there is still life in the person, but that of course isn't correct.'

Q: I want to be clear, this is where the body is lying, not being moved or touched?

Cooper: That is when the body is lying, yes.

In answer to a question about the sort of noise that occurs he said: 'A rumble, a groaning noise, perhaps a gurgle, yeah.'

Similarly, Dr Peter Ross, the scientist from Melbourne, told the jury how on one occasion when he was called to a crime scene while a dead person was still there, he got a terrible fright when that body, without being moved or handled, suddenly made noises out of the blue which could be described as gurgling or groaning sounds.

Mr Raftery's reference to 'gurgling' in his closing address at the retrial was somewhat watered down when compared with the dramatic statement made by Bill Wright all those years ago, and also from the Crown case as put by Robin Bates at the beginning of the retrial. Bates told the jury in his opening address: 'The Crown says to have heard that gurgling, the accused must have been near Laniet during the period between the first non-fatal shot and either of the second and third shots, or between those shots. This shows, the Crown says, that the accused murdered Laniet.'

Quoting directly from Mr Raftery's closing address, this is what was said three months later:

'From there he goes on to Laniet's room and this is in his scenario, coming back from the paper round, entirely innocently, Dad has murdered them all, and what does he do, he hears his own sister gurgling. What does he do, does he behave like a brother, does he go straight to the telephone and dial 111 to get some help? Does he do a thing for 15 or 20 minutes? He does nothing to help his sister who is gurgling, who is giving, in layman's terms, signs of life. He is no pathologist. He is no expert. He hears something that any family member hearing gurgling, muffled by what sounded like water, as a sign of life. And if you are genuinely home from the paper run and hear that sign of life, you would do what any human being would do, you would strain heaven and earth to get someone there as fast as possible. My sister is still alive. The rest seem to be dead but she is still alive. Get here as fast as you can. But no, he waits 15 or 20 minutes before he telephones and tells the 111 people … "They are all dead." Well, by the time he left it for 15 to 20 minutes, they certainly were. There wasn't a chance of Laniet being alive.'

Raftery went on to say that the idea that David came home and heard her gurgling is totally untrue, totally untenable and is one of those Freudian slips. To Raftery, it indicated David was talking about the time during the course of the murders he was committing, and not about any other time.

The reference to 'Freudian slip' was in defiance of the evidence before the jury which was that David in fact had written a note to Michael Guest long before the first trial telling him that when he went into Laniet's room he heard her making noises that sounded like 'groaning muffled by water'.

It was no Freudian slip: as always, David had been doing everything in his power to truthfully recall what he could remember. Neither was there any evidence to support the claim that he had waited 15 or 20 minutes after hearing this noise to make the 111 call. As David had frankly told the police and the jury his recollection of the 15 or 20 minutes was extremely patchy and unreliable. He could not remember going from room to room. He could not remember leaving any rooms or entering any rooms. After having been helped by Dr Paul Mullen, the forensic psychiatrist from Australia, he had flashes of being in the rooms but that was all. The only thing he could remember for certain was finding his mother dead; everything after that was a blur.

As Jim Doyle conceded in his evidence, and as common sense would tell us, any person coming upon a scene such as this would very likely have fainted and this could have happened when he first saw his mother, which may have accounted for nearly all of the 15 or 20 minutes. It is also common knowledge that when a person faints they don't know for how long they have been unconscious.

And so from trial one where David *must* have been the killer, according to the Crown because he said he had heard these noises, the best they could do at the retrial was say that he was not a very considerate brother because he waited for 15 minutes before making a phone call after having heard them, which in itself was yet another proposition not supported by the evidence.

THE FULL BLADDER THEORY

It is remarkable that when those who advance their belief that David Bain is the guilty party, one of the main points they rely on is the condition of Robin's bladder. Indeed, Michael Reed has told me that many people he has spoken to, when expressing doubt that David is actually innocent, very often raise the issue of the 'full bladder' as being, to them, the strongest piece of evidence against him. Naturally, in the circles in which Reed mixes, many of these people are in the legal profession.

The proposition basically goes like this: Dr Dempster had recorded that Robin had approximately 400 ml of urine in his bladder and that was consistent with overnight collection. This amount then morphed in the Crown submissions into being 'a full bladder', which in turn was relied on to say that a person would not be able to commit four murders and then kill himself while in such a condition. Surely, he would relieve himself first, the argument went.

What is even more remarkable, given the extent to which this myth has embedded itself in the public psyche, is that in the entire Bain case it was not until nearly the very last day of the second trial almost 15 years after the deaths that any expert evidence was heard on the subject. The defence called Grant Russell, a urologist from Wellington, to provide an expert perspective. It has already been mentioned that Dempster, during the retrial cross-examination, disowned himself from the theory that the 400 ml of urine he found in Robin Bain's bladder was worthy of any inference whatsoever. He also said that he would defer to the opinion of a urologist on the matter because it is a complex and specialized area of medicine.

One aspect of the theory that illustrates its fallacy is that it fails to account for the other side of the coin, so to speak, for it was the Crown case that Robin was coming in to the lounge to kneel down in prayer for 20 minutes, in what they said was his custom. If he was in such need of relieving himself surely he would have done so before commencing his prayers you may think. The expert evidence puts the whole matter into perspective.

Grant Russell took the stand at the retrial and explained that he was a consultant urologist, that he had graduated from the University of Otago in 1979 and got full membership of the Urological Society in 1987, and that he now practised in Wellington in both the public and private sectors.

The following excerpt from Bates' opening address to the jury about three months earlier was put to Russell:

'As I mentioned, Robin Bain's bladder contained about 400 ml of concentrated urine consistent with overnight collection, the approximate amount an individual passes on getting up in the morning. Given that the murderer had a prolonged struggle with Stephen and spent some time cleaning up afterwards, the Crown says the presence of this full bladder isn't consistent with Robin Bain being involved in those events and therefore being the murderer.'

It was this proposition that Russell was asked to consider and he stated straight out: 'You can't conclude anything from 400 ml of urine in the bladder.' When asked for an explanation, Russell stated: 'This relates to a fairly complex matter of bladder function and it's bladder function that's the determinant here. Certainly, in some people, in many people in fact, 400 mls

307

would create urgency and a need to pass urine. But in many others this is not the case and we've got to consider here an ageing male with an enlarging prostate and I would suggest to you that 400 mls may be well tolerated and may not cause any urgency at all.'

He went on to say in respect to the functioning level of the bladder: 'It's not uncommon to admit ageing men with two, three, four, five litres of urine sitting in the bladder that they are not even aware of.'

He further said that 400 ml may well be tolerated by many men and that there are men who would get up in the morning and having passed urine still be left with 400 ml in their bladder. The likelihood would be enhanced by the fact that Robin was reported by Dempster to have a slightly enlarged prostate, he said. Another point he made was that an increase in adrenaline will decrease urine production and also the ability to store urine. As far as the concentrated colour of urine was concerned, he said that no conclusions could be drawn from that for a number of reasons, one of which was that the colour would change during the hours after death and as Robin Bain's postmortem was not done until 12 hours after his death, then nothing could be inferred from the colour. It will probably be no surprise that Robin Bain's bladder condition was not mentioned in the Crown's closing address.

It is incredible to think that a person could spend 13 years in prison in part because of the arrant nonsense postulated about Mr Bain's 'full bladder'.

CLOTHING, BEDDING, SELLOTAPE ...
EXHIBIT 520: THE GREEN TOWEL
This towel from the laundry was said to be heavily bloodstained. This was put to David on the day of his arrest as an incriminating piece of evidence against him, for which an explanation was demanded. DNA testing on instructions from the police in 2003 by Dr Sue Vintiner from the ESR found that this blood contained Robin Bain's DNA. It is no wonder David could not provide an explanation.

THE WHITE *GONDOLIERS* SWEATSHIRT
This was the shirt found in the laundry basket which was said to have diluted blood on it. David had told the police that he had been wearing it on the Sunday and that he had left it in the laundry basket on Sunday night. The Crown's evidence in the first trial was that it appeared as if somebody

had tried to sponge the blood off. That resulted in the Crown submission to the jury that David Bain tried to sponge the blood from this garment because it was white and he could not put it in the washing machine with the 'coloured' clothes.

DNA testing at the ESR failed to yield any result showing that human blood was on this garment. Also, it may be recalled that when it was examined by Detective Weir and another detective at about 4.30 p.m. on the day of the deaths it was recorded as being dry. How does that fit with it having been sponged that morning?

THE DUVET FROM DAVID'S BED

The spots of blood on the duvet from David's bed, used by Wright, on the basis they may have been Stephen's blood, you may recall, to say that David may have gone back to bed after the first four killings, were also tested during the 2003 tests at the ESR and found to be David's own, and therefore of no relevance to the killings.

SELLOTAPE ON STOCK OF RIFLE

Adjacent to David's fingerprints on the rifle, Jones had affixed a label indicating the fingerprints. The label was held in place by a Sellotape wrapping. The 2003 ESR tests found the profile of two males under this Sellotape, neither of which belonged to the Bain family. Stephen's DNA was not detected.

BLOODY FOOTPRINTS

At the first trial, the first mention of the five sock-clad footprints found in the house came from Detective Weir, who assisted Peter Hentschel with the luminol tests on that first Monday night of the inquiry. Weir described the footprints when he saw them luminesce as looking like the print you would see when someone barefoot walks in sand. Everybody is familiar with what he was talking about, particularly in New Zealand where most people have spent many holidays running around on sandy beaches.

Hentschel then gave evidence that three of these footprints were partial footprints which did not include the toes, but two of them were 'complete' footprints from the heel to toe. The partial ones he measured at 240 mm and the complete footprints were 280 mm long. All the footprints were from a right foot, and the difference in length between three of them and the two complete ones was because the toes were missing from the partial ones, which therefore were only measured from the ball of the foot to the back of the heel. Hentschel's evidence was that all the prints could have been made by the same foot, a view accepted by both sides.

The foot length measurements of David and Robin were not put before the jury in trial one. Instead, the measurements of the socks that Robin was wearing and the socks that David was wearing were used as a comparison. Robin Bain's socks, according to Hentschel, were 240 mm long; and David's socks, the white ones that he was found wearing, were 270 mm long. On the basis of this it will be recalled that the Crown submitted to the jury that Robin Bain's foot was too small to have made these footprints and they must have been made by David Bain.

Both of David's socks showed luminescence across the whole of the sole when luminol was applied to them by Hentschel, and yet only a right footprint was found when the carpet luminol tests were done. Michael Guest accepted that these footprints must have been made by his client, but he offered an innocent explanation: David would have made them when he came home and found his family dead. He would have got blood on the soles of the socks while in Stephen's room, and then left the footprints where they were found, which was at the exit to Stephen's room as it went through Margaret's room into the hallway and at the doorway of Laniet's room.

The first trial was told that the photographs taken of these luminol footprints did not come out, no drawings were made, the carpet was destroyed, and so the only evidence available was the verbal description of Weir and Hentschel.

The Bain defence team recognized the fallacy of comparing the size of a footprint with the size of the sock. Everyone knows that socks stretch when put on a foot, sometimes even nearly doubling in size depending upon what they are made of. It was also known that two or three pairs of socks had been through the washing machine and that it seemed rather odd that David Bain, if he was the maker of these footprints, did not leave both left and right foot impressions, bearing in mind that both of his white socks glowed when treated with luminol by Hentschel.

The luminol tests were done on the Monday night. Investigations by the defence into the documentation revealed that at about 10 a.m. on the Tuesday morning, Detective Lodge, the OC body of Robin Bain, went back to the mortuary and measured Robin Bain's feet. This measurement is recorded by Lodge at 270 mm and that is while Robin Bain is lying flat in the mortuary. He did not tell the jury that he had done this measurement and they never heard evidence of the size of Robin's feet. In 1997 the defence decided to measure David Bain's feet and when this was done they were found to be 300 mm in length.

Moving slightly away from the evidence, and giving you the opportunity of playing detective for a moment, as the Bain defence team did, we wondered, as you may well be doing, how a 300 mm foot when walking through a house on carpet could leave a complete impression which was smaller than the size of the foot. Any person can give this a try either walking on a sandy beach or getting a piece of carpet and spreading something on it which would cause an impression to remain, or alternatively do the reverse and put something on the sole of the sock before walking across a piece of carpet.

Invariably a person walking on carpet leaves a print which is larger than the foot, by virtue of the motion of walking. But regardless of that, it is impossible to leave a *complete* impression of your foot, or indeed of any object, which is smaller than itself. This is self-evident. The Crown had excluded Robin from being the maker of these footprints by virtue of the size of the socks when they knew full well that his foot was exactly the right size to make the footprints that Hentschel and Weir found. Later, when David's foot was measured it was too big. The Bain defence put this evidence to the police and Police Complaints Authority during the 1997 review.

As a result, the police arranged for Kevan Walsh from the ESR in Auckland to do a series of tests in 1997. As it turned out Walsh, who is rather a big chap, used his own foot, which measured 298 mm, to replicate David's foot size. The purpose of the tests was to see whether or not a 300 mm sock-clad foot would leave a complete impression of 280 mm which would be detected by luminol.

The short answer to his tests was that nearly every footprint he left on the carpet was greater than the size of his foot. And yet after having stated that he would expect a 300 mm foot to leave a footprint greater in size than 300 mm, he cryptically wrote in the conclusion that he believed it was possible to leave one of 280 mm. The Court of Appeal used this apparent disclaimer as the basis for saying David could have made the prints.

In 2007 in preparation for the Privy Council hearing, the defence visited Kevan Walsh to ask him about this proposition. As a result Walsh swore an affidavit to clarify what he meant in his 1997 report. The affidavit said that if a 300 mm foot left a 280 mm print then 20 mm at least of the foot must be missing and therefore it would not be a complete footprint.

At the Privy Council hearing, the Crown, represented by the Solicitor General, David Collins QC, accepted in answer to a question from the Law Lords, that the Crown case could not accommodate even one of these footprints having been made by Robin Bain, because it was the Crown case that he innocently came into the house to say his prayers when he was ambushed and shot by his son without going to any other room. The Privy Council, in its decision, ruled that this was one of the nine pieces of evidence that combined to cause the substantial miscarriage of justice. It stated:

> At trial, it was asserted and accepted that the 280 mm complete toe to heel sock print, found outside Margaret's room, seen and measured by Mr Hentschel, was David's because it was too big to be Robin's. The fresh evidence throws real doubt on the correctness of that assumption. The jury could reasonably infer that the print, if a complete print, was about the length of print that Robin would have made and too short to have been made by David.

The Board went on to say in its conclusion at paragraph 107 of the decision:

> If the jury had concluded that the print had, or might have, been made by Robin, the jury might have thought this significant for three reasons. First, it would indicate that Robin had been to parts of the house on the morning of 20 June which, on the Crown case, he would never have visited. Secondly, it would establish that Robin had changed out of blood-stained socks, since if he made the print he must have been wearing blood-stained socks and the socks he was wearing when he was found dead in the lounge were not blood-stained. Thirdly, if he changed his socks, the jury might not think it fanciful to infer that he changed other garments as well, as (on David's case) he had. The implausibility of Robin changing his clothes if he was about to commit suicide was a

point strongly relied upon by the Crown, as something a normal and rational person would not have done. But the jury might conclude that whoever committed these killings was not acting normally or rationally.

In 2008, in preparation for the second trial, the police commissioned Kevan Walsh to do a further series of tests, this time using a foot the same size as Robin's — 270 mm. These tests unsurprisingly resulted in the average size footprints being made by a 270 mm foot walking on carpet of 280 mm, a precise match for those Hentschel found in the house. The defence attended and watched the whole process, which included making the footprints by walking on carpet and the subsequent darkening of the room when the footprints were sprayed with luminol and measured by Walsh.

The police now had two sets of results done by their own expert Walsh, which showed firstly that David Bain could not have been the person who made the prints and, secondly, that a foot exactly the size of Robin Bain's would be expected to make the prints that Weir and Hentschel discovered. Walsh confirmed that if the carpet on which the footprints were made had been properly preserved in the normal manner then there would be no reason why many years later the luminol tests would not be repeatable. This evidence was confirmed at the trial before the jury and just went to show how much crucial information was lost when the police negligently allowed the carpet where the footprints were found to be burnt, instead of retaining it as they should have done. Doyle, remember, agreed.

When this second report of ESR scientist Walsh came to hand, it seemed to the defence that the combination of Hentschel's measurements at the house and his testimony in the first trial and before the Court of Appeal that the footprints were complete 'from the top of the toe to the heel', as well as the frank concession from the Solicitor General at the Privy Council that if even one of these footprints was Robin Bain's then their case was over, rendered the retrial prosecution untenable.

In the lead-up to the second trial after Walsh's second lot of tests were reported, representations were made by the Bain defence to Mr Raftery, the lead prosecutor for the Crown, that this evidence (which, keep in mind, was the Crown's own evidence), when coupled with the fact that David Bain could not have turned on the computer and other matters contained in this book which the Crown knew would be put before the jury, meant that they should agree with the defence to make an application to the court to have the charges against David Bain dismissed. It seemed so painfully obvious a long time before the trial that it was impossible for them to get a guilty verdict against David, and equally obvious that their own evidence implicated the other suspect identified by the police on the first day of the investigation some 15 years earlier.

These representations fell on deaf ears. The Crown pressed on with its prosecution without providing any response. The prosecution guidelines in New Zealand, certainly at this time at least, include the provision of evidential sufficiency, meaning evidence likely to be accepted by a jury which would lead to a conviction. Well, the defence had just highlighted to Raftery evidence of his own experts which on the Solicitor General's statement to the Privy Council had destroyed any possibility of a conviction or convictions. Interestingly, Bates made no mention of the 'luminol footprints' in the Crown's opening address.

Under these circumstances the defence decided to do its own tests, and so a forensic scientist was engaged to do luminol tests on David Bain's own foot walking on carpet. These were done with identical methods to those used by Walsh, and David's average walking footprint was about 310 mm. There were no complete footprints, or prints that could be regarded as even remotely complete to the extent of showing the toes and heel as Hentschel said they did, that were less than about 297 mm.

At the retrial, Hentschel, in a departure from his brief of evidence, blurted out unexpectedly, à la Jones's 'red' assertion about the fingerprints, that the prints he saw in the house were made by a foot larger than those prints. He had never said this before and no reasoning accompanied the assertion.

In cross-examination, however, Hentschel agreed that this was the first time in 15 years that he had ever ventured such an opinion. He then tried to justify it by talking of some tests he had done in the past using fingerprint ink and standing on paper and lino. He admitted that he kept no notes of this test and that because it was not done walking on carpet it did not properly represent the case in question. He conceded that the scientific quality of those tests 'was not at a level you would expect for trying to determine blood-soaked stockinged feet walking on carpet'. He also conceded that if all of the (subsequent) tests showed that the foot that made the complete prints could only be smaller than the size of the print, then his opinion must be wrong.

Kevan Walsh presented the results of the tests he had carried out, but then muddied the waters sufficiently to allow for the possibility that Hentschel was correct in the proposition that David could have made the prints that were smaller than his foot. This statement is a reference to the following excerpt from his evidence in chief:

Q: And from those experiments, what conclusion were you able to draw?
Walsh: I drew the conclusion from that that a walking person with a 300 mm foot making sock prints with a sock completely bloodied would be expected to make a print greater than 280 mm.
Q: But could a print of 280 mm be made?
Walsh: Yes, I believe so, but it wouldn't be the complete extremities of the toe and heel. [In other words it would *not* be a complete footprint.]

The defence expert, Dr Anna Sandiford, presented an array of photos of her tests showing that David himself, which surely was the proof of the pudding, could not make a complete print of 280 mm no matter how hard he tried, which would of course be the case with anybody trying to make a complete print 20 mm smaller than the size of their foot.

Justice Pankhurst repeatedly made the comment that the tests done by both Walsh and Sandiford were invalid because they did not properly represent what happened in the house. His point was that the scientists had immersed the sole of the sock in blood by stepping into a tray of blood a couple of millimetres deep. Justice Pankhurst's point had some merit in that nobody was suggesting that the footprints made in the Bain house were made by a sock where the sole had been soaked in blood. Of course, if it had been soaked in blood, the footprints would have been visible as red marks on the floor and would not have required the use of luminol to find them.

But what the judge did not mention, or possibly failed to appreciate, was the fact that in the course of doing the tests (in respect to those of Walsh and Sandiford), the blood on the sock dried so that about half of the footprints that were left during the course of the testing procedure did not leave any visible impression on the carpet. There was no difference in the size of the footprints made by the wet sock and the dry one after it was sprayed with luminol. This is significant because it gives the answer to the judge's query of the validity of the tests and shows that even a sock dried to the point of leaving no visible print nevertheless left complete prints as shown in the photos.

About three pages of Raftery's closing address are devoted to discrediting the footprint evidence. To do that he had to discredit tests done by Walsh as well as those done by the defence expert Sandiford.

He told the jury, picking up on Justice Pankhurst's comment, that there was no valid comparison between the tests done by the forensic scientists in the laboratory and what actually happened in that house that night or the early hours of the morning.

He said: 'The murderer was not trying to make the largest footprints he could. He wasn't trying to emulate the Sandiford/Walsh tests; he was creeping stealthily about the house killing members of his family.' That was perhaps the most accurate statement in his entire address, but how it would change the size of a complete print was not explained. If the killer had been on tiptoes as it seems was being suggested, then obviously he would have left only toe prints, not the complete prints that were found.

Raftery said nothing about how it could be that David, who had blood on both socks, did not leave left footprints as well, and neither did he refer to the cross-examination of Mr Hentschel on that subject. He relied solely on Hentschel's belated claim that the foot must have been bigger. It must be remembered that Mr Hentschel had perhaps lost credibility as an authority because of other deficiencies exposed in his evidence such as to do with the bullet fragments with fibres and weave impressions on them, the blood from Robin's hands and fingernail scrapings which went unreported, the blood on top of Robin Bain's shoe that he did not see or report — and so his claim, unsupported by any logic or generic data as it was, did not resonate as particularly convincing.

Raftery also failed to address the point that Weir made about the appearance of these footprints, which was that 'they looked like a print in sand'. The only thing he really went to was the unscientific assertion by Hentschel that the prints were made by a foot which was larger than 280 mm, and the explanation put forward by Hentschel about his use of the word 'complete' to describe the footprints. He had said that he used that word to distinguish between those prints and the other prints which were partial prints, rather than meaning that they were actually complete. He did not really mean complete in the normal use of that word, said Raftery.

It was the defence submission in its closing address that these footprints cannot have been made by David Bain and yet at the same time they had to be made by the killer. Ergo, David was not the killer. They happen to match precisely Robin's foot size.

Indeed that was the only proposition on the footprints that was supported by evidence. You will recall that Doyle said he relied on advice from Hentschel that the socks were a valid comparison to ascertain who made the prints. Hentschel, at the retrial, though, had to recant on his previous evidence to the first jury and the Court of Appeal that these were 'complete prints from the top of the toes to the heel'. The history of the evidence involving the footprints, from the failures at the beginning where the photos did not come out, the prints were not marked by drawing pins or some other suitable system such as a marker pen, the carpet was destroyed almost immediately, to the first trial where they were compared to sock size rather than foot size, to the ever-oscillating version of what the examining scientist meant by the word 'complete', along with the other nuances discussed herein, may be honestly perceived as not only a shameful moment in the annals of the criminal justice system in New Zealand, but an embarrassment for expert forensic scientists all over the world.

FAILURE TO FOLLOW PROCEDURE

One final comment on this matter relates to another incomprehensible failure to follow procedure. It goes further than that, though. Surely, it is simple common sense to retain something as vital as bloody footprints on carpet at a murder scene? Of course it is, and usually this would be done. It seems the Bain case, in this as in so many other respects, is the exception that proves the rule.

The disconcerting thing is that the police went to some trouble to retain other items of much less probative significance. For example, they chainsawed off whole door jambs that had blood on them when they could have removed the blood in the normal way and used photographs to show what was there. The *Criminal Investigation Manual* clearly states that in circumstances such as those relating to the carpet where the footprints were found, the material should be seized and secured as an exhibit in the proper way. Jim Doyle, as recounted, agreed with that.

Most of these inexplicable failures to follow procedure were admitted at the retrial, many of them having caused shock and concern when they became known. Remarkably, every single mistake or failure impacts adversely on David in that it reduces the ability to firm up evidence that would exonerate him and/or prove that it was Robin. Remember Peter Robinson's admission that it would have been advisable to take the blood from Robin's hands to Melbourne for testing. But, again, on that occasion they only took items that could assist in the prosecution of David. Seemingly, nothing that could be used against David went missing, was lost, destroyed or not tested.

Rather pointedly, one might think, the more recent DNA testing on items that had not been destroyed, like the skin, the fingerprints on the rifle, the green towel, Robin's shoes, the duvet from David's bed and the *Gondoliers* sweatshirt *all* provided results in favour of David's innocence.

CHAPTER 18

SPECTACLES, LENS ...

THE BROKEN SPECTACLES

The background to this evidence was that on a chair in David's room a pair of broken metal-framed spectacles was found, first being noticed by Constable Van Turnhout at about 9 a.m. on the morning of the deaths. The right lens and the metal frame were on the chair and the lens was not in the frame. The left lens was found by Detective Weir in Stephen Bain's bedroom at 8.46 p.m. on the Thursday night following the deaths. The Crown's allegation became that these were an old pair of David's glasses that he had been wearing because his good ones were broken and were at the optometrist's for repair, and that during the fight with Stephen the glasses were knocked off, causing damage to the frame when the lenses were dislodged. According to the Crown allegation, David left the left lens on the floor, where Weir eventually found it, and took the frame and the other lens back to his bedroom and put them on the red chair just inside the door.

Events subsequent to the first trial raised huge issues about the authenticity and credibility of the evidence relating to the spectacles in general. Those issues relate to the finding of the lens in Stephen's room, the ownership of the broken spectacles, and the allegation that David had been wearing them over the weekend while his were in the optometrist's being repaired. The first two of those issues were identified by the Privy Council as being two of the nine reasons for the substantial miscarriage of justice.

CROSS-EXAMINATION OF DS WEIR

At the heart of these credibility issues was Detective Sergeant Milton Weir, the officer in charge of the crime scene investigation and one of the officers in charge of presenting the Crown case at the first trial.

At the retrial the former detective's integrity came under scrutiny on a number of matters apart from his connection with the two issues identified by the Privy Council. He was queried in relation to his association with prostitutes, the fact that he had painted a sign on the front of his house saying 'Hang Bain' when he had a party celebrating the Court of Appeal decision declining David Bain's appeal in 2003, that he could not recall the names of any of the other police officers at that party and that by the time he left the police he had lost the trust of his superior officers. All of these matters were admitted by him during cross-examination barring his denial about knowing a particular prostitute. He was also accused of having actually planted the lens and lying about where he found it, both of which he denied.

He admitted that he was familiar with visiting brothels as part of his duties in the police to monitor them. The issue of a prostitute having delivered a present to the Dunedin CIB for him was then discussed. The package contained a pair of socks and a note and Detective George who received it recorded that the prostitute who gave it to him said, 'It's a gift from Petra to Milton, can you take it to him?'

Weir's response to this was: 'Firstly, the socks weren't being returned to me. For some reason this prostitute turned up at the police station and handed over a pair of socks to me. It was bizarre at the time and the socks were exhibited.'

Q: And a personal note?

Weir: I don't remember the personal note.

Q: Do you suggest that Detective George is wrong when he records this?

Weir: No, I'm not suggesting that he was wrong.

Q: It's not a thing you'd be likely to forget is it, when a prostitute gives a pair of socks to a police officer to pass specially to you together with a note?

Weir: It seemed bizarre at the time. As I say, I instructed Detective George to exhibit them and they were placed in the exhibit store.

Q: Well, you see, the wording of Detective George, it says: 'It's a gift from Petra to Milton of a pair of socks.'

Weir: Exactly — exactly and that's bizarre.

Q: Why would a prostitute give a police officer a gift of a pair of socks?

Weir: I have absolutely no idea, no idea at all.

Q: Had you ever inspected these premises?

Weir: That this particular prostitute worked at, yes I had.

Q: Did you know a prostitute called Petra?

Weir: No, I did not.

Q: So, some unknown prostitute you've never met but from a brothel that you had inspected makes a gift to you of a pair of socks and gives you a personal note?

Weir: I'm not suggesting that I'd never met her; I'm just saying I didn't know a prostitute named Petra.

Q: Well, did you know of a prostitute called Petra?

Weir: No, I didn't.

The reference to inspecting brothels is to do with the fact that Weir was a member of a group of detectives who visited massage parlours, as they were known then, although they were really a front for brothels, to monitor in particular the staff employed in the business. These monitoring visits were conducted on a very regular basis and involved checking the register of employees to make sure that they were not underage or otherwise unsuitable.

In regard to the *Hang Bain* sign painted on his house, which included a stick drawing under it supposedly representing David Bain in a hangman's noose, he claimed that it was there for only one day but then subsequently agreed, following further questions, that it may have been longer than that. In regard to the party referred to, the following is recorded:

Q: So, after the Court of Appeal decision where you thought you'd finally put this to bed, you have a celebration. Other police officers there? Who was there? Come on, Mr Weir, you must remember the celebration?

Weir: Well, I'm just trying to remember if other police officers were there, I'm sure there probably would have been.

Q: Right, well, who were they?

Weir: I don't remember.

Q: Come on, Mr Weir ...

Weir: I don't remember, Mr Reed.

Q: You would know who some of them were?

Weir: It was a long time ago; it was a small function of a group of people.

The questioning continued and he was directly asked whether Kallum Croudis or Jim Doyle had been at the party. He said that he did not believe that Croudis was there but that Doyle may have been, but he wasn't sure.

And then there was the question of his relationship with fellow officers. After a long series of questions during which he admitted that he had taken a hidden dictaphone with him when he was being interviewed at a performance appraisal meeting, it came down to this:

> *Q:* At that time before leaving the police, you believed that you were being viewed with suspicion by your supervisors — is that a fair statement?
> *Weir:* Yes, it is.
> *Q:* You thought you were being made the scapegoat?
> *Weir:* I don't remember if I said that.
> *Q:* You perceived a generalized lack of trust from your superiors? That's what you perceived at the time, didn't you, before you left the police?
> *Weir:* Possibly, yes.

There was further questioning in the same vein and then:

> *Q:* You felt you had reached a point where your relationship with other significant officers within the organization were increasingly strained. Would that be fair?
> *Weir:* Yes, that's right.
> *Q:* It led to an unhealthy degree of suspiciousness and a frank lack of trust, that's of you, correct?
> *Weir:* Correct.

It was confirmed with Weir that he had left the police under the police early-retirement scheme and that the matters that had been put to him were contained in his application. The questioning continued.

> *Q:* These were your concerns that, in relation to [a particular] investigation a police officer didn't trust you, in relation to your superiors some of them didn't trust you, and so on. That's the position you outlined to the police?
> *Weir:* Yes.

Q: It's not someone else making these allegations, it's you making them?

Weir: Correct.

Q: Given all those circumstances Mr Weir, we have a number of issues where the defence challenges you as to your credibility and your reliability. You understand that?

Weir: Yes, I do.

Q: And all those matters have been put squarely to you in relation to Mr Sanderson? [You will recall Sanderson was the ophthalmologist in the first trial about whom the jury asked a question.]

Weir: Yes.

Q: You were in court, you've told us, most of the time. You're aware, aren't you, that I have read to you that the jury asked a question relating to these glasses?

Weir: Yes.

Q: Were you in court when that occurred?

Weir: I don't recall.

It is fair to say that significant questions had been raised as to the former detective sergeant's reliability and trustworthiness.

FINDING THE LENS

Getting back to the broken glasses, the first point is that Weir's evidence about his discovery of the lens in Stephen's room was wrong and misled the jury. The Privy Council summarized the matter as follows:

Detective Sergeant Weir told the jury that he had found the left-hand lens in a visible and exposed position in which, as is now accepted, he had not seen or found it. His evidence to the jury was more consistent with the Crown's case that the lens had become dislodged during a struggle, than the finding of the lens, covered in dust, under other articles on the floor. The third Court of Appeal accepted that the jury had undoubtedly been misled by the officer's evidence. From the jury's point of view it did not matter that, as the court also held, the misleading was not deliberate. Nor, in the Board's view, with respect, is a determination that the glasses and the lens had not featured significantly in the third Court of Appeal's analysis of the strength of the case against David. What matters is what the trial jury made of the incorrect evidence and, even more importantly, what they would have made of the correct evidence.

Subsequent to the first trial, and as a result of the exposé in *David and Goliath*, Weir sued me, alleging that I had defamed him by alleging that he had committed perjury. The jury at that trial at the Auckland High Court in 2000 found in favour of my honest belief that perjury had been committed.

Weir admitted that Photo 62 — which you will recall he took great trouble to show to the judge and jury in the first trial to 'prove' where he found the lens — did not show a lens at all, but rather a specular reflection. What he said was a lens was actually light bouncing off some plastic. His explanation for his earlier inaccurate evidence is that he thought that Photo 62 showed the lens exactly where he had found it even though it had never been there. Therefore, he said, it was an honest mistake. The circumstances in which he found the lens led me to seriously doubt the veracity of that explanation.

Photo 62 was controversial anyway because it was a late addition to the photos produced for the trial, and no explanation was provided to the defence for its inclusion. The importance of Photo 62 was that the specular effect that Weir claimed to be the lens in exactly the position he found it was totally visible in front of the ice-skate boot, very near Stephen Bain's body. The fact that the body is in the photo illustrates that this photo was taken before any disturbance of the scene had occurred. As the Privy Council said, the lens in full view with the body supported the Crown theory of the case much better than if it had been under all those other things under a bunk as the real lens actually was.

However, the fact is, as Weir admitted at the retrial, he did not see the lens until after he had uplifted the ice-skate boot, which itself was underneath a folded raincoat, both of which were jammed between a small suitcase and a shoe rack under the bunk. The point made to him in cross-examination at the retrial was that when he saw the reflection in Photo 62 he must have known that even though it may have looked like a lens, it could not have been the lens he found. If it was, he would have seen it, as would other officers who had been searching in that area, before he removed the raincoat and the ice-skate boot.

Weir's deposition statement confirmed that the lens had been found under items including an ice-skate boot and a folded up raincoat, which in turn were under the set of bunks in that room. It also confirmed, as did his notes, that he did not find it until after he had removed the other items.

RETRIAL CROSS-EXAMINATION

A very long cross-examination on all these matters took place at the retrial in Christchurch in 2009.

In particular, Weir's evidence from the first trial was put to him where he stated: 'On the Thursday, the lens, as seen in Photo 62, that is *exactly* the position I found it when I found it on the Thursday.'

It is now known, and accepted by Weir, that that statement is false. He claims it was an innocent mistake. The defence position and my own opinion is that it was a deliberate false statement for the reasons given above. An excerpt from the retrial cross-examination of Weir exemplifies the position.

Q: But your notes record quite carefully that you removed all those items of clothing and then and only then found a lens underneath the boot.

Weir: And that's correct, and when I found Photograph 62 and believed that to be the lens, I assumed at that stage that when I had been searching and gone back to the area that I hadn't seen the lens at the front of the boot.

Q: Well, you see, Mr Weir, that cannot be a truthful answer, can it?

Weir: Well, it is.

Q: Well, let me put it to you this way. If that fake lens had been there on the Monday, if it had been, it would've sat there from Monday right through until Thursday night, wouldn't it, before—

Weir: Yes, it would have.

Q: We know from the photograph, the specular effect, that you can see it without moving anything, right?

Weir: Yes.

Q: And I'm putting it to you that you had Mr Legros and other people carefully inspecting that area by putting little arrows on items, right?

Weir: Correct, that's correct.

Q: Mr Legros must have had his nose right by the specular effect?

Weir: Quite possibly.

The explanation above, that he *assumed* he had missed the lens the first time, seems unlikely because it was a very significant find, and arguably all he had to do was check his notebook entries and deposition statement and he would have known absolutely that that was not where he found it. One might expect that his first thoughts when seeing the specular effect would have been something like the following: *Oh my god, this is strange! How could that lens have been sitting there all week and no one has seen it?*

Remember also that the police had debriefs at least once each day that first week and they knew that a lens was missing from as early as 9 a.m. that first morning. It would have been high on the agenda: *Look out for a left spectacle lens.*

The fact is that the photo and his identification of the lens in it were not communicated to Guest in the way that other fresh evidence was in the letter sent by Wright just before trial. If the handling of this photo and associated evidence had been consistent with the intentions of the letter (to advise of changes in the evidence), it should have pointed out what was said to be the lens and Weir's new evidence about where it *exactly* was when he found it. The silence on the matter may be considered akin to the silence from the police and prosecutor about the 'hidden' statement they had from Denise Laney.

The lens's true position may have raised questions about how it got under everything where he really found it and that scrutiny may have thrown doubt on whether the specular reflection was indeed the lens, which highlights the advantage gained by his claim that that was *exactly* where it was.

The focus at the retrial also turned to a nuance in the photographic record which indicated that a 'hole' had appeared among the clothing under which the lens had actually been found. This hole showed up as a white gap in photos taken after Stephen's body had been removed but before Weir found the lens.

Q: We see that someone has made a hole there and moved the Mac back from that left shoe. We can see it, can't we?

Weir: It seems to have moved, yes it does.

Q: Well, not seems to. Someone has moved it, haven't they? Let's be clear.

Weir: It seems to have moved, yes.

Q: Someone has moved it, Mr Weir, can't have moved of its own accord, there wasn't a gale through there or anything, was there?

Weir: Well, it could have been moved as a result of somebody touching the other end of the rack or anything, Mr Reed.

Q: Mr Weir, that gap there is precisely where you would put a hand in if you are going to put the lens in there, do you see that? Because that precisely is in line with where you say you found the real lens, right there?

Weir: It is close, I accept that, yes.

Q: It's not only close, Mr Weir, it is right alongside where the real lens was found and I put it to you, Mr Weir, that you put your hand in there and put that lens in there?

Weir: And I categorically deny that.

Q: Well, you have to deny it, Mr Weir, but the fact is you have not been truthful in relation to Mr Sanderson's explanation about the dust on the lens? [See next section.]

Weir: Well, I have been truthful in relation to that.

Q: You certainly agree you misled the first jury?

Weir: Unintentionally, yes.

The allegation put to Mr Weir at the retrial that he, in effect, planted the lens underneath clothing and the ice-skate boot was fairly put in the circumstances and on the evidence available at the time. The 'white hole' referred to was indeed suspicious, but as we know in respect to Photo 62 (said to show a lens which was in fact a reflection), photos can lie!

The passage from the trial transcript above about planting is included as one of the allegations put to Weir about his integrity, and for the sake of completeness. In the defence closing address, it was made very clear that the lens found by Weir was *either* there before Stephen was shot and is a complete red herring, or it may have been put there afterwards.

I should make it clear that I have never promoted the view that Weir 'planted' the lens and I'm not doing so now. It is my view that when all of the circumstances relating to the lens found in Stephen's room are considered — that it was hidden away underneath the boot and clothing, which did not appear to have been moved in the struggle; that neither this lens nor the frame and other lens found in David's room had any human material on them which could be associated with the bloody struggle in Stephen's room — there is not sufficient evidence of a reliable nature to form a strong view about how and when the lenses and frame came to be found as they were. There are many theories, and certainly one possibility is that the lens was planted by someone, but that, along with others, is speculative, in that the evidence on the whole issue is so fraught with contradictions.

However, as I've already said, I am firmly of the view that Milton Weir deliberately misled the jury at the trial in 1995 in respect to the *exact position in which he found the lens*. In this regard, I made a complaint to the Solicitor General and the New Zealand Police in 2001. The complaint was supported by a report from John Haigh QC, dated 9 August 2001, who was commissioned by the Bain defence to consider the evidence in relation to the finding of the lens. His report expressed the view 'that there is a very strong prima facie case in support of a charge that Weir committed perjury, and in the absence of a credible and acceptable explanation as to his actions, sufficient evidence to prove such charge beyond reasonable doubt'. He said he was of the view that Weir's defence would focus on 'innocent error'.

My complaint, although it was investigated by the police and was the subject of a report from a very senior ranking police officer, was never finalized. The report did not even have its facts correct. Crucially, its identification of where the lens was said to be (the specular reflection) compared to where it actually was (totally out of sight under the boot which was under a folded raincoat) was seriously astray.

OWNERSHIP OF THE BROKEN GLASSES

The second issue went to the ownership of the broken glasses.

At the first trial, Gordon Sanderson was the ophthalmologist called by the Crown to give evidence in relation to the broken glasses and David's eyesight in general. During its deliberations, the jury asked four questions seeking clarifications, one of which was: 'Whose glasses were they according to the ophthalmologist?' His evidence that when he examined these glasses he believed them to be an earlier prescription for David was read to the jury along with David's evidence that the glasses were an old pair of his mother's and that the ophthalmologist was wrong. Bill Wright, you will remember, cross-examined David vigorously on this point, highlighting the fact that David's evidence was in dispute with that of Sanderson.

However, fresh evidence in the form of an affidavit from Gordon Sanderson for the defence in 1997 was to the effect that before the trial he had been shown a photo by the police in which Margaret Bain was wearing these glasses many years previously, conclusively showing him that they were an earlier pair of her glasses. He went on to say that he approached Weir before the trial and asked him to ensure that his brief of evidence was altered to reflect the fact that although when he first examined the broken glasses he thought they may have been an older prescription of David's, they were actually an old pair of Margaret's.

However, this never happened. He was led through his evidence according to his deposition statement which had been completed before he became aware that the glasses were Margaret Bain's and not an earlier prescription of David's.

It was not until the book *David and Goliath* was published in 1997, highlighting the fact that the jury had asked a question about the ownership of the glasses, that Sanderson became aware that the very issue which he had asked Detective Weir to ensure was accurately reflected in his evidence had become a matter of concern to the jury, and that the answer given to the jury was untrue. It was this realization that caused Sanderson to make himself known to the Bain defence team in 1997, and swear his affidavit.

At that time he told of another matter that caused him concern, being that Weir told him dust was on the lens when it was found but that Weir then said, according to Sanderson, 'We'll just ignore that.' This allegation was also included in Sanderson's 1997 affidavit.

The Privy Council commented on the issue with the following passage in its conclusion.

> The Crown is right in its contention that the ownership of the glasses, as opposed to the wearing of them on the morning of 20 June, was not in itself a live issue at the trial. But Mr Sanderson was understood to say that the glasses were David's, David said they were not his but his mother's, and David was then cross-examined in a way that (as the third Court of Appeal accepted) impugned his credibility. If ownership of the glasses was in itself an immaterial matter, David's credibility was certainly not: the central question the jury had to resolve was whether they could be sure that David's account of events was untrue. While it cannot be known what motivated the jury to ask the question as to whose the glasses were, according to Mr Sanderson, it may have been

because they saw in this a valuable indication of David's credibility or lack of it. If Mr Sanderson's fresh evidence be accepted, the jury were given an answer which did not reflect his revised opinion and could have led the jury, reasonably in the circumstances, to draw an inference unfairly adverse to David.

Gordon Sanderson is a professor in the Department of Ophthalmology at the Dunedin School of Medicine, Otago University. He is not a forensic scientist and this is probably the only case in which he has given evidence in a court of law. Certainly, in the evidence he gave to the Court of Appeal in 2003 and at the retrial, he explained that he was not used to the procedures involved.

When the retrial was ordered the Bain defence was curious as to how the Crown would deal with Sanderson. On the one hand they would know that if they didn't call him the defence certainly would, whereas on the other what he had to say was far more damaging to them than to David. It was with some mirth that his brief of evidence was received in due course.

His evidence in chief at the retrial included a description of the eyesight of Margaret, David and Robin Bain, explaining the differences and the problems they had. He made it quite clear that Robin Bain simply needed reading glasses and that the broken glasses would have been of no use to him. He explained that both David and Margaret were myopic, which means short-sighted, and also suffered from astigmatism. He explained how the broken glasses' lens included a correction for astigmatism that did not coincide with David's eyesight and this was one of the reasons that caused concern about whose glasses they were. However, it was the photograph of Margaret wearing the glasses that convinced him.

Under cross-examination at the retrial Sanderson explained it this way:

'I wasn't clear on the court procedure. I didn't know whether the jury had been given a copy of my affidavit, I didn't know, and I did read from parts of it at the time I believe — and forgive me if I am somewhat vague, it's a long time ago. I also thought there would be questions of a nature which would enable me to clarify that position, that didn't appear to occur. I answered the questions that were put to me on the basis that the jury had already been informed of this matter, not, as I say, not being familiar with court procedure.'

He went on to say that he was shocked to learn later (after reading *David and Goliath*) that the jury had asked that question and not been given the truthful answer.

He was also adamant that Weir had said to him words to the effect: 'We will just ignore that when the lens was found it was covered in dust.' In regard to that, he said at the retrial:

'I thought it was an unusual way to handle evidence.'

When it was put to him that Weir denied making this statement, he agreed he knew of those denials and said: 'No, and I've never had any doubt that the comment was made because I spent a considerable period of time investigating the electrostatic properties of glass so I wouldn't have done that had I not been prompted by his question.' This was a reference to Weir's query of Sanderson as to whether glasses lenses have electrostatic properties that would attract dust to their surface.

Interestingly, Weir admitted that Sanderson may well have asked to have his evidence changed to reflect the fact that he knew that the broken glasses were an old pair of Margaret Bain's. A portion of Weir's cross-examination went like this:

Q: Well, you see if he did say that about he wanted his evidence changed and you did nothing about it, that is dishonest as well, Mr Weir?

Weir: At that stage there was a discussion with the Crown in relation to that and the Crown had a stance in relation to it.

Q: All right, well, that's a movement on from before, let's investigate that. So now you are admitting that Mr Sanderson was right when he asked for his evidence to be changed?

Weir: No, I'm not, when I showed Mr Sanderson the glasses that Margaret Bain was wearing, that information was given to the Crown and the Crown had a stance in relation to it.

Q: Mr Sanderson says that he came to you and asked for his evidence to be changed and you agreed you'd take it up and do something about it, that's his evidence in my words.

Weir: Right.

Q: You've said that you had no present recollection of that yesterday?

Weir: And that is the case.

Q: Now you are saying that you do have some recollection that he might have said that, is that what you're saying?

331

Weir: No, I'm not. What I'm saying—

Q: Well, you were saying that you took it up with—

Weir: What I'm saying was, in relation to when he was shown the glasses that Margaret Bain was wearing in the photograph, that information was passed onto the Crown and the Crown had a stance in relation to the glasses and that was their stance.

Q: Well, the stance, if that is the case, must have been taken by the Crown prosecutor Mr Wright?'

Weir: Correct.

Q: David Bain at that trial was asked questions as to the ownership of the glasses.

Weir: I believe so, yes.

It is now acknowledged by the Crown that the photo showing Margaret Bain wearing the broken glasses was never disclosed to the defence, which focuses attention on what Weir refers to as the 'Crown stance' on the matter. Weir had no hesitation in agreeing that whatever this stance was, it emanated from the Crown prosecutor Bill Wright. From the evidence of police officers at the retrial, Wright is now implicated in misleading the defence and the court on at least three matters.

1. In respect to Denise Laney, firstly that she provided extra evidence just before the trial and, secondly, as to the nature of that evidence going to the identification of the person she saw and the time of the sighting.
2. The position the lens was found; remember his opening address stated that it was on top of things, not under anything, and the failure to describe Photo 62 in the letter to the court.
3. The ownership of the broken glasses, by not disclosing the photo and by having what Weir called a 'stance' on the matter.

Guest maintains that it was agreed at the trial that the glasses were an old pair of Margaret's, but then he also thought, according to his submissions to the Court of Appeal, that it was agreed that the person seen by Mrs Laney was David. In any case, as we now know from other matters, Guest's assertions, at best, must be viewed with some suspicion.

THE ASSERTION THAT DAVID WAS WEARING THE GLASSES

The third matter on the spectacles issue relates right back to one of Croudis's original questions, one of those that Guest refused to allow David to answer on the day of his arrest. The allegation was: 'A lens from the set of glasses *you have been wearing* was found in Stephen's room.'

In his evidence at the first trial, David stated that he had not been wearing those glasses for a long period before the tragic events of 20 June 1994. No evidence was called by either side indicating whether David had been seen wearing these glasses in the period from the Thursday when his ones were broken until the Monday morning when the police arrived at the house.

At the retrial, however, that was not the case. It will be recalled that in the deposition statement of Crown witness Miss X, she had stated that David was not wearing glasses on the Sunday when she saw him after the polar plunge and took him to the university for rehearsals. This evidence was not given to the jury at the first trial but she confirmed it at the retrial.

In the lead-up to the retrial the police made contact with a woman who had been in the rehearsal at the university with David on the Sunday afternoon before the tragedy. She gave a very supportive account of David's personality and behaviour and also told the police that he had not been wearing glasses that afternoon and that that was a clear recollection. The statement was supplied to the defence among the discovery documents. As the Crown did not call her as a witness, the defence made contact. Through this contact a second person from the rehearsals who was also in the play was contacted and both witnesses gave evidence for the defence at the second trial that David was not wearing glasses on Sunday afternoon at the rehearsal.

In addition to that, the defence called Wallace Chapman, a broadcasting personality these days, who testified that he had told the police a few days after the events in 1994 that he had been out with David on the Friday night, 17 June, recording a video and generally having a good time, and that David was not wearing glasses throughout that evening.

Another witness, Lindsay Robertson, was with them on the Friday night and also gave that evidence.

But then for the Crown at the retrial, David's aunt, Jan Clark, gave evidence on the subject. She testified that while David was staying at her house he told her that he had been wearing those broken glasses over the weekend. The interesting thing about this evidence was that it was not part of her extensive testimony at the first trial. The first time she mentioned this was in a statement she gave to the police about five years later. She and David were extremely traumatized that week. Is it possible that her recollection five years later may have been wrong? She was adamant that it wasn't. But as the extensive research on memory recall shows, people's memories can be influenced by later information having a suggestive impact on the recollection, as genuine as that recollection may be.

VAN TURNHOUT'S OBSERVATION

The final element of doubt relating to the spectacles arose at the retrial in extremely unexpected circumstances. It related to Constable Van Turnhout when he gave evidence early on in the trial. To explain the significance of what happened, reference again must be made to the book *David and Goliath*, when all of the anomalies about the lens and glasses issue were first highlighted. A passage was quoted from Van Turnhout's notebook in which he made very detailed entries of his observations while in David's room. You may remember that he actually drew little diagrams of items in the room and counted the exact number of bullets on the floor.

The book recited an entry in his notebook written in response to David asking for glasses at about 9.30 a.m:

> Beside me and to my right as I faced David was a chair. Sitting on that chair which was at the entrance to the room was a pair of glasses. They appeared broken and there were no lenses in them. There was also a small brown glasses case sitting beside the glasses. There were other objects on the chair. The frame of the glasses appeared to be a metal frame and there were no lenses in them.

The passage was highlighted because in the photo of the chair taken later that day, between the glasses frame and case was the right lens, but this is not referred to at all in Van Turnhout's note above. It seemed odd that, firstly, no reference was made to the lens that was there; and, secondly, that the reference to the absence of lens was in the plural: 'lenses', suggesting that there was either two lenses there or both lenses were missing.

Van Turnhout subsequently swore an affidavit and gave evidence at the defamation trial in 2000 that he did see the right lens on the chair and that it was the only lens there. There definitely were not two lenses on the chair, he said.

We jump forward now to Monday, 16 March 2009, at the Christchurch retrial when Van Turnhout was to be called to the witness box. That morning the defence received a handwritten statement made out and signed by Van Turnhout at 8.30 a.m. that day in which he stated that when David had asked for the glasses he picked them up and put them down again.

Paul Morten cross-examined Van Turnhout:

Q: Now, you've given evidence about the glasses on the chair. As I understand it, you prepared your handwritten notes on the 20th of June, you had the notes typed, you gave the 25 June statement to Detective Fitchett, you gave a depositions statement in October 1994 and you also gave evidence at trial. Is that right?

Van Turnhout: I did.

Q: And not once on any of those occasions did you record that you saw a lens on the chair?

Van Turnhout: The lens on the chair was never an issue at that stage. It didn't become an issue until 1997.

Q: Thank you for that, officer, but could you answer the question. Not once—

Van Turnhout: I did not.

Q. —in that period did you record the lens on the chair?

Van Turnhout: I did not.

Q: Now after that, you also assisted at the Police Complaints Authority inquiry. You gave an affidavit in the Court of Appeal and you gave evidence in another jury trial in Auckland, didn't you?

Van Turnhout: I did.

Q: And today is the first occasion when you said that you picked up the glasses, isn't it?

Van Turnhout: Correct.

Q: So not only did you not tell Detective Sergeant Weir that you'd picked up the glasses but you didn't tell the courts either, did you?

Van Turnhout: I was never asked.

Q: But you didn't tell them?

Van Turnhout: I did not.

335

The point has been made in relation to other witnesses, including police officers, about the oath and its requirement, 'To tell the *whole* truth and nothing but the truth'. At the first trial in his evidence Van Turnhout actually stated that he told Weir that nothing in David's room had been handled apart from the pillow from the bed.

It was never established why Van Turnhout decided on the day of his evidence 15 years after the event to suddenly disclose that he had handled the glasses. However, the belated disclosure had the effect of casting some doubt on the balance of his evidence. The interesting thing was that he conceded that he had been instructed not to touch anything but just to watch and observe. However, such an innocent thing as what he disclosed could hardly have got him into trouble, one would think, if he had told of it right from the beginning.

BROKEN GLASSES EVIDENCE: AN 'UNSPEAKABLE MESS'

The entire evidence about the broken glasses, then, is fraught with so many inconsistencies that it raises more questions than answers. To use the words of another expert citing scientific evidence from the Crown in this case, it is an unspeakable mess. Some of the matters that spring to mind are listed below.

- The glasses were picked up before being photographed but the police officer who did that never disclosed the fact for 15 years.
- There was dust on the lens found in Stephen's room, but apparently, according to Sanderson under oath, Weir decided that should be ignored.
- The photo showing Margaret Bain wearing the glasses was not disclosed to the defence. This is confirmed in the Court of Appeal decision of 2003, but they dismissed it as irrelevant.
- A key Crown witness wanted his evidence changed to reflect more accurately what he believed to be the truth but it wasn't done.
- According to Weir, the Crown prosecutor had a 'stance' on the issue — it is not known what that stance was, but in evidence at the retrial it went like this. Weir in answer to Reed: 'What I'm saying was, in relation to when he [Sanderson] was shown the glasses that Margaret Bain was wearing in the photograph, that information was passed on to the Crown and the Crown had a stance in relation to the glasses and

that was their stance.' Reed: 'Well the stance, if that is the case, must have been taken by the Crown prosecutor Mr Wright?' Weir: 'Correct.' Reed: 'David Bain at that trial was asked questions as to the ownership of the glasses.' Weir: 'I believe so, yes.'

- The jury at the first trial asked a question during deliberations about whose they were according to Dr Sanderson. Despite the police and, if Weir's evidence is accurate, the Crown knowing that he had said the glasses were Margaret Bain's (and not David's as he had previously thought), they still failed to ensure the jury were informed and allowed the dispute between David and Sanderson to remain.
- Weir admits and the Crown concedes that his evidence about where the lens was actually found was wrong and misled the first jury.
- Photo 62 was not described properly to the defence and was put in evidence at the very last minute by Weir and Wright.
- Photo 62 does not show a lens but Weir nevertheless went up to the judge and jury at the first trial and pointed out the false image as being the lens, and saying that the false image 'was *exactly* where he found it'.
- In one photo, a 'hole' is identified which Weir agreed was in exactly the position that a person would put their hand in if the lens had been put there after the events (planted).
- At the first trial there was no evidence as to whether David had been wearing any glasses since his were broken on the Thursday before the tragedy, despite the police having statements from at least three witnesses to that effect. Five witnesses at the second trial said that David was not wearing glasses on the Friday night and all day Sunday. Each of them gave this evidence to the police in the first instance. These witnesses were called by the defence.
- Jan Clark claimed about five years after the first trial that David said he was wearing them that weekend.
- David gave evidence that he wasn't wearing them.
- The Crown allege they were knocked off and broken in the bloody struggle but not a scrap of blood was found on them, or any evidence to link them to the struggle. The damage is on the left side, the bruise on David's face is on the right side.
- It is another example where the Crown theory is in itself contradictory. The theory requires David to have picked up one lens and the frame

and put them on the chair in his room after the fight with Stephen. Why on earth would he do that? What could be the use to anyone of a bent frame with no lens in it?

- On the one hand they say he is a cunning, clever killer with a sophisticated masterplan to escape detection, but then they say he takes that frame and one lens and puts them on the chair in his room without leaving a trace of evidence, that he did so despite his hands, according the theory of the Crown case, being covered in blood.

- The Court of Appeal in 2003 supported the Crown's approach, for after accepting that Weir's evidence was wrong and misled the jury, that the photograph of Margaret wearing the glasses was not disclosed to the defence and that David's credibility was improperly impugned, it concluded: 'We do not consider that the Crown's approach to this aspect of the case has caused any miscarriage of justice.'

It would be possible to speculate ad infinitum about the probative value of the broken glasses and their relevance to the deaths. All we can do is rely on what we actually know, and even that doesn't take matters very far.

There is no doubt that David was not wearing glasses on the Friday night and all day Sunday. He said he drove to get the fish and chips with Laniet on the Sunday night without glasses. There has been no evidence disputing that. It seems clearly contradictory to say that having gone about his daily business for three days without the use of these glasses, he would then seek them out or even need them to kill people at *point blank range in the dark*.

After all, on the Crown's theory, he is supposed to have killed his father with an extremely precise contact shot to the front of the head in the dark without glasses, for on the Crown's case they had been broken about three hours earlier.

More significantly, there was nothing to link them to the events in Stephen's room. Think about this for a moment. In that room was a violent, bloody, hand-to-hand struggle, according to the police, with blood flying to every corner from the wounds to Stephen's hand and head. Their theory goes on that the glasses were knocked off and then trampled on or otherwise subjected to pressure, causing the lens to fall out and the metal frame to be severely twisted on the left side. Sanderson said that would take quite some force. Yet, not a skerrick of blood or anything else on any part of the glasses?

Then, with his hands saturated in his brother's blood after taking off the gloves, David is supposed to have taken one lens and the frame back to his room. Apart from the obvious question of why he would do this, how come there is no blood or hairs or anything on them? Did he pick them up with tweezers — which have never been found either? Remember the evidence was that they appeared as though they had not been worn for a long time. There was no evidence to suggest they had been washed or cleaned; indeed the opposite is the inference.

What can also be said is that if other evidence shows that David was not responsible for the killings, then some explanation for the broken glasses other than the Crown theory must exist. Who knows, in another 15 years one of the detectives might come forward with some more evidence à la Van Turnhout's belated confession.

339

CHAPTER 19

DAVID'S 'FAKE FIT', INJURIES, FINGERPRINTS, NEWSPAPER ...

DAVID'S FAKE FIT

In regard to the so-called fake fit, the Crown were nearly right. They were correct in that it was not a fit. But they were wrong that it was some kind of pretence. It was simply that David fainted; well, that was the evidence of the only expert called, Christchurch neurologist Dr Tim Anderson. Dr Anderson is impeccably qualified to provide such evidence, especially when compared to Constable Andrew, one may think, whose expertise related to the fact that there was a child in his class at school who was an epileptic. Tim Anderson told the second jury that he was a Professor of Medicine at the University of Otago, had a private practice and worked at Christchurch Hospital as well. He had been working as a neurologist for 19 years.

He had no exposure at all to the Bain case until, during the retrial, he agreed to review the evidence of Constable Andrew and the ambulance staff who were with David that cold morning all those years ago.

The defence contacted him on the urging of Helen Cull QC who had been responsible for cross-examining the witnesses involved. She had 'smelt a rat', one might say, and recommended that the evidence should be reviewed by an appropriate expert.

All the symptoms described by those in attendance with David were, according to Dr Anderson, symptomatic of a fainting experience and he even gave an example that everyday people could relate to involving his own daughter. His evidence was not seriously contested. He graphically described the difference between a faint and a fit to the jury. It should be pointed out that Dr Anderson was simply given the relevant evidence to consider. There were no discussions with him about the concerns of the defence. He came to his conclusions entirely of his own accord. He did not take issue with the observations that had been made by the various Crown witnesses, simply their interpretation of those observations.

Then there was the operations manager from St John Ambulance, Mr Cooper, who, as has been recited, gave evidence about dead bodies gurgling.

He stated that he observed David at about 7.50 a.m. that morning and he described him as being 'in a very distressed state'. He said David was sitting at the end of the bed with a blanket wrapped right round him and he was 'whimpering, crying, shaking and quivering'. He disagreed with the proposition that David had suffered a seizure or fit.

The fact that the defence had to call Mr Cooper at the retrial was yet another example of what the defence called the 'cherry-picking' exercise conducted by the Crown, where the witness was contacted and interviewed by the police before the defence had ever heard of him but because they did not like what he said it was left to the defence to get the evidence before the jury.

INJURIES TO DAVID

When Dr Pryde examined David at about 11.20 a.m. on 20 June 1994, he described the injuries as recent. He was referring to the light bruising on the right side of David's head just above and below his eye and the superficial graze to his knee.

Constable Andrew described how not long after he got into the room where David was sitting on the floor when the police first made entry, David tried to get up but crashed down onto the floor between the wall and the bed, ending up on his back with his knee straight out between the piece of furniture and the end of the bed. Remember that immediately before this happened, David was confronted by Stapp pointing a revolver right in his face.

Andrew could only see his legs from where he was standing, meaning he could not see if or where his head hit the wall or the floor. Remember the room was very, very dimly lit as well. Andrew graphically described in his evidence at the retrial how he went over and grabbed David Bain by the left arm and left leg and pulled him out between the chest of drawers and the bottom of the bed. When he did so, obviously the right side of David's head was dragging on the ground and had to squeeze between the very narrow gap between the end of the bed and the chest of drawers.

341

After pulling him out from that position Andrew then spun him right around, still with his right side on the floor, and placed him in the recovery position at the end of the bed with his head facing the bed. Looking into David's room towards the end of the bed, David's head was at the right-hand side of the bed and his feet were over towards the wall. Andrew admitted at the retrial that he would not have noticed if David's body had contacted something as he was pulling him around the foot of the bed into the recovery position.

The first evidence of anybody noticing the bruise to David's head was not until 8.47 a.m., over an hour later. Van Turnhout arrived in David's room just after 8 a.m. and stayed with him the entire time before he was carried out to the ambulance. At 8.47 a.m., when David complained of having a sore head, he had a close look and noticed the bruise on his forehead.

Wombwell was the first ambulance officer to visit David at about 7.40 a.m. He checked David with his torch, actually shining his torch onto David's face. He did not see any injuries. If they had occurred three or four hours earlier as the Crown proposed, they should have been clearly visible at this time.

Ambulance Officer Anderson came in immediately after Wombwell, before Scott and Dick arrived. He said in evidence that he gave David a quick once over and had a good look all around him, including brushing his finger across David's eyelashes to see whether he was conscious. He did not notice any injuries on David's face.

Ambulance Officer Dick had been with David from about 7.50 a.m. and he did not note any injuries. Ambulance Officer Scott arrived at the same time as Dick.

The bruising to David's face is on the right side, not the left side. It is inconsistent with the damage to the glasses frame, which is damaged on the left side. All the evidence suggests that there was no bruising on David's face or head when the police and ambulance first arrived because it had only happened one or two minutes earlier when David crashed down between the bed and the wall and was dragged out by Andrew.

The skin from Stephen's room, as we now know, was not David's. David was wearing shorts; the graze was superficial, involving only the outer layer of skin and not even bleeding, according to Dr Pryde. It could have happened when he was being dragged out or alternatively in the process of stumbling about in confusion and distress after finding his mother.

Another point is that when questioned by the police about this bruising all he could say was that he knew he did not have it when he got home from his paper round. Surely, if he was the cunning psychopathic killer they allege, he would have said that he tripped over at some point, and tried to provide an innocent explanation for the injuries?

At the retrial the police also called evidence from a prison officer who claimed that when he admitted David to prison upon his arrest on Friday afternoon, 24 June 1994, David was stripped and searched. He claimed to have seen scratches and bruises on the right side of David's chest which looked like fingernail scratches. He also said they looked about three days old. This information was given to the police for the first time in 2007 after the order of the retrial.

Dr Pryde, however, had done a strip-search of David on the Monday morning; whatever these scratches and bruises seen by the prison officer were, they were not there then. When Dr Pryde examined David he used a standard police form which included a diagram of a male torso, front and back, on which the doctor marked those matters of interest which he saw at the time of the examination. This included the bruising to the head and the graze on the knee. It also included a tattoo on the left arm above the bicep very near the shoulder.

When Dr Pryde strip-searched David, DS Dunne and Constable Van Turnhout were present. They gave evidence in both trials. In particular at the second trial, because Dr Pryde was dead by then and could not give evidence, the opportunity was available for them to deny that the doctor had strip-searched David or, alternatively, to say that the scratches were there but the doctor had failed to record them on the diagram or note them on his examination form. They did neither. Doyle confirmed in his evidence that Dr Pryde strip-searched David. Interestingly, there were two prison officers present when David was admitted. The prison officer who gave evidence 'could not remember' who the other prison officer was. No notes or records were kept at the time and neither were any photos taken of the alleged scratches.

ROBIN BAIN'S FINGERPRINTS NOT ON RIFLE

Another thing much touted at the first trial and by some commentators since the retrial is that Robin Bain's fingerprints were not found on the rifle.

In response, the first point is that there were nine separate lots of finger marks on the rifle. One was on the wood beside the trigger and it was very prominent when the rifle was first examined by Kim Jones. Jones's evidence was that none of these provided fingerprints that were good enough for identification purposes.

Unfortunately, yet again, they were not photographed or protected for evidential purposes. They were not said to be in blood, which presumably means they had a different appearance to David's prints in the pick-up position on the front of the fore-stock, ironically meaning that they may well have been in blood, bearing in mind that Jones thought blood fluoresced at that time.

Carl Lloyd, the defence fingerprint expert from the UK, made the point at the retrial that had they been lifted and photographed as they should have been, then it might have been possible to show that they were *not* the prints of one person or another. At least eight points of correspondence must be found to legally prove a match in fingerprints. But just one piece that does not correspond can prove that they are not a particular person's prints.

In other words, even if they did not have sufficient detail to prove, for instance, they were Robin's, there may have been enough to say they were not David's. If there was even one print on that rifle that was not David's then the case against him could never have got off the ground. But that evidence, too, was lost forever soon after the deaths.

The second point is that in the petition to the Governor General and in evidence to the Court of Appeal and Privy Council, the defence presented generic evidence from Australian and American authorities showing that in less than 10 per cent of firearms deaths are the fingerprints of the perpetrator found on the weapon. The Crown obviously accepted this evidence and so dropped this argument completely.

Confirmation of this common misapprehension came in an inquest in February 2011 into the deaths of a man and his wife and his wife's father in Feilding near Palmerston North. The Palmerston North coroner Tim Scott found that the husband had killed his wife and her father and then shot himself with a rifle. Of some note at the hearing was the fact that the husband's fingerprints were not found on the rifle even though he had shot two other people and himself with it. The police officer told the coroner that this was not uncommon. It appears from the reports available that the coroner agreed.

On this point, TVNZ screened a documentary during 2010 purporting to examine the defence case that Robin Bain was responsible for his own death and those of his family. One of the principal points of this documentary was on this subject.

It claimed that if Robin Bain had been responsible, he must have left blood marks on the rifle from his fingers because they must have been 'dripping' in blood when he shot himself. The documentary made somewhat tasteless theatre of this, even to the point of doing a demonstration by immersing the presenter's fingers in his own blood. Of course, if his fingers were dripping in blood when he shot himself he would have left finger marks. You don't have to be a scientist to work that out.

But the proposition was ridiculous because Robin's hands were never said by the defence to be 'dripping in blood'. The producer of the documentary ignored the fact that it has always been maintained by the defence that he had cleaned up before he committed suicide. It is just that he did not scrub his hands all over, meaning that residues of the bloodstains remained, as described by Crown witnesses at the trial.

THE *ODT*: WHO BROUGHT IT IN?

Some comment has been made, and Kieran Raftery made something of it in his closing address, that if Robin Bain collected the newspaper from the letterbox at 65 Every Street on that Monday morning, then that would be inconsistent with the actions of a man killing his family and committing suicide. This argument has some merit — but what is the evidence relating to the matter? The morning paper was found by the police on a bookshelf in the hallway.

In the second statement David made to DS Dunne on Tuesday, 21 June he was asked about the newspaper.

Q: When you came home did you bring a paper with you?
David: No.
Q: Is one delivered?
David: Yes, it's delivered by Kieran Garbutt of 6 Mahon Street to the letterbox at home. He's usually past our gate at quarter to six.
Q: Did you take that paper inside on Monday from the letterbox?
David: No, I didn't.
Q: [Just thinking]

David: I haven't thought about it until now. I normally would take it in but
    sometimes, if I walk my run, Dad may get it at 7 a.m.

Q: Do you remember if the paper was in the letterbox?

David: No I don't.

This is the sum total of the evidence relied upon by those who say David did
not bring in the paper and so Robin must have got it; a statement taken on
the day after the tragedy. The newspaper would have been the last thing on
David's mind on Tuesday, 21 June 1994. Routine matters are often hard to
recall. Things like car keys, for example: when they are not where they are
normally kept, you try to remember what you did with them the last time the
car was used, which is not easy even in normal circumstances.

The topic gained some traction when Justice Pankhurst used the matter
to explain to the jury the 'drawing of inferences' in his summing up. After
his summing up was completed the judge was requested by the defence to
recall the jury to correct a number of errors in his summing up, one of which
was related to this issue. The jury was recalled about 30 minutes later and on
advice from the defence the judge informed them of two matters which had
come out in evidence, and he told them:

'It has been drawn to my attention that at page 1503 in the notes of
evidence there is evidence that Robin Bain's hands were swabbed and that no
ink was detected on his hands. Secondly, in relation to this aspect, if I implied
that there was some invariable habit in relation to his getting the paper from
the gate it's, of course, very relevant to note that he's at Taieri Mouth for at
least three days, three mornings, Wednesday, Thursday, Friday ... and maybe
Tuesday as well. So that is relevant also.'

At the first trial this proposition did not feature at all. It may be considered
that it only surfaced out of desperation at the second one. We will never know
for certain who brought in the newspaper, but personally I don't discount
the likelihood that David himself brought it in as he usually did, and simply
and understandably had no recall of doing so in the aftermath of what
happened next.

NOBLE CAUSE CORRUPTION?

Noble cause corruption refers to corruption committed in the name of
worthy causes or good ends — corruption when officers do bad things

because they believe that the outcomes will be good. Maybe they truly believed that David was guilty and that he should have been arrested when he was so that he could not take part in the funeral services the following day. Even if that was the case, it is no excuse for taking short cuts or for not remaining fair and objective throughout the investigation and conduct of proceedings.

So let's go back to 24 June 1994 when Bob Clark was with Jim Doyle having a coffee on the fifth floor of the electricity department building and David was down the corridor with Detectives Croudis and Lowden.

As we revisit this life-changing interview with the benefit of hindsight, we should bear in mind that at that time, as we now know, theories had not been tested by reconstruction as stipulated by the *Manual* and neither did they have the benefit of scientific analysis. All they really had at this stage was Kim Jones's Polilight examination of the rifle and the statements of an extremely traumatized 22 year old.

Let's look at how the police mindset, as it can be ascertained from the contents of that interview, has stood the test of time. As we do so and evaluate the answers, bear in mind the comments of Judge Callander and John Haigh QC in relation to Operation Vine, recounted in Chapter 2.

Judge Callander's inquiry, it may be recalled, concluded that:

1. *The investigating team erred in that many available witnesses were not interviewed;*
2. *They formed a mindset that the accused were guilty;*
3. *The prosecution criteria for laying charges were not properly regarded.*

John Haigh QC wrote: 'In regard to investigations that lead to charges and prosecution, what is required however is a degree of objectivity in every investigation. Where a mindset has developed as to the guilt of a suspect there can be no such objectivity.'

The first point put to David was that his fingerprints had been found in blood on his rifle. Apart from Kim Jones's belated assertion at the end of the second trial that he could see red pigment (in contradiction to what he told Michael Guest and the first trial judge and all his other evidence over the years), there is not one scrap of evidence that these fingerprints were made in blood. Repeated intensive DNA testing by the Crown over the following 14 years did not detect any human DNA, let alone blood, in the area where those fingerprints were found. The only evidence the police had at this time that the fingerprints were in blood was from Jones as a result of his examination with the Polilight, which at best is only an indicator for blood. The situation is actually worse than that because, according to his own statements to the jury at the first trial, Jones thought in 1994 that blood fluoresced under the Polilight, when in fact it doesn't.

The second point, put by Croudis, was that the 'missing 20 minutes' was an explanation for what happened to the family. We know that the Crown themselves subsequently abandoned this proposition as untenable.

The third point was that there was a bloodstained fingerprint on the washing machine. First of all, it was a partial palm print, not a fingerprint; and secondly, bearing in mind that it was not red in colour (according to Jones) even though it was on a white hob, it may not have been blood. The tests applied to it suggesting it was blood were indicative tests only. But even if it was blood, there is an entirely innocent explanation: that David inadvertently and without knowing handled a bloody item as he was loading the washing machine in a dark, dank laundry with a flooded floor.

The fourth was a request for David to explain why bloodstained clothing had been washed. David said that he did not know why, which of course was true.

Croudis then asked him if he accepted that he washed the clothes, in particular a pair of socks, a sweatshirt belonging to him, and a dark jersey belonging to Arawa. Of course David agreed, because he had already told the police voluntarily that he had done so.

Croudis next asked David for an explanation for the blood on the sole of the socks, the back of his T-shirt and the crotch of his shorts. In particular, Croudis put to him that if his statements to DS Dunne were true, there should be no reason for this blood to be on his clothes. Croudis was referring to the fact that David had told Dunne he had only seen his mother and father. The response to this requires a diversion. We know that he told the 111 people that he came home and found them 'all' dead. We know also that when the police made entry, Sergeant Stapp confronted David with a pistol in his face. David then fainted when Andrew was in the room. It is very likely that David would have fainted after he discovered his mother dead too. We then know from Dunne's evidence that after David had been carried out of the house at about 10.20 a.m., but before Dr Pryde began his examination at about 11 a.m., David asked Dunne what had happened. Dunne told David that 'his mother and father were dead'. Later that afternoon during the very long interview, Dunne repeated that, and it is only after this David said that he had only seen his mother and father. One cannot help but wonder, with the tricks that a mind can play on itself when it has suffered great shock and trauma, whether Dunne's statement to him that his mother and father were dead was all that stayed in his mind because his mind had blacked out the memory of the gruesome and terrifying discovery of his whole family dead. This phenomenon was explained by Professor Mullen and is referred to as dissociative amnesia.

Nevertheless, when being interviewed by Croudis, David would have had no idea that when he had been in the laundry there was extensive blood staining and bloodstained clothing on the floor. We know that the floor was saturated and that when it was sprayed with luminol the whole floor speckled, suggesting that blood had got mixed with the water on the floor.

At this point, it seemed the police believed David was lying about where he had been and gave no thought to the effects on the mind of a person subjected to the terrifying experience that David claimed to have encountered. Croudis was asking the questions as though David had been investigating the crime scene. For example, David was asked: 'We have located blood on the sole of the sock. How did [it] get there?'

David: I don't know.
Croudis: If your statement to Detective Sergeant Dunne is truthful there is no reason for you to have bloodstained clothing.
David: Unless I stood in blood.
Croudis: Where might you have stood in blood?
David: I don't know.

Well, of course David did not know whether there was blood on the floor, and if there was, where it was.

Croudis then asked David how a considerable amount of blood got on the large towel hanging in the bathroom. David again said that he did not know. Well, as we now know, of course, David did not know because that blood all turned out to be Robin Bain's blood.

David was then asked how the blood got on the door jambs and he said that he did not know.

He was asked what gloves he owned and straightaway without any prompting he replied: 'Purple woollen gloves, fingerless green gloves and I've recently bought new white dress gloves for a ball at Larnach Castle.'

A series of questions followed about gloves before David was asked if he knew anything about the heavily bloodstained white gloves found in Stephen's room. David said that he did not know anything about those gloves and at that point asked to have a solicitor present.

One would have to question whether a cunning, callous, cold-blooded killer would have been quite so forthcoming about the gloves as he was.

Then came the questions which Guest refused to allow David to answer, the first of which was: 'A lens from the set of glasses you have been wearing was found in Stephen's room.' As far as can be ascertained, the police had no information about whether David had been wearing glasses at this time. Over the next few days and weeks they obtained statements that he was not wearing any glasses on the Friday night or the Sunday. David himself had not been questioned by the police during the week about the glasses.

The second of the unanswered questions was: 'Did you tell Val Boyd: it could have been me. I don't know if it was me or Dad?' As has been recounted earlier, Val Boyd gave evidence in both trials and has not made this allegation on either of those occasions. There appears to be no foundation for this allegation.

The next question was a request for David to explain the piece of skin found in Stephen's room, with the allegation it matched the graze on his knee. We now know the answer to that — it was Stephen's skin, as was discovered in DNA tests in 2008.

And then the last question: 'A computer message was typed at 6.44 a.m. after you got home. Did you type it?' We know that proposition is wrong on two counts. Firstly, the police have never known when the message was typed and, secondly, they were claiming that David got home before 6.44 a.m. But of course at this time, because of the typing error in Darling's notebook, they had not interviewed Denise Laney and neither had they done the time check on Anderson's wristwatch that had been requested by Martin Cox the previous Tuesday. They relied on David's statement that he was at Heath Street at 6.40 a.m., but they never checked his watch either.

Were it not that the inquiry was besieged by a guilty mindset as discussed by the experts in Operation Vine, they would have obtained the proper answers to all these questions before they arrested David, rather than 15 years later.

It is now abundantly clear that at the time of the arrest, the police investigation was in its infancy and in a state of confusion caused by failures to follow the specified procedures in their own *Manual*, along with misinformation and lack of information due to the fact that many witnesses had not even been interviewed. There was a dearth of hard evidence and a wealth of speculation, which for the most part turned out to be wrong.

They believed, without having done any reconstructions or properly collated the evidence, that everybody had been killed in the missing 20 minutes, and at that point, as Jim Doyle stated at the retrial 15 years later, the focus of the investigation shifted onto David and away from Robin.

REMNANTS OF THE CASE AGAINST DAVID

What then of the other evidence called in support of David's guilt? As will be recounted later, in the case of David Dougherty, he was found guilty by a jury 'beyond reasonable doubt' when in fact he was totally innocent; meaning that the evidence upon which he was found guilty had an innocent explanation.

All of the other evidence against David Bain is capable of an innocent explanation and the innocent explanation makes more sense and is much simpler than the Crown allegation about it. Take the blood on the clothes he was found in, by way of example. The very light smearing on his black shorts and white T-shirt did not carry the hallmarks of airborne blood spatter or, as the Crown expert Dr Harbison said, blood that has soaked through a garment. There was actually nothing sinister in it at all. In fact, it would be highly suspicious if, after claiming he discovered his family dead, he did not have some bloodstains of the nature described.

This highlights the inherent contradictions in the Crown case. They believe him when it suits them, and say he is lying when it doesn't. If he was such a cunning murderer with an elaborate plan of deception as they suggest, why would he wash some clothes but not others? Would he *really* be sponging a white sweater because he can't put it in with the coloureds? Would he be telling the police no one else knew where the key to the rifle was?

The blood on the soles of the socks cannot have got there before he went on his paper round because there was no blood on the insoles of the shoes he wore. The two spots of blood did not drop from above as had been alleged in trial one, but got there when he stood in blood. Common sense. Nearly all the forensic evidence at the first trial was shown to be defective.

The remaining evidence against David is largely of the speculative variety, relying on people's interpretations, often when they were under stress themselves, to do with how he looked at certain times, his behaviour on occasions before and after the tragedy, whether he cried when he should have and so on. Many of them only surfaced after the Privy Council decision in 2007. They have not been considered worthy of consideration in this book. They may well represent the genuine belief of the witness in question, but then those witnesses' recollections may be clouded by the pressure of the occasion and the effect of the long-term exposure the case has had on the memory in question. Take, for example, some of the evidence about how David seemed cool and aloof to the family in discussing the funeral arrangements. It is completely contradicted by Derek Hope, the funeral director (see Chapter 22), in the statement he gave the police at the time. He is a much more detached witness with far more experience of an individual's behaviour in times of grief. His evidence was not heard at the first trial.

Similarly, the Crown relied heavily on the fact that David was unable to explain things to the police. However, and very obviously, an inability to explain something can result from the fact that the person genuinely doesn't know the answer. If David was not there, as the Crown's evidence ultimately demonstrates, then clearly he cannot explain things that happened in his absence — much as David Dougherty was unable to explain how the 11-year-old girl identified him as the rapist when he had nothing to do with the rape in question.

CHAPTER 20

FAMILICIDE

UNDERSTANDING FAMILICIDE

Homicide is the intentional killing of one human being by another. Homicides, as we know, are committed by people from all walks of life and are the subject of a vast amount of literature, movies and documentaries, and they form the basis of high-profile television programmes such as *CSI* and the like. Whether it is Sherlock Holmes, Agatha Christie or modern-day fiction writers of crime novels, a gruesome, unusual homicide is usually the foundation for the story.

Homicides generally are difficult to classify. Some are capable of classification such as those committed by contract hit-men or professional killers. There are the instances of mass murder where a gunman goes crazy, randomly killing everybody in the vicinity. These seem to happen quite regularly in the United States at schools and universities, but New Zealand and Australia are not exempt. In particular, in 1990 in New Zealand, the Aramoana tragedy near Dunedin was a typical example. There were the slayings in Raurimu which involved family members and others. In Australia in 1996 there was a similar incident involving the deaths of many more people in Tasmania. So, there is a general acceptance that they can happen anytime, anywhere and among all classes of people, from the rich and famous like OJ Simpson, through to the killings of prostitutes and other social outcasts. Nobody is exempt.

There is one specific category of homicide which makes up a very small percentage of the total number of killings perpetrated by human beings on each other which, although rare, happen all too regularly. They are extremely shocking and very difficult for society to comprehend. They are what is called *familicide*, the term used to describe a multiple killing of members of a family by another member of the family. Usually, but not always, familicide is followed by the suicide or attempted suicide of the perpetrator. The Bain case was a case of familicide.

There have been a number of academic studies completed throughout the world from which data relating to familicides can be plotted. A review of this data has disclosed findings that may help to understand the causal factors of the Bain familicide tragedy. The research screened thousands of potential studies and academic papers for relevance, which resulted in about 130 being included (see Appendix C).

This review found that familicide is almost always perpetrated by a parent or someone in a parental role, such as an adult child acting as caregiver for elderly parents. By way of example, Statistics Canada, in their fact sheet *Family Homicides* (2006), reported that between 1997 and 2006, 56 per cent of children killed by a family member were killed by their fathers, 33 per cent by their mothers and only the remaining 10 per cent by other family members including siblings, grandparents, cousins and so on (numbers are rounded to the nearest whole number).

Where the familicide includes the death of *both* parents along with the children, it is almost always a familicide-suicide by the father. For example, a 2005 study by Hatters Friedman, Hrouda, Holden, Noffsinger and Resnick of 7040 homicides found that in family killings, 65 per cent of fathers who killed their children also attempted to kill their spouse, 55 per cent successfully. By contrast, none of the mothers killing their children attempted to kill their partner. Similarly, the review found that most perpetrators of homicide-suicide are men who killed their partner and sometimes their children too; and a greatly increased likelihood of suicide following homicide is predicted by a close relationship between the perpetrator and victim.

Familicide by a child where both parents and siblings are killed is extremely rare, so much so that no data could be found reporting the rate of this occurrence as a proportion of familicides as a whole. For example, a study by Mouzos and Rushforth, published in 2003 by the Australian Institute of Criminology, found the killing of siblings to be the least common form of family homicide.

Parricide is the term used to describe the killing of a parent by its child; the killing of both parents is known as double parricide. In cases of familicide where both parents are killed, either as the only two deaths or along with other family members, the review found that of 293 international examples, 99 per cent were familicide-suicide committed by the father and only 1 per cent committed by a son. In the 1 per cent committed by a son, these were cases of double parricide and did not include the killing of brothers and sisters as well, so strictly speaking cannot be classified as familicides.

The review found the research has identified very significant differences in the characteristics of the perpetrators of familicide when the perpetrator is a father compared with when it is an adult son. The majority of perpetrators of double parricide and familicide by an adult child are male. They are either seriously mentally disordered, mostly with some form of psychosis, or they have a psychopathic personality disorder. Many are also victims of prolonged severe abuse by the parents. When siblings are killed alongside parents, it is because the siblings are seen as supporting the abuse by a hostile father. A good example of these findings is the highly publicized Menendez case in the United States where two sons conspired to kill both their mother and father. The sons had both been involved in serious criminal activity in the years leading up to the event and had consistently and openly conveyed a hatred for the parents, caused by the domineering and abusive nature of their father's behaviour. They were also said to display signs of 'psychopathy'. 'Psychopath' is a popular term used for people with a particular set of antisocial personality traits, including a serious lack of empathy, compassion and remorse, as well as a proclivity for lying, cruelty and exploitation of others.

The literature consistently reports that all adult sons who commit familicide and double parricide fall into one or more of three categories: they have either suffered chronic, severe abuse from one or both parents; have a severe mental illness or disorder; or have antisocial personality disorder (which we generally refer to as being a psychopath). The odd cases where this is not so are 'mercy killings', such as when a son has taken on the role as caregiver for an elderly parent who is suffering an anguished illness and is near to dying. In such cases, the son frequently also commits suicide.

CONCLUSIONS FROM THE RESEARCH LITERATURE

The review found that 13 specific conclusions could be drawn from the research literature. They are identified as follows:

355

1. FATHER

Familicide where both parents and some or all children die is almost always perpetrated by the father. Although there are extremely rare cases where such familicide is committed by the mother or some other member of the family, more than 95 per cent are committed by the father.

2. ADULT SONS

On the very rare occasions when adult sons are the perpetrators, they are either seriously mentally ill, disordered, or psychopathic. Only about 1 per cent of cases of familicide are committed by a child of the family, and when they are committed by an adult son, he almost always commits suicide too. In cases where sons killed both parents, the research indicates that the perpetrator is always either severely abused, suffering from severe mental disorders (usually psychotic), or psychopathic. There are no identified cases where the son exhibits none of these pathologies and does not commit suicide.

3. PERPETRATORS OF FAMILICIDE-SUICIDE

The perpetrators of familicide-suicide conform to types on a continuum from angry at one end to despairing at the other, and the two types are identifiably different. A typology of perpetrators has evolved over the past two decades of study of familicide-suicide, which shows the angry type is hostile, angry, aggressive, usually of low socioeconomic status, often with drug and/or alcohol abuse problems. For him the familicide is a hostile act of revenge or punishment. The despairing type is non-hostile, controlled, conventional, of good standing in the community, and his role as a husband and father is very important to his identity. For him the familicide is an escape for himself and his family from an intolerable future. The types are not separate, but the two extremes of a continuum. Most perpetrators will show aspects of both types, but can be placed closer to one side than the other.

4. PERSONALITY OF FATHER

Fathers who commit familicide-suicide have specific personality traits that contribute to the familicide. These men are very controlling of themselves and their families, viewing themselves as the head of the family; they are usually authoritarian fathers and expect their spouse to be submissive. They are, however, extremely dependent on their spouse and their role as father for their self-esteem and sense of identity. They are often narcissistic, feeling that they are entitled to better and often constantly striving for that better; and they are frustrated that their skills and abilities are not appropriately recognized or rewarded. Ultimately, these men are chronically disappointed, failing to achieve or maintain a high status to which they feel entitled in the unrealistic goals they set themselves and their family members. They control the impressions that they and their family present to those around them as closely as they can to maintain the image of a happy and successful family.

5. MENTAL ILLNESS NOT ALWAYS PRESENT

A large proportion of fathers who commit familicide-suicide will not have any history of treatment for mental illness. More than 30 per cent of perpetrators have no record of diagnosis or treatment for mental illness. However, many will have shown symptoms of mental illness, particularly of depression, often over many years and back into adolescence. These men control the outer image closely, rarely confiding in people or seeking help.

6. PARENTING EXPERIENCE

There is a shared pattern of parenting experienced in childhood by men who commit familicide-suicide. These men generally had fathers who were emotionally withdrawn, authoritarian, controlling and with unreasonably high expectations of their sons: quick to scorn but stinting with praise. The father may have been physically abusive: this is more likely in the case of the angry perpetrator than the despairing type. The mother, on the other hand, is likely to have been loving, indulgent and protective, trying to compensate for his father's harshness or absence. However, the mother would have been on eggshells around the father, submitting to his rules; and so any protection was likely to be covert rather than explicit. The men themselves, however, often do not recognize their father as having been anything other than an ordinary father.

7. MOTIVES FOR FAMILICIDE-SUICIDE

Familicide is caused by a lethal mixture of causal events, societal mores and personal characteristics of the perpetrator. The precipitating event is not of itself the cause of the familicide, as such events occur with many men who do not kill their families. For the familicide perpetrators, these events occur in the context of the industries, personalities, beliefs and self-constructed identities of the individual men, and in that context they create a lethal mix.

8. MOTIVES FRAMED AS LOSSES

Motives for familicide can be framed as losses of various types. The most frequent factor leading to familicide was a loss or imminent loss of spouse and family: over 50 per cent of familicide perpetrators were experiencing marital breakdown. Financial loss, such as bankruptcy or other loss of assets or income, was the second most prevalent factor. Loss of employment status was also very common, whether this loss was of their job, a failure to receive a promotion or appointment, a demotion, or a cut in hours. Connected with these were loss of control, with the perpetrator having lost control over his spouse, family, or the image projected of self and family; and loss of social status. This last took various forms: the threat or existence of judicial proceedings for some wrongdoing; financial losses meaning that the lifestyle could not be maintained; or being seen as a failure as a husband and father.

9. BUILD-UP OF SHAME AND DESPAIR

Familicide is preceded by a prolonged build-up of shame and despair. Perpetrators of familicide have experienced severe damage to their own sense of self-worth resulting from a long-term accumulation of shame. Eventually, the accumulated frustrations, failures and losses reach a crisis point where any more disappointments are catastrophic; and the perpetrator becomes hopeless and despairing. Suicide may be perceived as an escape, perhaps even a respectable way out; and the family dying is part of an extended suicide. Alternatively, the angry perpetrators blame their wives for their plight, and the familicide is an act of revenge.

A study by Duwe in 2004 looking at mass murder in the United States noted an interesting connection between the rates of familicide and the incidence of divorce. As the rate of divorce goes up, so does the incidence of familicide. This is compatible with information derived from the review that marital breakdown is a significant factor in familicides.

10. A FINAL STRAW

There is usually a specific event that is the final straw triggering the familicide, one that leads in the perpetrator's mind to ignominy: a terminal public shame, mortification and self-disgust. This final triggering event differs, but it is always one over which the perpetrator has little control, and is going to publicly expose his failure.

11. CHARACTERISTICS OF FAMILICIDE-SUICIDE

Familicidal killings have specific characteristics. Familicide-suicide almost always takes place in the family home; victims are most often killed in their own bedrooms; and the perpetrator usually commits suicide in the same place or close by. 'Angry' perpetrators tend to show more aggression and may use more brutal methods of killing. 'Despairing' perpetrators tend to use efficient methods, and are likely to have killed the victims while they were asleep; they may also arrange the bodies decently and leave candles or flowers at the scene. Some men also use a disguise or some sort of role play.

12. SIGNS OF PREMEDITATION

Over a third of familicide perpetrators show signs of premeditation, which may be practical arrangements such as cancelling appointments or updating wills, disclosure of the intention before the event, or explanation and a suicide note. Only about 15 per cent of perpetrators leave suicide notes. The research reports that when suicide notes are left, or the perpetrators have survived a suicide attempt and are then able to be interviewed, they universally use language indicating that they see death as a transition rather than an end: the terms they use include 'going', 'staying/being left behind', and 'taking the family with them'.

13. AFTERMATH OF FAMILICIDE

In the aftermath of a familicide, there are predictable reactions from the media and from family and friends of the perpetrator and victims. Familicide is an event that is shocking and provokes outrage. Media coverage tends to be distorting and to discredit the perpetrator, but to a lesser extent and generating less fear in the public than with other forms of mass killing. Satisfactory answers are rarely found or published to the question of why a familicide-suicide has occurred. One of the reasons for this is that in most familicides the perpetrator is dead after having committed suicide himself, and so there is no public trial. The inquest that follows, certainly in New Zealand law, suppresses most evidence to do with the suicide aspect of what took place.

The responses of family and friends of the perpetrator and victims differ according to the type of perpetrator. With angry perpetrators the act is seen as the culmination of a recognizable behaviour. However, when the perpetrator is of the despairing type, the extended family and friends usually have difficulty accepting that the person they knew was capable of such an act, and the familicide may cause problems between family members.

MEN WHO COMMIT FAMILICIDE-SUICIDE

So, as we can see, there are, broadly, two types of fathers who commit familicide-suicide. Although different terminology is used in the papers they can be satisfactorily characterized under the headings of 'angry' types on the one hand and 'despairing' types on the other. As has been said, the types are a continuum but nevertheless in most cases the perpetrator of familicide-suicide can be aligned more with one category than the other.

I have outlined these types above, but as their descriptions are important I will expand on them here. The 'angry' types tend to come from a lower socioeconomic grouping. These angry men blame someone else, usually their partner, for the dire circumstances that led to the familicide. The actual act of familicide is generally driven by resentment, anger and jealousy. There is usually a history which indicates that the men perceive the children to have sided with their mother who he perceives as his antagonist. Usually, these men will have a history of aggression and violence which will be known in a general sense by friends and family, and often the killings themselves may be brutal. These perpetrators are more likely to have been treated for mental health problems and they often have a history of drug and/or alcohol abuse. Unsurprisingly, after the event people who knew the perpetrator are often able to recognize signs of violence and aggression and even notice changes in the perpetrator in the build-up to the violent climax.

On the other hand, the 'despairing' perpetrators of familicide-suicide tend to be middle-class men who have been well educated and employed in white-collar professional roles. As a rule they have a strong sense of duty and responsibility in their patriarchal or paternal role and see themselves as providers for and protectors of their families. They are very likely to be in traditional relationships where they are the sole or main provider and their wife is a homemaker. They see their wife as dependent upon them. Very often the men of this type are well integrated into their communities, fulfilling roles in community groups such as churches and local councils. Almost without fail the despairing type has no history of violence or aggression and the killings themselves are carried out with the minimum of aggression, either killing the victims while they are asleep or finding other non-violent means such as using poison. These men perceive themselves as having failed, or are in the process of failing at achieving or maintaining the façade upon which their social status has been founded. The research shows that these men feel that they have reached the end of their endurance, that their life has become irredeemably intolerable for some reason or another, or a combination of reasons. Although there may be mental health issues such as depression, they may often be untreated and unrecognized, particularly by the people close to the perpetrator. For obvious reasons familicide-suicide committed by these type of men is very difficult for friends, colleagues and families to comprehend and accept because the act seems so completely out of character.

A further common thread relates to the perception of the perpetrators by their friends and colleagues. Angry perpetrators were likely to have been recognized by others as volatile and aggressive, whereas the despairing type was seen as calm, dutiful and conventional. A number of the studies found that angry perpetrators were known by at least some people outside of the family to be volatile, violent, quick-tempered and were likely to have expressed their anger to others about their partner, their situation and the way they believed they had been treated.

Contrastingly, people rarely knew of the difficulties in which the despairing perpetrators found themselves. These men rarely confided in people, preferring to maintain the image of the family as successful, and when they did confide, tended to play down the extent of their concerns. They were generally respected in the community and reported as appearing quiet, often slightly reserved, peaceable and easy-going. They were also frequently described as responsible or devoted partners and parents who cared for their families and who loved their partner or at least maintained an amicable partnership in raising their children.

MOTIVATIONS

The motivation of men who commit familicide-suicide was usually a combination of factors, and when familicide is committed by the despairing type, the motives are usually difficult for those people well acquainted with the perpetrator to comprehend. Basically, familicide-suicide is motivated by a combination of losses: loss of family, loss of finances, loss of status and control, all of which lead to a build-up of shame and despair. Then, usually, some ignominious event will provide the trigger for the actual familicide itself. There is very rarely a single motive or cause, but rather the act is the result of a combination of personality, mood, upbringing, expectations and beliefs. Dominant themes, however, include loss, failure, shame and financial stress.

At the head of the loss factors that are likely to lead to familicide is the loss of family and partner. The review showed that the research was consistent in identifying separation, divorce or estrangement from an intimate partner as being the most significant issue in most cases. In essence, the loss of the man's role as husband and father provided a fundamental threat to his perception of his identity.

Loss of control is also a common characteristic, and it appears to be a strong feature in the build-up to the familicidal act. This may be a loss of control over the spouse and family through rejection and separation, but also could be a loss of control over the impression that people have of them and their families through exposure or disgrace.

Studies also show that shame and ignominy are common causes of the familicidal act. Shame, a negative perception of one's self-worth and ignominy, a nearly total loss of dignity and self-respect, are seen as strong driving factors leading to despair, and to familicide in these men, who may have been or are about to be exposed in such a way as to cause humiliation and embarrassment to themselves and their extended family. The data shows that there has usually been a long-term accumulation of shame with the associated damage to their sense of self-worth. Usually, immediately prior to the familicide there will be some precipitating event which would lead in the perpetrator's minds to a terminal public shame, mortification and self-disgust. Neil Websdale, in his book on familicidal men published in 2010, described it in the following terms:

> This ignominy represents an intensification and transcendence of the chronic and sometimes acute and toxic shame that permeated the perpetrators' lives. The appearance of ignominy marked another stage in the death of the self, the numbing of the emotions, the mortification of the spirit.
>
> ...
>
> [Cases show] some kind of terminal disgrace or mortifying humiliation — days of enjoying some semblance of honour or the esteem of those around them were about to vanish. In the light of fast-disappearing material resources, it was this final episode of shame that threatened to expose the [perpetrators] and their families to gossip, possible scorn, and the reality that they would no longer occupy the cherished place in the social order.

Websdale reports this as a significant factor in 92 per cent of the despairing type (which he termed 'civic-reputable') of familicide-suicide perpetrator; and that the principal sources of such shame were the failure of their marriages, which caused the perpetrators to feel unlovable and unworthy. He also identified other matters such as professional or financial failure or legal action likely to lead to public disgrace.

It is important to understand that the precipitating events are not by themselves the *cause* of familicide. In almost every case of familicide-suicide, the contributing causal factors included a combination of losses resulting in shame and despair in the mind of the perpetrator. Having said that, there was usually some trigger event which, when set against the background and personality of the perpetrator, led to the final act.

WHAT THIS TELLS US ABOUT THE BAIN CASE

Relating all this information to the familicide which happened at 65 Every Street in Dunedin, a couple of points become obvious.

The first one is that there is no known case in the international reported literature of a familicide committed by an adult son who does not commit suicide or who is not seriously mentally disordered and/or psychopathic. Of course, we know that David Bain did not commit suicide. There has never been any indication or suggestion that he was abused, and as we shall see there is substantial evidence from a number of expert sources that he is not mentally disordered or psychopathic.

The second one follows on from the first, and is that, when one looks only at familicides where both parents die, nearly all are perpetrated by fathers who commit suicide following the event.

It will be recalled that in the evidence at the first trial in 1995, the jury were not informed about and therefore could not take into account very significant factors relating to the family dynamics. They were aware that Robin and Margaret were experiencing marital difficulties, but beyond that little was known. Barbara Neasmith explained how Margaret was indulging in New Age spiritual beliefs and practices such as her use of the pendulum. The evidence about Robin suggested that he was a proud and much-loved school teacher who was doing a very good job. As to David, he was the only person who spoke on his own behalf. Professor Mullen, the psychiatrist, could only give evidence that David Bain was not insane and that he was suffering post-traumatic stress disorder, a complaint that both perpetrators and victims of terrifying events experience.

The intervening years of investigation resulted in evidence at the retrial that provides a much more complete picture. A brief review of that evidence will help the reader to align the family dynamics with the information from the international data regarding familicides. First, we will look at the evidence relating to Robin Bain.

CHAPTER 21

PSYCHOLOGICAL EVIDENCE: ROBIN BAIN

WITNESS TESTIMONY

MICHAEL BAIN

Michael Bain, Robin's youngest brother, did not give evidence at the first trial but was called by the Crown at the retrial. He told how Robin first went to Papua New Guinea in 1964. He did not describe what Robin was doing there in 1964, but it is understood he went there on behalf of the Presbyterian Church. Robin and Margaret married in Dunedin in 1969, and Michael Bain told the court that they stayed in Papua New Guinea from 1972 until 1988 when they returned. He said they came back to New Zealand on three occasions in 1978, 1981 and 1983. He talked about where Robin lived and the various jobs he had in Papua New Guinea that, he said, led to Robin being appointed as a senior lecturer in education at the teachers college at Boroko.

He saw them on each of the three occasions that they came back to New Zealand, and then again when they returned in 1988. However, since their return at Christmas of 1988, Michael Bain had not seen the family together at all. During the five years after the Bain family returned to Dunedin, he saw David on one occasion in 1992 when he took his mother, David's grandmother, to attend the graduation at the Outward Bound School. He saw Arawa once when she accompanied Robin to a family wedding in Auckland. He never saw Margaret, Stephen or Laniet again after their return to New Zealand. He saw Robin only twice during the five-year period, the last occasion being in January of 1994 when Robin stayed with his mother at Otaki and the brothers painted her house together.

An interesting point is Michael Bain's perception of his brother's state of mind on that occasion in January 1994, as he told the jury in his evidence in chief: 'The following morning when I delivered [Robin] to the airport we just carried on the family discussion and then he left in a very good-humoured way.' After some further comments about the bag Robin was carrying he was asked:

> Q: Did he make any comment to you just before he left that was, that you didn't quite understand or …?
>
> *Michael Bain:* Yes, he said to me just as he was about to board, 'Well, here I go again back to that situation' or words to that effect.
>
> Q: Did you know what he was referring to at that time?
>
> *Michael Bain:* Well, I had understood that there was a problem between him and Margaret but I didn't know the depth of it and I only surmised that because my mother had wanted to go down and visit the family in Dunedin several times but Robin had always put her off on the grounds that the time was not yet right and so she, I don't think she knew the depths of what was happening and neither did I, but I assumed that that was what he was referring to when he made that comment. I didn't inquire what he meant and he didn't elucidate any further than that.

He told the jury how Robin was very interested in computers and that he introduced a new Internet system for use at the school which got reported in the newspaper. Raftery asked how Robin talked about his children and his attitude and relationship towards them.

Michael Bain: 'He was very proud of all of them in fact, um, Robin was a humble man who — who — he wasn't proud of his own achievements, actually, but he was proud of his family's achievements, um, he was proud of Arawa and how she was progressing at school, she was actually head girl at Bayfield High and she was following him into the teaching profession and he was very proud of that fact.'

In respect to Laniet, Michael Bain said: 'He didn't actually say very much about Laniet to me but I knew Laniet as being a girl who — who needed affection from a very young age. She was a delightful girl who was full of light and full of laughter and she was a very, very pretty, and very pleasant and happy little girl. I noticed during her growing up period and she always wanted a cuddle, she just loved — liked being loved really, um, and Robin never really discussed what was happening with Laniet to us. I don't know that — what she was achieving.'

He said young Stephen was a bit of a larrikin and that Robin was proud that Stephen had become a musician who played the trumpet. He was then asked about how Robin described David.

'Robin was proud that David was singing. David and Robin were both in the Royal Dunedin Male Voice Choir together, and that really gave Robin a thrill to be able to have David along in the choir. David had a good singing voice and Robin had a good singing voice and, um, also Robin did tell us that David was graduating at the Outward Bound School, 1992 I think it was, and my mother and I decided to visit at the graduation, and Robin and Margaret were both very pleased that we were going to support the family by visiting. So other than that I don't recollect any other comments that Robin made about David.'

In cross-examination he was asked: 'You've said that Robin was the sort of person who kept problems to himself?'

Michael Bain: Yes.

Q: So he was putting on a bit of a brave face really with his mother, wasn't he, in those letters for instance?

Michael Bain: In retrospect I would say that's probably correct yes, but he was the sort of person who is able to cope and deal with problems, after all, he had a career of counselling and dealing with people with problems and so I believe that in fact he was coping and he certainly put on — he gave my mother the impression that things were going well because he didn't want to worry her, I am sure, but that's — I am surmising there, actually, because he never discussed his problems with me either.

In respect to the comment 'Well, here I go again back to that situation' that Michael Bain had said in his evidence in chief, it was put to him that it was a depressing prospect that Robin was facing. He answered: 'That's what I felt at the time, yes. I felt he was saddened by the fact that he had had such a wonderful holiday and such a relaxing time and now he had to go back and face it all again, whatever it was he was referring to, he didn't elucidate.'

He was asked whether or not he knew the state of the marriage prior to the deaths. His answer was: 'No, in fact I don't believe he had separated, he was living in the caravan but that is not a separation, because initially I believe that Margaret was living in the caravan and then she transferred into the house and then Robin moved into the caravan but I don't believe there was any separation — Robin was still maintaining his responsibility for the family and returning home like — commuting from his work to the family as many people do and if there was tensions at home Robin was coping with them.'

Pressed on the matter that the Crown witnesses had actually said that Robin and Margaret had separated, Michael Bain told the jury that he wasn't aware of any separation and that 'as far as I am concerned they were still a family unit'.

Michael Bain admitted that in the six months after Robin went home in January 1994 he had no idea what had happened because he had not seen Robin. It was put to him that Robin's standard of dress was very shabby and he replied, 'Well, yeah, I've heard those comments and I don't agree with them myself', and went on to say that he thought Robin's standard of dress was relaxed rather than shabby. Further questioning revealed that he knew little of Robin's living conditions at the school where Robin lived in a van in a paddock without any ablution facilities. He was also unaware of the plans to build a new house.

The reader may discern the correlation between common factors related with familicide from the description of Michael Bain, his brother, alone. Of course it is natural that Michael Bain would stand up for his elder brother and honourable that he should do so. Nevertheless, his own evidence makes it clear that from 1973 until 1994 he had very little to do with Robin and his family, and had almost no knowledge of the actual dynamics playing out in the family and in Robin Bain's own life. Nonetheless, the fact that Robin was said by his brother to be a man who put on a brave face and could cope strongly correlates to the same traits in the despairing type of familicide perpetrators as described in the research.

The first cluster of witnesses were involved with Robin through work and education and some of them knew Margaret as well.

MR STONE

The first was Malin Stone, a school principal who first met Robin in 1991 when he said he used Robin as a sort of a mentor because at that time he himself was a new principal. Mr Stone was the principal of a small, two-teacher school near where Robin's school was. He described how Robin was extremely involved with computers and then went on to tell of how the two schools combined to go on a school camp together in 1994. He was asked to describe to the jury how he found Robin at this camp in 1994.

'In '94, he was just quiet, um, he seemed to be involved with his own thoughts, he wasn't motivated. Just he seemed to have lost a lot of interest in — in the schooling and life, ah, as a principal. I think he was very discouraged by the fact that he couldn't, ah, progress any further in his career ... I know he had applied for several jobs to get out of Taieri Beach but it hadn't eventuated.'

Mr Stone was asked about an occasion when he and Robin attended a course together not long before the tragedy and he told the jury: '... one of the discussions one night was on the appointments procedure for boards of trustees, and we were discussing it and Robin became very, very angry about the whole process and was arguing with the lecturer and became very embarrassing because he was actually verbally abusing him and I know that I sort of sat back 'cos I felt a little bit embarrassed about the situation, I was sitting right beside him, as did many others ... [It] was totally out of character for Robin. Robin was one of those calm sort of all-together people that — that I really enjoyed being around, but at this stage his character had changed quite dramatically. He was still angry when we travelled home in the car.'

Q: When you talk about being aggressive and angry, I mean how was this, was it really marked or just normal?

Mr Stone: Oh yes you could see it, I mean his voice was raised and you could see it in his face, the anger in his face, you know how somebody goes a little bit red when their blood pressure is rising.

Q: How did that compare with the Robin you used to know back in '91, '92?

Mr Stone: The Robin I used to know was fazed by nothing, he was always calm and collected and he would just laugh something off or just joke about it.

Mr Stone went on to say that Robin never talked about family matters with him. He then described how he went over and helped out at the school the day after the tragedy.

'What I encountered there was basically nothing. There were no programmes at work, um, when I asked the children to get their reading boxes or their reading books, or where was their maths material, or pretty much anything, they didn't know where it was and couldn't find it. And I found no evidence of planning, any evidence of programming, I didn't know where the children were at as far as their reading ages were, or what levels of achievement they had at maths. So we basically had to sort out and find out where the children were so that we could set up a programme for them.'

He was talking about the children from Robin's class who were 10 and 11 year olds. He went on to describe that their literacy level was below average and he described the classroom as 'a shambles'. He said the whole scene in terms of its presentation (referring to the teacher's table and the desks and the school) was a mess and that the resources were chaotic in general. He said everything was disorganized and that he couldn't find his way around. He went on to say that Robin had lost pride in the way he dressed and that even at the school camp he didn't take interest in his appearance. Mr Stone was finally asked how Robin looked to him, to which he answered: 'He looked very gaunt and very tired and, like I say, just very unmotivated. Completely different from the person I first knew.'

KEVIN MacKENZIE

The next witness was Kevin MacKenzie, who in 1994 was the president of the Taieri Principals Association. He also described how Robin was very computer-literate and far ahead of most teachers of his day in that regard, in particular teachers of his age. MacKenzie said that in 1994 the members of the Principals Association became very concerned that Robin seemed to be depressed and going through a tough time, having difficulty coping with the Tomorrow's Schools programme (a sweeping set of education reforms that had been introduced in 1989) and the like. They actually organized a seminar to be held in July that was mainly arranged as a result of their impression that Robin could not cope. MacKenzie described Robin at the last major meeting of the Association as being quite dishevelled with his hair all over the place and that he wasn't dressed like a professional colleague. He said that meeting was the first time that he noticed that Robin was a bit smelly. He had known Robin since the early 90s but noticed a big change from mid-1993 to May 1994. He said that on the Thursday after the tragedy he went out to the school with another local headmaster and that he found the place messy and shambolic in the same way that Mr Stone described it.

MRS DAVIDSON

Mrs Davidson was the principal of Brighton School, just up the road from Taieri Beach, and she too gave evidence for the defence on very much the same lines as the two previous witnesses. She described Robin as looking worn out and bedraggled and that the change began in 1993. She said: 'He was obviously in need of a shower when you were sitting close to him at a meeting, particularly in the winter when people have heating going.'

She also said that Robin had become very frustrated because he had applied for jobs everywhere and complained that he didn't even get an interview. She described the day that she spent at the school on the Thursday after the deaths and talked about going into Robin Bain's office: 'I can describe quite clearly in my mind what we saw that day. Piles and piles, there was mail ... high as anything ... it was on the table, it was on the chairs, it was underneath the chairs, stuff stacked in corners, it was unbelievable, and I could also see some of the Ministry of Education edges of the envelopes, unopened.'

CYRIL WILDEN

Cyril Wilden, the next witness, was a registered psychologist working for the Special Education Services of the Ministry of Education. Wilden, it must be pointed out, had known Robin and Margaret Bain for 20 or 30 years and considered them to be friends. In fact all of these witnesses were giving evidence as colleagues of Robin, not adversaries, because they had noticed such dramatic changes in Robin Bain in the year or so before the tragedy. Wilden had been called to the school during 1993 and 1994 because there were three or four children who needed special assistance. He described Robin as looking gaunt and that he thought he was not well. He said: 'Physically, I thought he wasn't well, that was the first thing I noticed, and my impression was that he had some sort of communication problem because it was difficult to engage him and talk about the issues that I wanted to talk about. He was quite happy to either not talk at all or talk about things that he was concerned about. So I was concerned about his physical appearance, his demeanour, some of the things he said just didn't sound right and I was concerned about the state of the school that I was sort of picking up on, it was rather chaotic and disorganized.'

He went on to say: 'My abiding impression was that [Robin] was suffering from some sort of reactive depression or situational depression.' He also said that Robin Bain had told him that he was becoming increasingly frustrated about all of the jobs he had applied for, which did not seem to be happening.

Wilden was asked about Robin Bain's mental health, and whether he ever discussed his medical position or condition and whether he needed any medical help. He replied: 'I was looking to find some way to communicate to him about the stress he was under and all I can remember is whether he had been to his GP, I mean as a psychologist, generally we would ask a teacher or a principal if we thought there was a health issue, we would ask them automatically virtually, have you got a GP, have you got any medical needs that we should be considering that haven't been met in a sense, is the way perhaps I could put it, and asked him whether he was getting any medical help and he was quite dismissive and said yes he was, as far as I can recall.'

Pressed on the issue, he said that Robin really didn't want to talk about it.

He also said that two of the children that he had been asked to consult had complained that the principal Robin Bain had lost his cool and hit them. Wilden went on to say that it was a relatively minor incident but that in his mind it reflected that Robin was under a lot of stress and strain at that time. He certainly did not make a big play of the fact and said that in 1994 it was a very minor matter, but that in combination with other things it concerned him. Of further concern to Wilden was that when he got to the school on the day of the tragedy, he found the same disorganized mess and piles of unopened mail as had Mrs Davidson, and everything was in a chaotic state.

Wilden went on to describe that while he was there that week, he came across a school newsletter that had been sent out to the parents the week before the tragedy. In that newsletter there were a series of stories written by the children, three of which were of a nature that concerned him considerably. The stories, written by nine and 10 year olds, described family killings, stabbings, shootings and other violence. The bulletin in which the stories were published was headed up with the words, 'Here are some stories which were ready for publication. We will include more with each newsletter. Each author is proud of their work. (Read a warning — some topics may disturb adult viewers).'

The three stories of concern were written by children about nine years old. Excerpts from the first story are as follows:

> He went home and got his gun he shot 100 cops and broke into a shop, got some bombs and he bombed the cop shop … He went back to the street, the cops were there so he went to jail. When he got out he got his big red motorbike and he crashed into a wall but it was the wall of a house and he did not know it was his Mum and dad's house. So he nicked a TV and it went well but he got madder and shot his mum 'it was fun' so he shot his dad 'it was funnier' so he shot everyone he saw. The cops came and put back in jail.

Story two:

> Once there was a man called Tim. That was his nickname. He lived in a house at number 13. One day he went to the loo. It was dark while he was on it. He noticed that the toilet paper was gone. He noticed a ghost dancing around by the window outside. Then it picked up some flowers and threw them away. Then the ghost vanished into thin air. He went back downstairs to watch TV. Then the trouble began. He went into the kitchen to cook dinner. He cooked dinner then went to get a knife. Then the ghost came back and killed him. They buried him one month later. A lady saw a ghost — he had risen from the dead. One of the people next door had stolen the picture. They put the picture back and the ghost lived happily ever after.

Story three:

> Once upon a time there was a girl who loved porcelain dolls so her mother got her a porcelain doll for her birthday and she played with it

and took really good care of it. Her name was Rose. One day she got a new doll for her birthday. She played with it all day for months and months. She shifted the old porcelain doll to another place and put the new doll on the place where she kept the old doll and she never dusted the old doll or played with it. The old doll got mad so one night the girl was in bed and she heard a scream. In the morning she woke up and went into her mum and dad's room and her dad had a rifle stuck through his head and she went back into her room and the porcelain doll had a fingernail missing. Then the next night she went to bed and she heard a scream and she went into her mum's room and she had a knife stuck through her heart. So she went into her room and another fingernail was missing. Now that was getting strange so she went to bed that night and she heard another scream and it was her sister this time. She had been stabbed through the leg and the heart 10 times. She went into her room to get her new doll and she found another fingernail missing. Now there were three fingernails missing and three nights. She was thinking it strange. So she went to bed and heard another scream and it was her brother — he had been shot in the head and his heart. She found four fingernail is missing. She went to bed and she woke up in the middle of the night and the porcelain doll was missing and then she heard a cry and she fell asleep again. Then she woke up in the morning and she looked at her porcelain doll and there were five fingernails missing so she went into her baby sister's room and her head was smashed through the cot. So she got her porcelain doll and went to the garden and buried her old porcelain doll. Then another family moved into that house and looked after Rose. One day the mother was doing the gardening and came upon a porcelain doll and she thought it was beautiful and she cleaned it up and gave it to the children and killed all the people in the family apart from Rose. The end.

All of the educational experts said in evidence that the publication of these stories was a profound error of judgment by a principal in 1994. What particularly concerned Wilden and the other headmasters who commented on the stories was that a school teacher of long-standing experience like Robin Bain should have known he should never include such stories for publication in a school newsletter. To them it indicated, as one of them put it, that 'Robin had lost touch with reality'. MacKenzie described it in the following words: 'It's totally weird and unprofessional for any principal who … I just don't know of any principal who would publish the stories. And I think if you did then I would have a major concern about the mental health of the principal.' All six of the education witnesses called by the defence were extremely alarmed that a principal would include the stories in a public newsletter to the parents.

The Crown called witnesses from the school Board of Trustees who said Robin was a caring and diligent teacher, much liked by parents and children alike. This is not disputed. However, it does not detract from the factual matters illustrating the dramatic degeneration of aspects of his life.

The next witness was another psychologist from the Special Education Services, Maryanne Pease, who accompanied Wilden and gave evidence which in effect confirmed the evidence of Wilden and everyone else that had gone before him.

Of course, as stated earlier, all of these witnesses were cross-examined very closely by the Crown, who naturally could not let these views go by uncontested. The difficulty the Crown had was that even leaving aside any opinions expressed (such as to the propriety of sending out the school newsletter), the chaotic state of the school, the unopened mail, the lack of planning, Robin's presentation and poor hygiene and his expressed anger and frustration about his employment prospects were matters of fact which spoke for themselves. This is not hearsay. This is how it was. It should also be noted that these witnesses had no allegiance to David. In fact most of them considered themselves friends of Robin and had never met David. They were simply attesting to the facts as they were in 1994. These witnesses describe a man who was losing control, much as would be expected from the description of 'despairing type' familicidal men in the research.

JOAN WITHERS

Then the defence called Mrs Joan Withers from Hamilton, who was a senior adviser with the Ministry of Education and who conducted a review for the Education Review Office (ERO) at Taieri Beach School in 1993. In a nutshell, Withers told the court that the review conducted in 1993 was very critical of the operation of the school. She described how on the first day she arrived Robin Bain was on the computer while all of the children were talking to each other and running about playing in what she described as a very chaotic scene. She said that she would have hoped it would have been the children on the computer, not the teacher. She also confirmed what the other teachers had said: that there was very little evidence of the curriculum being implemented and of the normal work she would expect to see in the children's books.

She also describes her impressions of Robin Bain as a result of meeting with him and expressing these concerns. In her own words: 'He was — he was very impassive about the whole thing and it was something that quite troubled me because his demeanour showed no emotion and I tried to lighten things up a bit but it was still this very bland, unemotional face that … and the responses were just robotic like and just had no feeling with them. So it was most unusual.'

She went on to say: 'I believed him to be the most unusual person I've ever met in my work and I described him to my colleague Pat as a walking cadaver because he seemed to be dead behind his eyes. There was just no flicker of light there.'

Although the follow-up ERO review in early 1994 showed general improvement at the school, the situation found at the school immediately after Robin's death demonstrates that in a personal sense he was not coping.

DARYL YOUNG

Another example of Robin Bain neglecting his professional duties came from Daryl Young, the photocopier salesman whose company had supplied a photocopier to the school while Robin Bain was the headmaster. He described how he had been to the school on three occasions and that on one occasion, which he thought was in 1992 or 1993, he went to the school for a prearranged meeting with Robin Bain which was set for nine o'clock but when he arrived Robin Bain was not at the school. He said the children were running around the classroom unattended. He was informed that he might find Robin in his Commer van at the old Taieri Beach camping ground (effectively a paddock) and so he went down there, and seeing the van he banged on the back door. His evidence states: 'I heard voices and then I sort of, once I heard the voices, I sort of moved away sort of five or 10 metres.' He said he thought he heard two different voices but was unable to determine the sex of the second voice but just assumed it was a female. He said that Robin Bain came out of the back of the van completely naked with just a towel wrapped around him. When he came out of the van, Young said that he smelt alcohol and thought that that's why he (Robin) wasn't at school. The reference to 'back of the van' is not to the actual back door, but the sliding door in the rear section of the van as opposed to either the passenger or the driver's door.

PREVIOUS PRINCIPAL

There was also evidence that Robin himself was aware he had a problem. Another headmaster called by the defence told how he was the principal at Taieri Beach from 2001 to 2004. His evidence was simply that when some members of the Board at the school were cleaning out an old storage cupboard they came across a document which was a request from Robin Bain seeking stress leave, written not long before the tragedy. The Board member in question gave evidence that she found the letter which she said was signed by Robin Bain. She stated: 'The letter was from Mr Bain asking for and I don't remember all the words, he was asking to be released from his duties as principal because of stress.'

MICHAEL MAYSON

Michael Mayson, a consulting engineer who was Robin Bain's first cousin, was called by the defence. His mother and Robin's mother were sisters. Robin Bain had lived with Michael Mayson and his wife for several months in Dunedin in about 1967. Michael and Robin had gone to the gym together at that stage and later Michael went to Robin and Margaret's wedding. He said that after Robin and Margaret went to Papua New Guinea in 1972 he lost contact with them and only ever saw them once again together as a family in 1989. However, at the beginning of 1994 on the occasion that Michael Bain had described when he and Robin had painted his mother's house in January in Otaki, Michael Mayson described how Robin had come to visit his mother, and that he called in while he was there.

Mayson was asked to describe how Robin looked and he stated: 'Well, I was shocked, actually. I have this image in my head of him sitting at the head of my mother's kitchen table, against the wall, and it's ah, it's a shocking image that's stayed with me ever since, he looked gaunt, ill, wasted. In fact my first thought was that he had some sort of terminal illness, he looked terrible. But I was assured that he was all right. I have a lot of regret that I didn't actually take him to one side at that time and try to find out what the problem was, but he was a seriously ill looking person.'

KYLE CUNNINGHAM

Kyle Cunningham, the young man living with Robin and Laniet at the schoolhouse for the few weeks before the tragedy, was also called by the defence. He was asked about the sort of clothes that Robin Bain wore and said that Robin was a fairly scruffily dressed man who was 'different' in his demeanour. He stated: '... he certainly wasn't, um, your average person by any stretch. I mean I saw on the news the other day a lady likened him to a cadaver, and I mean that was a pretty good conclusion to his appearance and, just overall aura that he gave away. I mean he was very distant.' His evidence was not of special importance because it was such a long time ago; however, his general impression of Robin Bain as a man who was somewhat empty emotionally fitted a general picture.

METER READER

Further evidence that all was not well with Robin came from the man who was responsible for reading the meters at Taieri Beach in 1994. He said that a week or two before the tragedy he had called to read the meter at the school. He described Robin Bain's demeanour and appearance in the following words: 'After meeting the principal of the Taieri Beach School for the first time, I would have said he came across as being quite depressed to me. Not, not who — the type of person I would have thought, that was involved with kids and that type of thing, someone who would be more outgoing I would suppose.'

MRS DUNN

The research shows that men who commit familicide-suicide often have symptoms of depression going back many years. In the Bain case, another witness who came forward to the defence was a Mrs Dunn, who had been the wife of a Presbyterian minister who was deceased by the time of the trial. She and her husband had lived in Alexandra and got to know David's mother and her sisters and their mother very well during that time. Later they were transferred to St Andrew's Presbyterian Church in Dunedin when they befriended Robin and Margaret. She described how in 1978 and 1991, when Robin and Margaret returned to New Zealand on holiday, they visited her and her husband and that on one occasion during the 1978 visit she and Margaret were talking about family things and the like when Margaret told her that she was very worried about Robin because of his depression.

It should be pointed out that the Crown called a number of witnesses from Taieri Beach and the school Board of Trustees who all spoke glowingly of Robin in the same way that Michael Bain did. They worked with him and knew that he was a decent, hard-working man at heart and attributed many of the observations made by the defence witnesses to simply being idiosyncrasies associated with Robin's methods and personality. These people's observations were put to the defence witnesses in cross-examination by the Crown.

As the research shows, the fact that these other witnesses noticed nothing unusual in Robin Bain is consistent with the findings about men of this despairing type who have committed familicide-suicide, where usually many people are unable to identify any sign of impending crisis; and demonstrates how good these men are at managing their outward image. Such evidence does not contradict the fact that some people who knew Robin very well did have concerns, and the defence witnesses did not, under cross-examination, change their view of what they saw in Robin over the years and months leading up to the tragedy.

SIGNS OF PREPARATION?

The review of the research literature found that many men who commit familicide-suicide make preparations: cancelling appointments, settling accounts and so on before the killings. Such signs may have been shown by Robin Bain, according to the accounts of these witnesses.

Christine Rout, who had done a lot of relief teaching at Taieri Beach School from 1991 until 1993, was another witness called by the defence. She said that Robin Bain had rung her a number of times in the first six months of 1994 to ask if she could relieve, but she was booked at other schools each time. She went on to say that the last time he called was the week before the deaths. She said that when Robin rang, her daughter answered the phone and put a message on the wall and as a result of that message she rang him back. She said that Robin wanted her to relieve for the week starting 20 June, but again she was unable to do that because at that time she was working long term at another school. Christine Rout had been interviewed by the police during the week of 20 June 1994, and given them this information in her statement. Yet again, it took the defence at the retrial to call her evidence.

The man responsible for reading the power meters at Taieri Beach in 1994, whose description of Robin we saw above, also told the court that when he called to read the meter at the school, he was approached by a man as he was walking across the playground. '... he stood there with his hands in his pockets and his head down, and he didn't sort of look at me when he was talking ... He asked me if I could do a final reading on the school house, um, that was — the name on the account was under Bain, I don't remember any initials, and he said, um, "I want to put the power back into the Board of Trustees' name".' He went on to explain that the man told him he was moving back to town. The man explained that he was just the meter reader and that he could not do final readings.

Another witness, who owned a dairy across the road from where Laniet had been living in Russell Street, Dunedin, also gave evidence. He said that on the afternoon of Sunday, 19 June — the day before the killings — Robin came to the shop and insisted on paying off the money that Laniet owed on account. The witness (whose name is suppressed) described how Laniet was a customer who came in very regularly and as she was unemployed she would often pop in wearing her pyjamas. He said that she was very chatty and personable and they got to know her reasonably well. He said that she was not usually in a hurry and he learned that she was unemployed, had difficulties at home and some relationship issues. She would usually buy bread, milk and cigarettes and often didn't have enough money so they ran an informal account for her. He went on to say that she would generally come and pay her account on a weekly basis, but sometimes it went longer than that. He said he did not know Robin personally but knew who he was because on weekends he would come and make sundry purchases. He then stated: 'The Sunday before it was announced in the papers that the family had been murdered, Robin Bain came into the store, made some purchases and asked to clear Laniet's account in full, was adamant that the account needed to be paid in full.'

Q: Did that strike you as usual?

Dairy owner: He didn't normally pay her accounts. She was normally responsible for them.

Q: Did he give any reason why on that Sunday he suddenly came in and wanted to clear her account?

Dairy owner: No.

IGNOMINY: A TRIGGER EVENT

As discussed, the research shows that familicide-suicide tends to be preceded by a triggering event that occurs on top of a long build-up of disappointment, loss and failure. This trigger event is often something that the perpetrator fears will expose him and his family to public shame and scandal. There are some indications of what the trigger may have been for Robin Bain: the final breakdown of his marriage, or something even more shaming.

It will be remembered that at the first trial there was no evidence at all that Laniet had been working as a prostitute for the previous nine or 10 months, and nor was there any evidence that she had been making allegations to people that an incestuous relationship existed with her father. But the fact of her prostitution was common ground at the second trial.

The dairy owner described how one day Laniet came into the store crying, very distressed and upset, and he asked her if she was all right. She told him 'that she was having an affair with her father'. He said he was completely gobsmacked and didn't know how to respond. He said her exact words were: 'I'm having an affair with my father.'

There were a number of witnesses apart from the dairy owner who also gave evidence about the incest allegations made by Laniet about her father and herself. One was a man who in 1994 owned a superette not far from where the Bains lived. He said that he had given Laniet Bain a part-time job because some girls who worked for him, who were friends of Laniet, had approached him to help her because she was trying to turn her life around. He couldn't remember the dates but thought it was early in 1994 that this happened. He said she only worked there for a few weeks but it was just a small shop and often there was down time when he would talk to her about her life. He said that she told him her father had been having sex with her in Papua New Guinea, and that it was still continuing. He said he told her she should go to the police and that he would go with her as a support person. This man did not come forward until 2006 after reading about the Privy Council decision, when he sent an email to the *Otago Daily Times* regarding his involvement with Laniet and they interviewed him: the story was published in the newspaper with a photo of him.

Another fellow who gave evidence had lived at the Russell Street boarding house where Laniet also lived for a time. One evening she had been upset and they had quite a long discussion which went on till the early hours of the morning. His memory was that it was in the month prior to the deaths. She told him, he said, that she was a prostitute and he went into some detail about the conversation. He described how in the process of this long conversation she became very upset and got onto the subject of her father and said that when she was younger he would go into her room and touch her inappropriately. He claimed that she was worried that the same thing may have happened to Arawa, her sister. This witness had told a friend of his about this years ago and, in turn, this friend had told somebody from one of the television channels which was how he came to be interviewed about it.

A female witness who also has name suppression had also lived at the Russell Street flats during 1993 and 1994, and became a close friend of Laniet. This witness came to the attention of the defence because she had been contacted by the police in 2007 when they took a statement from her. The police originally listed her as being a witness for the Crown, but in the lead-up to the trial they decided not to call her. The defence made contact with her and arranged for her to give evidence of her knowledge and friendship with Laniet, and she told how she knew that Laniet had a cellphone which she used in her job as a prostitute. She knew that the cellphone belonged to Dean Cottle.

She said that while they were living in Russell Street together, Laniet told her she had been having sex with her father, although she never specified how long it had been going on for. Laniet also told her she had a baby in Papua New Guinea and the father was a family friend. She said that Laniet showed her a photo which she claimed was the baby; and she described the baby in the photo as 'whitish' with Laniet's hair. This witness said she and Laniet shared bathroom facilities and she often saw Laniet naked, and Laniet had stretch-marks down her stomach.

She then said that she had not seen Laniet for quite some time, but bumped into her in the Octagon on the Thursday before the murders. During a chat on this occasion, Laniet said to her 'that she was working in the Museum café, that she had given up work as a sex worker and that she was going home that weekend to blow the whistle on her being a sex worker and that she had been having an incestuous relationship with her father'. She said that Laniet had told her of the incestuous relationship while they were living together at the Russell Street flat. In cross-examination she said that David also wanted to see the whole family that weekend but she did not know why.

Two further witnesses, who had been prostitutes working with Laniet before her death, had both been to the police initially with their information that Laniet had told them that her father had been having sex with her for years.

In one instance, the woman in question claimed that she went with a friend into the Dunedin CIB not long after the deaths of the family but after David was arrested. She said the police were not interested in her information. When the retrial was ordered in 2007 she wrote to me personally with her information. The conversation when Laniet told her about the incest came about because it was quite a common topic among prostitutes. In her words, the majority of the women have been raped or molested or abused in some form and so it is quite often therapeutic for them to talk together. This woman did not mention anything about stretch-marks.

The other woman first went to the police in 1998 and told them of her association with Laniet. The police referred her to the Bain defence team and to Mr Withnall in particular. She said that she had 'done doubles' with Laniet, and that she had definitely seen stretch-marks on those occasions, indicating that she had had a baby. The stretch-marks were down the middle of the abdominal region and she was sure they were the type of stretch-marks that related to childbirth. This evidence about stretch-marks is direct observation. It is not hearsay. Could all these women be wrong? They did not know each other so had not collaborated.

The 'why' questions

A couple of questions are often asked and they were put up by the Crown. They are 'why' questions. Why would Robin change his clothes if he intended to commit suicide? Why would Robin spare David? The first answer to these questions is that we don't know. We cannot know what is in the mind of another person and why they do what they do, particularly if it is something of which we have no personal experience. In some ways the questions are best answered with another question.

A few years ago, during the 2008 financial crisis, a successful banking executive in England got up one morning, dressed in his smart suit, told his wife that he would meet her at their country house that evening, set off for work in his expensive car and sent her a text not long after confirming the evening's arrangements.

A few minutes after sending the text message, he parked his car and lay down on a railway line in front of an oncoming train and was killed. Why would he have texted his wife arranging to meet her that evening, just minutes before committing suicide? It is incomprehensible. Does that question answer the question? What more can be said?

It may be that when the killing rampage began Robin did not intend to spare David but then changed his mind while waiting for him to get back. It is one thing killing people asleep in the dark. It is maybe another to kill your eldest son when he is going about his daily business. But this is speculation as is any other counter-proposition.

However, although the actual reasons cannot be known, the data does provide some insight into these points. Men who commit familicide-suicide are known to 'tidy up' before killing themselves, often cleaning and arranging the scene, changing their clothes and so on. You will recall that Ratima, after killing his three sons, arranged them neatly on a bed with a Bible. Although this may seem bizarre in someone whose intention is to kill himself, it might also be seen as consistent with the respectability of the 'despairing' perpetrators; that is, it is one last act of impression management.

Similarly, any attempt to explain why Robin would spare David alone of all the family necessarily involves speculation, for the reasons stated at the outset — that it is impossible to know what is going on in the mind of a person. However, the data shows that the survival of adult children of perpetrators of familicide-suicide is not uncommon. The fathers often 'spare' adult children. It may be because they are adults and are therefore no longer seen as dependants.

Who knows what Mr Bain was experiencing mentally and emotionally that morning? One thing we do know is that he could not have got the gun and ammunition until after David had left on his paper round. We know from the evidence on familicides perpetrated by men who are not of a violent or abusive nature that the killings are driven by the sort of compulsion that drives suicide rather than by those that drive homicide. It may be that when Robin Bain settled on taking his own life that was all he had in mind. We will never know.

Maybe on this matter the Privy Council expressed it with most precision: 'But the jury might consider that whoever committed these killings was not acting normally or rationally.'

CHAPTER 22

PSYCHOLOGICAL EVIDENCE: DAVID BAIN

DAVID'S STATE OF MIND

When the Crown changed its original 'missing 20 minutes' theory to the 'four before, one after' scenario on which David was convicted and which the Crown pursued thereafter and at the retrial, one of the major impacts of that dramatic change relates to the psychology of the case.

After David's arrest, speculation was rife among the police, Michael Guest, family members, the media and others in the know about the killings as to what may have caused David to go on the killing spree, if indeed he had. Was it simply the brain explosion of a mentally disturbed young man who, when he came back to his senses, did not even know what he had done? Or was it some evil spirit, an occult force, that had developed while he lived in the tropics all those years? Support for this theory was generated by David's comments about black hands and the fact that Papua New Guinea is known to be a place where black magic and similar workings of the spirits are common in the native culture. It was also known that David had suffered from malaria while living in the tropics. Was it a legacy of that disease, or a combination of all the above? Whatever it was, it was a mystery to all involved. Even by the end of the first trial nobody was any wiser. Remember Wright's words at the beginning of his closing address: 'It is beyond our comprehension. We can't understand it. We will probably never know why it occurred much less understand it.'

If it was some psychotic outburst, brain explosion, call it what you will, involving temporary insanity or even some evil spirit followed by a blackout that caused all this, then did David come to his senses afterwards and rather clumsily try to cover up what he had done by writing a message on the computer and doing the washing and claiming they were all dead when he got home? This does not fit — but then, there is no explaining what such a mentally deranged person may do.

As we know, the scenario ultimately put to the jury was the opposite of this. It was not a brain explosion, a psychotic frenzied outburst, but rather a cold-blooded, cunning, premeditated plan.

These musings and posturings led Michael Guest to make contact with Dr Phil Brinded, New Zealand's most eminent criminal psychiatrist, soon after David's arrest and engage him to interview David and provide an assessment as to mental and personal stability. Dr Brinded met David twice within a month or so of the arrest and formally reported to Guest that he could find no abnormalities either mentally or in his personality traits.

As time went on, Guest considered various defences such as automatism, which is the term used to describe actions carried out when a person is acting like a robot with no conscious volition at all. This defence would have embraced the evil spirit scenario where some kind of occult power had occupied David's mind, compelling him to do things that he did not even know that he was doing.

However, David's absolute refusal to accept that he had done anything except find his family dead, along with such things as the message on the computer and the doing of the washing, meant this theory fell to the ground and was not pursued by Michael Guest.

In the months leading up to the trial Guest suggested to David that if he pleaded temporary insanity then Guest believed that he would probably get a few years in a mental institution instead of a possible life term in prison. David's response was unequivocal, to the effect that as he did not kill anyone he would not be pleading anything in mitigation because he was entirely innocent of any wrongdoing or involvement in the killings.

When, after the depositions, Dr Paul Mullen, the Australian psychiatrist, was brought in during December of 1994, his mission was largely to see if he could extract from David some recovery in memory of that missing 20 minutes, simply because that period of time was believed to hold the key to the whole case.

In the light of subsequent events, this meant that Mullen was instructed on a false premise, albeit that Guest could not have known then that it was false. If at that time Michael Guest had known that the Crown case was that these killings were premeditated by David, planned in a cruel and evil way and that the killings took place for all those in the house at around 4 a.m., and that his father would be killed when he got home, then the instructions to Professor Mullen would have been totally reversed. Rather than looking for some psychosis involving a blackout or whatever, he would have been looking for personality disorders of the type that in colloquial language are associated with psychopaths.

Mullen nonetheless noted in his report to Michael Guest, as has been heard in the evidence he gave to the jury, that David Bain had no personality disorders of any description, let alone psychopathic tendencies. But of course the fact that David was not psychopathic was of no help to them in defending the proposition that this was all done in some kind of bizarre trance during the missing 20 minutes.

Here lies one of the fundamental differences from trial one to the retrial. By the time of the retrial in 2009 it was well and truly entrenched that David had to be a very seriously disturbed person, what we colloquially call a psychopath, to have carried out the evil, cunning plan postulated by the Crown. The trouble was that nobody who had come in contact with David either before the terrible events of that day or since his arrest — whether they were professionals, laypeople, workmates, house-mates or social acquaintances — has ever seen anything even remotely associated with the mental defects and personality disorders that the Crown case demanded.

PSYCHOLOGICAL EVIDENCE REGARDING DAVID

What follows is all of the professional evidence pertaining to David's mental condition and personality traits, including two reports that have come to light since the retrial. Both of these new psychiatric reports on David were conducted by medical experts *on instructions from the Crown*.

SENTENCING REPORT

The first is from a doctor who was the Director of Forensic Psychiatry for Healthcare Otago, who interviewed David first in July 1994 at the request of prison staff to assess his suicide risk when he was first charged; and then again after David was convicted in 1995 to complete a psychiatric assessment for sentencing purposes under Section 121 2(b) of the Criminal Justice Act. The doctor interviewed David on 13 and 14 June 1995 in respect to those instructions. In his report addressed to the presiding judge in the Dunedin High Court, the doctor noted that EEG, CT and MRI scans had been arranged to look for significant neurological abnormalities. These had been considered by the doctor and other expert medical staff and found to be utterly negative.

The report to the presiding judge dated 15 June 1995 is comprehensive, as one would expect in the grave circumstances facing the judge in sentencing a man convicted of five murders. As well as interviewing David, the doctor had been provided with access to the court files, evidence regarding David's personal functioning given by friends and relatives at the court, all of which were considered in the compilation of the report. The report begins by presenting a summary of David's account to the psychiatrist of the family history involving life growing up in Papua New Guinea, the difficulties associated with shifting back to a more modern society for David himself and the family in general. It covered his first attempt at university to study zoology, which he lost interest in before discovering has passion for music and drama, and returning to university in 1994 to study classics. David's account to the doctor mirrored what the court had heard.

The report states that David openly talked about his knowledge and understanding of the estrangement between his parents upon the family's return to New Zealand.

The report states:

He described tension in the family, the parents' marital situation never having been completely resolved by a final separation, and a sense of his father continuing to try to involve himself in family matters and assert affectionate and paternal bonds with the children in a way that led to increasing awkwardness.

It goes on to say:

He described his mother's increasing interest in 'new age' spirituality and techniques for personal growth and healing, and the widening gap between that and his father's more conservative religious beliefs. He said he himself had been comfortable with most of his mother's beliefs except her use of a pendulum for decision-making. He described his strong belief that he was innocent, and his intention to pursue legal means to prove that.

The report, after recounting this background, went on to what it called 'mental state examination', which was the doctor's assessment of David based upon the information and interviews conducted. The following passages are taken directly from the report.

> Mr Bain presented as pleasant and fluent at interview, with no evidence of major mental disorder in terms of either disturbance of the function of mood, or disturbance of the function of thinking and reasoning. He is clearly of above-average intelligence from his verbal skills, and there was no evidence of impairment of memory or concentration or the capacity for abstract reasoning.
>
> Mr Bain's own perception of the situation is that he is innocent of the charges for which he has been found guilty, and that he will eventually be able to prove this. His religious beliefs include the belief that God has a purpose for him, and that this may involve his having to endure prison for a time, but will eventually lead to the proof of his innocence.
>
> Mr Bain does not present significant features of an antisocial personality. There is no history of antisocial behaviour in the past, he demonstrates concern for others and some ability to empathize or put himself in someone else's shoes in an imaginative way. Mr Bain also does not present significant features of a narcissistic personality, in that he does not present with abnormal ideas of his own self-worth, nor abnormal notions of what he is entitled to from other people.

CORRECTIONS REPORT

Following David's sentencing to life imprisonment with a minimum parole period of 16 years, he was incarcerated at Christchurch men's prison. The Corrections Department required another psychiatric assessment to assist them in formulating the kind of care that he would require and this was conducted by the senior psychologist for the psychological services of the Department of Justice in Christchurch. The doctor interviewed David on 27 July 1995 and completed his report on 2 August 1995. This would be the fourth psychiatric assessment of David by a professional person and the second conducted for a Crown authority since the events of 20 June 1994.

The report states that the doctor explained to David that his reasons for seeing him were to assess his reaction to such a lengthy sentence, to evaluate his adjustment to prison life and to determine his needs during the initial phase of his sentence. It continues:

Although Mr Bain's demeanour at the beginning of the interview was reserved, he established rapport fairly quickly and as our discussion proceeded he seemed to be glad of the opportunity to discuss matters of significance for him. He answered my questions thoughtfully, and I believed openly and honestly, and I was left with the impression of a young man of some maturity and sincerity.

Mr Bain was fully aware of my reasons for seeing him, and at the outset acknowledged that there must be some concern as to his potential for self-harm, particularly were his appeal to be unsuccessful. He volunteered, without any questioning on my behalf, that the last year had been extremely traumatic, and following his conviction he had considered suicide and the implications which this would have, both for his resolutely maintained assertion of innocence, and also for others who had supported him following the deaths of all his close family members. He told me that suicide was not an option for him, particularly as a successful attempt would be seen by some as a confirmation of his guilt. He argued that, notwithstanding his current situation and the potentially negative outcome of this current appeal, he still had his life to lead, and that when he was eventually released he intended to devote his energies to exonerate himself of the murders for which he was convicted.

In response to my inquiry as to the basis of his appeal, he advised that the judge had made certain rulings in relation to the admissibility of evidence which had been uncovered in the course of the police investigations, and that he and his counsel considered that the trial judge had been in error in finding one particular item inadmissible. He discussed the particular details of this item with me, and I consider that his opinion about the importance of the judge's refusal to allow this matter to be raised is not unreasonable.

He acknowledged that he was anxious about how he would be received on his arrival, and commented that the number of convictions, coupled with the publicity given to his trial, had the effect of other inmates initially regarding him with a degree of suspicion and caution, doubtless resulting from the inferences which they had drawn about his state of mind. His high level of social and interpersonal skills, however, appear to have enabled him to establish reasonable and cordial relationships with other inmates and the staff of the wing.

The report goes on to describe that the doctor required David to complete psychometric testing.

David Bain, throughout the entire interview, was reasonable, insightful, and rational. He impressed as a young man of intelligence, maturity, and sincerity. He appreciates the impact of the stresses to which he has been subjected, and has some understanding of the considerable emotional issues which he must now attempt to resolve. I have no doubt that he believes that he is innocent of the charges, and in the event of his appeal against conviction being dismissed, which is probable, then ongoing supportive treatment from this service is warranted. I have discussed that eventuality with Mr Bain, and he expressed a desire to continue to see me on a fortnightly basis in the meantime.

DR PHIL BRINDED

The doctor from the psychological services continued to visit David for some time according to his undertaking, but then the role was assumed by Dr Philip Brinded. Dr Brinded continued to visit David continuously almost up until the time that he was released from prison and also gave evidence to the Ministry of Justice at the time of the petition to the Governor General and also to the Court of Appeal and finally at the retrial in 2009.

There are limitations on the evidence that is admissible from psychiatrists in criminal trials, but those limitations did not apply to the petition to the Governor General in 1998. Dr Brinded provided a report for that petition in which he said the following:

My sessions with David have shown him to be totally consistent in his recounting of what he does and doesn't remember regarding the day of the killings. *I have never detected nor do I believe that there has been any attempt on his part to fabricate information.* I believe the consistency of the story, over a long period of time, *is due to the fact that he is being truthful about the events.* Consequently, I believe his period of amnesia to be entirely genuine and consistent with the descriptions of the associated amnesia found in the psychiatric literature. This view I believe to be far more credible than the alternative, that he has been able to lie with great conviction, accuracy and credibility for over four years.

At the retrial in 2009 Dr Phillip Brinded told the jury that he was Professor in Forensic Psychiatry at the Christchurch School of Medicine and the Chief of Psychiatry for the Canterbury District Health Board. He was led through his evidence by Helen Cull QC.

Dr Brinded described how he was asked to examine David and do a mental status examination of him in July and August of 1994. He told of his conclusions from those two interviews:

'The overall conclusion that I drew following the two interviews was that I felt that David, in terms of his history, showed no previous signs of mental disorder. He showed no signs of personality disorder, most particularly at the time of the alleged offending. I could find nothing to suggest that leading up to that David was suffering from mental illness and in that regard I advised his counsel [Guest] that I did not believe that an insanity defence would be available.'

He then went on to describe how in 1996 after David began his sentence at Christchurch Prison he became David's regular therapist and saw him regularly every two or three weeks for the following three years. He clarified with the court that all of those discussions were in confidence on the basis of the professional relationship between David and him as David's then doctor.

However, in something of a bombshell for the Crown, Helen Cull QC, who was leading him through his evidence, advised that David had waived that privilege and that Dr Brinded was free to discuss with her *and in cross-examination* anything and everything that took place between them. This meant, for example, that the Crown could have required the doctor to produce his medical files relating to David.

This in itself was quite startling because as one could imagine a person with anything to hide would be very unlikely to allow their psychiatrist free rein in the witness box, particularly under cross-examination. Brinded stated that David at that time, 1996, showed very significant signs of post-traumatic stress and said that he would always become very distressed when talking about the events of the day his family died.

However, he said: 'His accounts of that always remained consistent with what he had told me actually at the time of the trial.' He went on to explain the effect of acute stress reaction and post-traumatic stress disorder on a person's recollection of the trauma that caused the disorder. He said that dissociative amnesia is the medical term for this sort of memory loss and that it is very common in people suffering post-traumatic stress disorder.

'It's thought to be really the brain's way of defending the sufferer from the most painful or most dreadful memories or thoughts of the trauma that they experienced. And so dissociative amnesia usually isn't complete, usually there are fragments of memory which a person can't put together in a sequential story but they remember bits and pieces.'

He explained to the court that déjà vu experiences and the trance described by one of the witnesses were common, particularly in young people, and not something that would be considered to be a psychiatric condition or disorder. He was asked to describe the types of disorders or psychiatric illnesses that are commonly found or that a forensic psychiatrist is looking for in cases of this type when he is consulted as an expert. He said:

'Broadly one looks for the common psychiatric illnesses or major disorders like major depressive disorder, bipolar disorder, major depression, schizophrenia, and one also looks at the other aspect which is about people's personality. You're trying to tell whether their actions or the alleged actions are part and parcel of a mental illness or the way they are in terms of their personality, and if their personality is particularly unusual, then a personality disorder or whether it might be a combination of the two.'

He went on to say that in terms of violent crimes or homicide the most likely personality disorder is what he said in common parlance is known as psychopathy, which he described as follows:

'Somebody who is severely antisocial or a psychopath [has] different emotional responses from most. They lack empathy, they lacked consideration for others, they're indifferent to other people's experiences or suffering, they're often repeatedly antisocial in terms of breaking the law and offending, they're deceitful and what makes that out to be a personality disorder is that those characteristics are actually enduring — they're inflexible, they're part of the way the person sees themselves and interacts with the world. And so it

394

is a personality disorder, it's not an illness and *it's usually lifelong.*'

He went on to discuss in quite some detail various types of disorders and then said:

'So in summary, I didn't detect any of those things as David reported them in the months and days leading up to the alleged offending and at the time that I saw him, the predominant features were those of post-traumatic stress, although as I said he developed some element of depression ... but not that actually required medication.'

Helen Cull then asked him: 'So can I just be clear with this witness, there was no psychopathic tendencies or characteristics that you ever saw in David Bain, is that correct?'

Dr Brinded answered: 'That's correct.'

He was then asked whether he had considered the evidence of the ambulance officers and others regarding that period when David was said to have been shaking in his bedroom that morning. Dr Brinded said that the evidence appeared to him to be entirely consistent with somebody who is very shocked or traumatized.

In cross-examination, Kieran Raftery was very brief. The only subject that he had Dr Brinded confirm was that which Professor Mullen had told of at the first trial — that post-traumatic stress disorder can happen in both the discoverer of a horrible scene as well as the person who actually committed the crime.

It was obvious that Dr Brinded would never have been called by the defence with a waiver of privilege from David if he had the slightest doubt whatsoever as to David's innocence. Indeed the fact that Raftery's cross-examination was so brief confirms that he did not wish to broach the subject.

What has never been professionally appropriate for him to include in a formal document is what Dr Brinded has told me personally many times over the past 14 years, which is that he believes that David Bain is innocent and has told the truth.

There were many witnesses at the retrial who gave evidence about David Bain's personality and behaviour. There were Crown witnesses called to give evidence intended to cast him in a bad light that came to very little.

There were three witnesses called by the defence whose evidence may well be considered the most objective of all. The reason is that each of them was interviewed in 1994 when they gave statements to the police which they signed. They were called to give evidence at the retrial 15 years later by the defence, but nobody from the defence had ever met with them in the intervening years.

John Barsby

The first of these was Professor John Barsby who was Emeritus Professor of Classics at Otago University. He explained to the court that as a result of the police inquiry he was asked to supply them with a letter, which he did on 16 September 1994, and that in that letter he confirmed that David had been enrolled in his department doing just one paper, which was the literature paper of classical studies. He explained that David had been elected by the class to be the class representative, whose job it is to report to the Head of Department several times a year on how the class is progressing. He said that he met with David on 22 April 1994, and had been asked by police for his impressions of David at that time. 'In that interview I actually found him quite impressive,' Professor Barsby said. 'He was slightly older than other class reps, but I was impressed by the fact that what he had to say was sensible and constructive and as I say, really, very impressive.'

He went on to say that he did not actually teach David but in the course of writing this letter to the police he consulted with two of his colleagues who were involved in lecturing David and in his tutorial group. He said: 'They were both very positive in what they said. I mean, David had been attending lectures and he was contributing well to tutorials, so all of the reports were very positive.'

It was put to him that over the years David had been portrayed in the press as a geeky, nerdy sort of person. Professor Barsby said: 'All I can say is that there was absolutely no sign of that in the dealings that I had with him or in what my colleagues reported.'

Harold Love

Then there was Dr Harold Love, the person that David had said to Constable Van Turnhout on the morning of the deaths that he needed to contact to tell that he would be absent. Dr Love explained that he had a PhD in dramatic theory from the University of Keele in England and that he had been a teacher at universities in England, Ireland and at Otago. He went on to explain that he met David Bain when he auditioned for a part in the chorus of a play. He said that David was an impressive singer who had a very good voice and presence and so he went straight into the chorus. He said that his experience of knowing David was over a period of about a month during 10 or 12 rehearsals for the play during May of 1994. He said: 'He would apply himself very well, he was always very reliable, he was always there which is not always something you can count on, um, and — well, he being I guess rather more experienced than some of his co-chorus members, he did become a leader or a co-leader of it. But I had no problems or difficulties or anything at all.'

He confirmed that there was a rehearsal for the play on the Sunday afternoon of 19 June 1994 and that on 28 February 1995 he was interviewed by the police. He said there was nothing unusual or abnormal about David's behaviour on that Sunday afternoon and he described David as being 'fairly relaxed and convivial and horsing about with the others in quite the normal manner' on the Sunday afternoon before the tragedy. The final question Mr Reed put to him was: 'Now, some people are likeable, others are not; how would you describe him?'

'Yes, perfectly likeable and approachable, yes,' Harry Love answered.

The cross-examination conducted by Mr Bates was one of the few light-hearted moments at the retrial. It finally came to an end when the judge realized that Mr Bates was in way over his head and said, 'I think that's probably enough, doctor.' The production David was involved in and Dr Love was producing was *Oedipus Rex*, and Bates attempted to convey a link between the subject matter of the play and the deaths of the family the following morning. He put to Harry Love that the play was a dark tragedy and called that description an understatement. Dr Love described it as a deep sort of tragedy and was then asked by Bates to briefly describe the theme of the play. Dr Love began his answer by saying, 'Yes, I see where this is going.' And so did everybody else, which brought a chuckle to the courtroom. He went on to describe the Greek myth and then Bates asked if there was a reference in the play to black hands. He was told that there was no reference to black hands, so then he asked, 'Is there a reference to a black sca?' There was an objection at that stage, but Bates persisted and was asked by Harry Love whose translation of the play he was referring to. The roles had reversed, and in answer to that question Bates said, 'It is obviously an

English translation: "Tested in the lives I cut down with these hands, what a Black Sea of terror has overwhelmed him." Now, this is a phrase that the chorus would be singing?'

'Not in the production we had,' Dr Love replied. 'The translation we used was my own one, and I certainly wouldn't have put that. It's terrible.'

Bates then tried to get some link between black gloves and a sea of black in Harry Love's production, but Dr Love told him that the play was being done with colourful Greek costumes and the chorus were dressed in creamy light-coloured attire. Just before the judge finally had enough, Bates said that the killing of the father in the play was done with the purest of motives but came back to haunt *Oedipus*. Everybody except the police officers and Bates' fellow prosecutors could hardly contain themselves by this stage and before Dr Love was able to finish his answer, the judge put Bates out of his misery.

DEREK HOPE, FUNERAL DIRECTOR

The third witness in this group of witnesses was led through his evidence by Helen Cull QC, whom he had never met until the day in question, which was 13 May 2009. Derek Hope explained to the court that he was retired and lived in Wanaka but that in 1994 he was a funeral director in Dunedin. He said that the business had been a family business which was founded in 1887 and that he served for 42 years in the company. He was contacted by Bob Clark on 21 June 1994 and went to meet the members of the family at three o'clock that afternoon. He confirmed that he was interviewed by a police officer in September 1994 and that he did not give evidence at the first trial and that the police had not contacted him in the lead-up to the second trial.

He said when he arrived at the Clarks' David was being interviewed by the police. It wasn't until about 5.30 p.m. that the police officers finished with David and he met him for the first time.

Helen Cull asked Hope if he could describe David's demeanour at that time. 'Well,' he said, 'David I think was — I would describe as a person probably in deep shock. Um, very emotionless, um, probably a kind of, zombie-like.' He said that a discussion followed with all of the people in the room and during this discussion David sat very quietly. He only reacted when he was spoken to and was acquiescing to a lot of discussion, decisions and thoughts that were being expressed. There was a further meeting on the Thursday two days later which he thinks was again at three o'clock with members of the family and David to finalize the funeral arrangements. On this occasion he described David in the following words: 'Well, he was — my recollection was that I think that he actually sat looking out the window, that he didn't actually look at me once the whole interview. But when he was asked a question he answered.'

Hope was asked: 'Did you notice a difference between Tuesday and Thursday?'

He replied: 'I would have said perhaps he was even — even in deeper shock perhaps, um, and he certainly wasn't — you know he was still zombie-like as far as I'm concerned, yeah.'

He told the court that in 1994 he had been a funeral director for 30-something years. He was asked, 'In your experience dealing with people who are grieving, how would you describe David's reactions to you?'

Mr Hope answered: 'Well, in a sense, um, normal that I would expect in the traumatic circumstances of what he had been involved in. You know, he was um [in] what I thought deep shock and, um, very unresponsive to me particularly, um, I got no feedback at all, I was just fortunate that I had all the other family members to deal with, who were able to assist and make decisions.'

The cross-examination by the Deputy Solicitor General Cameron Mander served only to confirm Derek Hope's view that David was a person in deep shock, unresponsive and not being able to participate in the normal way, which he said was because 'people react so differently to death'.

The fact that the defence called these witnesses who had been interviewed by the police following David's arrest and whose evidence contrasted so dramatically with the family's observations was very compelling.

There were a number of other witnesses who gave evidence about David's character and personality and in particular how well he got on with his family and friends — Catherine Spencer who met him at university and his friends from Opera Live, Patti Napier and Lindsay Robertson.

Geoff Swift was a family friend and he called in and had a cup of tea with Margaret on Friday, 17 June 1994. David was about to leave for university and as he left he happily gave his mum a kiss goodbye, Swift told the jury.

Margaret was very enthusiastic in showing Swift the plans for the new house.

A very close friend of Arawa's described their friendship and particularly how close David and Arawa were to each other. She knew all of the family.

Miss X from the first trial was again called by the Crown. She had not seen David since she gave evidence in 1995, 14 years earlier. Her body language towards David was unmistakably warm and friendly. She smiled gracefully at him as she left the stand.

ARTHUR WELLS

In 2003 David requested through his friends that he would like to have a Quaker elder visit him. Arrangements were made with a Mr Arthur Wells who lived in Christchurch to take up this role. Arthur Wells has two MA degrees, both with first-class honours, and also a graduate diploma in social work. He had been a counsellor and group worker in the men's programme of the family mental health service of the Canterbury District Health Board and for 23 years had worked for 'stopping violence' services in Christchurch, leading group programmes for men. For many years Wells had been training people to do this work involved in developing programmes to facilitate the prevention of violence by men. Wells also co-edited two books on family violence and had worked extensively with suicidal people as a staff member of Lifeline in Christchurch. In addition to that he was a part-time clinical lecturer in family violence at the Christchurch School of Medicine, a branch of the University of Otago.

Wells compiled a report to the David Bain defence team in the course of preparation for the retrial. The excerpts below are taken from the document.

Wells states that as a young man he had been a close friend of David's mother and for that reason the family history and dynamics have held special interest and concern for him. His personal impressions and assessment of David occupy the initial portion of his report.

When I first went out to the prison to visit David I did so intrigued, expecting to find a very disturbed and unbalanced, probably psychopathic young man, who had committed a crime much more horrific than I had previously had dealings with. What made it harder was that one of his victims, his mother, had been such a close and dearly loved friend of mine when I was aged from 18 to 21 years old.

When I actually met David, I had to come to terms rapidly with the discovery that this calm, clear-eyed young man was completely sane, balanced, and obviously truthful. Nothing added up. I could not see how a person of such obvious sincerity, decency and integrity could be guilty. My confusion did not last for more than a few weeks. I was quickly reassured that he is not guilty when I began to study the evidence from a psychological point of view, first of all by reading James McNeish's book *The Mask of Sanity*, which, although it poses as a psychological inquiry, is obviously bogus to anyone trained in the area. He said David was insane, but everything in the book told me it was Robin who became insane, and that David was completely normal.

In my experience, most people realize that David is innocent almost instantaneously on meeting. Fortunately, this is how it usually goes in his social and working contacts in the three years since he has left prison. David has a transparent personality, with no hint of dissembling or calculation, and people warm to him immediately, sensing his goodwill towards them and his lively intelligence and humour. I noticed that this was the case in prison, too.

It would be reasonable for anyone to wonder whether I am a gullible kind of person, since I speak about David's innocence with such a high level of certainty. I can only say that it has been almost a daily experience for me, as a counsellor of violent and abusive men, to sit patiently while they tell me a whole bunch of lies about the violence towards their families.

Over many years I have carried out hundreds of mental state and risk assessments of such men, and have developed a capacity to maintain objectivity, and to lay aside my own feelings of warmth towards these men, as I take into account things they have been hiding, often which are only discovered through talking to other members of their families. In the early years, two decades or more ago, I was sometimes taken in by the lies these men tell, but not so often these days. I generally now pick up quickly on whether they are minimizing or denying what they have done.

Yet in all my hundreds of hours talking to David there has not been a single moment in which he has given me a reason to doubt his innocence. Not even a single fleeting shadow of suspicion has crossed our many in-depth conversations about the members of his family and how he remembers them and felt about them. It would be extraordinary if this is all just a consummate act he is putting on, which has successfully fooled not just me but dozens of others, consistently, without a single slip-up, over many, many years of close contact and friendship.

I can say, and feel completely at ease in saying, that I know that David is innocent. I know it with the kind of unshakeable confidence I have that certain people are good and genuine people, or that my wife and children love me. There is a knowledge that goes deeper than the mere observation of people's behaviour on the surface.

PRISON REFERENCES

After the Privy Council quashed David's convictions, the defence team applied to get bail and some character references were necessary. A request was put through to the prison management where David had been for the previous 12 years and various staff who had been closely associated with David provided glowing testimonials for the court in respect to the caring, cooperative and responsible nature of his character and personality.

POST RELEASE

Since he has been out of prison he has lived with a number of people and formed enduring friendships with each of those families. He worked full-time for the two years before the trial while on bail and formed lasting friendships with the staff and suppliers of that company.

He also joined a 'hunt' club in West Auckland whose members include a cross-section of people including some from the legal profession. David has now been involved with this equestrian group for nearly four years. He participates in all of their activities like everyone else, and is a popular member of the club. After his brief trip overseas following his acquittal in 2009 he went on the dole for a few weeks but soon found employment in a very fashionable interior design and home staging company that operated out of a warehouse in Auckland's trendy Parnell. He has made friends with the staff from there and regularly sees the owner on a social basis.

But his main interest is in engineering and design and when a position came up in a medium-sized engineering workshop in West Auckland nearer to where he lives he was delighted to accept the offer of a job. He has been employed there now for over a year and is a much-liked and respected member of the staff.

The personality disorders associated with what we colloquially call psychopaths are generally referred to in professional circles as 'Cluster B' personality disorders. The type of behavioural characteristics commonly coming under this heading are such things as lack of empathy, disregard for the law and the rights of others, and generally narcissistic, self-centred attitudes. These are not like the common cold where you go to bed for a day and it disappears. These are permanent deteriorating conditions. They manifest in daily life and are obvious for all to see. They are not a temporary condition.

Putting it in blunt lay terms and relating it to the circumstances of this case, it is not possible that David could be a normal person in his interactions with family, society and in other endeavours for 22 years, turn into a psychopath overnight and then return to being normal again for the following 15 years.

And so whereas at the first trial when Guest was ambushed by the proposition that David was a psychopath, or putting it another way, that the crimes said to have been committed by David required blatant psychopathic personality disorders, the Bain defence teams since then have been fully alert to this fundamental flaw in the allegations upon which he was convicted.

PART FIVE

INNOCENCE

CHAPTER 23

WEIGHING THE EVIDENCE

It may seem obvious to say that when there is evidence that proves a person cannot have done something, then evidence suggesting he has done it must have an innocent explanation. But sometimes the obvious gets lost in the maelstrom of evidence that constitutes a criminal proceeding, particularly one that has become as complicated and commented upon as the case in question.

THE CASE OF DAVID DOUGHERTY

A good example of this is the case of David Dougherty, convicted of the abduction and rape of an 11-year-old girl who lived next door to him in West Auckland. Dougherty went to a jury trial where he was convicted and sentenced to a lengthy term in prison. The evidence against him was predominantly founded upon the identification of him by the little girl who had been raped. In addition to that, there was DNA evidence obtained for the police by the ESR which could not rule out Dougherty and was said to be sufficiently cogent to be incriminating against him. This DNA evidence related to semen samples obtained at the time of the crime. The evidence was vigorously disputed after David Dougherty was convicted and eventually, following a second Court of Appeal hearing, a retrial was ordered.

The Crown pursued the retrial with determination to uphold the original police investigation and scientific evidence, despite new DNA evidence showing that at least one of the samples which yielded a DNA profile was not that of David Dougherty. At the retrial they said David Dougherty must have had an unknown accomplice, and ran their case on that basis, despite the fact that the complainant had never suggested that there were two rapists.

The retrial was a dingdong battle, but eventually resulted in an acquittal for Dougherty. By this time he had spent over three years in prison. The intervention of Dr Arie Geursen, a genetic biologist at that time working in the public sector and only taking an interest in the case because the science of DNA technology was his particular specialty, was crucial to the eventual acquittal of Dougherty. In fact, had it not been for Dr Geursen it is unlikely there ever would have been a retrial.

Subsequent to his acquittal an application was made to the government for compensation for his wrongful conviction and incarceration. The investigation conducted on behalf of the government lasted for some years and in the first instance was unable to reach a conclusion as to whether Dougherty was actually innocent of the crimes, or even innocent on the balance of probabilities. However, DNA testing on a sample that had not previously been tested was able to conclusively show that the semen was from someone other than Dougherty and could not have been his. It should be noted that, by this time, it was some seven or eight years after the original incident.

The DNA profile obtained from the latest testing was compared with the police database and a match was found with a person who had convictions for other rapes. This person admitted to being the sole rapist in the Dougherty case and confirmed Dougherty's claims of absolute innocence. He was, as he had always claimed, home with his wife in bed when the alleged offences happened.

As a result of these findings he was handsomely compensated for the three years he spent in prison as a result of the wrongful conviction.

So here we have an entirely innocent person who had been enmeshed by the police and scientific evidence in a false fabric of guilt sufficiently well woven to gain a conviction before a jury and almost capable of surviving the application for compensation. Had the crime scene samples and exhibits been destroyed, it is almost certain that the government would have concluded that Dougherty had not been able to establish that he was 'probably' innocent, despite his *actual* innocence.

MAKING SENSE OF THE EVENTS

This just serves to exemplify the point that, with all the resources available to it, if the Crown is determined to build a case against a person it can almost invariably succeed, regardless of the person's culpability or otherwise, and this emphasizes the need for extreme caution when charges are laid. Reliance on one or two detectives' 'sniff test' as a criterion for charging someone is almost always the genesis for every miscarriage of justice. Prime well-known international examples of this are Lindy Chamberlain, Rubin Carter and the parents of JonBenét Ramsey. There are numerous cases in New Zealand continuing up to the present day.

We have seen, and it is frankly acknowledged, that such a fabric of guilt was woven around David Bain at the first trial. At that time it did not appear to be a false fabric. As stated near the beginning of this book, the evidence against David at that trial was compelling and for the most part uncontested, leaving the jury with no option but to convict.

However, we have seen that since those convictions in 1995 a vastly different picture has emerged which has given rise to a number of matters that exclude David Bain from guilt, let alone being the cold-blooded, cunning and determined killer that the evidence in the first trial caused the trial judge at sentencing to say that he was. In this case, there is no single DNA test which can prove David Bain's innocence because the relevant samples either were never collected in the first place or have been deliberately destroyed by the police.

As unfortunate and disgraceful as that may be, DNA evidence is not the only evidence available that can prove someone's innocence or guilt.

It is pertinent to point out that the matters relied on below to show that David is totally innocent do not rely on defence evidence but are founded on the Crown's own evidence. Another point that should be kept in mind when considering the following matters is that this is a case of *either* it was David *or* it was Robin. One is exclusive of the other. That was the police case from day one and there has never been any suggestion to the contrary.

Any evidence that proves it cannot have been one in effect proves it was the other. In this regard it should also be remembered that it was the police who decided this was the case, not David. At no time, either before his arrest or since, has David pointed the finger at his father. It was the police who put that to David. The responses he made could not be construed as trying to implicate his father. Indeed the opposite was true.

The following matters are not listed in any particular order of importance or preference. Each of them on its own, just like the one DNA profile that proved David Dougherty's innocence, is capable of showing David is innocent. The combination of them leaves absolutely no doubt whatsoever. Indeed, when placed in context with the known data about perpetrators of familicide it is the only scenario that makes any sense of the tragedy.

TIME OF DEATH

There is the matter of the times of the deaths. When the police arrested David, they believed that all five people died between about 6.45 a.m. and 7 o'clock, the 'missing 20 minutes'. This belief was endorsed at the second trial by the evidence of Chief Ambulance Officer Wombwell who told the police that all the bodies were still warm and in his opinion had died within the last hour and a half before he touched them. Without for one moment suggesting that his time of 90 minutes is precise to the minute, he touched them at about 7.45 a.m., which means that everybody had died after about 6.15 a.m., or let's say six o'clock in the morning, on his evidence.

We have seen that Bill Wright and Jim Doyle revisited the timing evidence just before the first trial, resulting in a realization that the police theory regarding the 'missing 20 minutes' did not fit. Wombwell's description at the first trial changed in relation to the first four deaths. When interviewed by the police at the time of the events in June 1994 he said all the bodies were *warm*, but at trial this became *cool but not cold*. Wright then argued that there was a big time gap between those four deaths and the death of Robin. This fitted with the now discredited evidence about the age of bruising given by Dr Pryde, and supported Wright's new four-before-and-one-after scenario.

However, with the second trial evidence, the truth is now on the table. There was no large gap between the four deaths and Robin. Robin was warm and the four others were relatively warm but not as warm as Robin. In addition, and most significantly, the almost naked, uncovered body of Stephen was of the *same* warmth as his mother and sister who were clothed and tucked up in bed. The two Crown pathologists, Dr Dempster and Dr Thomson, both agreed that Stephen Bain would have been likely to cool very quickly compared to the others. He had not cooled and so he cannot have died at some time between 1 and 5 a.m. when the Crown case requires that he did.

Putting it another way, on the Crown's own evidence Stephen can't have been killed after the paper round during the missing 20 minutes and nor can he have been killed before the paper round; he must have been killed during the paper round when of course David was miles from home delivering the papers, providing the opportunity for Robin to access the rifle and ammunition from his bedroom wardrobe.

SUICIDE

There is the matter of the death of Robin Bain himself. Was he murdered, or was it suicide? The evidence as it now stands is almost unequivocal. Again, most of this evidence is accepted by the Crown or is otherwise Crown evidence. First of all, it was a contact wound that killed him and contact wounds to the front of the head are almost *exclusively diagnostic of suicide*. Dr Dempster stated that 90 per cent of such wounds are suicidal. Indeed, one of the most extensive studies ever carried out relative to the circumstances of Robin Bain's death was conducted by Vincent J. Di Maio, in conjunction with Dr Kimberly Molina. Di Maio is generally recognized as the leading international authority on gunshot wounds. Published in 2008 in the *American Journal of Forensic Medicine and Pathology*, it made a study of 509 cases of death by rifle shot to the head. The authors stated that the study was 'designed to examine the characteristics of rifle wounds to determine if we could predict manner of death (suicide or murder) using the range and location of a rifle wound'. They did this study because they said that no other study in the English language could be found which focused exclusively on rifle wounds (that is, did not include handguns).

The 509 cases that were the subject of the study represented every death by rifle reported from the Bexar County Medical Examiner's Office, San Antonio, Texas between 1988 and 2004, of which 233 were suicides and 266 homicides. Contact shots comprised 95.7 per cent of the suicides. However, 2.6 per cent were not determined so virtually all suicides were contact wounds if one said that 95.7 per cent of that 2.6 per cent were also contact wounds. The two most common sites of those suicides were the mouth and the temple area at 32 per cent each. In all, 80 per cent of suicide wounds were to the head. The other 20 per cent were mostly to the chest. By contrast only 21 per cent of homicide wounds were to the head and the most common sites of murderous shots to the head were the back, the top and the face. Only 5 per cent of the homicides involved a contact wound.

It can safely be said that Robin Bain's wound, being that it was in the temple region and it was a contact shot, overwhelmingly supports a conclusion of suicide, and conversely, with equal force, does not fit with being a murder.

Then there are the general circumstances and other evidential factors to consider.

DEEP IN PRAYER?

The blood splatter found in 2008 by the defence scientist on the top of Robin Bain's right shoe proves that he cannot have been kneeling down when he was killed. This blows the Crown theory out of the water. It was their proposition that Robin was kneeling, deep in prayer, which laid the platform for the Crown to argue that David would be able to poke the rifle through the curtains against his head without him realizing what was happening.

SITTING DOWN?

The location and direction of the blood spatter containing brain and bone matter on the curtains precludes the possibility that he could have been sitting on either the beanbag or the floor at the time he was shot. The Crown has never suggested he was sitting in the beanbag because they know that it is incompatible with the crime scene blood profile. However, when kneeling was ruled out at the retrial after Dr Manlove provided the evidence about the blood on the top of the shoe, they put up a drawing of him sitting on the floor, but that does not fit with the evidence either because the drops on the curtain are falling downwards and so, as all experts agreed, his head had to be higher than the highest of those drops of blood. When this drawing was put to defence scientist Dr John Manlove, an expert in blood spatter, he said that position was 'inconceivable'.

STANDING

Robin must have been standing. The first obvious point resulting from the application of common sense to this point is that if a person is standing they are in a conscious state. Such a person is unlikely to stand motionless in front of and facing curtains at seven o'clock in the morning in the dark. But even if he were, it would be expected that there would be some reaction of a defensive nature when a gun starts approaching his head.

But then his position while standing needs to accommodate the blood spatter evidence. The inference to be drawn from the nature of the blood spatter on the top of the shoe and the evidence that a splash of blood on the upper thigh region of his trousers was heading upwards as opposed to falling down were agreed to by Crown experts. The inferences result in two likely conclusions: the first being that Robin Bain's right leg was bent at right angles at the knee, thereby creating the situation for the blood to fall downwards below the knee but upwards above the knee as it spurted from his head wound; and the second is that, as the experts explained, the nature of the blood spots on the shoe strongly suggest that his right foot must have been no further than a metre from his head when the shot was fired. Each of these propositions supports the other.

Combining the known factors, therefore, it is highly likely that Robin Bain was standing in front of the red chair adjacent to the curtains with his right foot on the chair with his head bowed towards his left at the moment the fatal bullet entered his left temple. This is the only position that is compatible with the evidence as explained. Not only did Dr Dempster agree that this position was perfectly feasible and as demonstrated properly replicated the site of entry and the angle and trajectory of the shot, but he explicitly agreed that it was quite a natural position that did not require any difficult contortions.

In addition to these specific scientific findings, there is the noise of the computer fan which could be heard by Dr Dempster when he first entered the room, as well as the light from the screen that would have been shining out from under the curtains. Can we really believe that Robin ignored that as well?

Finally, there is the bullet lying on the floor beside the gun that did not feed out of the magazine correctly. Would the cunning killer, lying in wait, be able to fiddle about, reloading the gun without alerting the intended victim standing on the other side of the curtain?

In summary, then, on the death of Robin Bain it cannot be reasonably disputed that for Robin's death to be murder, the murderer successfully replicated with absolute precision the factors that would exist if it was a self-inflicted shot: a contact wound to the temple of a conscious, upright, wide-awake victim, and on the Crown case, did so without the benefit of glasses even though he couldn't see clearly beyond 30 cm. Dr Jim Gwynne, the forensic pathologist who had been Dr Dempster's boss, provided affidavits to this effect to the Governor General, Court of Appeal and Privy Council. Unfortunately, Dr Gwynne was very ill by the time of the retrial and could not give evidence. He has since died. It was this aspect that troubled him so much — that anyone, let alone a 22-year-old kid inexperienced with firearms, could achieve the appearance of suicide so perfectly.

On the subject of suicide and the evidence about Robin's death, comment was noticeably limited in the Crown's closing address at the retrial. Kieran Raftery did agree that Robin must have been close to the green curtain when shot. In regards to the evidence about the contact shot, he said, 'There's something for everybody in there.' Not quite the same as the first trial when suicide was ruled out as virtually impossible.

Sadly, Robin Bain surely killed himself.

ALIBI

There is the fact, effectively conceded by the Crown in their closing address based upon their witnesses Martin Cox and Denise Laney, that David was not home when the computer was turned on. It is granted there is no evidence to show who actually wrote the message on the computer. However, when one considers the overall circumstances it is far-fetched if not totally implausible to suggest that that person is not the same one who turned it on.

Robin Bates in his opening address told the jury that the Crown would prove it was impossible for Robin to have shot himself. On the pathology of his death, Raftery said 'there's something for everybody in there'. On what happened he said, 'We don't know for certain exactly what happened in that room.'

Raftery in his closing address was unable to explain how Robin Bain died. He conceded that Robin may well have turned on the computer. He gave no explanation of how David was supposed to have got past his father with the gun into the computer alcove after Robin turned on the computer. Nor did he attempt to explain the implications that would arise from Robin being up and about in the house and turning on the computer before David got home. It would mean that Robin must have entered the house from the caravan, fully dressed, sometime between 6.30 a.m. and 6.40 a.m. and turned on the computer, but did not notice or sense anything amiss. If it is suggested that

Robin was still in the computer alcove preparing to do some work on the computer when David got home, then one has to ask how David got in there with the gun. If he by some miracle managed that, the next question is why and how Robin moved out from the alcove to the front of the curtains and stood with his foot on the chair while David stayed in the alcove behind the curtains and shot him. If Robin was not in the computer alcove when David got home, then where was he? What was he doing? Surely he might sense something was not right? Why would he turn on the computer and then go walkabout? How did David manage to come inside, take off his shoes and yellow *ODT* bag, go downstairs, wash his hands of the printer's ink and then get back to the computer room with the gun without his father's intervention? There was no mention of any of these problems in Raftery's closing address.

Until the retrial when Martin Cox and Denise Laney's evidence was properly tested before a jury, the Crown case had always been that whoever *turned on* the computer was the killer. It was only after the evidence relating to the time the computer was turned on (that is, at 6.41 a.m., not 6.44 a.m.) and that it was David (not an unknown person) seen at the gate by Denise Laney at 6.45 a.m. that they said it did not matter who turned it on. However, for the reasons listed above, the person who turned it on and the killer are one and the same. Any suggestion to the contrary is ridiculous and cannot be sustained on the evidence or by the application of common sense.

There is one final point on this computer message which may have been forgotten, which is that it was well known and accepted as recounted by a number of witnesses that Robin was a computer fanatic. It is not proof of anything but in the circumstances should not be dismissed as having some relevance.

FOOTPRINTS

There were two 280 mm 'complete' footprints made by the right foot of a person wearing a sock which was covered on the sole with blood. The prints were leading out of Stephen's room towards and into the hallway. Two major testing procedures undertaken by the ESR on instructions from the police involving, firstly, feet the size of David's and, secondly, the size of Robin's, proved the obvious point that a foot cannot make a complete impression of itself which is smaller than its own size. Poignantly, the tests done on a foot the size of Robin's concluded that the footprints averaged 282 mm, almost exactly the size of the complete footprints found in the house by Detective Weir and Peter Hentschel. The only answer to this evidence put up by the Crown was Hentschel's belated claim that the foot which made the prints must have been bigger because the prints were *not* complete prints after all. This was a direct contradiction of his evidence at the first trial, to questions from the first trial judge and at the Court of Appeal. When questioned by Justice Williamson he said that the two prints of 280 mm were *complete prints from the top of the toe to the heel.*

The Crown acknowledged the obvious to the Law Lords at the Privy Council, being that they could not accommodate even one of the footprints being made by Robin. Both of David's socks reacted to luminol but only a right print was left in the carpet. Robin made the footprints and on the Crown's own admission that makes him the killer.

BLOOD ON ROBIN'S HANDS

Perhaps the most compelling matter that incriminates Robin is the blood on his hands and the blood (if the 'blood-like substance' was blood) seen in his fingernail scrapings. As we know, none of this blood was tested because for the most part it was not even collected. Of the nine discrete areas of blood that were described at the retrial, only two were collected and they were destroyed without being tested. The photographic record was also extremely flimsy, but the photo finally put before the jury at the retrial by Dr Dempster showing what appears and was agreed to be a rim of residual blood around the tip of his left thumb is very telling.

People involved in such activities as hunting or fishing may relate very well to what is described here as 'residual blood staining'. This is where hands have been completely covered in blood which then dries and is embedded in the pores of the skin. A quick rinse does not remove all the blood. Unless the hands are thoroughly washed and scrubbed with soap, bloodstains remain in those areas where the skin is wrinkled or less likely to be rubbed with a quick rinse. Pathologists at the retrial explained how difficult it can be to clean dried blood from the pores of the skin. This blood cannot have got there from his own wound. The same can be said for the smear of blood on the heel of his thumb and base of his little finger. DSS Jim Doyle agreed at the retrial that these blood smears are 'unexplained'.

In the circumstances, the only reasonable explanation for this residual blood embedded in the pores of the skin is that this hand has been covered in blood which has dried, and then been rinsed without being scrubbed thoroughly.

It is an accepted fact of the case that the killer discarded white gloves in Stephen's room that were saturated in blood. There is no evidence that David had worn these gloves. The blood smears on Robin's hand provide very strong evidence that he did.

Readers and students of human behaviour, which we all are to some extent or another, will have their own opinions as to the relevance and importance of the various matters of evidence listed, as is their wont. Often such opinions may result from experiences you have had in your own life. Some people, for example, might get bogged down with the business of the computer timing and think, well it is only five or six minutes — we can't decide a multiple murder case on this. Some may be attracted to the psychology of the case; others may think that is all mumbo-jumbo. People who spend a lot of time walking on a sandy beach may find the footprint evidence compelling by virtue of that experience. Anybody who has lived in a very cold climate, or farmers from cold climates who handle animals that have died, may relate particularly to the warmth of Stephen's body as it was described lying almost naked on the floor in freezing cold, draughty conditions.

'WHO DID IT? DAVID BAIN? ROBIN BAIN?'

These were the first words of the judge's summing up at the first trial.

There is the evidence from both professional and lay people that David does not suffer from any mental illness or personality disorder. In this respect attention is drawn first to the assessment by Professor Paul Mullen, which was not only based on the five interviews he had with David but also on electronic brain scans. Secondly, to the separate assessments made of him by two professional psychiatrists instructed by the Crown, initially in respect to the sentencing and later on behalf of the Corrections Department after his convictions. Then there is Dr Phil Brinded, one of New Zealand's pre-eminent forensic psychiatrists who was employed by the Crown in a very senior position in its mental health service. Dr Brinded's testimony is not based on a single assessment or interview but many years of assessing and counselling David from the time of his arrest right through to while he was imprisoned in Christchurch. Dr Brinded is unequivocal in his belief that David is innocent and that he exhibits none of the personality traits associated with what we commonly call psychopathic behaviour. Psychiatric professionals in New Zealand refer to what the popular media call psychopathic behaviour as 'Cluster B' personality disorders. This includes things such as a lack of empathy, disregard for the law and the rights of others, shallow or exaggerated emotions, attention-seeking behaviour, grandiosity and a need for admiration, and inappropriate sexual behaviour.

Of course, these traits are common to all of us in varying degrees. However, in the case of a disorder, such traits are pronounced and have a profound effect on the person's behaviour and the people around them. None of the professionals found any such disorder in David. His normality in this regard is borne out in daily life. Putting it bluntly, the evidence both from the trial and the hundreds of others with whom he worked in the prison, including prison staff, and those with whom he has worked and socialized both before June 1994 and since he got out of prison is quite to the contrary. He is described as a very empathetic person, caring of the needs of others, a law-abiding citizen, cognizant and aware of the behaviour expected in any situation. Does he have idiosyncrasies? Of course he does, as we all do. But there is absolutely no doubt that he has no mental disorder or clinical mental illness. The Crown case that David killed four people and then took his dog on a paper round before coming home to kill his father and then leave a false trail, along with the other planning and deception they say is involved, is totally incompatible with the person David was and is.

On the other hand, Robin, as we have seen from the empirical data, and putting it in plain language, is a dead ringer for the profile of a despairing-type perpetrator of familicide. A proud man who sees himself as the head of the family, who has been rejected by his wife. A man who is becoming angry and frustrated at not finding the standard of employment he feels he deserves. A man suffering shame and ignominy from the lips of his own daughter; true or false as her stories may have been, the shame would be the same. A man who applied for stress leave not long before the tragedy. A man tidying up loose ends. A man said by his peers to have lost the ability to act rationally. A man who for years had been living in embarrassing conditions in a derelict van in a paddock with no ablution facilities. A man who according to his very loyal brother was going back home to 'face up to it all again', or words to that effect. A man who had been a hunter and user of firearms all his life. A man who had two books on his bedside table, each of which involved death as their main theme and the one he appeared to be reading entitled *Death Comes as the End*. A man who had a pile of bullet shells fired by the murder weapon on his dresser. A man who was a very experienced school teacher who sent out a school newsletter just days before the tragedy which included three stories written by his pupils about family slayings and prefaced them with the warning that they may disturb. A man with a bruise and abrasion on his right fist that had been sustained in the hours before his death. A man whose wife, 15 years earlier, told her close friend and confidant that she was extremely concerned about 'Robin's depression'.

A man who ultimately succumbed to the combination of factors that causes some men to take the ultimate revenge on life in the most inexplicable manner, by destroying his life and the lives of those he loves in an act of what we call familicide.

PIGS MIGHT FLY

Lord Nicholls of Birkenhead, one of the most senior Law Lords and former Vice Chancellor in the British House of Lords, wrote in 1996 in regard to the question of standards of proof:

> Although the result is much the same, this does not mean that where a serious allegation is an issue the standard of proof required is higher. It means only that the inherent probability or improbability of an event is itself a matter to be taken into account when weighting the probabilities and deciding whether on balance the event occurred. The more improbable the event the stronger must be the evidence that it did occur before, on the balance of probability, its occurrence will be established. The more serious the allegation the more cogent is the evidence required to overcome the unlikelihood of what is alleged and thus to prove it. (FLR 80 Act 96 E & F)

Putting this in plain language the Law Lord was saying that the more unlikely the event, the better the evidence must be to prove it. An analogy may be: if you are going to allege that you saw the proverbial pig flying, you had better have some very good proof.

Applying the principle to this case, being that the Crown's proposition means that David Bain is the only person in recorded history who as an adult son slaughtered his entire family but did not commit suicide, and also is neither psychopathic nor mentally deranged, then they would need some powerful, nay, irrevocable evidence in support. But, as we have seen, there is no such evidence.

This 'evidence' has always been no more than a house of cards. In many instances, it was shown to be so as long ago as 1997. That it took a further 12 years before David was acquitted should be a source of shame to all of the government agencies involved in the administration of justice in New Zealand.

APPENDIX A

Arrest statement

10237.ST.BAIN.D.KC7838.24069

5th floor
DCC Building
Cumberland Street
DUNEDIN

24.06.94
10:43

DAVID CULLEN BAIN STATES

My full name is David Cullen BAIN. I am 22 years of age being born on 27 march 1972. I lived at 65 Every Street, Dunedin and I am a student at Otago University.

I am speaking to Detective Sergeant CROUDIS and Detective LOWDEN regarding events at my address on Monday 20.6.94. I have been told that I'm not obliged to say anything and that anything I do say may be given in evidence. I have also been told that I'm entitled to consult and instruct a lawyer without delay.

Q   Do you understand.
A   Yes.

Q   Your fingerprints have been found in blood on your firearm, why are they there.
A   I don't know.

Q   When you say I don't know do you mean that you didn't touch the firearm, you didn't have blood on your hands or the forensic evidence is false.
A   I didn't touch the firearm to my knowledge. I didn't have blood on my hands as I'd washed them.

Q   Do you accept the forensic evidence I've outlined.
A   Yes.

Q   When we discussed that question earlier you stated you could not account for between 15-20 minutes. Is that an explanation for what happened to your family that morning.
A   No.

Q   What is it.
A   It's a question of what happened to me. After I saw my father I remember seeing um my family being pulled away from me by black hands.

2175₄

Q   There is a blood stained fingerprint on the washing machine. How did that get there.

A   I don't know.

Q   Are you saying you didn't make it.

A   I can't say that because if it is my fingerprint then it is my hand that has put it there.

Q   There are indications of blood from clothing that appears to have been pushed into the washing machine. Can you tell me why blood stained clothing had been washed.

A   No.

Q   Do you accept that you washed clothes on Monday morning.

A   Yes.

Q   And in those clothes was at least one pair of socks belonging to you.

A   Yes.

Q   A sweatshirt belonging to you.

A   Yes.

Q   A dark jersey belonging to Arawa.

A   Yes.

Q   When the police located you at the house, you were wearing a white t-shirt with a Queens Baton Relay emblem.

A   Yes.

Q   On the back of that shirt we have observed blood, how did that get there.

A   I don't know.

Q   If your previous statements to Detective Sergeant DUNNE are truthful, then there should be no reason for that blood to be on your shirt.

A   No.

Q   When you were located by the police you were wearing white socks.   We have located blood on the sole of the sock.   How did that get there.

A   I don't know.

Q   Again, if your statement to D/S DUNNE is truthful there is no reason for you to have blood stained clothing.

A   Unless I stood in some blood.

Q   Where might you have stood in blood.

A   I don't know.

Q   We have located a spot of blood on your black rugby shorts you were wearing. Explain to me how that got there.

A   I can't.

Q   There is blood on the porcelain handbasin in the bathroom, how did that get there.

A   I don't know.

Q   Did you put it there.

A   No.

Q   There's blood on a large towel hanging in the bathroom, a considerable amount of blood. How did that get there David.

A   I don't know.

Q   We found blood on the door surround in Stephen's room. It was a small amount compared with the amount of blood found inside Stephen's room. There had been a violent struggle in Stephen's room. Stephen had fought for his life. Can you tell me how that blood got there.

A   No.

Q   David do you own any gloves.

A   Purple woollen gloves, fingerless green gloves and I've recently bought new white dress gloves for a ball at Larnach Castle.

Q   Is that all.

A   Yes.

Q   Where are those gloves.

A   The purple ones should be in the top drawer of the wardrobe in my room, the green gloves are on the chair in my room. The white gloves are with my dress scarf in the same drawer as the purple drawers.

Q   Do you keep your dress clothes separate.

A   Not all of it.

Q   The white gloves, do they have a button or gap.

A   No they're plain.

Q   What are they made of.

A   Elasticated some sort, I don't know.

Q   Did anyone else in the house have dress gloves.

A   My father.

Q   Where would those be.

A   In the caravan, I don't know where.

Q   You're certain he keeps his formal gear in the caravan.

A   Yes.

Q   In Steven's room a pair of white formal type gloves were located. These were heavily blood stained. Do you know anything about these.

A   No.

Q   (David) Can I have a solicitor present?

A   Who do you want.

Q   I don't know.

5
1797

We will provide you with a list.

DOYLE and Bob CLARK enters. Michael GUEST to be contacted.

STATEMENT READ TO DAVID AND ASKED IF IT IS ACCURATE AND STATES:

A It is a fair record of the conversation but some questions had more of a preamble. But the answers are fairly recorded.

I HAVE READ THIS STATEMENT, AND IT IS A TRUE AND CORRECT STATEMENT.

'D BAIN'

Statement taken and witnessed by:

'N A LOWDEN'
Det 8396
1:06
24.06.94

Witnessed and taken by:

'K D CROUDIS
D/S 7838
24.06.94

425

10238.ST.ADDITION.KC7838.240694

1730

1   A lens from the set of glasses you have been wearing was found in Stephen's room

2   Did you tell Val BOYD:

      "It could have been me. I don't know if it was me or Dad".

3   A piece of skin similar to the piece missing from your knee was found in Stephen's room. Can you explain this.

4   A computer message was typed at 6.44 am after you got home, did you type it.

5   Did you shoot and kill the members of your immediate family.

Q   Are you prepared to answer these questions.
A   No.

Q   You have seen them and read the document given to you by Mr GUEST.
A   Yes.

Statement/Question put by:

K D CROUDIS
D/S 7838
24.06.94

1305 hrs - David reads

Q   Is that accurate.
A   Yes.

GUEST intervenes, client not prepared to sign this.

426

APPENDIX B

The submissions prepared by the author for the Privy Council listing errors and omissions in the Court of Appeal decision

The numbers in brackets refer to the relevant clause in the Court of Appeal decision.

APPENDIX 1: FACTUAL ERRORS AND OMISSIONS, AND SPECULATION BY THE COURT OF APPEAL:

1. Paragraph [32]: the spare key was found in an anorak in the family van on the following morning. Actually, it was found four days later, on 24 June 1994, on the same day that David was arrested. It was found in an anorak which had already been searched by two detectives on the day of the murders.

2. Paragraph [34]: That Robin had come to learn of the existence of the spare key "is no more than a speculative possibility". Keys tend to come in sets. It is not unlikely that Robin realised there was a spare. If Robin did not have access to it, what is the explanation for the 20 spent cartridge shells found in his caravan?

3. Same paragraph: David said the rifle had not been used since January or February 1994. In fact, he said he had not personally used it since then.

4. Paragraph [35]: Whether the opera gloves were removed to deal with a misfeed in the rifle "is of no great moment". It was of great moment at the trial, where the Crown submitted there was evidence of a rifle misfeed in Stephen's bedroom, and used that submission to link the bloody gloves to David Bain. In fact, there was no evidence of a misfeed in Stephen's room; no live round was discovered in the room, let alone a live round bearing damage marks from a misfeed. Yet this was an important part of the Crown's case, as the trial judge's summing up reflects.

5. Paragraph [37]: the fact that the clothing Robin Bain was wearing was less smart than the clothing he normally dressed in to go to school contradicts the thrust of the previous statements in paragraph [37]. If he was intending to go to school, why was he not dressed accordingly?

6. Paragraph [38]: the Court of Appeal concludes that the two drops on the underside of the socks dropped from above, and are more consistent with having got onto the socks during the fight with Stephen. How droplets can fall onto the soles of socks has not been explained. It defies gravity (as the

Court of Appeal readily agreed when shown photos of the socks by Mr Withnall QC). The absence of any blood on the upper surface of the socks suggests that these socks were not worn by whoever struggled with Stephen. Although the Crown said that David Bain murdered four members of this family, did the paper round, and then murdered his father, and that his socks were soaked in blood in the process, no blood has been found on the inside of any of David Bain's shoes (including the trainers he wore during the paper round).

7.   Paragraph [40]: "[David Bain's] track pants had been through the wash." He did not own the track pants. They belonged to Robin Bain.

8.   Paragraph [40]: The track pants may have been worn over the black shorts, "allowing only a small amount of blood to seep through": this is the type of speculation that the Court of Appeal has criticised the appellant for. If there had been that volume of seepage, you would expect the cycling shorts that David wore underneath the black shorts to have had blood on them. They did not. In fact, the single drop on the black rugby shorts is entirely consistent with accidental contact.

9.   Paragraph [44]: Whether the green jersey was too small [for David Bain] "in his view": It was not his view, because when put on at trial the jersey was demonstrably too small, as evidenced by the question in cross-examination: "Have you put weight on since then?": 2/1012, line 34; 2/1021, line 19.

10.   Paragraph [51]: "There is evidence that [the fact that Stephen's body, though naked, was not markedly colder than those of the other members of his family] might be explained by his violent struggle to survive. The statement that Stephen's body was not markedly colder than the others is incorrect. The evidence of the ambulance officer Wombwell at depositions was that when he checked the bodies at 7:45 a.m. all the bodies felt relatively warm to the touch. But in respect to the relative warmth of Margaret, Arawa, Laniet and Stephen, he was quite specific that they were

all the same. The Crown case was that Stephen was in a bloody struggle in which David sustained his injuries between 1:20 a.m. and 4:20 a.m. Stephen had therefore been dead at the very least three hours and 30 minutes by the time Wombwell touched him just before 8 a.m. Even a live body (let alone a dead one which had suffered severe blood loss) would not be warm to the touch if left for that period of time naked and motionless on the floor of a draughty house with no heating, where the temperature was at freezing point. Nor would a dead body be the same warmth as the bodies of Margaret and Laniet, who were in bed under the covers (Laniet was dressed, and Arawa was dressed as well). The suggestion that Stephen's body was kept warm by his struggle with the killer is simply speculative. The proper inference is that he was killed much later, while David was on his paper round.

11. Paragraph [53]: The court criticises the fact that David Bain was unable to explain how the frame from his mother's glasses and the right lens came to be in his room. One explanation for that is that he simply did not know.

12. Paragraph [53]: "It was suggested that the left lens had somehow become detached from the frame.. and been kicked under or otherwise found its way under the clothing." This is not correct: the Crown's case was that it had become detached while being worn during the struggle, and fallen on the floor out in the open beside Stephen's body. The optometrist's [undisclosed] view was that the lens was not detached during any struggle.

13. Paragraph [53]: "the Crown's suggestion was that as it was covered by clothing.. David could not immediately find it." That was not the Crown's case, which was that it was out in the open.

14. Paragraph [57]: "At trial it was taken for granted that the blood in which David's fingerprints were found was human blood." It was not taken for granted: that was the uncontested (but wrong) evidence. The Crown's experts told the jury that.

15. Paragraph [59]: "That is why everyone at trial treated it as being from the same source as the fingerprints." That is not the reason. The jury was told

4

by the Crown experts at trial that there was no other blood in the area where the fingerprints were found, and that the blood taken from the area of the fingerprints was labelled "fingerprint" and tested positive for human blood.

16.   Paragraph [60]: "We note that when the rifle was tested by the VIFS it had much less blood on it." In fact, it had no blood on it.

17.   Paragraph [60]: "But that was years later". That is wrong. It was tested in 1998 by the VIFS for the appellant just weeks after the ESR in Auckland had taken samples from 10 discrete areas of the rifle, all of which were found to contain human DNA except for the combined samples from the fingerprints labelled "Rifle 3 + 4".

18.   Paragraph [61]: "It matters not for this purpose whether the total coverage of the rifle with blood occurred as a result of the struggle with Stephen or, which seems more likely, as a result of the rifle being wiped with some form of material." The Court of Appeal's proposition is not supported by any evidence. The evidence at trial was that the rest of the rifle had many areas where fingerprints were visible, but they were of insufficient quality to be identifiable. That is proof that the rest of the rifle had not been wiped. The only place in the trial transcript where the word "wipe" is to be found is at 2/798/1 where Hentschel said: " And to me that indicated that that whole area had been shielded from blood being wiped across that surface. Was the blood on the rest of the rifle smeared or sprayed in appearance? It was smeared rather than sprayed." There is no evidence that the rifle was wiped.

19.   Paragraph [63]. "...the tenor of his evidence at trial was that the fingerprints made by David and that made by Stephen were of the same degree of recency." What he said was that he would have expected the prints to have deteriorated. The court speculates that that means the prints were recent. And see the subsequent affidavit evidence of Sergeant Claven (a policeman attached to the Victoria Forensic Science Centre in Melbourne) 6/2251 to which is attached a technical report published in the

5

Journal of Forensic Identification, stating unless there is a witness to the handling of a firearm, there is no way of knowing when the firearm was touched. It could be days, months, or years since the firearm was handled by an offender. Latent prints can survive for a long period, even in harsh conditions (6/2251). That the ageing of latent prints on firearms is virtually impossible is a point with which Mr Jones agreed, as the Court of Appeal records at paragraph [66].

20.   Paragraph [67]: "The evidence is that in suicide cases the victim's fingerprints are quite often not found on the firearm." In fact the evidence before the Court of Appeal was that in only 3% of cases were fingerprints identifiable, as Mr Claven stated.

21.   Paragraph [68]: "We note that David had been given some training in gun management by his father and to put the rifle away with animal blood on it would not be good gun management. It seems unlikely he would have done so." This is speculation on the part of the Court of Appeal. In the same speculative vein, it is likely that Robin discussed with his son the issue of security, and what to do with the trigger lock keys.

22.   Paragraph [70]: ".. the water pressure was low even for Every Street." Preston's evidence was that other properties he had been to in Every Street over the years had very high water pressure.

23.   Paragraph [73]: " In the light of this evidence the probabilities are that.. it would have taken one hour to complete its whole cycle." This is speculation by the Court, not supported by Preston's vague evidence.

24.   Paragraph [75]: " ..after the installation of new taps." The very fact that new taps had been installed before the later tests destroys the validity of those tests.

25.   Same paragraph: ".. Mr Preston indicated that in his experience the water pressure made little difference." That was not his evidence. He suspected the pressure would not be very different. He did not test any difference in pressure. He was surprised how low the water pressure was in the house.

26.   Paragraph [76]: "They both described David as wearing an anorak or a sweatshirt with a hood." Actually, they did not. The two witnesses are Richardson and Clark. Richardson at trial said David was wearing an anorak and washed out shorts. In cross-examination (2/893/11), he accepted that David was wearing a red sweatshirt, without a hood. Clark said the person she saw was wearing a black or navy blue sweatshirt with a hood, and dark coloured long trousers (2/901). There was no sweatshirt matching that description found at the house by the Police. She did not see this person's face. She did not see his yellow newspaper bag.

27.   Paragraph [77]: " All in all the evidence.. suggests that the washing machine was set in motion prior to David's departure on his paper round." Contrast the Court's statement in paragraph [74]:"While there can be no precision in the analysis.."

28.   Paragraph [78] "… with the bullet entering Robin's head on his left side and exiting on the right..." This is incorrect. There was no exit wound.

29.   Paragraph [79]. "We accept that such a suggested mechanism of suicide is reasonably possible, although we must say it does seem an unlikely mechanism in the circumstances." That is for the jury. The Court of Appeal does not make explicit the "circumstances" that make suicide unlikely; and a number of the appellant's experts say he committed suicide.

30.   Paragraph [80]: "The position of the magazine is such that the only explanation consistent with suicide is that for some reason Robin had the magazine in his right hand at the time he shot himself." This is not the only explanation given by the appellant's experts. In tests, the police managed to get the magazine to stand on its narrow edge on a number of occasions. There is no reason why Robin could not have put the magazine on the ground himself. To suggest Robin held the magazine in his right hand is simply speculation.

31.   Paragraph [86]: "..but the inference that the magazine was placed how and where it was, after the event, to make it look like suicide is, in our view, a strong one." This is not what the appellant's experts (Mr Cordner and Mr

Gwynne) considered. And if the murderer "placed" it there to make it look like suicide, it is puzzling why the magazine was not placed in Robin Bain's hand, or in his pocket, rather than in the position in which it was found.

32. Paragraph [88]: The issue of Robin's full bladder. I note that this matter was not considered important enough to be included in the Crown's 9 page 61 paragraph list of evidence which it considered implicated the appellant, tendered to the Court at the Court's request midway through the hearing.

33. Paragraph [90]: "Nevertheless the point must be regarded as significantly supporting the Crown's contention that David was the killer". This is completely speculative.

34. Paragraph [100]: "But the finish time of the saving process was not contemporaneously recorded.............. NZST." Mr Cox's evidence at trial was: "I had saved that message at 16 minutes past two on the afternoon of 21 June. This was noted". The impact of this on the jury must have been significant.

35. Paragraph [103]: "On that basis Mr. Cox deduced that the message was saved 31 hrs and 32 minutes after the Word program was started." This is not correct. In fact the clock had been running for 31 hrs and 32 minutes from the time the computer had been switched on. This elapsed time was then deducted from the save time of 1416 hrs on 21 June to arrive at a start time of 6-44 a.m on 20 June.

36. Paragraph [107]: This entire clause is a mish-mash of excerpts from the evidence, which the Court of Appeal acknowledges it has not set out in detail. The Crown accepts that the computer could have been turned on as early as 6-39-49 a.m. The judgment fails to address or mention the appellant's affidavit of Mr Tomlinson which sets out the whole time argument in graphic form. Tomlinson is a mathematician. He gave evidence at the 406(b) hearing. His name is not mentioned in the judgment. Defence criticism of the methodology of Kleintjes was based on Kleintjes' ignoring new evidence by Cox, the Crown's own witness, that he

took two minutes to save the message, perhaps only one minute. The Court of Appeal ignores that too.

37.   Paragraph [108]: "The discrepancy.. is largely related to the different estimates.. the defence alleging 30 seconds at the most and the Crown, based on the estimate of Mr Cox and Det Anderson, two minutes as most likely." Kleintjes does not take account of Cox's evidence in his calculations.

38.   Paragraph [109]: "The clock's digital nature immediately involves a potential imprecision of up to 59 seconds." This 59 seconds is allowed for in Mr Tomlinson's chart (at section E 6/2155).

39.   Paragraph [109]: "The greater detail in her second statement ..does not in our view, lead to any greater precision...She did not correlate her calculation with any objectively verifiable time signal..." The Court of Appeal fails to record the evidence of Detective Low, who checked the car clock against her watch and confirmed it to be 5 minutes fast (6/2081). That evidence was not before the jury. Just as the evidence that Anderson's watch was two minutes fast ought to have been before the jury, so ought Low's.

40.   Same paragraph: The Court does not refer to the fact that the jury asked to hear Laney's evidence again after 5 hours of deliberation. Nor do they acknowledge that her second statement identifies David as the person she saw whereas the first statement that the jury heard talks only about "a person". The point was made strongly in the appellant's submissions that the reason the jury wished to hear her evidence again was in regard to time evidence but also as to identification. In paragraph [159] the Court of Appeal recognised that this second statement "should have been disclosed", but again reiterates that "in their view it made no difference". It was clearly a matter that was of serious concern to the jury.

41.   Paragraph [117]: "On the evidence, we consider that the cheek shot was the first in time and the fact of blood on Laniet's hands shows that she survived that shot, lifting her hands to her face after it struck." This is a

9

speculative conclusion by the Court, which ignores evidence by Ross (supported by Cordner) that the first shot must have been to the top of the head.

42.   Paragraph [118]: "... the white cloth was never found..." That is because the police were not looking for it at the time. The cotton embedded in the lead bullets was not discovered for some years. The house had been burned down by then. The Crown's own witness (Ferris) said a bullet hole like that would have been extraordinary hard to find anyway.

43.   Paragraph [123]: "... the strong probability that the first shot was to the cheek and Laniet then made gurgling noises which David heard." This is entirely speculative. It involves the Court of Appeal picking and choosing which of the experts' evidence to prefer.

44.   Paragraph [127]: "We also regard as significant a following passage..." The description that Ferris (and the Court) rely on, which is "attributed" to David Bain, is not part of the evidence.

45.   Paragraph [128]-[129]: The Court of Appeal's conclusion is pure speculation. The Court of Appeal accepts unreservedly "the Crown's further evidence on this issue", untested though it is. Ferris' final affidavit, upon which the Court relies, supplemented his unsatisfactory oral evidence at the section 406(b) hearing. The Thompson affidavit upon which the Court relies simply exhibits a 1997 report, and does not refer to the (later) affidavits filed on behalf of David Bain by his experts.

46.   Paragraph [130]: "David's case in short is that his new evidence raises at least the reasonable possibility that his fingerprints were in animal blood. We find ourselves unable to accept that proposition when all aspects of the subject are borne in mind." At the earlier 406(b) hearing witnesses were cross examined at length on this issue before the Court. This finding is the complete opposite to the finding of the judges on the issue at the 406(b) hearing, despite the fact that the evidence was the same in both hearings.

47.   Paragraph [131]: "...the results of the pre-trial testing, confirming the blood taken from the fingerprints to be human, are open to challenge." They are not just "open to challenge". They are wrong, as there was no such pre-trial testing of the fingerprints, which was the point on appeal.

48.   Paragraph [131]: "For this reason a series of post trial tests was conducted." This is incorrect. It was not until August 1999 that Mr. Hentschel advised the Ministry of Justice that the sample labelled "fingerprint" which the jury was told was human blood was not in fact taken from the fingerprint at all. The post trial tests were conducted in 1997, well before that dramatic news, initially for the Police/PCA inquiry team, and then in 1998 by Dr. Geursen for the appellant.

49.   Paragraph [133]: "... any such evidential value would be negligible, given that the results cannot be seen as having scientific validity." The Court of Appeal has completely missed the point: if, as the appellant says, the sample tested by Dr Guersen was from the fingerprints, and was uncontaminated, his result (that the blood contained mammalian DNA) was scientifically valid, and established that the fingerprints had nothing to do with the murders, since they were not made contemporaneously.

50.   Paragraph [135]: ".. David's fingerprints were almost certainly deposited on the fore-end of the rifle contemporaneously with the murders." This is more speculation by the Court of Appeal.

51.   Paragraph [138]: "He was cross-examined in a way which could have suggested he was not correct in this evidence." In fact, it was directly put to him that he was in dispute with the optometrist. The Crown wanted to paint him as a liar.

52.   Same paragraph: "The ownership of the glasses was thus apparently put an issue". It was not just apparent, ownership was clearly put in issue by the Crown, as the jury realised.

53.   Same paragraph: "The jury seems to have thought so..." This is an extremely cautious way to view the jury question, which makes it clear

that the jury was concerned about ownership of the glasses, rather than (as the Crown now suggests) whether David would deprive any benefit out of wearing the glasses.

54.   Paragraph [139]: "...Dr. Sanderson subsequently swore two affidavits." He swore three. The third and most significant of the affidavits claims that Detective Sergeant Weir knowingly allowed him to give misleading evidence. The allegations in the third affidavit are not addressed in the Court of Appeal's judgment, despite considerable oral discussion regarding the third affidavit at the hearing.

55.   Paragraph [140]: "The real point was that the glasses were of no use to Robin..." That was not the real point that the jury perceived, nor was it the point the Crown was trying to make.

56.   Paragraph [145]: ".. a reasonable jury could well still consider that David's own mental state was at least as relevant as that of Robin." That is not the test. Nor is it an accurate balance by the Court of new evidence from a variety of witnesses, including an educational psychologist who met with Robin Bain before the murders and who knew about Robin's depression (for which he was on medication) and his failure to cope at school. The Court of Appeal described Robin Bain at [142] as having lost touch with reality. There was no evidence at trial mental state, other than that he had had a minor argument with his father about a chainsaw, and some déjà vu experiences .

57.   Paragraph [146]: "This evidence was of course hearsay and excluded as such by the trial judge...based on his perception that Dean Cottle's evidence was not sufficiently reliable to justify admission in spite of its hearsay nature." It was not excluded because of its hearsay nature. It was excluded because the trial judge considered Cottle to be an unreliable witness.

58.   Paragraph [150]: "The most important of these are the location and state of the entry and exit wounds on Robin's head...." There was no exit wound.

12

The Court of Appeal's conclusion is speculative, and requires it to pick and choose which experts' evidence to accept.

59. Paragraph [153]: the Court of Appeal said new evidence showing Robin's shoe prints in David's room, in places consistent with his having been there to collect the rifle and ammunition, was "unsurprising", and not inconsistent with the Crown contention that Robin had not been into any of the rooms. The conclusion is illogical. His foot prints were right in front of the cupboard where the rifle was stored.

60. Paragraph [155]: Robin's feet were measured in the mortuary at 275 mm. They were 270 mm.

61. Paragraph [156]: ".. Mr Walsh has said that a 300 mm stocking foot could make a print of about 280 mm... David could well have made the footprints in question." Walsh's evidence was that a walking foot print on carpet (which was the trial evidence about the 280 mm long bloodied stock print) could not make a complete from heel to toe 280 mm foot print. The luminol footprints clearly belonged to Robin Bain.

62. Paragraph [157]: "...we have noted the submission concerning the possible presence of blood under Robin's fingernails and the absence of Robin's fingerprints on the rifle... neither individually nor collectively do these various points give more than a speculative basis for saying that there is now further evidence affirmatively implicating Robin." That misses the point, with respect. The absence of Robin's fingerprints on the rifle was one of the 10 points of evidence specifically listed by the trial judge in his summing up at trial. The lack of Robin Bain's fingerprints must have counted significantly against David Bain. We now know that identifiable fingerprints are seldom found. The impact on the jury of evidence that Robin may have had traces of blood under his fingernails is likely to have been significant, in the context of "Who did it? Robin or David?"

63. Paragraph [157]: in light of [156] and Mr Walsh's evidence, the Court of Appeal's conclusion that none of the new evidence implicated Robin is simply wrong.

64.   Paragraph [158-162]: the Court of Appeal completely overlooks submissions made by the appellant about Mr Dempster's notes that were not disclosed to the appellant that recorded he thought suicide was feasible; and the inference that his unexplained change of mind about that at trial was based on Ngamoki's incorrect measurement of the rifle. The Court of Appeal also fails to address the submission that the undisclosed statement the Police took from Denise Laney was important not only because of the time issue but also because of the identity issue.

65.   Paragraph [167]: The computer switch on issue does prove physical impossibility. On the Crown's own evidence, the most likely computer switch on time was 6:42:30. Laney saw David Bain at the gate at 6:45. No printer's ink was found on the computer. It must have been some time before David could possibly have reached the computer to turn it on. He cannot have been the murderer. The Court of Appeal's conclusion shows it has misdirected itself on the facts.

66.   Paragraph [168]: "There is no evidence positively implicating Robin Bain on any tenable basis." Although the onus is not on the appellant to establish that Robin Bain committed the murders, new evidence implicates him (for instance the socks) and excludes David.

Appendix C

References

Amorado, RM, Lin, C-Y, and Hsu, H-F (2008). Parricide: an analysis of offender characteristics and crime scene behaviors of adult and juvenile offenders. *Asian Journal of Family Violence and Sexual Assault, 4*(2): 1–32.

Anderson, P (2009). Parents who kill their children not psychopaths but have emotional dysfunction. *Medscape Medical News,* 29 May: 13–16.

Auchter, B (2010). Men who murder their families: what the research tells us. *NIJ Journal,* (266): 10–12.

Banks, L, Crandall, C, Sklar, D, and Bauer, M (2008). A comparison of intimate partner homicide to intimate partner homicide-suicide: one hundred and twenty-four New Mexico cases. *Violence Against Women, 14*(9): 1065–78.

Barraclough, B, and Harris, EC (2002). Suicide preceded by murder: the epidemiology of homicide-suicide in England and Wales 1988–92. *Psychological Medicine, 32*(4): 577–84.

Barthell, VR, and Shelton, KM (2009). Familicide: risk factors, characteristics of the offender, characteristics of the crime of familicide, and the prevalence of suicide following familicide. Research proposal, University of New Hampshire.

Bernhard, B (2009). Family killers reveal patterns. *St Louis Post-Dispatch,* 28 May.

Block, CR, and Block, RL (2008). Homicides connected to other homicides: an examination of the Chicago Homicide Dataset. *2008 National Conference, Using Data to Improve Justice Policy and Practice*: 1–26.

Boots, DP, and Heide, KM (2006). Parricides in the media: a content analysis of available reports across cultures. *International Journal of Offender Therapy and Comparative Criminology, 50*(4): 418–45.

Bossarte, RM, Simon, TR, and Barker, L (2006). Characteristics of homicide followed by suicide incidents in multiple states, 2003–04. *Injury Prevention: Journal of the International Society for Child and Adolescent Injury Prevention, 12 Suppl. 2*: ii33–ii38.

Bouchard, J-P, and Bachelier, A-S (2004). Schizophrenia and double parricide: about a clinical observation. *Annales Médico-psychologiques, 162*(8): 626–33.

Bourget, D, Gagné, P, and Labelle, M-E (2007). Parricide: a comparative study of matricide versus patricide. *The Journal of the American Academy of Psychiatry and the Law, 35*(3): 306–12.

Bridges, FS, and Lester, D (2010). Homicide-suicide in the United States, 1968–1975. *Forensic Science International*: 1–5.

Brock, K (2002). American roulette: the untold story of murder-suicide in the United States: 20. Violence Policy Center, Washington DC.

Byard, RW (2005). Murder-suicide an overview. *Forensic Pathology Reviews*, *3*: 337–47.

Byard, RW, Knight, D, James, RA, and Gilbert, JD (1999). Murder-suicides involving children: a 29-year study. *American Journal of Forensic Medicine and Pathology*, *20*(4): 323–27.

Campanelli, C, and Gilson, T (2002). Murder-suicide in New Hampshire, 1995–2000. *American Journal of Forensic Medicine and Pathology*, *23*(3): 248–51.

Canadian Centre for Justice Statistics (2005). Family violence in Canada: a statistical profile 2005. *Canadian Centre for Justice Statistics*. Retrieved from www.statcan.ca.

Carcach, C (1987). Youth as victims and offenders of homicide. *Trends and Issues in Crime and Criminal Justice*: 6. Canberra, Australia.

Carcach, C, and Grabosky, PN (1998). Murder-suicide in Australia. *Australian Institute of Criminology: Trends and Issues in Crime and Criminal Justice*, *82* (March).

Carcach, C, James, M, and Graycar, A (1996). Homicide between intimate partners in Australia. *Trends and Issues in Crime and Criminal Justice*: 6. Canberra, Australia.

Chan, C (2003). Homicide-suicide in Hong Kong, 1989–1998. *Forensic Science International*, *137*(2–3): 165–71.

Chan, CY, Beh, SL, and Broadhurst, RG (2004). Homicide-suicide in Hong Kong, 1989–98: a preliminary analysis. In RG Broadhurst (Ed.), *Crime and Its Control in the People's Republic of China Proceedings of the University of Hong Kong Annual Symposia 2000–2002*. Hong Kong: Centre for Criminology, the University of Hong Kong.

Chan, CYA (2007). Hostility in homicide-suicide events: a typological analysis with data from a Chinese society, Hong Kong, 1989–2003. *Asian Journal of Criminology*, *2*(1): 1–18.

Chong Ho Shon, P, and Roberts, MA (2010). An archival exploration of homicide-suicide and mass murder in the context of 19th-century American parricides. *International Journal of Offender Therapy and Comparative Criminology*, *54*: 43–60.

Christiansen, S, Rollmann, D, Leth, P, and Thomsen, J (2007). Children as victims of homicide 1972–2005. *Ugeskr Laeger*, *169*(47): 4070–74.

Cohen, D, Llorente, M, and Eisdorfer, C (1998). Homicide-suicide in older persons. *The American Journal of Psychiatry*, *155*(3): 390–96.

Daly, M, and Wilson, MI (1994). Some differential attributes of lethal assaults on small children by stepfathers versus genetic fathers. *Ethology and Sociobiology*, *15*(4): 207–17.

Dawson, JM, and Angan, PA (1994). *Special report: murder in families*: 13. Bureau of Justice Statistics.

Delisi, M, and Scherer, AM (2006). Multiple homicide offenders: offense characteristics, social correlates, and criminal careers. *Criminal Justice and Behavior, 33*(3): 367–91.

Dobash, RP, Dobash, RE, Wilson, M, and Daly, M (1992). The myth of sexual symmetry in marital violence. *Social Problems, 39*(1): 71–91.

Duwe, G (2004). The patterns and prevalence of mass murder in twentieth-century America. *Justice Quarterly, 21*(4): 729–61.

Duwe, G (2005). A circle of distortion: the social construction of mass murder in the United States. *Western Criminology Review, 6*(1): 59–78.

Eliason, S (2009). Murder-suicide: a review of the recent literature. *The Journal of the American Academy of Psychiatry and the Law, 37*(3): 371–76.

Ewing, C (1997). *Fatal families: the dynamics of intrafamilial homicide.* Thousand Oaks, CA: Sage.

Ferguson, S, Blakely, T, Allan, B, and Collings, S (2003). *Suicide rates in New Zealand: exploring associations with social and economic factors. Health (San Francisco).* Wellington, New Zealand.

Fox, JA, and Levin, J (1998). Multiple homicide: patterns of serial and mass murder. *Crime and Justice, 23*(1998): 407–55.

Fox, JA, and Levin, J (2005). *Extreme killing: understanding serial and mass murder.* Thousand Oaks, CA: Sage.

Gallacher, S (1993). *Publishing our own dishonour: the criminalisation of incest in New Zealand and the judicial response.* Otago University.

Galta, K, Olsen, SL, and Wik, G (2005). Murder followed by suicide: Norwegian data and international literature. *Forensic Pathology Reviews, 3*(8): 337–47.

Goldman, R (2007). Why parents kill kids and themselves. ABC News (25 June). Retrieved 20 September 2010, from http://abcnews.go.com/US/story?id=3307902.

Goldney, RD (1977). Family murder followed by suicide. *Forensic Science, 9*: 219–28.

Haines, J, Williams, CL, and Lester, D (2010). Murder-suicide: a reaction to interpersonal crises. *Forensic Science International, 202*(1–3): 93–96.

Hannah, SG, Turf, EE, and Fierro, MF (1998). Murder-suicide in Central Virginia: a descriptive epidemiologic study and empiric validation of the Hanzlick-Koponen Typology. *American Journal of Forensic Medicine and Pathology, 19*(3): 275–83.

Harper, DW, and Voigt, L (2007). Homicide followed by suicide: an integrated theoretical perspective. *Homicide Studies, 11*(4): 295–318.

Harris, G, Hilton, N, Rice, M, and Eke, A (2007). Children killed by genetic parents versus stepparents. *Evolution and Human Behavior, 28*(2): 85–95.

Harris Johnson, C (2008). Intimate partner homicide and familicide in Western Australia. In Australian Institute of Criminology (Eds), *Domestic-related homicide: keynote papers from the 2008 international conference on homicide*: 37–48. Canberra, Australia: Australian Institute of Criminology.

Hatters Friedman, S, and Friedman, JB (2010). Parents who kill their children. *Pediatrics in review/American Academy of Pediatrics, 31*(2): e10–6.

Hatters Friedman, S, Hrouda, DR, Holden, CE, Noffsinger, SG, and Resnick, PJ (2005). Filicide-suicide: common factors in parents who kill their children and themselves. *The Journal of the American Academy of Psychiatry and the Law, 33*(4): 496–504.

Havasi, B, Mágori, K, Tóth, A, and Kiss, L (2005). Fatal suicide cases from 1991 to 2000 in Szeged, Hungary. *Forensic Science International, 147 Suppl.*: S25–8.

Heide, KM, and Boots, DP (2007). A comparative analysis of media reports of U.S. parricide cases with officially reported national crime data and the psychiatric and psychological literature. *International Journal of Offender Therapy and Comparative Criminology, 51*(6): 646–75.

Heide, KM, and Petee, TA (2007). Parricide: an empirical analysis of 24 years of U.S. data. *Journal of Interpersonal Violence, 22*(11): 1382–99.

Hillbrand, M, Alexandre, JW, Young, JL, and Spitz, RT (1999). Parricides: characteristics of offenders and victims, legal factors, and treatment issues. *Aggression and Violent Behavior, 4*(2): 179–90.

Hillbrand, M, and Cipriano, T (2007). Commentary: parricides unanswered questions, methodological obstacles, and legal considerations. *The Journal of the American Academy of Psychiatry and the Law, 35*(3): 313–16.

Hodges, M, and Calhoun, E (2006). *A Christmas Family Tragedy*. FACETS.

Holdt, J (1998). *The incest report: 1997* clients: 12. Auckland, New Zealand.

James, M, and Carcach, C (1997). *Homicide in Australia 1989–96*. Canberra, Australia.

Jena, S, Mountany, L, and Muller, A (2009). A demographic study of homicide-suicide in the Pretoria region over a 5 year period. *Journal of Forensic and Legal Medicine, 16*(5): 261–65.

Jensen, LL, Gilbert, JD, and Byard, RW (2009). Coincident deaths: double suicide or murder-suicide? *Medical Science and the Law, 49*(27): 32.

Johnson, CH (2006). Familicide and custody disputes — dispelling the myths (a study of filicide-suicide following separation). *Family Court Review, 44*(3): 448–63.

Julich, SJ (2006). Views of justice among survivors of historical child sexual abuse. *Theoretical Criminology, 10*(1): 125–38.

Kauppi, A, Kumpulainen, K, Karkola, K, Vanamo, T, and Merikanto, J (2010). Maternal and paternal filicides: a retrospective review of filicides in Finland. *Journal of the American Academy of Psychiatry and the Law, 38*(2): 229–38.

Large, M, Smith, G, and Nielssen, O (2009). The epidemiology of homicide followed by suicide: a systematic and quantitative review. *Suicide and life-threatening behavior, 39*(3): 294–306.

Lecomte, D, and Fornes, P (1998). Homicide followed by suicide: Paris and its suburbs, 1991–1996. *Journal of Forensic Sciences, 43*(4): 760–64.

Lee, JH (1999). *The Treatment of Psychopathic and Antisocial Personality Disorders: A Review. Health (San Francisco)*: 1–33. Crowethorne, Berks.

LeFevre Sillito, C (2010). Intimate partner murder-suicide. *Social Dialogue, 1*(1): 8–10.

Léveillée, S, and Lefebvre, J (2008). *Rapport de recherche — Étude des homicides intrafamiliaux commis par des personnes souffrant d'un trouble mental*: 1–73.

Léveillée, S, Lefebvre, J, and Marleau, J-D (2009). Profil psychosocial des familicides commis au Québec — 1986 à 2000. *Annales Médico-psychologiques, Revue Psychiatrique, 167*(8): 591–96.

Léveillée, S, Lefebvre, J, and Vaillancourt, J-P (2010). Parricide commis par des hommes adultes: variables descriptives et motivations sous-jacentes au passage à l'acte. *L'Évolution Psychiatrique, 75*(1): 77–91.

Léveillée, S, Marleau, JD, and Dubé, M (2007). Filicide: a comparison by sex and presence or absence of self-destructive behavior. *Journal of Family Violence, 22*(5): 287–95.

Léveillée, S, Marleau, J, and Lefebvre, J (2010). Passage à l'acte familicide et filicide: deux réalités distinctes? *L'Évolution Psychiatrique, 75*(1): 19–33.

Levin, J, and Madfis, E (2009). Mass murder at school and cumulative strain: a sequential model. *American Behavioral Scientist, 52*(9): 1227–45.

Liem, M (2009). Homicide followed by suicide: a unique type of lethal violence. In Australian Institute of Criminology (Eds), *2008 International Conference on Homicide*: 25–35. Canberra, Australia: AIC Reports: Research and Public Policy Series 104. Retrieved from www.aic.gov.au.

Liem, M (2010a). *Homicide Followed by Suicide. An Empirical Analysis. PhD thesis.* Utrecht University, the Netherlands.

Liem, M (2010b). Homicide followed by suicide: a review. *Aggression and Violent Behavior, 15*(3): 153–61. Elsevier Ltd.

Liem, M, Hengeveld, M, and Koenraadt, F (2009). Domestic homicide followed by parasuicide: a comparison with homicide and parasuicide. *International Journal of Offender Therapy and Comparative Criminology, 53*(5): 497–516.

Liem, M, Koenraadt, F, and Pompe, W (2008). Familicide: a comparison with spousal and child homicide by mentally disordered perpetrators. *Criminal Behaviour and Mental Health, 318*: 306–18.

Liem, M, Postulart, M, and Nieuwbeerta, P (2009). Homicide-suicide in the Netherlands: an epidemiology. *Homicide Studies, 13*(2): 99–123.

Lindqvist, P, and Gustafsson, L (1995). Homicide followed by the offender's suicide in northern Sweden. *Nordic Journal of Psychiatry, 49*(1): 17–25.

Logan, J, Hill, HA, Black, ML, Crosby, AE, Karch, DL, Barnes, JD, et al. (2008). Characteristics of perpetrators in homicide-followed-by-suicide incidents: national violent death reporting system — 17 US States, 2003–2005. *American Journal of Epidemiology, 168*(9): 1056–64.

MaGPIe Research Group (2003). The nature and prevalence of psychological problems in New Zealand primary healthcare: a report on Mental Health and General Practice Investigation (MaGPIe), the MaGPIe Research Group. *Journal of the New Zealand Medical Association, 116*(1171).

Marleau, JD, Auclair, N, and Millaud, F (2006). Comparison of factors associated with parricide in adults and adolescents. *Journal of Family Violence, 21*(5): 321–25.

Marleau, JD, Poulin, B, Webanck, T, Roy, R, and Laporte, L (1999). Paternal filicide: a study of 10 men. *Canadian Journal of Psychiatry, 44*(1): 57–63.

Martin, J, and Pritchard, R (2010). *Learning from Tragedy: Homicide within Families in New Zealand. MSD Report* (Vol. 1). Wellington, New Zealand.

Marzuk, PM, Tardiff, K, and Hirsch, CS (1992). The epidemiology of murder-suicide. *Journal of the American Medical Association, 267*(23): 3179–83.

McGreevey, JE, Levin, SB, and Atwood, B (2003). *New Jersey Domestic Violence Fatality Review Board Report February 2003. Review Literature and Arts of the Americas*: 31.

Messing, JT, and Heeren, JW (2004). Another side of multiple murder: women killers in the domestic context. *Homicide Studies, 8*(2): 123–58.

Milroy, CM (1995). Reasons for homicide and suicide in episodes of dyadic death in Yorkshire and Humberside. *Medical Science and the Law, 35*: 213–17.

Milroy, CM (1998). Homicide followed by suicide: remorse or revenge? *Journal of Clinical Forensic Medicine, 5*(2): 61–64.

Ministry of Health (2006). *New Zealand Suicide Trends: Mortality 1921–2003, Hospitalisations for Intentional Self-harm 1978–2004. Public Health.* Wellington, New Zealand.

Moskowitz, A, Simpson, A, McKenna, B, Skipworth, J, and Barry-Walsh, J (2006). The role of mental illness in homicide-suicide in New Zealand, 1991–2000. *Journal of Forensic Psychiatry and Psychology, 17*(3): 417–30.

Mouzos, J (2000). *Homicidal Encounters. A Study of Homicide in Australia 1989–1999. Public Policy:* 238. Canberra, Australia. Retrieved from http://www.aic.gov.au.

Mouzos, J, and Graycar, A (2001). *Homicide in Australia 1999–2000. Trends and Issues in Criminal Justice, Vol. 187:* 6. Canberra, Australia.

Mouzos, J, and Houliaras, T (2006). *Homicide in Australia: 2004–05 National Homicide Monitoring Program (NHMP) Annual Report. AIC.* Canberra.

Mouzos, J, and Rushforth, C (2003). *Family Homicide in Australia. Australian Institute of Criminology Trends and Issues, Vol. June:* 6. Canberra, Australia. Retrieved from http://www.aic.gov.au.

National Institute of Justice (NIJ) (2009). Murder-suicide in families. *National Institute of Justice (NIJ).* Retrieved 20 September 2010, from http://www.ojp.usdoj.gov/nij/.

Newhill, CE (1996). Parricide. *Journal of Family Violence, 6*(4): 375–94.

Palermo, GB (1997). The Berserk Syndrome: a review of mass murder. *Aggression and Violent Behavior, 2*(1): 1–8.

Palermo, GB (2010). Parricide: a crime against nature. *International Journal of Offender Therapy and Comparative Criminology, 54*(1): 3–5.

Perri, FS, Lichtenwald, TG, and Mackenzie, P (2008). The lull before the storm: adult children who kill their parents. *The Forensic Examiner, Fall* (417): 40–54.

Polland, M, Cameron, A, Wong, K, and Fletcher, M (2007). *Moving On: Changes in a Year in Family Living Arrangements.* Wellington, New Zealand.

Porch, TL (1990). *Attitudes of New Zealand Police and Social Workers toward Child Sexual Abuse.* University of South Dakota.

Putkonen, H, Amon, S, Almiron, MP, Cederwall, JY, Eronen, M, Klier, C, et al. (2009). Filicide in Austria and Finland — a register-based study on all filicide cases in Austria and Finland 1995–2005. *BMC Psychiatry, 9:* 74.

Ramsland, K (2010). Fathers Who Kill. *Trutv Crime Library (Web).* Retrieved 20 September 2010, from http://www.trutv.com/library/crime/criminal_mind/psychology/fathers_who_kill/index.html.

Riedel, M (2010). Homicide-suicide in the United States: a review of the literature. *Sociology Compass, 4*(7): 440–31.

Roberts, C (1998). It's okay to talk about incest. *Social Work Now, 10*: 36–39.

Sacco, L (2009). *Unspeakable: Father-Daughter Incest in American History*: 368. Washington: Johns Hopkins University Press.

Saint-Martin, P, Bouyssy, M, and O'Byrne, P (2008). Homicide-suicide in Tours, France (2000–2005) — description of 10 cases and a review of the literature. *Journal of Forensic and Legal Medicine, 15*(2): 104–9.

Saleva, O, Putkonen, H, Kiviruusu, O, and Lönnqvist, J (2007). Homicide-suicide — an event hard to prevent and separate from homicide or suicide. *Forensic Science International, 166*(2–3): 204–8.

Scourfield, J (2005). Suicidal masculinities. *Sociological Research Online, 10*(2).

Serran, G (2004). Intimate partner homicide: a review of the male proprietariness and the self-defense theories. *Aggression and Violent Behavior, 9*(1): 1–15.

Shiferaw, K, Burkhardt, S, Lardi, C, Mangin, P, and La Harpe, R (2010). A half century retrospective study of homicide-suicide in Geneva — Switzerland: 1956–2005. *Journal of Forensic and Legal Medicine, 17*(2): 62–66.

Simpson, AIF, Skipworth, J, McKenna, B, Moskowitz, A, and Barry-Walsh, J (2006). Mentally abnormal homicide in New Zealand as defined by legal and clinical criteria: a national study. *The Australian and New Zealand Journal of Psychiatry, 40*(9): 804–9.

Singhall, S, and Dutta, A (1990). Who commits patricide? *Acta Psychiatrica Scandinavica, 82*(1): 40–43.

Stack, S (1997). Homicide followed by suicide: analysis of Chicago data. *Criminology, 35*(3): 435–54.

Statistics Canada (2006). Fact sheet: family homicides. *Statistics Canada Fact Sheets*. Retrieved from http://www.statcan.gc.ca/.

Strang, H (1996). Children as victims of homicide. *Trends and Issues in Crime and Criminal Justice, Vol. 169*: 6. Canberra, Australia.

Tanay, E (1973). Adolescents who kill parents — reactive parricide. *Australian and New Zealand Journal of Psychiatry, 7*(4): 263–77.

Van Wormer, K, and Odiah, C (1999). The psychology of suicide-murder and the death penalty. *Journal of Criminal Justice, 27*(4): 361–70.

Vaughn, MG, DeLisi, M, Beaver, KM, and Howard, MO (2009). Multiple murder and criminal careers: a latent class analysis of multiple homicide offenders. *Forensic Science International, 183*(1–3): 67–73.

Vicente, B, Kohn, R, Rioseco, P, Saldivia, S, Levav, I, and Torres, S (2006). Lifetime and 12-month prevalence of DSM-III-R disorders in the Chile psychiatric prevalence study. *The American Journal of Psychiatry, 163*(8): 1362–70.

Violence Policy Center (2006). *American Roulette: Murder-Suicide in the United States 2006. Violence Policy Center.* 21. Washington, DC. Retrieved from www.vpc.org.

Violence Policy Center (2008). *American Roulette: Murder-Suicide in the United States 2008. Violence Policy Center.* 18. Washington DC. Retrieved from http://www.vpc. org/studyndx.htm.

Websdale, N (2006). Understanding familicide. *Fatality Review Bulletin, Summer.* 4–7. Retrieved from www.apiahf.org.

Websdale, N (2010). *Familicidal Hearts: The Emotional Styles of 211 Killers*: 335. New York: Oxford University Press.

Weisman, AM, Ehrenclou, MG, and Sharma, KK (2002). Double parricide: forensic analysis and psycholegal implications. *Journal of Forensic Sciences, 47*(2): 313–17.

Weisman, AM, and Sharma, KK (1997). Forensic analysis and psycholegal implications of parricide and attempted parricide. *Journal of Forensic Sciences, 42*(6): 1107–13.

West, SG (2010). Parricide: characteristics of sons and daughters who kill their parents. *Current Psychiatry, 9*(11).

West, S, Friedman, S, and Resnick, P (2009). Fathers who kill their children: an analysis of the literature. *Journal of Forensic Sciences, 54*(2): 463–68.

Wilson, M, and Daly, M (1995). Familicide: uxoricide plus filicide? *Lethal Violence: Proceedings of the 1995 Meeting of the Homicide Research Working Group*: 159–69. Ottawa, Canada: National Institute of Justice. Retrieved from http://www.ncjrs.org.

Wilson, MI, and Daly, M (1992). Who kills whom in spouse killings? On the exceptional sex ratio of spousal homicides in the United States. *Criminology, 30*(2): 189–216.

Wilson, M, Daly, M, and Daniele, A (1995). Familicide: the killing of spouse and children. *Aggressive Behavior, 21*(4): 275–91.

Wood Harper, D, and Voigt, L (2007). Homicide followed by suicide: an integrated theoretical perspective. *Homicide Studies, 11*(4): 295–318.

Wormer, K van (2008). The dynamics of murder-suicide in domestic situations. *Brief Treatment and Crisis Intervention, 8*(3): 274–82.